The History of
William Marshal

The History of William Marshal

Translated by

Nigel Bryant

THE BOYDELL PRESS

© Nigel Bryant 2016

All Rights Reserved. Except as permitted under current legislation no part of this work may be photocopied, stored in a retrieval system, published, performed in public, adapted, broadcast, transmitted, recorded or reproduced in any form or by any means, without the prior permission of the copyright owner

The right of Nigel Bryant to be identified as
the author of this work has been asserted in accordance with
sections 77 and 78 of the Copyright, Designs and Patents Act 1988

First published 2016
The Boydell Press, Woodbridge
Paperback edition 2018

ISBN 978 1 78327 131 3 hardback
ISBN 978 1 78327 303 4 paperback

The Boydell Press is an imprint of Boydell & Brewer Ltd
PO Box 9, Woodbridge, Suffolk IP12 3DF, UK
and of Boydell & Brewer Inc.
668 Mt Hope Avenue, Rochester, NY 14620–2731, USA
website: www.boydellandbrewer.com

A catalogue record for this book is available
from the British Library

The publisher has no responsibility for the continued existence or accuracy of URLs for external or third-party internet websites referred to in this book, and does not guarantee that any content on such websites is, or will remain, accurate or appropriate

Typeset by
www.thewordservice.com

Contents

Maps
    Northern France   xi
    Normandy and its Borders   xii
    England   xiv
    The Battle of Lincoln   xv

Introduction   1
    Envy   2
    Respect   4
    Credibility I   5
    Justification   9
    Credibility II   14
    Character   17
    Authorship and Date   22
    Editions and Further Reading   25

The History of William Marshal

Prologue   27
    The author promises a true account, to counter tales prompted by envy (verses 1–22)

Marshal's Father   27
    John Marshal supports the Empress Matilda in her war against King Stephen (23–166); to rescue her after the siege of Winchester he makes an heroic stand at Wherwell (167–278); he ambushes King Stephen and the earl of Salisbury (279–354); he divorces his wife and marries Salisbury's sister to end the conflict between them (355–377)

Young William   31
    William is John's second born son (378–398); he is given to King Stephen as a hostage at the siege of Newbury and narrowly escapes death (399–714); he is trained as a squire and knighted in Normandy by the Chamberlain of Tancarville (715–804); he has his first experience of battle at Neufchâtel-en-Bray (805–1162)

Marshal's First Tournaments   39
    William wins handsomely at his first two tournaments (1163–1512)

War in Poitou   43
William accompanies his uncle the earl of Salisbury on Henry II's campaign in Poitou (1513–1622); the earl is killed (1623–1652); William is wounded and captured as he seeks revenge (1653–1857); he is ransomed by Queen Eleanor (1858–1904)

Henry the Young King   47
Henry II crowns his eldest son and William becomes his instructor in arms (1905–1974); a rift develops between king and son (1975–2070); William knights the Young King (2071–2106); King Henry has the better of the conflict and the Young King's supporters are ruined (2107–2384); William guides the Young King as he engages in tournament after tournament (2385–2636); the Young King becomes a model of chivalry for all great lords (2637–2712); at William's urging, the Young King adopts the tournament tactics of Count Philip of Flanders (2713–2874)

The Tournament at Pleurs   57
William is awarded a pike as a prize for his performance (2875–3164)

The Tournament at Eu   60
William wins numerous prisoners and horses – one of them twice (3165–3425)

The Tournament at Joigny   63
William triumphs at another tournament, in which ladies are an inspiration for the knights (3426–3571)

The Tournament between Maintenon and Nogent   64
William is the Young King's guide and protector; he captures Sir Renaud de Nevers (3572–3880)

The Tournament between Anet and Sorel   68
William loses two horses, but wins back one with a dice-throw and the other with canny bargaining (3881–4284)

The Tournament at Épernon   72
William recovers his horse from a thief (4285–4456)

The Tournament at Lagny   74
At the greatest tournament ever seen, William rescues the Young King (4457–5050)

Rift with the Young King   80
A treacherous plot is hatched to break the Young King's trust in William (5051–5748); William seeks to prove his innocence in a trial by

combat, but none will accept the challenge (5749–5840); he leaves the Young King, and great lords everywhere crave his service (5841–6178); he goes on a pilgrimage to Cologne (6179–6298)

War between King Henry's Sons   93
The plot against William is exposed (6299–6512); the Young King recalls him to his side to support him in his war against his father and his brother Richard (6513–6664); on the way back William meets a monk eloping with a young lady (6665–6864)

The Death of the Young King   99
As the Young King dies at Martel, he asks William to bear his crusader's cross to the Holy Land; William takes the Young King's body to King Henry, then to Rouen for burial (6865–7232)

The Holy Land   103
William takes the Young King's cross to the Holy Land; he spends two years there; on his return he joins King Henry's household (7233–7318)

War Between King Henry and King Philip   104
Henry II and Philip Augustus agree to take the cross but fall out and go to war in Normandy (7319–7875); William makes a daring charge on a bridge at Montmirail (7876–8048); Henry's son Richard sides with the king of France against him and blocks all moves for peace (8049–8310); Philip's attack on Le Mans ends with the city in flames (8311–8790); William kills Richard's horse when they meet in combat (8791–8906)

The Death of King Henry   120
King Henry falls ill as he and Philip meet to parley (8907–9038); he hears that Prince John as well as Richard has betrayed him (9039–9083); he dies at Chinon in a pitiful state, stripped of all his clothes and money (9084–9164); William helps to carry his body to Fontevrault (9165–9290); Richard sends William to England to take charge of his affairs (9291–9450)

Marshal's Marriage   126
William marries Isabel de Clare in London (9451–9550); Prince John is reluctant to return William's rightful inheritance in Ireland (9551–9630)

In King Richard's Absence   128
Richard sets off on the Third Crusade (9631–9742); the Chancellor Stephen Langton and then Prince John try to exploit the king's absence (9743–9964); a ransom is raised to free Richard from captivity (9965–10017)

King Richard's Return 132
William is distressed at his brother's death but delighted by the king's return to England (10018–10152); Richard captures Nottingham Castle from John's forces (10153–10288); William refuses to pay Richard homage for his land in Ireland, having already paid homage to John (10289–10340)

King Richard's War in Normandy 136
Richard crosses to Normandy; he forgives his brother John (10341–10428); he relieves Verneuil, under siege from Philip (10429–10508); he makes great advances and routs the French at Fréteval, where William leads a fine rearguard (10509–10676); Richard allies with Count Baldwin of Flanders, and William goes to support the count against the French, who retreat without a fight (10677–10923); Richard drives Philip's army from Gisors (10924–11084); William fights valiantly at the storming of Milly-sur-Thérain (11085–11310); Richard negotiates angrily with the papal legate to secure a favourable truce (11311–11744)

The Death of King Richard 149
Richard is mortally wounded by a poisoned bolt; he places William in charge of his treasury at Rouen; William advises that John, not Arthur of Brittany, should succeed as king (11745–11908)

King John's Wars in France 151
John is made duke of Normandy and then crowned king of England (11909–11982); he divorces his first wife and marries a second (11983–12004); he makes repeated concessions to the king of France, but wins a notable victory at Mirebeau, capturing Arthur of Brittany (12005–12404); his arrogance grows and he breaks promises made to William des Roches (12405–12550); he steadily loses support and trusts no one; he slips back to England (12551–12838)

Crisis in Normandy 161
Rouen falls to King Philip and Normandy is close to being lost (12839–12932); William is sent as an envoy to Philip, having made it clear to John that he needs to pay homage to Philip for his land in Normandy; William's mission is wrecked by the archbishop of Canterbury; William is accused of betraying John, whose mood towards him turns hostile (12933–13310)

Marshal in Ireland 166
John reluctantly gives William leave to go to his estate in Leinster; Meiler FitzHenry prompts John to recall William from Ireland (13311–13550); in William's absence Meiler's followers wreak havoc there; William's men in Ireland realise that John means to ruin them,

but they stay loyal to William; they seek the aid of the earl of Ulster; Meiler is defeated (13551–13930); William returns to Ireland and forgives the traitors (13931–14136); John banishes William of Briouze, who takes refuge with William in Leinster; John accuses William of treachery and demands hostages of him (14137–14490)

The Battles of Damme and Bouvines   178
Philip of France plans an invasion of England; John is urged to recall William from Ireland; the English destroy the French fleet at Damme (14491–14671); John mounts a campaign in Poitou while his allies in Flanders are crushed at Bouvines (14672–14859)

Marshal's Children   183
William's five sons and five daughters, and the fine marriages he arranges (14860–15030)

The Barons' War   184
Many of John's barons ally against him and bring Prince Louis of France to England; William remains strictly loyal to John; John falls gravely ill and dies at Newark; he is buried at Worcester (15031–15228)

Protector of King and Realm   187
William knights the nine-year-old Henry III, who is crowned at Gloucester; the loyal magnates plead with William to be the king's protector; he reluctantly agrees (15229–15708); he advances on Louis of France and corners him at Winchelsea; Louis narrowly escapes back to France (15709–15869); a series of castles surrender to William's forces before Louis returns with a great army (15870–16114)

The Battle of Lincoln   195
William and those loyal to King Henry are outnumbered by the French and the English rebels, but win a stunning victory at Lincoln (16115–17030)

The Battle of Sandwich   205
Louis takes refuge in London and sends to France for aid; the great fleet of reinforcements is destroyed by the English at Sandwich (17031–17576); Louis is escorted to Dover and returns to France (17577–17736); Morgan of Caerleon refuses to observe the ensuing truce (17737–17879)

Marshal's Death   213
Marshal falls ill and doctors cannot help; he is taken to his home at Caversham, where he is visited by the king and magnates; William proposes that the king be entrusted to the guardianship of the papal legate (17880–18118); he completes the making of his will, providing

first for his children; he wishes to be buried in the Temple Church; he gives instruction for alms to be distributed to the poor, and endows abbeys and their chapters; he distributes gowns to his knights (18119–18737); the abbot of Reading gives him absolution and he dies (18738–18982); he is taken to London and buried in the Temple Church (18983–19214)

Glossary   229

Index   233

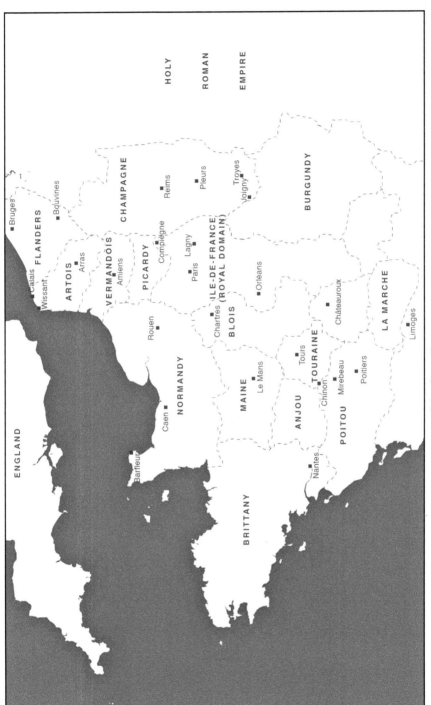

Northern France

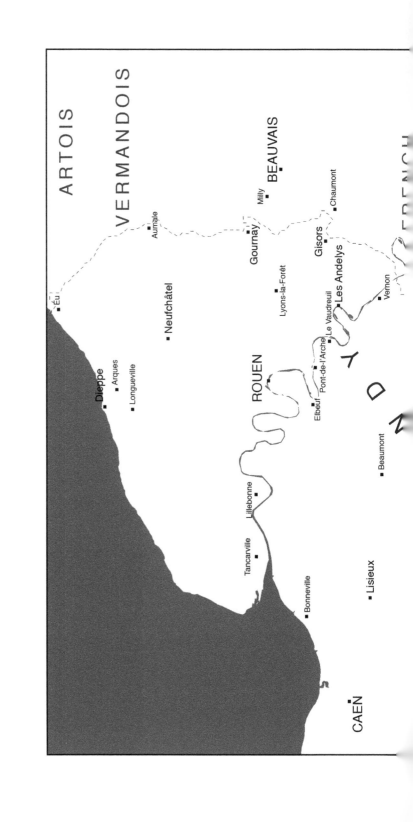

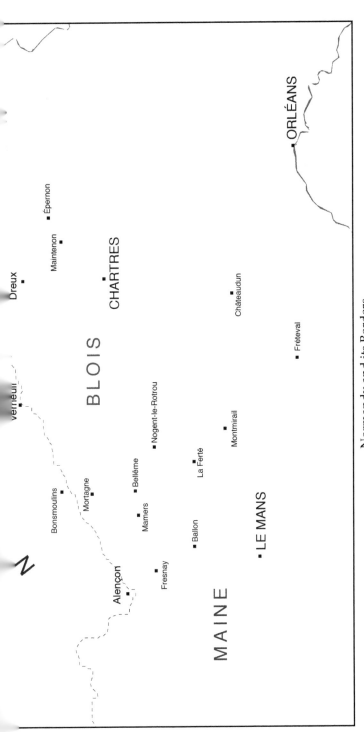

Normandy and its Borders

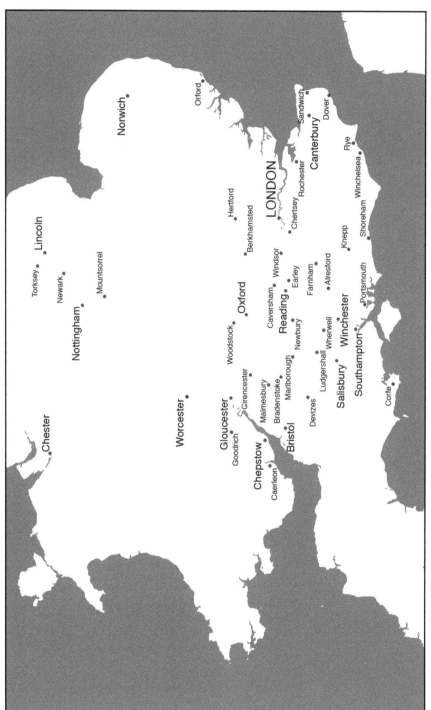

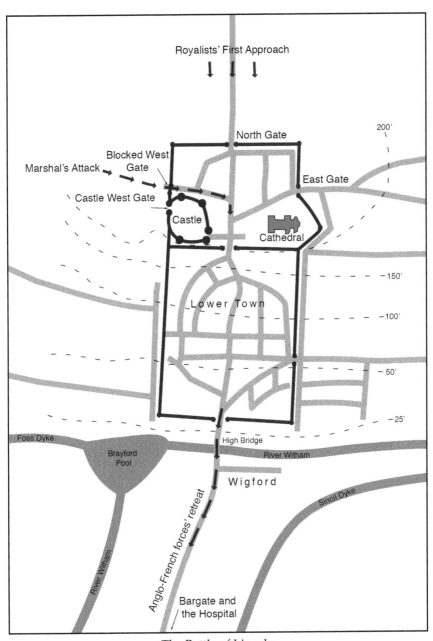

The Battle of Lincoln

For Sally

Introduction

The History of William Marshal is the earliest surviving biography of a medieval knight – indeed, it is the first biography of a layman in the vernacular in European history. Composed in verse in the 1220s just a few years after his death, it is a major primary source not simply for its subject's life but for the exceptionally stormy period he had had to navigate. It could hardly be other than major, given that its subject was regarded as the greatest knight who ever lived and that he rose in the course of his long life to be a central figure in the reigns of no fewer than four kings: Henry II, Richard Lionheart, John and Henry III. This remarkable biography was brought to light in the late nineteenth century thanks to a determined hunt for the manuscript by its first editor, the eminent French scholar Paul Meyer.[1] It gives a vigorous account of events, full of vivid detail, passionate comment and frequent flashes of humour. And it gives revelatory insights into the attitudes and perceptions of the time, especially into the experience and nature of warfare in the late twelfth and early thirteenth centuries.

But while its quality and value have been long acknowledged, the poem has generally been deemed less than impartial and objective. Commissioned as it was by Marshal's own son, and intended not least for his family's fond enjoyment, it is little surprise that the poem's adulation of its subject is rarely (if ever) qualified by regrets for failings or what are nowadays referred to as 'errors of judgement'. Marshal is presented as – to all intents and purposes – flawless: not simply a magnificent warrior, supreme in tournaments and battles alike, but a paragon of the key chivalric virtues of prowess, largesse and unfailing loyalty. A typical view of many historians, therefore, is that expressed by Dan Jones, who has commented that 'a dramatic and highly self-serving 19,000-line Life of Marshal is, despite its obvious exaggerations and distortions, still one of the most enjoyable and interesting sources for this period of English history'.[2]

While most readers will hopefully agree that it is indeed dramatic, enjoyable and interesting, I would suggest that the 'exaggerations and distortions' have themselves been exaggerated. The work does at times treat Marshal and his deeds as heroic in the manner (and on the scale) of the *chansons de geste* or the romance of Alexander, but of course it does: not only were such works the obvious model, the vocabulary, the idiom for recounting the deeds of a great achiever; they were also, in all probability, the model to which Marshal was aspiring in his life – and successfully, to the point where he could become such a model himself. For achieve greatly he undeniably did: he was by any standards extraordinary and seen as such by his contemporaries, and we should beware of responding with

---

[1] For a splendid account of Meyer's heroic search, see the Preface of *The Greatest Knight*, Thomas Asbridge (London, 2015), pp. xiii–xviii.
[2] Dan Jones, *Magna Carta* (London, 2014), p. 151.

too much twenty-first-century cynicism or scepticism, and of looking too eagerly for flaws in him and deliberate omissions or evasions in this work; the values and expectations of his time were not our own. I would also argue that this biography is 'self-serving' only insofar as it was designed not simply to commemorate a life which was outstandingly worthy of record and celebration, but also to refute contemporary allegations against Marshal that his family – and the author – felt were unjustified and in need of rebuttal.

Envy

It would be easy to glance over the stock words of the author's short prologue, in which he declares his duty to ensure that his work 'chimes with the truth, irreproachably'. But what immediately follows is in fact crucial: he says that other writers 'are inclined to undertake such tasks with lesser intentions: they just want to run men down! And what is it that drives them? Envy – whose tongue, prompted by its bitter heart, can never stop sniping: it resents any sign of outstanding goodness.'[3] This, I would suggest, is an important motive in the poem's whole composition. Time and again Marshal (not to mention his father and Henry II and Richard Lionheart) is depicted as the victim of enemies driven by *envy*. From his earliest years his rivals are jealous: jealous of the favour shown him by the Chamberlain of Tancarville, who takes a shine to him when he's in training as a knight; jealous of the honour and prestige he wins with his series of tournament triumphs; and then, when he's given the great honour of knighting Henry the Young King (even though Marshal 'owned not a single strip of land: all that he had was his chivalry'), we're told that 'many men were jealous of him, though they kept quiet, not daring to say a word'.[4] But they say words soon enough: as he grows ever closer to the Young King, the envious hatch a slanderous plot to poison relations between them, prompting the author to launch into an impassioned diatribe:

> This life is blighted by Envy: there are many men so riddled with it that it's close to killing them. Envy will happily burn its own house down to set fire to its neighbour's ... A curse upon it! ... And men diseased with envy were jealous at seeing the Marshal thrive and prosper and so cherished by his lord. They seethed with resentment, almost bursting with frustration at finding no way to do him down: night and day they brooded over how to bring him into conflict with his lord.[5]

But this envy, however unworthy, is all too understandable in an age when material wealth was dependent on the largesse of princes and on what could be acquired through military action and marriage. The author – quite unconsciously, as it is an ever-present fact of life in his world – makes us

[3] Below, p. 27.
[4] p. 49.
[5] p. 81.

sharply aware that men such as William Marshal, the landless younger son of a middle-ranking English noble, could survive in the world only by what they won in combat by capturing knights and booty, and by gaining positions in the retinues of the magnates – and, above all, kings – in whose gift all land and wealth essentially resided. At the very outset, when we see King Stephen laying siege to John Marshal's castle near Newbury, he tells his men that: 'The first man inside will earn such a reward that he'll never want for anything again!' – whereupon we're told 'you should have seen the squires boldly leaping in the ditches and on to the ramparts!'[6] We visualise those squires, ravenous for income, attacking in a swarm.

And in his early career we repeatedly see Marshal – and others – just as hungry, with numerous brilliant vignettes of how knights make their way. Quite apart from all their haggling over captured gear and horses, there is the rather low-grade tournament at 'some out-of-the-way place in Normandy' where Marshal and two companions, Sir Baldwin and Sir Hugh, are indoors eating when jousting starts up outside. They hear a knight come crashing from his horse and cry out in pain. At this,

> Marshal went out and saw the knight lying there; he ran to him and swept him up and carried him, fully armed, into the house. What a fine fellow he is who brings such a gift! That bright and courteous knight said to his companions:
> 'Here – this should help to pay your dues!'
> 'Oh,' said Sir Hugh, 'well done, that man! I'll happily take your promise of ransom, sir – while I fill my mouth with fresh herrings! Come on – give us your oath!'
> And the captive duly gave his word of honour.[7]

This outrageously opportunistic piece of ransom-grabbing is not the only telling episode. There is an earlier passage, at the very start of Marshal's career, which gives a vivid picture of how a good many knights lived and what drove them to take part in tournaments. We're told that 'with peace prevailing tournaments now were held throughout the land' – how else, after all, were knights to pass the time, and how else were they to win booty? – and these tournaments were

> attended by any knight who sought to win renown and had the wherewithal. This was most frustrating for the Marshal, who was in a quandary: all he had was his palfrey, his destrier having died from its wounds ... But the Chamberlain didn't help him, showing him little regard and leaving him humiliated.

How vital, we're reminded, was the sponsorship of lords. And the author continues: 'as we all know, many a noble man has been undone by poverty, and so it was with the Marshal: he hadn't a penny to his name and was forced to sell the mantle he'd worn at his knighting'.[8]

---

[6] p. 31.
[7] pp. 102–3.
[8] p. 39.

When it was so easy to be 'undone by poverty', Marshal's singular success on the tournament grounds of Northern France and his outstanding success in winning the confidence of kings, not to mention his breathtaking success on the marriage front, couldn't fail to make him the object of the utmost envy.

Respect

Nonetheless, the author depicts Marshal as less materialistic than his fellows. Importantly, at the tournament at Pleurs

> he performed so many feats of arms that every great lord, every count and baron and knight, yearned to match him. And what a hard time he gave his jealous rivals! But he wasn't concerned with spoils: he was so intent on fighting well that he gave no thought to booty; he won something of far more value, for the man who wins honour has made a rich profit indeed.[9]

Later, at a tournament between Anet and Sorel, he saves no fewer than fifteen knights from capture and

> once they were safe they offered again, quite properly, to surrender themselves to him – but he declined to take anything from them and declared them completely free. This earned their warmest thanks and admiration, and they promised to be his knights wherever they met in future; he asked for nothing more.[10]

And when King Richard routs the French at Fréteval Marshal and his men take no part in the bountiful plunder, mounting instead – echoing Charlemagne's nephew Roland or Alexander's general Emenidus – a fine rearguard to ensure Richard's army's safety:

> Loot and drink the English won in abundance – and food! Gorgeous fish and meat a-plenty! But the Marshal and his men, let me tell you, gave no thought to booty, only to guarding the king's army ... When [the others] took to their lodgings that night they all boasted before the king about their spoils, displaying their winnings; but the king said: 'The Marshal's done better than any of you ... He'd have bailed us all out if we'd been in trouble. That's why I rate his actions higher than any of ours.'[11]

And so it is, perhaps, that Marshal wins such exceptional respect, to the point where, according to the poet, Marshal's word alone is enough to satisfy the Young King's numerous creditors, as he tells them:

> 'My lord hasn't the money on him, but you'll have it within the month.'

---

[9] pp. 58–9.
[10] pp. 69–70.
[11] pp. 138–9.

INTRODUCTION

'Truly,' said the burghers, 'if the Marshal gives his guarantee we're not worried at all – it's as good as being paid!'

In cases such as this no respect or credit was shown to barons, counts or vavasors, but the Marshal, with no revenue or land behind him, was entirely trusted simply on account of his character, known to all.[12]

Is this, one might be forgiven for thinking, all too good to be true? An 'exaggeration and distortion'? After all, the author makes even more extravagant claims. He declares that Henry the Young King

> had no peer in prowess and largesse. Neither Arthur nor Alexander, who devoted their lives to prowess, achieved so much in so little time ... And how could it be otherwise? For his tutor in arms was the finest in his time or at any time since, so I find in my sources. It's the Marshal I mean, who without the slightest doubt gave him unfailing, devoted attention.[13]

The author makes Marshal, in other words, the ultimate inspiration for the great flowering of chivalry that takes place under the Young King, who (conveniently ignoring, it might be said, his irresponsibility and profligacy) is described by the author as 'the portal, the door, the gateway through which the spirit of knighthood returned; he was its standard-bearer'.[14] An implication of the whole work is likewise that Marshal is ultimately responsible for transforming the continent's perception of England as 'a land suited only to vavasors and men with no ambition'.[15]

Credibility

So how worthy of credence are these amazing claims, written for the subject's family – and not even in sober prose but in the rhyming octosyllabic verse strongly associated with fanciful romances? Its audience's familiarity with the latter is clear: the poem contains references not only to Arthur and the prophecies of Merlin but also to the *Roman d'Alexandre* and the *Roman de Renart* – and, in the cases of Alexander and Reynard, the references are so oblique that the familiarity is evidently great. But it is important not to be too distracted by the verse-form or the vocabulary of epic and romance. In her interesting study of chivalric biographies Elisabeth Gaucher notes, for example, how the *History of William Marshal*, like epics and romances, uses animal imagery – references to a lion, a boar, a sparrowhawk, an eagle – to convey its hero's bearing in combat,[16] and this is certainly true. It's true, too, that there is one episode, the tournament at Joigny, in which, in unmistakable romance fashion, knights are inspired to mighty feats by the presence of the countess and her female entourage:

---

[12] p. 81.
[13] pp. 64-5.
[14] p. 55.
[15] p. 43.
[16] Elisabeth Gaucher, *La biographie chevaleresque: Typologie d'un genre* (Paris, 1994), p. 113.

> The ladies redoubled the strength, the spirit, the courage and the heart of every knight present … As a thunderbolt smashes and crushes all it strikes, sparing nothing in its path, so the knights inspired by the ladies fell on all before them. It was a brilliant contest, with many fine deeds of arms that day, but the knights who'd enjoyed the company of the ladies overcame all opposition.[17]

But before these worryingly whimsical lines undermine the reader's confidence, it should be stressed that this episode is notable for being very untypical. In any case, it might also be argued that, looking at the memorably witty and specific incident at the heart of this episode (Marshal slipping away from pre-tournament dancing to win a horse in response to a good-humoured song about him), there is every reason to believe that it is all – however extraordinary it may seem to us – a perfectly accurate account of what happened, or at least of how it was perceived and understood by those involved.

It's true, too, that the author's description of Marshal's very first combat – in a fierce skirmish at Neufchâtel-en-Bray – teeters on the brink of fancy (and possibly topples in) when he describes the novice knight's inspirational intervention:

> Watching from the windows of upper chambers were knights and ladies and crowds of townsfolk, all distraught, beside themselves to see the Marshal stranded, without support. With one voice they cried:
> 'Knights of Normandy! Shame on you, not going to the Marshal's aid! It's dreadful to see him fighting against such odds!'
> Heralds and minstrels, keen to record and proclaim great deeds of arms they witnessed, flocked after him, crying: 'Come, see the good knight making the mighty squadrons reel!'
> When the Normans heard this wake-up call they struck out to right and left – their enemies didn't want to be anywhere near![18]

But let's not be too hasty. Just how fanciful *is* it? It may be expressed in somewhat romanticised terms, but, as with the passage about the ladies, perhaps we should beware of being too sceptical: the author may well be waxing lyrical (or, rather, epic) because he's so inspired by real events. Who is to say that he's wrong to claim that young Marshal's example turned the tide, or that the townsfolk, too, were 'inspired by this display of prowess [and] rushed to take up arms themselves'? And who is to say he's exaggerating when he tells us that Tancarville and his companions 'all declared – and rightly so, for they'd seen it with their own eyes – that the Marshal had fought better than anyone on either side that day, and he was awarded all the honour and esteem'?

In any case, this passage is untypical. The author's work is generally invaluable for specific, minute details of medieval combat. At Le Mans, for example,

> the Marshal reached out and seized Sir Andrew de Chauvigny's bridle and led him off; he hauled him back as far as the gate, and the horse, moving at speed,

---

[17] pp. 63–4.
[18] p. 37.

already had its head inside the gate when someone on the brattice flung down a massive stone that struck Sir Andrew on the arm, doing him no good at all – it broke his arm in two. Another man hurled a big, weighty lump that caught the horse on the head and made him rear so violently that the reins came loose in the Marshal's hand and he was left there while the horse shot away; so Sir Andrew was free and managed to escape, though he was sorely wounded. The Marshal dumped the bridle in the gateway to be collected by a boy; then he returned to the fray.[19]

And then, as fire takes hold of the city and Le Mans burns, the author describes how

they saw a woman in terrible distress, carrying her belongings from her house which had just caught fire. The Marshal, ever compassionate, was filled with sorrow and pity, and bade his squires dismount and go to her aid at once; he dismounted himself and gladly gave her all the help he could … He took hold of a feather mattress that was smouldering beneath: there was so much smoke that it got inside his helm and choked him and he was forced to take it off.[20]

These and many other passages have the absolute ring of truth, and their vivid visual – almost cinematic – quality makes the work a joy to read. The author's historically important account of the Battle of Lincoln, too, is dramatic, certainly, but the drama is in no way contrived, suggesting little in the way of 'exaggeration and distortion', and it is likewise full of detail that lends it a high degree of credibility. As the French and the rebel barons take to flight

they had a hard time reaching the outer gate, and there they fell foul of a wretched stroke of luck: a cow had wandered through the gate and triggered the bar, closing the gate so that no one on horseback could get through: they were well and truly stuck. In their desperation to escape they killed the cow, but that just made the shambles worse, and many of their knights were captured there, as easily as could be.[21]

And the dramatic death of the count of Perche in the fighting in front of Lincoln cathedral is recounted by the author with great precision and control: as Marshal reaches out to seize the count's bridle

the count had already taken a mortal wound from a sword, thrust in a fearful lunge through his visor by Sir Reginald Croc; and now, as he saw our forces driving his men back, he let go of his reins and gripped his sword in both hands; then William the Marshal dealt him three successive blows upon the helm, so fierce and strong that they left clear marks upon it, whereupon the count collapsed and went tumbling from his horse. Seeing him fall, the Earl Marshal thought he'd lost consciousness and feared he'd be held to blame. He said to William de Montigny:

---

[19] p. 118.
[20] p. 119.
[21] pp. 203–4.

> 'Dismount and take off his helm – it's giving him trouble: I fear he can't stand up.'
>
> When the helmet was removed and the Marshal, at his side, saw that he was stone-cold dead, there was much consternation; but from the moment the blade had been pulled from the wound dealt through his visor, his death had been inevitable. It was a grievous pity that he died so.[22]

This graphic reportage (though admittedly involving a possible element of blame-shifting)[23] is far more typical of the author's work than his description of Marshal's youthful combat at Neufchâtel.

The reason may of course be that his sources by that point were more reliable.[24] For the early part of the work (Marshal's childhood and youth and the life of his father John), the author was dependent on the distant reminiscences, probably retold and embroidered at second- and even third-hand, of Marshal's family; but as the work progresses the author is clearly drawing on first-hand, eye-witness accounts, notably of Marshal's son (William Marshal II) and of his squire and constant companion John of Earley. He is also drawing on documents, both tournament rolls and clerical records: if some of Marshal's tournament winnings seem improbably rich, it's worth noting that Marshal and Roger de Gaugy

> were companions for two years, and at every tournament they attended they won richer spoils than six or eight others put together. That's not a wild and naïve guess: it's exactly what was recorded by the clerks of the court who kept accounts – Wigan, the clerk of the kitchen, and others indeed, recorded that between Pentecost and Lent they captured precisely one hundred and three knights; and that's not to mention the horses and equipment they won, of which the clerks kept no account.[25]

---

[22] p. 201.

[23] It is, of course, interesting to see that, even in a pitched battle, killing an opponent of the count's status was not necessarily desirable: the object was to capture. It's also interesting to compare the author's animated and detailed account (and indeed his involvement of Marshal) with that of Roger of Wendover, who, in his Chronicle, after describing English crossbowmen killing large numbers of the enemies' horses, records in somewhat leaden terms: 'the party of the barons was greatly weakened, for when the horses fell to the earth slain, their riders were taken prisoners, as there was no one to rescue them. At length, when the barons were thus weakened, and great numbers of their soldiers had been made prisoners and safely secured, the king's knights rushed in a close body on the count of Perche, entirely surrounding him; and as he could not withstand their force as they rushed him, they called on him to surrender, that he might escape with his life. He, however, swore that he could not surrender to the English, who were traitors to their lawful king. On hearing this a knight rushed on him, and striking him in the eye, pierced his brain, on which he fell to the ground without uttering another word.' *Roger of Wendover's Flowers of History*, Vol. 2, tr. J. A. Giles (London, 1849), p. 395.

[24] For an excellent discussion of the author's sources see D. Crouch, 'Writing a Biography in the Thirteenth Century: The Construction and Composition of *The History of William Marshal*', in *Writing Medieval Biography, 750–1250: Essays in Honour of Professor Frank Barlow* (Woodbridge, 2006), pp. 221–35.

[25] p. 63.

The author's declared intention to see that his work 'chimes with the truth, irreproachably' is underlined in his account of the Battle of Sandwich, where he tells us that 'according to eye-witnesses, it's reckoned there were at least four thousand slain, not counting those who leapt in the sea to drown, whose numbers no one knows. But I wasn't there myself, and I'm not going to make rash claims when numbers are uncertain: no one likes or respects a man who strays into falsehood and speculation.'[26] And, of the Battle of Lincoln, he says that

> I should add at this point that those who've given me accounts of what followed don't all agree, and I can't comply with them all – I'd lose track of myself and be less worthy of credence. No one should tell untruths when recording proper history: falsehoods have no place in such a celebrated story, heard about and witnessed by so many.[27]

And that, surely, is a crucial point: Marshal's life was 'witnessed by so many', was lived so much in the public eye, and the events involved were of such magnitude, that excessive claims – let alone downright falsehoods – in this biography would have struck his contemporaries as risible and shameful, and, far from impressing and earning him the respect and adulation of posterity, would have been a matter of dishonour.

Justification

Little wonder, then, that the author is at pains throughout to justify all assertions, to give evidence – and, as it were, witnesses – to legitimise all of Marshal's claims and to repudiate implied accusations against him. Lest anyone should have been tempted to believe the slanderous charge of his adultery with the Young King's queen (Margaret, daughter of Louis of France), the author stresses that letters patent in support of Marshal were sent by no lesser persons than the French king himself, the counts of Dreux and Blois and the archbishop of Reims – they clearly believed not a word of it; and the Young King's subsequent devotion to Marshal, even entrusting him on his death-bed with carrying his cross to the Holy Land, makes it plain that his doubts of Marshal's fidelity had vanished. Similarly, lest there should have been any question about Marshal's deserving of the hand of the fabulously wealthy heiress Isabel de Clare ('the damsel of Striguil')[28] – or any cynical observation that he'd waited and waited till the best possible heiress was on offer (though why shouldn't he?) – the author makes it a royal gift twice over as he shows Richard Lionheart, shortly after Henry II's death, confirming and thoroughly approving the arrangement:

---

[26] p. 209.
[27] p. 198.
[28] A striking reminder that a wealthy heiress was a priceless (and vulnerable) commodity is the fact that when Marshal goes to claim his bride, the inheritrix of vast estates, she is residing for safe keeping in the Tower of London.

'My lord,' said the Chancellor, 'I hope you'll not object: I wish to remind you that the king gave the Marshal the damsel of Striguil.'

'God's legs, no, he didn't!' said Count Richard. 'He merely promised to! But I do give her to him absolutely – the young lady and her estate. I know they'll be well and truly safe in his hands.'[29]

This is rapidly followed by the author's depiction of what is virtually a legal debate, in which he shows King Richard confirming Marshal's right to the vast estate in Leinster that he'd inherited from his 'forebear' (his new wife's late father), but which was being withheld by the Lord of Ireland, Richard's brother (soon to be king) John:

The Marshal came to King Richard and requested him to ask his brother John to give him back his land in Ireland – and a very reasonable request it was, I'd say, for it had been conquered by his forebear. The king did ask this of his brother, but he didn't warm to the idea at all; he wouldn't consider it.

'What?' said the king. 'John! You surely don't mean to withhold what's rightfully his? He can't expect any favours from you if you won't even give him what he owns! But you shall indeed, for God's legs, that's my will!'

'I'll do so,' John replied, 'on condition that the gifts of land I've made to my men are allowed to stand.'

'That's not possible,' said the king. 'What would he be left with? You've given it all to your followers, every bit!'

'In that case, sire, if you insist, I ask merely that he leaves Theobald my butler the land I placed in his possession.'

'Very well,' the king replied, 'provided he holds it as the Marshal's vassal – otherwise it'll be a grievous loss to him. But he's not to acknowledge any other gift of land you've made – only that one.'[30]

Vindications, justifications and explanations come thick and fast. Should anyone have listened to sniping about Marshal staying at home and not joining the Third Crusade (in which a staggering number of figures who appear in the first half of the *History* were to die), the author points out that Marshal had 'already made the journey to the Holy Land to seek God's mercy, faithfully taking there his lord the Young King's cross and, thanks be to God, fulfilling his mission admirably and to the letter. Whatever anyone else may tell you, that's how it was.'[31] The phrase 'whatever anyone else may tell you' is more than a little suggestive. And there may well have been serious sniping about Marshal having paid homage to the king of France, an apparently treasonous act against King John, for the author devotes a lengthy episode to insisting that John himself had given Marshal permission to do just that – to pay King Philip homage for his land in Normandy (again acquired through marriage to Isabel de Clare). Marshal had said:

---

[29] p. 125.
[30] pp. 127–8.
[31] p. 129.

'If I don't pay homage for it to the king of France it'll be disastrous for me – it'll be lost beyond recovery. What can I do?'

'I know you to be so loyal,' King John replied, 'that you could never bring yourself to desert me at any price. I'm perfectly willing for you to pay him homage and avoid such loss – I don't want you to lose the capacity to serve me! I'm well aware that the more you own, the better service you can give!'[32]

Typically (the author implies), John then forgets this happy conversation and, listening to the weasel words of malicious, envious courtiers, is soon deliberately turning the screw on Marshal. He accuses him of siding with the king of France against him when Marshal refuses to campaign in Poitou now that he's Philip's liegeman, having paid him homage for his Norman land. John tells Marshal:

'I want you to fight against the king of France, to whom you paid homage, to win back my inheritance!'

'Ah, my lord!' said the Marshal. 'I crave your mercy, in God's name! It would be wrong of me to oppose him when I'm his liegeman!'[33]

Is this a clever evasion by Marshal, to avoid taking sides when the fate of Normandy is unsure? Or is it steadfast adherence to feudal rules? He is certainly having to play the rules with care, as King Philip, having demanded homage as he has, has placed Marshal in a near-impossible position. And Marshal certainly knows how to play the rules to his advantage when it suits him: when he harbours John's enemy William of Briouze in Ireland he tells the king: 'you shouldn't take it ill that I gave him shelter. I didn't think I was doing wrong – he was my friend *and my lord* and I'd no idea you'd fallen out with him!'[34] 'My lord' in this case is probably a legal nicety about Briouze being overlord of the Marshal manor at Speen in Berkshire. But perhaps a cynical interpretation, assuming Marshal to be a wily operator, would be anachronistic. Marshal is living in an age of oaths, and he keeps his. His unfailing commitment to loyalty is repeatedly stressed: he has earlier refused to pay homage to Richard for his land in Leinster precisely because he'd already done so to John as Lord of Ireland; he tells Richard:

'I'll do no such thing, so help me God! I'll not be so base: no one will see me do wrong! I paid homage to your brother for what I hold from him. No one will accuse me of falseness.'

'God save me,' said the king, 'that's well spoken!'

All the barons present approved and praised him for his words and said he was a worthy man indeed. The Chancellor looked thunderous ... [but] the Marshal said:

'I tell you straight: if any man alive tried to take Ireland, I'd do all in my power to aid the lord [John] to whom I've paid homage. You'll have no blan-

---

[32] pp. 162–3.
[33] p. 164.
[34] p. 176.

dishments from me; I stand before our lord King Richard whom I've served in all good faith for what I hold as *his* vassal, so I've nothing to fear.'[35]

In other words, the author shows Marshal winning the highest station with successive kings because they know they can trust him; they can depend on his strict adherence to the rules, on his total loyalty.

In some ways the whole *History* is a paean to that great knightly virtue, a study in the crucial importance of loyalty in the feudal world and the baleful effects of the opposite. Marshal's relationship with King John is typical: he is loyal in spite of a very great deal. He was instrumental, we are told, in bringing John to the throne despite Richard having once named Arthur of Brittany his successor, and a cynical view might have it that Marshal did so with a shrewd and devious eye to personal advantage. He says that Arthur is 'surrounded by treacherous counsellors and he's arrogant and aloof. If we give him lordship over us he'll seek to do us down: he feels no love for the English'; in other words, a cynic might say, Marshal feared that with Arthur he would find it harder to gain favour. But the fact that John promptly made Marshal an earl – which he did – does not necessarily mean that reward was Marshal's motive. We should, I think, trust that he was thinking of the common good – Arthur would 'seek to do the English down' – and also that he gave his support to John's claim to the throne for the simple reason that it was – according to the rules – the right thing to do, even though he could foresee potential problems. He tells the archbishop of Canterbury:

> 'I think it's only right [that John, not Arthur of Brittany, should be king]. Without question, the son is the nearer heir to his father's land than the grandson. We should see that that's observed.'
> 'And so it shall be, Marshal. But I tell you truly, you'll never have regretted anything you've done so much.'
> 'I hear you,' said the Marshal, 'but I still say it should be so.'[36]

To be precise, the rules of feudal succession were not that clear: according to Norman custom (and the conversation is taking place in Normandy) Marshal was right – Norman law favoured Henry II's eldest surviving son, but Angevin law favoured the heir of the elder brother.

In any event, if Marshal *had* seen personal advantage in supporting John he is quickly disabused. He is soon under no illusions about John's tyrannical tendencies and is a victim of them himself; and when, in the presence of a host of barons, he is on the end of a particular injustice at the king's hands, Marshal

---

[35] p. 135. Thomas Asbridge (*op. cit.*, pp. 243–4) suggests that Marshal was cannily 'preparing the ground for future reward', but in 1194 William had no reason to suppose that John would ever be king at all, let alone only five years later. At this point in the *History* we see the Chancellor (the archbishop of Canterbury, Hubert Walter) accusing Marshal of just such devious thinking, and Marshal tells him he shouldn't assume he shares his methods (see below, p. 135 and note 345).
[36] p. 151.

looked straight up and placed his finger to his forehead and said: 'Look at me, sirs, for this day I am the mirror and the model of you all. And take good note of the king: what he plans to do with me he'll do with every man – or worse! – if he has the power.'[37]

But no matter how faithless and harsh John is to him, Marshal remains absolutely steadfast. When the French invade in 1216,

> once King John was out of cash, few of those who'd come for money hung around! Off they went with their booty! But the loyal-hearted, constant Marshal stayed with him through the darkest, hardest times. He wouldn't desert him, and his heart never wavered: he served him in good faith as his lord and king. He never left him till the day he died, and I declare he stayed with him and his followers even then, in death as well as life, good and loyal man that he was. It's a proven fact, very frequently observed, that, no matter how he'd been treated by the king, he could never be persuaded to forsake him.[38]

According to the author John finally admits this on his death-bed, in a passage which introduces the mighty subject of how Marshal came to be nothing less than regent of England. And, in case any contemporaries accused him of ambition, the author makes plain at all points that the colossal burden of the regency was laid upon Marshal by others – and against his will.[39] Beginning with a profound apology for all the wrongs he'd done Marshal, the dying King John makes him his young son's protector, saying:

> 'Marshal has always served me faithfully and never wronged me no matter what I've done or said to him. By God who made the world, sirs, crave his pardon. And because I trust in his loyalty above all others, I pray you, let him be my son's protector, his guide and guardian in all matters: without his help and his help alone, he'll never govern these lands of mine.'[40]

We are then shown the child-king Henry III accepting Marshal as his guardian, in words as fulsome as John's death-bed speech, as he greets him with:

> 'Welcome, sir. I entrust myself, truly, to God and to you, praying you in God's name to care for me; and may the true God who bestows all blessings grant that you manage our affairs successfully and keep us safe.'[41]

Then, when it comes to the question of who should crown the new king, the author tells us that members of the council all agreed it should be

---

[37] p. 165.
[38] p. 185.
[39] It is worth noting that, in the course of his regency, Marshal showed very modest favour to his family and retinue and took very little for himself.
[40] Below, p. 186.
[41] p. 187.

'who else but the one – even if there were a thousand of us – who's more worthy than any, of higher standing, and has done more deeds of valour? That's William the Marshal, who girded the sword of the Young King. God has favoured him so much – none of us can match him!'[42]

But the author is just as adamant that Marshal is reluctant to accept the protectorship, and the passage describing the process of persuasion is long and detailed. Marshal protests that he is much too old (he was by this time around 70) and, although his nephew and his follower Ralph Musard (the latter for venal reasons!) encourage him to accept the honour, his faithful companion John of Earley agrees with him that 'your body's strength is waning – through exertion and through age. And the king has scant resources, so anyone wanting anything from him will be coming to beg it from *you*! I'm very worried: I fear the pressure and the trouble will be hard for you to bear.'[43] The author shows the magnates struggling desperately to change Marshal's mind and it is only the intervention of the papal legate, Guala Bicchieri, which finally has any effect:

The legate took charge and implored the Marshal in God's name to assume the guardianship in return for forgiveness and remission of his sins, for which he granted him total absolution before God on Judgement Day.
  'In the Lord's name,' said the Marshal, 'if it saves me from my sins, this office suits me well! Much as it pains me, I'll accept it!'[44]

Credibility II

Now, this is all very well, but how dependable, the sceptical historian might ask, is all this dialogue? Elisabeth Gaucher rightly points out[45] that, when Philip of France hears of the French defeat at Lincoln, the author preposterously writes an exchange of dialogue in which Philip is unaware of King John's death, which had occurred the previous year.[46] But this clearly fictitious passage is no more than the screenwriter of a modern biopic might feel the need to insert for narrative purposes; it doesn't mean that what follows – Philip being daunted by the prospect of Marshal as England's protector – is necessarily false and it absolutely doesn't mean that all other passages of dialogue are suspect. I would repeat that the events involved were 'witnessed by so many'; any marked exaggeration or distortion would have earned the *History* ridicule and dishonour. Eye-(and ear-)witnesses are the author's major source, and although eye-witnesses are, of course, far from infallible, a great deal of the dialogue in the *History* is striking for its ring of authenticity. One can hear, for example, Marshal himself telling his son or John of Earley how, on a peace mission to Philip of France, the 'insatiably greedy' French king

---

[42] p. 187.
[43] p. 189.
[44] p. 190.
[45] Gaucher, *op. cit.*, p. 449.
[46] Below, p. 205.

raised all possible obstacles, till the Marshal realised there was no chance of peace. Then he said:

'Good sire, I'd appreciate it if you'd explain one thing: in France it's the custom for traitors to be treated as scum – burnt at the stake or pulled apart by horses! But now they're part of the establishment: they're all lords and masters!'

'That's fair enough,' the king replied. 'It's all a question of business now – and they're like shit-rags: once you've done your business, you chuck them down the privy.'[47]

This sounds near-verbatim: if it isn't exactly what they said, it's what Marshal said they said; and the reader should perhaps trust that, given the honour on which the reputation of knights genuinely depended, Marshal (and other witnesses) accurately reported the essence of what was spoken.

Can we, then, trust the author's every claim? The *History* would have us believe that Marshal was central to so many events and decisions: it presents him as a key arbiter of who should succeed the childless Richard and as being able to give clear-sighted advice to Henry II when the rest of his noble counsellors were useless ('they might have been deaf or dumb'),[48] while his guidance on military strategy is respected throughout – in foreign parts, too, his counsel being valued just as much when he's on campaign with the Flemish: 'after he'd spoken, all agreed with the Marshal's words, saying: "Bless a worthy man's counsel!" It was a great honour for the Marshal that day to win everyone's approval, and all the nobles praised him highly for his commitment to securing their rights when he wasn't from their land.'[49] Is there really no 'exaggeration and distortion' at all?

It's hard to deny that the author's work has occasional moments of hagiography. Consider, for example, the famous episode in which, during Henry II's retreat from his son Richard at Le Mans, Marshal kills Lionheart's horse beneath him to ward off his pursuit: 'he drove his lance clean through Count Richard's horse, killing it on the spot: it didn't move another step – it fell dead and the count fell with it'. The author's comment on this is (to say the least) surprising: 'It's my firm belief,' he tells us, 'that no single lance-blow achieved so great a rescue, saving men doomed to loss and pain and woe, since God in His Passion allowed Himself to be stricken with the lance.'[50] And, after Marshal's death, as alms are distributed to the thronging poor at his funeral in London, something uncannily akin to a miracle occurs: 'wondrously, almighty God saw to it that there was enough of all for everyone, and when the sharing of alms was over not a coin or scrap of bread remained: there had been just the right amount. And when gowns were given to one hundred paupers, faithfully following the Marshal's bidding, it was found that there were three still left.'[51]

And then there is the question of omissions: the author does on more than one occasion conveniently avoid an issue. 'The *History*', observes David Crouch,

[47] p. 160.
[48] p. 106.
[49] p. 141.
[50] p. 120.
[51] p. 225.

'has a distinct aversion to tales of failure and defeat',[52] and the author makes no mention of Marshal's notable defeat at the hands of William des Barres when he tried to recover Château-Gaillard in 1203; he says nothing of the hostility Marshal met on his first visit to his lands in Ireland;[53] he avoids any reference to the murder of Arthur of Brittany, in which Elisabeth Gaucher (somewhat harshly, it might be said) suggests that Marshal, by his non-intervention, had made himself complicit.[54] But are these evasions by the author unreasonable? Even in the present, when we are generally obsessed with finding flaws in our heroes, would the biographer of, for example, an otherwise role-model, exceptionally successful footballer feel obliged to mention the occasional (and inevitable) shock defeat or missed open goal, or the fact that he wasn't universally loved, or was associated with someone less admirable than himself? And, although the picture would be marginally less complete, would such omissions make the rest of the account less worthy of credence, or the player's achievements and qualities less remarkable and real?

It could, it's true, be rightly pointed out that, given the supreme importance of loyalty, it's unfortunate that Marshal's brother had rebelled and held Marlborough Castle against King Richard, and the author's evasive discussion of this brother's death, probably as a result of wounds sustained during the castle's capture, sidesteps any mention of this.[55] He likewise blithely avoids the even more unfortunate fact that Marshal's eldest son had supported the invading Louis of France against King John before deciding to change sides.[56]

But this only serves to highlight the fact that Marshal's own loyalty was unwavering, even when he had everything to gain by being other than loyal. It was truly exceptional. And, if that loyalty proved to earn him great rewards, there is no reason to be cynical and assume that his decision to be faithful to successive kings was based on personal interests: rather, his loyalty at times cost him a good deal of suffering and seriously endangered his life and fortune. He stood by Henry II and John in desperate straits when self-interest would have yelled that he do otherwise. First broadcast on BBC Radio 4 in 1993, a play by Peter Roberts, significantly entitled *Holy Fool*, was well aware of this, and presented John of Earley as downright shocked and exasperated by Marshal's idealistic, otherworldly adherence to loyalty when any sane man would have looked after number one. It is a fine play and well researched, but John's frustration with his lord, although very funny, is, if not anachronistic, certainly not borne out by the *History*, where Earley himself follows Marshal's example and shows total loyalty at all points, notably when asked to offer himself as a hostage for Marshal to King John: 'In faith, my lord,' John of Earley said, 'I am the king's man and yours at all times and in all places. If that's the king's will I'll gladly accept, for he's no true friend who fails his lord in time of need, wherever

---

[52] D. Crouch, *William Marshal: Knighthood, War and Chivalry, 1147–1219* (2nd edition, London, 2002), p. 91.
[53] Ibid., pp. 88–9.
[54] Gaucher, *op. cit.*, p. 455.
[55] Below, pp. 132–3.
[56] p. 193.

he may be, near or far.'⁵⁷ And, indeed, the dramatist Roberts is equally aware of Earley's ultimate admiration for his lord's unshakeable, astonishing fidelity.

Character

In the end, of course, much depends on the reader's perception of Marshal's character. David Crouch has argued eloquently that 'the Marshal was one of the great practitioners of courtliness of his age. His political conduct was studied, sophisticated and devious.'⁵⁸ So extraordinary were Marshal's rise and fortune that it is certainly possible – even tempting – to interpret him not simply as lucky or deserving but as a mightily skilled operator, and to assume that the motives for his loyalty were calculated, canny and self-serving. But unless the author was painting a wildly inaccurate portrait of his subject – and why would he, when his audience would surely have been embarrassed (and bored) by an extravagant, cosmetic treatment which they knew to be untrue? – it is hard to avoid the conclusion that Marshal was simply exceptional, and indeed strange. What will surely strike most readers is the near-naivety of his behaviour. After his first major action, at Neufchâtel-en-Bray, his obliviousness to the thought that he might have taken booty is treated by William de Mandeville as material for a joke, in the course of which he asks Marshal for 'a crupper, or at least a spare halter'. To this we're told:

> the *honest, guileless, modest* Marshal answered: 'God bless me, I've never had a spare in all my life.'⁵⁹

Honest, guileless and modest are adjectives which may well strike the reader as applicable to him throughout. The author's depiction of Marshal is extremely consistent. At tournament after tournament he is single-minded in his focus on performing well or on looking after the Young King, and if he does make a profit from captured horses and knights, as he certainly does, the spoils appear to be an afterthought. His willingness to throw dice to win what is already his is almost childlike. Childlike, too, is his reaction to the teasing, good-humoured song about his ability to win horses, which has the refrain 'Give me a good horse, Marshal!'; on hearing it he dashes straight off to win one. Time after time he hurls himself into danger in blinkered fashion: one of John of Earley's first memories of him will have been his extraordinary charge on the bridge at Montmirail, a bridge which

> sloped steeply at both ends. Without a second thought the Marshal charged up the steep incline of the bridge, which spanned a yawning ditch more than sixty feet deep; no one on earth would have fallen in more than once! But the Mar-

---

⁵⁷ p. 177.
⁵⁸ Crouch, *op. cit.*, p. 7.
⁵⁹ p. 39.

shal gave it no thought or heed; he didn't care; he spurred up the slope as fast as his horse could go. The knights on the bridge met him with a solid, fearful body of lances, thrusting out at his horse's chest; but God in His might saw to it that the horse kept its feet and turned smartly back down the slope unscathed.

So he manages to survive, but even his own companions think he was mad:

> Had the horse veered inches in either direction he'd have plummeted from the bridge to the ditch's bottom, hewn sixty feet deep from the solid rock. They accused the Marshal of recklessness: Sir Hugh de Hamelincourt and Baldwin de Béthune ran to him … and scolded and chid him for what he'd done. They asked him why he'd acted so: they thought it needlessly rash.
> 'Can't you see,' he said, 'why I made that charge? There was a mounted knight among them, and if I'd caught him by the bridle I'd have brought him back with me for sure: he couldn't have pulled back on a bridge that steep!'
> 'So help me Christ,' said Baldwin, 'there was no point in a gamble like that!'[60]

Marshal's behaviour strikes his companions as extraordinary. And he doesn't change: at Lincoln, when he's seventy years old, he's so excited that he starts charging into battle without a helmet. There is something odd, childlike and guileless, too, in his reaction to the plan to betray him; while Peter de Préaux has the mature wit to advise him to protect himself from the Young King's wrath by forestalling any allegations the slanderers might make, Marshal simply replies:

> 'I, sir? God desert me if I raise the subject of something I've not done! It would be shameful to refute a charge that hasn't yet been made! I'd be ashamed even to speak of it! I'll not say a word till I hear an allegation; then I'll trust my fate to God. Treason is a heinous crime, but the truth will always out. And when the treachery comes to light, the hatchers of the foul plot will be revealed in all their shame!'[61]

In absolute terms Marshal may be right, but the innocence of his response leads him into desperate trouble. The same ingenuous quality is evident soon after, when he bears no grudge for the Young King's cruel spurning of him and comes to support him in a tournament as soon as he's summoned: 'Marshal was duly found and he came without demur: he let nothing get in the way – the moment he heard the king's summons he considered it a command.'[62]

Most striking of all is the famous scene after he's killed Richard Lionheart's horse: here Marshal speaks in a direct, literal manner, making no concession to politic good sense. At this point, just as Richard is about to be king, Marshal has everything to gain by asking forgiveness and everything to lose by being truculent. But see how he behaves. Richard – with mature and less than honest guile – says: 'Marshal, my good sir, the other day you tried to kill me, and would

---

[60] p. 111.
[61] p. 83.
[62] p. 85.

have done so for sure if I hadn't turned your lance away with my arm.' Marshal appears not to understand the rules of such a subtle and dishonest social game; he responds in terms reminiscent of the naïve Perceval when he challenges and kills the Red Knight in a blackly comic scene of Chrétien de Troyes' *Story of the Grail*. He says:

> 'Sir, I'd no intention of killing you and didn't try. I'm quite strong enough to direct a lance, whether I'm armed or not – even more so when I'm not, and I wasn't at the time – and if I'd wanted I'd have buried it in your body as I buried it in your horse. I don't think I was wrong to kill your mount and I'm not sorry I did.'
>
> Those were his very words. And the count replied, most decently: 'You're forgiven, Marshal: I shan't hold it against you.'
>
> 'Thank you, my dear lord,' the Marshal said. 'I have never wished to see you dead.'[63]

We may find all this improbable, and may choose to disbelieve it, but 'those', we are told, 'were his very words'. And we may equally choose to trust that they were, and to think that they were memorable and worth quoting because their honest, guileless simplicity were remarkable – and typical of his nature. None of this is meant to suggest for a moment that Marshal lacks intelligence: he clearly has outstanding skills as a fighting knight and, later, a mastery of military planning. But a sophisticated politician he is not. A modern psychologist might even be inclined to see autistic traits.

But that is unnecessary. Marshal's absolute, literal-minded playing by the rules, his absolute adherence to loyalty and honour, may be alien to us but were appreciated as ideals of his time. When Henry II is in conflict with his son the Young King, Marshal sends him letters asking for his permission to return to the Young King's side without incurring his displeasure. It is interesting to see Henry's response to this honest courtesy:

> When King Henry heard these pleas on the Marshal's behalf he gladly complied, and sent greetings and assurances of his love and approved his return to his lord the Young King. Indeed, I understand King Henry went further, giving the Marshal full leave to wage war against him with fire and sword, to do all in his power – such grace would he be granted by the king that he would bear him no ill will for opposing him at all: he was to have it in letters patent, plain and clear.[64]

This can be interpreted, cynically, as a canny rebuttal by the author of any criticism of the Marshal for having opposed King Henry; but alternatively it can be recognised as a fine example of how men of Marshal's time appreciated and valued his remarkable straightness and adherence to the loyalty he owed his liege lord the Young King. The past is a foreign country – they do things differ-

---

[63] p. 124.
[64] pp. 96–7.

ently there. In a brilliant evocation of Henry II's court, Thomas Asbridge has pointed out that Marshal had to negotiate 'a place of danger and insecurity – a viper's nest of gossip, intrigue and duplicity, where a single misstep or ill-chosen word could threaten ruin'; he had to 'move with exceptional caution. At knightly tournaments he had been expected to conform to the emerging code of chivalry. Now, success depended on his ability to interpret and absorb the unwritten rules of the court, to be able to follow the precepts of *"courtesie"* ("courtesy", or, quite literally, "how to behave at court").'[65] This might lead the reader to assume that, given Marshal's extraordinary rise to favour, he must have been the devious, sophisticated courtier proposed by David Crouch; and, indeed, Asbridge adds that 'it would be naïve to assume that William's conduct as a courtier was thoroughly admirable. In truth, it was probably impossible to climb through the ranks as he did without a degree of obsequious duplicity and scheming ambition.'[66] At the risk of being charged with naivety I would suggest that, if the image of Marshal depicted in the *History* (not least his manner of speaking) is at all accurate, there is another possibility entirely: that Marshal was valued and successful at court precisely because he did *not* scheme, was *not* obsequious, was not one of the flattering, manipulative, self-seeking *'losengiers'* who abounded. Not only did he stand out as an exceptional, daunting warrior whom anyone would want on his side (and magnates all over France and Flanders did, according to the *History*, offering him fabulous inducements without being asked); at court he stood out also because of his striking – and sometimes positively strange – honesty and frank directness, qualities which made him an invaluable counsellor: he could be absolutely trusted to be playing by the rules, to have no hidden agenda and to be proposing whatever he proposed for no other reason than because it was the right thing to do.[67]

The astonishing heights to which he rose in life, and the astonishing personal fortune he accrued, should not lead us to assume that he sought them. True, he fought hard to keep what came to him, but as a feudal lord that was his job: he was looking after his *mesnie* and the future of his dynasty.[68] True, he doubtless

---

[65] Asbridge, *op. cit.*, pp. 178–9.
[66] Ibid., p. 181.
[67] He seems to have expected others to be equally honest and to do the right thing. It may be significant that in 1217, having decisively defeated Louis of France, Marshal trusted him too much. In return for a 'substantial sum of money' (below, p. 211) given by the English to Louis for returning to France, he promised Marshal that he would persuade his father King Philip to restore to young Henry III the Angevin lands taken from King John. Louis promptly reneged on the oath. It is hard not to feel that the trust shown by Marshal was admirable but rather less than sophisticated. Regarding this generous deal with the defeated French dauphin, Elisabeth Gaucher (*op.cit.*, p. 462) mentions Matthew Paris's citing of King Philip, on hearing that Louis was in Marshal's hands after the defeat, saying: 'in that case I have no fear for my son'; she takes this as a sign that Marshal was potentially disloyal, but it could just as easily be seen as a sign of Philip's certainty that Marshal would behave with straightforward generosity and chivalry.
[68] And he had hard-nosed counsellors ready to step in if he was tempted to be too easy-going. In the dispute over land seized from his neighbour Morgan of Caerleon, the author assures us that 'had [his counsellors] so advised, the Marshal wouldn't have hesitated to hand over what Morgan had asked; but that's not what they advised at all: rather, they immediately set forth all the reasons why he should keep it for himself' (below, p. 212).

pressed for – and made sure he was given – the rewards befitting his service and support, but that was simply right and proper and no different from asking the Chamberlain of Tancarville for a horse as he completed his training as a knight: it was the expected norm in the relationship between lord and liegeman. There is no reason to assume that he 'applied wheedling pressure for reward [from John] … currying favour and bidding for preferment'.[69] What need did he have to curry favour? Who in his right mind wouldn't want Marshal's support and counsel? He of all people had no need to wheedle.

One thing is certain: his unwavering loyalty to John in the crisis at the end of his reign cannot have been motivated by the prospect of gain. Marshal had every reason to turn against him as so many of the barons (at least two-thirds of them) did: John had treated him abysmally; the loyalists were militarily weak and had no money and no allies – they seemed bound to lose; moreover, if Marshal had been politically devious he would surely have thought that, having paid homage to King Philip for his Norman land, he might gain richly from backing the Capetians and siding with Prince Louis, who, if he became the new king of England, would have rich prizes to offer. But no: what was *really* at stake for Marshal was his *honour*. He had served the Angevin dynasty his whole life; to turn against John would have destroyed at the very end of it the reputation for absolute loyalty which was central to his image and, in all probability, to his vision of himself.

First and foremost, naïve though it may seem, Marshal sought honour and sought to be loyal; and if position and fortune came to him as a result, without their having been his primary goals, it simply makes the story of the strange knight William Marshal even more remarkable, as something akin to a morality play.

Despite the extraordinary claims it makes for Marshal's character and achievements, I suggest that the 'exaggerations and distortions' involved in this biography are surprisingly and improbably minor. The exuberance of the author's style can sometimes lead a reader to feel he is lapsing into the phraseology or the tropes of an epic or a romance. But the likeness to such works is a large part of the point: medieval romances and epics were in no small measure didactic, providing models for princes and models for knights, and if William Marshal through his remarkable career could earn depiction as a mirror of Emenidus or Roland, then he in turn provided a model for those to come. If he, a landless younger son of a middle-ranking noble, could earn representation as a hero, then so could others. To use an anachronistic phrase, the medium was the message: a knight's life could be an epic.

In any case, I would argue that the substance is altogether more reliable than it may appear to the modern mind, and that most of the *History*, aware as the author was that he was describing events (and a person) 'witnessed by many', is worthy of a high degree of trust and credence. This is true not least of the final tributes paid to Marshal after his death. It is interesting that these are attributed not to

[69] Asbridge, *op. cit.*, p. 261.

fellow English or Norman knights but – as a mark of how chivalry transcended realm and faction – to the French. When news of his death reaches King Philip's court, the great French knight William des Barres says:

> 'Truly, sire, that is a great pity. In our time there has been no finer knight anywhere nor one who so excelled in arms, so talented a warrior.'
> 'What's that you said?' said the king.
> 'I said, sire, so help me God, that I've never seen a greater knight in all my life. I don't know what more I can say.'
> 'You've said a lot, in faith, and said it well! The Marshal, I swear, was the most loyal knight I ever met in all my travels.'[70]

It would be a great shame if the essence of this dialogue was fictitious. It would also be surprising: des Barres, if not King Philip, was still alive to deny and mock it.

Authorship and Date

So who was the author of this invaluable record? There is a passage in the poem's brief epilogue which has led some readers to understand that the author was a poet named John. This may be right; but the flow of the lines is in that case very odd and, distractingly, includes a reference also to John of Earley. It reads:

> It's been plain throughout that the one who arranged the material and has seen the work to fruition, thank God, loved his lord the Marshal dearly: that, truly, is John of Earley, who has devoted heart and thought and money to it for sure – let no one be in any doubt. Sincere love, they say, is proven through good deeds; and it's no idle adage: John has proven his in his making and composing of this book.[71]

The repetitions of 'John' and 'love' have led other readers of the *History* to assume, not unreasonably, that John of Earley is the John who composed the poem. But just two brief quotes suggest strongly that this cannot be the case. Firstly, the author refers to himself at one point as one of those who 'want to live by the pen'[72] – hardly a description of John of Earley; and, even more conclusively, during the fighting at Le Mans, when two knights throw off their horses' bridles to evade capture by Marshal, the author remarks that 'John of Earley, to whom, I think, the bridles were given, attests to this – and being the recipient, we can surely trust that he saw and heard all that happened.'[73] Only the most extravagant use of the Caesaresque third person could allow for John of Earley being the writer. On the other hand, the reference to 'sincere love' is not the most natural and expected of remarks from a commissioned poet, especially one who repeat-

---

[70] Below, p. 226.
[71] p. 226.
[72] p. 143. The French is '*de trouver volt vivre*' – i.e. wants to live as a *trouvère*, composing verse.
[73] p. 118.

edly acknowledges that his sources are either eye-witnesses other than himself or the written records of others, with little suggestion that he knew Marshal personally to the point where he would feel 'sincere love'. I would suggest instead that the second 'John' referred to in the epilogue *is* still John of Earley, but he is not the author; the reference to his 'love being proven in his making and composing of this book' is not to be taken too literally – he did not necessarily put pen to parchment and compose the verses – but as an acknowledgement that he was very closely involved not only in the provision of material but also in the structure and the detailed content, even some of the phraseology, throughout.[74] The alternative – that the poet suddenly dropped in his own name 'John' in a frankly strange and clumsy way – is much less satisfactory as a reading.

The date of the *History*'s composition is far more certain. It is clear from the references to John of Earley that he was alive at the time of the poem's completion, so it must have been written before his death in 1229; there are references to William Longsword, earl of Salisbury, which suggest that he was alive while the author was writing about the battle at Mirebeau,[75] but recently dead when he wrote about the Battle of Lincoln,[76] and he died in March 1226; and Marshal's eldest son, who commissioned the work, was away in Ireland from June 1224 until June 1226. It seems most likely, therefore, that the work was commissioned (and perhaps begun) before he left in 1224, and completed during the summer of 1226.

The *History* has survived in just one manuscript, M.888 of the Pierpont Morgan Library in New York; but at least three other copies, now lost, are known to have been made: they are included in medieval catalogues of Westminster Abbey and St Augustine's Abbey at Canterbury and in a fourteenth-century inventory of the library of Thomas duke of Gloucester. Although the most recent edition was published by the Anglo-Norman Text Society, its editor A. J. Holden comments that 'the language of the scribe is unmistakably Anglo-Norman ... [but the poem employs] the standard literary idiom used in the west of France at the end of the twelfth and beginning of the thirteenth centuries ...; Anglo-Norman features are not present'; and he is 'inclined to identify the author's language, tentatively, with that of Touraine or Anjou'.[77]

This is certainly not the language of John of Earley in Berkshire, and the author remains anonymous. He is a very engaging writer, though not always the most stylish: he is guilty at times of awkward rhymes, of clumsy sentence structures (though at least some of these are attributable to the scribe) and of a loose, patchwork approach to his narrative. But that is because he seems, self-effacingly, far more interested in content (and respect for his sources) than in technique. There is an energy and pace, an enthusiasm and directness to his

---

74   Significantly, the French has it that John of Earley '*la matire en a portrète*', which I have translated as 'arranged the material'. The meaning of '*portraire*' is multiple: it means to finish and achieve, but also to fashion, form, shape.

75   p. 154.

76   pp. 197 and 200.

77   *The History of William Marshal*, ed. Holden, Gregory and Crouch, Vol. 3 (London, 2006), pp. 21–2.

work which make it an appealing read. And if finally his work is a triumph of substance over style, we should be extremely grateful to him – and to Paul Meyer for tracking down the manuscript – for a work so rich in insights into an intensely dramatic period and a truly extraordinary man.

Editions

L'Histoire de Guillaume le Maréchal, comte de Striguil et de Pembroke, régent d'Angleterre de 1216 à 1219, ed. Paul Meyer, 3 volumes (Paris, 1891–1901).
The History of William Marshal, ed. A. J. Holden, with English translation by S. Gregory and historical notes by D. Crouch, 3 volumes (London, 2002–6).

Further Reading

Asbridge, T., *The Greatest Knight* (London, 2015).
Barber, R., *The Knight and Chivalry* (2nd edition, Woodbridge, 1995).
Barber, R. and Barker, J., *Tournaments* (Woodbridge, 1989).
Benson, L. D., 'The Tournament in the Romances of Chrétien de Troyes and *L'Histoire de Guillaume le Maréchal*', in *Chivalric Literature, Studies in Medieval Culture 14* (Kalamazoo, 1980), pp. 1–24.
Carpenter, D. A., *The Minority of Henry III* (London, 1990).
Chronicles of the Reigns of Stephen, Henry II and Richard, ed. R. Howlett, 4 volumes (Rolls Series, 1884–9).
Church, S., *King John: England, Magna Carta and the Making of a Tyrant* (London, 2015).
Crosland, J., *William the Marshal, the last great feudal baron* (London, 1962).
Crouch, D., *William Marshal: Knighthood, War and Chivalry, 1147–1219* (2nd edition, London, 2002).
Crouch, D., 'Writing a Biography in the Thirteenth Century: The Construction and Composition of *The History of William Marshal*', in *Writing Medieval Biography, 750–1250: Essays in Honour of Professor Frank Barlow*, ed. D. Bates, J. Crick and S. Hamilton (Woodbridge, 2006), pp. 221–35.
Gaucher, E., *La biographie chevaleresque: Typologie d'un genre* (Paris, 1994).
Gillingham, J., 'War and Chivalry in *The History of William Marshal*', in *Anglo-Norman Warfare*, ed. M. Strickland (Woodbridge, 1992), pp. 251–63.
Gillingham, J., *Richard I* (New Haven and London, 1999).
Green, J. A., *The Aristocracy of Norman England* (Cambridge, 2002).
Histoire des ducs de Normandie et des rois d'Angleterre, ed. F. Michel (Société de L'Histoire de France, 1840).
Kaeuper, R., *Chivalry and Violence in Medieval Europe* (Oxford, 1999).
Kaeuper, R., 'William Marshal, Lancelot and the Issue of Chivalric Identity', in *Essays in Medieval Studies* 22 (2005), pp. 1–19.
Keen, M., *Chivalry* (New Haven and London, 1984).
Loengard, J. S. (ed.), *Magna Carta and the England of King John* (Woodbridge, 2010).
McGlynn, S., *Blood Cries Afar: The Forgotten Invasion of England 1216* (Stroud, 2011).
Morris, M., *King John: Treachery, Tyranny and the Road to Magna Carta* (London, 2015).
Painter, S., *William Marshal: Knight Errant, Baron and Regent of England* (Baltimore, 1933).
Power, D., *The Norman Frontier in the Twelfth and Early Thirteenth Centuries* (Cambridge, 2008).

Roger of Howden, *Chronica*, ed. W. Stubbs, 4 volumes (Rolls Series, 1868–71).
Roger of Wendover, *Chronica*, ed. H. G. Hewlett, 3 volumes (Rolls Series, 1886–9).
Saul, N., *For Honour and Fame: Chivalry in England, 1066–1500* (London, 2011).
Strickland, M., *War and Chivalry: The Conduct and Perception of War in England and Normandy, 1066–1217* (Cambridge, 1996).
Warren, W. L., *King John* (2nd edition, London, 1978).
Warren, W. L., *Henry II* (London, 1973).

The History of William Marshal

Anyone with a worthy subject should see he treats it in such a way that, if it starts well, it's carried through to a good conclusion – and that it chimes with the truth, irreproachably; for some are inclined to undertake such tasks with lesser intentions: they just want to run men down! And what is it that drives them? Envy – whose tongue, prompted by its bitter heart, can never stop sniping: it resents any sign of outstanding goodness. But to come straight to the point: my subject concerns the worthiest man who ever was in our time, so help me God – and may God grant me grace and the wit to treat it so that it will give pleasure and enjoyment to all who hear it in the proper spirit.

Marshal's Father

In the time of King Stephen,[1] who struggled to keep England and whose hold on Normandy was so weak that he lost it through incompetence, there was a brave and trusty knight, Sir John the Marshal, so spirited, bold and tireless in his ventures that good men flocked to him – not that he was an earl or a baron of great wealth, but he bestowed largesse on such an ever-growing scale that it was a marvel to all: even those with no love for him, beset by envy as they were, were obliged to speak well of him often. He was seneschal of England; but in his time there was a mighty war between the king and the Empress,[2] which raged on until King Stephen at last had the worst of it, the reason in our view being that the good Marshal sided firmly with the rightful heir to the crown – and that, without doubt, was the Empress Matilda. Many an action and many a battle he fought on her behalf – and much hardship and suffering he endured – before the conflict was finally resolved. The noble Marshal had three hundred knights in his retinue, and he clothed them, paid them, provisioned them, shod their horses, treated them with good cheer and generous gifts: he knew how to attract and keep good men!

I shall say no more for a moment about the land's affairs – the war and the ensuing peace. Instead I'll focus on my subject: the wise, courtly, worthy Marshal. He took a wife of high lineage: fair she was, and good, bright, vivacious and cultured. They lived happily together for a long while, it seems, until the

---

[1] i.e. Stephen of Blois, king of England 1135–54.
[2] The 'Empress' Matilda – so called because she had married the Holy Roman Emperor Henry V.

lady bore him two sons, and you'd find none so fair from here to Compostela: as they grew in age and understanding they delighted all with their handsome looks, their valour, intelligence, fine manners and thorough aptitude. One was named Gilbert and the other Walter the Marshal. They were equally fine youths, and together they grew and matured till they were knighted. They promised so much, and would have continued to lead fine lives if they'd lived long; but Death, resenting the good as She does, couldn't bear to see them thrive! This is what happened: one, I've been told, fell ill at Salisbury; no doctor could help, nor could anything else – his intelligence, courage, wealth were of no avail: nothing could save him from Death. His servants were distraught to see him die: how bitterly they wept, nearly crazed with grief; their lamenting was dreadful and profound. His brother at the time was playing chess; he saw a servant heading his way and asked at once:

'Have you news of my brother?'

With a tortured heart and a face dark with anguish, the servant replied: 'If it be God's will, he'll be in bliss.'

'Ah!' he cried. 'My brother's dead! He was my delight, my comfort, the source of all my joy! I'll never know happiness again!'

Such were his words as he gave way to grief; he never ate or drank again: he died of distress for his brother. Their father and mother were woebegone – with every reason: Nature, which gives the heart capacity for sorrow and joy alike, demands it. But I tell you truly, no heart should grieve or rejoice excessively.

If you want to hear more about John the good Marshal, it would take me all year to recount his mighty deeds and exploits: indeed, I haven't heard them all myself! But in his time England was plunged in misery and strife, the kingdom torn by conflict: no peace, truce or agreement could be sustained, nor rule of law – only war, so savage and incessant that many people suffered; for some of the barons sided with King Stephen, doing all they could to maintain his position and rule since he'd been anointed king, while others declared that the crown and realm should go to the Empress, direct issue of the late king.[3] So the conflict raged between them, unstoppably, parting thousands of souls from bodies. In the course of it, I understand, Earl Patrick of Salisbury[4] waged frequent war against the Marshal, inflicting much damage and harm. The Marshal paid him back in kind – that tends to be the way of it: you win some, you lose some! But that's enough – I shan't go on – it could get tedious relating every clash and fight and ambush; but many lances were shattered, many shields were smashed, many hauberks*[5] drenched in blood, many a soul and body parted, many good and valued knights wounded, killed and captured, many ladies widowed and destitute and many a maid left orphaned and forced to a shameful recourse for want of a husband. That's how it was: there was no remedy.

---

[3] Matilda was daughter of the late Henry I, while Stephen of Blois, her cousin, was only Henry's nephew.
[4] Patrick, 1st earl of Salisbury (c. 1122–68).
[5] An asterisk indicates that a word or term is explained in the Glossary below, pp. 229–31.

JOHN MARSHAL'S STAND AT WHERWELL

The Empress laid siege to Winchester. With her was the Marshal, ever loyal, and a good number of other barons were ranged around the city, bent on its capture. But it was defended by good knights and brave men who, eager to engage in feats of arms, rode out daily to tourney with the besiegers. Philip de Colombières[6] was always at the forefront; young and valiant, he surpassed all, from both sides.

The king hurriedly mustered a mighty force to go to the aid of his good men and rescue Winchester. When the Empress heard he was coming with a massive army, determined to attack and kill or capture her – and that she hadn't one tenth as many men as he – she was far from happy, and even her most eminent counsellors were at a loss; all, that is, except the Marshal, who had her make straight for Ludgershall.[7] But it was a grim day's ride: the king and all his army went in hot pursuit; the lady's men turned frequently to face them, and in those clashes many saddles were emptied, many knights unhorsed and captured. At last her men could resist no more and fled as best they could, spurring with free rein till they reached Wherwell. But the Empress was slowing them down a good deal, riding side-saddle as women do; and the Marshal, unimpressed, said to her:

'By Christ, lady, you can't spur when you're seated so! You'll have to part your legs and swing over the saddle!'

And so she did, whether she liked it or not, for the enemy were hot on their heels and harrying them hard.

The Marshal didn't know what to do or say: he could see no hope of aid or rescue. He entrusted the lady to Brian of Wallingford,[8] bidding him, if he cared for his soul, not to stop on any account, no matter what, until they reached Ludgershall. He promptly and readily obeyed. Then the Marshal made a stand at the ford[9] and did all in his power to hold them off. But the whole enemy army fell on him, with such mighty force that he could resist no more – it was too much; he took refuge in a church,[10] alone with just one other knight. The king's men, seeing this, cried:

'Fire! Bring fire! The traitor won't escape!'

As the church caught fire the Marshal set off up the tower stairs. The other knight said:

'Good sir, we're going to be burnt alive – a dismal, sinful, shameful death! We'd better surrender!'

The Marshal responded fiercely: 'I forbid you to say so! Another word like that and I'll kill you myself!'

---

[6] One of a notable family from Normandy (Colombières lies west of Bayeux).
[7] On the border of Wiltshire and Hampshire; the remains of Ludgershall Castle survive. According to the *Annals of Winchester* it belonged to John Marshal at that time.
[8] A major figure at the court of Henry I. It seems unlikely that John Marshal was in any position to give orders to a man of Brian's status.
[9] Over the River Test.
[10] This is Wherwell Abbey. Remains of earthworks constructed by Matilda's forces can still be seen. The abbey was rebuilt after the fire which is about to be described, and survived until the Dissolution of the Monasteries.

As the fire took raging hold it brought molten lead pouring from the tower's roof; some fell on the Marshal's face with horrible results: it cost him an eye; he thought it was the end of him, but thanks be to God he lived. The king's men, thinking he'd been burnt to death, started back to Winchester. But he wasn't finished: he'd survived; and as the blaze began to abate he struggled out as best he could, though he was in a bad way, and he and the knight had to limp and trudge right through the night till they came at last to Marlborough. When the people of the castle[11] saw them they greeted them with all joy and honour.

And let me assure you, he then assembled a mighty force with which he caused the king and his party no end of trouble. He was at Ludgershall; it was there he'd gathered great numbers. The king meanwhile was at Winchester; he'd had the Marshal carefully watched, and now sent word that, if he was willing to await him at Ludgershall, he'd see him there next day. That wasn't what the Marshal had in mind, and he returned word that he'd no intention of waiting for him – a waiter he was not! He had other plans! When the king's men heard his reply they were rash enough to be jubilant, and said they'd go next day and take him by force. The Marshal, well prepared for this, wouldn't leave his good men vulnerable; they armed at midnight and rode stealthily to a valley where, as day drew near, they lay in ambush, waiting for the king's forces. With the coming of the dawn the king and the great army he'd mustered rode from Winchester, so full of reckless confidence that they were only lightly armed; and they found what they were looking for rather sooner than they'd expected – waiting in their path! Their ambushers – fully armed – fell on their lightly clad quarry more fiercely than a lion on its prey. Without any word of challenge, warning, boast or taunt they clashed with heads of spears and lances; it was merciless: many were captured, many were lost, many were killed and maimed; many brains were scattered, bowels spilt, and many a fine destrier* charged riderless about the field – no one thought to catch them: they had more pressing concerns! In any event, the king's men, caught unarmed, had no choice but to run; they couldn't resist their armed attackers: they were helpless and had to turn tail. Anyone who wanted a prisoner had only to reach out and grab his reins – the king's men were defenceless! That's what comes of recklessness. It was a cruel day: Earl Patrick of Salisbury lost his most valued companions; I know their names but I'm not going to list them here – I don't want to slow my story down. The Marshal's men carried off handsome spoils, and he saw the booty fairly and generously shared: they considered their service richly paid, and were very glad they'd come!

But Fortune, never resting, endlessly turning Her wheel first up and then down, has brought many an unsuspecting man suddenly tumbling from the heights; and the Marshal was unsuspecting as the earl of Salisbury raised a huge army of his own men and others – at the prompting and expense of the king who gave him great support – and launched a series of fierce attacks, inflicting

---

[11] The motte of Marlborough Castle survives. King Stephen appointed John Marshal its castellan in 1138, but within a year Marshal had changed sides: in 1139 John of Worcester's chronicle records an unsuccessful siege of the castle by Stephen's forces.

dreadful damage on the Marshal: he was a fearsome adversary indeed, and the Marshal came off worse. He was now advised, I understand, to divorce his wife and marry the damsel Sybil, Earl Patrick's sister: he did so willingly, to bring an end to the conflict between them; and indeed, it led to lifelong friendship and concord.

Young William

I should now tell you of the fine children he fathered upon this lady. The first she bore was named John after him. The second was named William, and I promise you that in all this realm – and in twenty days' ride in every direction beyond! – there was no man so worthy in his time. The third was named Ansel, a handsome and good-hearted man. The fourth was named Henry, renowned for his exceptional qualities: an erudite clerk he was, of fine manners befitting a noble man, and he was later to be bishop of Exeter. And they had two very lovely sisters, courtly damsels of immaculate appearance who made illustrious marriages.

The time then came, very notably, when the king laid siege to Newbury[12] with a mighty host – quite without warning, taking the castle's defenders unawares; they suddenly saw the scouts and archers, then the whole great army arrive and pitch their tents and pavilions. They realised they'd been taken by surprise – and it wasn't a pleasant one, for the garrison was small and provisions were running low. The king sent an able messenger to ask the constable[13] if he would surrender the castle or meant to resist. The decision was quickly made:

'We're not so beleaguered that we can't mount a defence! We've no intention of yielding; our resolve is such that there'll be many battered heads and bodies, many pierced with spear or lance, many left in such a state that all they'll be needing is a bier!'

At this the king's heart hardened, and he swore by God's birth: 'I'll take full revenge on these base rogues! I want every last one in my clutches! To arms, brave squires, soldiers, archers! Let them do their worst, we'll have them all! The first man inside will earn such a reward that he'll never want for anything again!'

You should have seen the squires boldly leaping in the ditches and on to the ramparts! But the defenders fought back valiantly, meeting them with a furious hail of bolts and darts and massive beams of wood to fell them: they made them pay dearly for the assault, determined that it should fail. You'd have seen so many stagger, pitch and fall, so many wounded, senseless. You couldn't blame

---

[12] This refers to events in 1152. John Marshal had built a new fortified outpost to command the important crossroads at Newbury, where the Oxford–Winchester road cuts across the major route from London to the west. Its exact position is uncertain, but 'given the lack of any archaeological evidence [at Newbury itself], the castle may perhaps be identified with a sizeable motte that can still be found nestled atop a natural slope less than a mile east of John's existing castle at Hamstead Marshall'. Thomas Asbridge, *The Greatest Knight* (London, 2015), p. 26.

[13] The officer commanding the garrison. See 'constable' in the Glossary.

the defenders for fighting so: they'd no foreseeable hope of help. The attackers came off much the worse, and the perilous assault was stopped. The king was enraged, and swore the tables would be turned: he wouldn't leave till he'd seized the keep and dealt with the defenders.

The men of the castle, good men that they were, discussed their position and decided to ask for a truce; in the meantime they would send word to their lord and master and tell him exactly how things stood. So they called for a truce and it was granted, and with all possible speed they informed their lord that the truce they'd secured was for just one day, and begged him to come to their rescue if he could, for the castle was devoid of provisions. The Marshal acted instantly, sending a letter to the king asking him to extend the truce till he'd spoken with his lady the Empress. The king was reluctant to agree, regardless of any word or promise: he didn't trust him and would accept no oath or pledge, but would grant his request if he gave him the hostages he wished. The deal was duly struck – and it was to lead to trouble, for the Marshal gave him as a hostage one of his sons: not the first-born but the second, William,[14] about whom you'll hear many great adventures if you've a mind. In return the siege was lifted, whereupon the Marshal reprovisioned his castle – he found it very short of supplies – and strengthened the garrison with good knights and men-at-arms and archers, all committed to its defence with no intention of yielding: the Marshal wasn't interested in peace! His son was now at dreadful risk, for the king realised he'd been tricked: when the time came for the castle to be handed over, there was no question of surrender – if he wanted it, he'd have to take it as best he could!

Then some wicked, fawning villains came to the king and said he should hang the boy! His father was made well aware of this, but he said he didn't care about the child, for he still had the anvils and hammers to forge yet better ones! When this was reported to the king he was incensed, and gave orders for the boy to be taken to the gibbet and strung up. To the gallows he duly sent him – with a mighty escort, being very afraid of ambush.

As the child was led along, oblivious that he was going to his death, he saw the earl of Arundel holding a handsome javelin; with boyish excitement he said:

'Let me have a go with that spear, sir!'

When the king heard his innocent glee he wouldn't have had him hanged that day for all the gold in France! His heart overcome with warm compassion, he picked up the child and said:

'You're reprieved! You'll not die today, truly!'

And they went back and rejoined the army, who were readying a catapult to bombard the keep and the surrounding walls. The king's toadies now came and said he should put the boy in the sling and fling him into the castle to shock and awe the defenders. So the innocent child, quite unaware, was led towards the catapult; and when he saw the machine and its massive arm he took a step back and said:

'Oh, my! What a see-saw! I must have a go on that!'

---

[14] At this point William was about five years old.

He was about to jump on when the king cried: 'Stop! Stop him! Only the hardest heart could let him die this dreadful death! What a sweet innocent he is! Bring up stones and mangonels[15] and bombard the walls and battlements with all the force you can – that'll do more damage than the boy!'

While they saw to the bombardment, others built a wicker shelter[16] to launch an attack on the gate. Some rogue now pulled the child forward and yelled:

'Constable! Are you watching? We've got your lord's son here! He's going to die a hideous death – he's going on top of the shelter!'

'Are you serious?' cried the constable.

'Absolutely!'

'Then by my life, he'll die! We've a present for him that'll crush him as flat as a pancake! You're wasting your time with these tricks of yours – he's going to die and that's that!'

He had a huge millstone suspended from the battlement, ready to drop; so the boy asked what this new game was, hanging stones from windows! When the king heard this he roared with laughter, and said:

'Oh, William, it's not a game you'd find much fun! It's a sinful shame to treat you so – you've done nothing wrong. This sport's not for you: I'm getting you out of this – you'll not die on my account.'

Then one day, as the king continued his siege, he was sitting in his pavilion. It was strewn with grass and flowers of various colours, and William was rummaging through the flowers on the floor, merrily intent on collecting 'knights' – the tall, upright stalks of the ribwort plantain with its sharp, broad-bladed leaves. When he'd gathered a good fistful he said to the king:

'Sir, do you want to play knights?'

'Why, yes, dear boy!' he replied.

So he put some of the ribwort in the king's lap and said: 'Who'll strike first?'

'You, my boy!' said the king.

So William's 'knight' swung into action and the king set his to parry; and as they clashed the king's 'knight' lost his head: William was jubilant! The king picked out another; but just as William was about to strike again he chanced to glimpse through a gap in the tent a youth he recognised: one of his mother's staff he was, come there to keep an eye on him – and an ear, to find out what was to be done with him, as his family were afraid he might be harmed. William was overjoyed to see him, and called out, not caring who might hear:

'Wilikin, old chap, it's good to see you! Who sent you here? Tell me, how's my mother? And my sisters and my brothers, how are they?'

The youth dashed off as fast as he could, slipping down a narrow alley and hiding behind a post. The king, hearing William's cheery words, asked him to tell him straight: who had he been speaking to? He'd heard him clearly enough.

'By the faith I owe my father it was one of my mother's servants,' he replied, 'peeping at me through that hole.'

---

15 '*perdrials*', one of a number of names for stone-throwing machines.
16 '*cleier*': a shelter to protect those manning a battering-ram, for instance, from missiles from above.

'Why didn't he come in through the door?' said the king. He sent men searching everywhere, but the youth was nowhere to be found.

These adventures of young William didn't all happen on one and the same day or in the course of two or three, but over more than two months.

And while the king maintained the siege, Henry the bishop of Winchester made strenuous efforts to broker a peace. He could no longer bear the bitter war that was ruining the land, leaving the people dead or devoid of hope, stifling all happiness, turning gain to loss and wealth to poverty; for when the poor folk can produce nothing and are unable to pay their rents they're forced to leave the land and seek a living elsewhere – so the lords, too, find their wealth declining and many are in serious want. And so it was that peace was made, and on very judicious terms: everyone would keep by right what he currently held, avoiding any cause for rancour or further discord, and all past wrongs would be forgotten. This peace was struck after the taking of Lincoln, where the king himself was captured[17] – a grievous blow to his prestige, leaving him with nothing more than his crown, and what's the use of a king who's in no position to give or take, to win or lose? His royal seal now counted for nothing: his power was dead; he was king in name only, with no authority. The parliament that concluded the peace was held at Stockbridge,[18] truly. The king was exchanged for the earl of Gloucester[19] but had the worst of the deal: he was effectively stripped of his power.

With the terms of peace set down in writing, all hostages and prisoners were released, and William returned to his father. His mother, his three brothers and his sisters were overjoyed – they'd been terribly distressed by all the reports they'd heard of the torments that he'd endured, from which God in His great mercy had preserved him; but as the saying goes, no harm or suffering can befall the ones whom God wishes to help.

In a few short years young William grew into such a fine figure of a man that no sculptor could have created one so perfect in every limb. I saw it with my own eyes and remember it well: such fair feet and hands – but they were as nothing compared with the rest of his handsome body! Anyone who beheld his shapely, upright figure would have declared, if he had any judgement, that there was none more finely built in the whole wide world. His hair was brown, his complexion good and swarthy,[20] and his bearing was worthy of an emperor of Rome, with a fine broad stride[21] and as impressively tall a stature as any truly noble man could wish. He was the work of a master sculptor indeed!

---

[17] The author's order of events is seriously awry. The Battle of Lincoln, where King Stephen was captured, took place in February 1141; but the peace to which he alludes was made in 1153, a year after the siege of Newbury.

[18] '*Estroburge*'; Stockbridge is north-west of Winchester, where other sources place the exchange of captives that is about to be described.

[19] Robert, 1st earl of Gloucester, was captured by Stephen's queen in September 1141; the exchange of prisoners took place shortly after, and again had nothing to do with the peace of 1153.

[20] Literally 'as was his face' (i.e. brown like his hair).

[21] Strictly speaking the word '*forcheüre*' means 'crutch', a broad one being a good attribute for a class defined by horse-riding; Marshal by implication was made to be a horseman.

And while William was growing, King Stephen died and King Henry was crowned.[22] He was valiant and courtly, and already had a wife and children, sons and daughters big and small.[23]

The Marshal now decided to send William to Tancarville in Normandy, to the Chamberlain,[24] who was certainly no discredit to his line but an honour and a boon; and he was the Marshal's first cousin. Thus resolved, he made preparations for William's journey befitting a noble youth about to venture abroad in search of honour and to make his name. William couldn't wait to go, but when it came to the leave-taking his mother and sisters and all his brothers wept piteously – as is natural; but he set off at once all the same. And he took with him just one young companion and a servant, for the world wasn't as vain as it is these days: even a king's son, free of all pretension, would travel with no more baggage than the cloak slung over his shoulder; nowadays just about every squire needs to take a packhorse!

I'm not going to expend my energies recounting William's time as a squire; but it's said he spent eight[25] whole years at it – which didn't go down well, as most of the time he did little but sleep and drink and eat! Base rascals used to jeer behind his back, asking one another:

'What in God's name's the point of our having this William Waste-o'-Food?'

The whole household said the same, and so did others. The Chamberlain was well aware of this – there were plenty of people saying to him:

'What use is he to you, this devilish, gluttonous, hopeless burden who's asleep when he's not stuffing himself? It's crazy to keep feeding him!'

This annoyed the Chamberlain, but he smiled to himself and kept quiet; then he simply said: 'He'll come up trumps yet. And he's my cousin's son and my friend. You don't realise who I'm feeding here!'

William was so indulged that he shared in the choicest portions laid before the lord! This infuriated others, who were bitterly jealous and thought so little of him. But William tended to keep his silence, being so easy-going and good-natured that he didn't react to the spiteful words aimed his way.

At this time King Henry was at war with King Louis;[26] no gift or pledge would secure peace: it was the fiercest war they ever waged with each other, and the borders between their lands were heavily fortified; from Bonsmoulins to Arques[27] every castle, be it of stone or wood, was well garrisoned.

The Chamberlain was at Drincourt,[28] where he'd been holding a splendid court. It was there that William the Marshal was knighted; he was elated to

---

[22] Stephen died on 25 October 1154; Henry II, the Empress Matilda's son, was crowned on 19 December. He was 21.
[23] In fact he had only one child at the time, and the first to survive childhood, Henry, was not born until the following year.
[24] The lords of Tancarville were the hereditary chamberlains of the dukes of Normandy.
[25] The MS says 'twenty', but this is surely a misreading of '*uint*' for '*uit*'.
[26] This refers to Henry II's conflict with Louis VII of France when the latter invaded the county of Eu in 1166. By this time William was nineteen or twenty.
[27] A considerable distance, from Lower Normandy near Alençon to the coast near Dieppe.
[28] Now Neufchâtel-en-Bray, south-east of Dieppe; Henry I of England had built a castle there which was originally called in French '*le Noef-castiel de Driencourt*'.

receive the God-given honour for which he'd been longing. The Chamberlain girded his sword – a sword with which he was to strike so many blows; and God bestowed such grace upon him that in all his deeds of arms he never failed to shine. The count of Eu[29] was present with a good number of Norman knights. The Constable of Normandy was there, too – but not for long! There were rumours flying everywhere that the count of Flanders was heading their way with the count of Ponthieu, Bernard of Saint-Valéry and Count Matthew of Boulogne,[30] and the moment he heard this the Constable was off! The alarm spread, with everyone crying:

'To arms! To arms! Constable,[31] why don't you arm? There are more than two thousand, about to attack and fire the town!'

Like the good men they were, they all armed as fast as they could and mounted at once. Down from the hall came the Chamberlain with a company of twenty-eight knights; as he reached the foot of the steps he ran into the Constable and said (and rightly – he should have taken it to heart):

'Constable, it would be a shameful deed to leave this town to burn.'

'You have a point, Chamberlain,' he replied. 'And if that's how you feel, you carry on and defend it!'

'Indeed I shall!' he said. 'I'll do my utmost, sir!'

So saying he rode down from the castle and into the town, and on the bridge he found William of Mandeville,[32] a man without guile, of total integrity; he'd dismounted there, determined to defend the bridge. The Chamberlain joined him with a great body of knights. The Marshal now rode forward till he was right alongside him, but he said:

'Stay back, William – don't be so presumptuous! Let these knights pass!'

William drew back, crestfallen and ashamed – he wished he'd never been born! He thought he was a knight himself! He let three knights ride past him, but then spurred his horse forward till he was at the very head of the party crossing the bridge! Come what may, if there was to be a clash or battle, if knights were going to join in combat, nothing would stop him being at the front! And on they rode, I understand, till they saw the enemy right before them, advancing in great numbers: they'd broken into the town. They went to meet them, and as the two forces closed they sent their horses charging forward, and with shields braced and lances levelled they struck each other with their utmost might, piercing and shattering shields, smashing and splintering their lances and battering each other with the stumps. So loud was the clashing din of their blows that it would have drowned God's thunder. You'd have heard the echoing clang and ring of helmets, battered down to the chainmail hoods. Gone were the boasts and claims made

---

[29] John, count of Eu 1140–70.
[30] Philip, count of Flanders and Matthew, count of Boulogne were brothers; Count Philip and John, count of Ponthieu were both to die in the epidemic that struck Acre in 1191 during the Third Crusade (as was Bernard of Saint-Valéry).
[31] The MS reads 'Count', which might refer to the count of Eu, but 'Constable' (though it wouldn't scan) makes more sense in the context of what follows.
[32] Literally, 'William, later to be earl de Mandeville'. William de Mandeville became earl of Essex in October 1166 and count of Aumale in 1180.

back indoors: rather more was called for now! And William the Marshal made a valiant show indeed: his lance broken, he drew his sword at once and plunged into the fray. No one seeing him would have thought him a novice in arms: he dealt and received so many blows before he was done – he'd no intention of leaving till he'd shown what he could do! Many found him a fearful foe as he cut through the press with awesome blows, so awesome indeed, and dealt with such force, that many gave way before him, terrified. They didn't fancy what he was dishing out! But unappealing though they found it, he carried on with gusto, giving them more than they'd bargained for! And the fact is, sirs, the prowess of a single valiant knight can embolden a whole army, and inspired by his example they fought so bravely that they were worth twice their number. They drove the enemy through the gate by main force, back the way they'd come, over the outer bridge and on to the road. They'd enhanced their honour greatly.

But they didn't have much respite: a huge new force was advancing down the road from Eu and fell on them in a mighty charge. They had no choice but to retreat, but as they did so they turned and fought, shields braced, and many fine deeds of arms were seen. But, outnumbered, they were driven back to the end of the main bridge. William was further up the street in a sheep-pen next to a house, and was dismayed of course to see his fellows being battered, so hard pressed. He'd chanced to find a lance, so he charged back into the street and struck a knight on the shield so mightily that he sent him and his horse crashing down together. He gave two cries of:

'Tancarville! This town is ours, sirs! And we'll show you a trick or two to see it stays that way, try what you may!'

Watching from the windows of upper chambers were knights and ladies and crowds of townsfolk, all distraught, beside themselves to see the Marshal stranded, without support. With one voice they cried:

'Knights of Normandy! Shame on you, not going to the Marshal's aid! It's dreadful to see him fighting against such odds!'

Heralds and minstrels, keen to record and proclaim great deeds of arms they witnessed, flocked after him, crying: 'Come, everyone! Come, see the good knight making the mighty squadrons reel! He doesn't hold back! He drives through the ranks! He lays about him on every side! No empty show! Neither iron nor wood withstands his blows! He's no intention of making peace!'

When the Normans heard this wake-up call they struck out to right and left – their enemies didn't want to be anywhere near! It was turmoil: everywhere hands were grabbing reins, and axes, lances, swords were flailing, thrusting, many knights were captured, wounded, slain – it was a fearsome battle. The Marshal was striking, hammering like a blacksmith upon iron: I don't believe Gadifer du Laris,[33] that knight of such high honour, ever performed so many feats of arms in a single day. Raining blows, the Normans drove the enemy back

---

[33] A memorable figure in the twelfth-century *Roman d'Alexandre*. A 'most valiant, worthy and courageous knight', Gadifer confronts Alexander at Gaza and unhorses him in a mighty battle before being dramatically slain. See *The Medieval Romance of Alexander*, trans. Bryant (Cambridge, 2012), pp. 63–8.

to where they'd come from, both sides fighting so furiously that they inflicted dreadful damage on each other.

The contest was on the brink of being won when Count Matthew of Boulogne appeared over a hill: had it not been for this unfortunate turn, the enemy were doomed to ignominious defeat. His men were fresh and rested – and everyone knew what fine warriors they were – while ours were battle-weary, battered and bruised. His bright new reinforcements rode straight to the attack, forcing our men to retreat – though they turned and fought back many times, emptying a good few saddles let me tell you, and they didn't withdraw in confusion but in tight order, mounting a resolute defence. But they couldn't hope to face them in the open field when numbers were so uneven, the enemy being six times as strong. But what's the point of dragging this out? Repetition makes a story boring, and it would take all day to describe every fine blow one by one. So let me put them all together and say that nowhere in the last forty years have so many been given, returned and repaid in so short a space, as four times they repulsed the foe, four times drove them back to the outer bridge and the road – they taught them the way sure enough! I tell you no word of a lie – it was well known and reported: the fact is that with the Marshal's help the men of the town managed to outfight their attackers.

The Marshal was on his way back to his refuge in the sheep-pen, to gather his strength, eager to inflict more damage on the foe, when he ran into a band of Flemish troops. They'd found a shafted iron hook – a demolition tool – and he couldn't fend off the blow as they hooked him through the shoulder. Thirteen or more banded together to try and haul him from his horse, but he clung on to the breast-strap and thrust in his spurs. They were heaving like fury, tearing off a dozen rings of mail and leaving a scar in his flesh that lasted long, but he managed to break free, and the men with the hook paid dearly as he belaboured them with a rain of ferocious blows. But as he rode away his horse was in a sorry state, with blood streaming from countless wounds, losing so much it was sure to die.

The townsfolk, inspired by this display of prowess, rushed to take up arms themselves – swords, axes, gisarmes;* the women burst from their houses wielding sticks and clubs; and with swords and cudgels alike the townsfolk chased the enemy through the streets, giving them a shameful battering till they'd cleared them from the town with the aid of the knights – foremost among them the Marshal.

Once the town had been saved by the lord of Tancarville and his companions, they all declared – and rightly so, for they'd seen it with their own eyes – that the Marshal had fought better than anyone on either side that day, and he was awarded all the honour and esteem. The French concurred, who previously had held him in little regard till they'd experienced his treatment for themselves!

That same day the Chamberlain held a great court to which everyone was invited. No expense was spared – if there was good food to be had it was promptly bought at a fair price with good coin. As the feast began there were fully four score knights in attendance, and they ate and drank their fill of whatever they wished. The door was barred to no one, and you should have seen the gifts brought by the burghers and all the other folk – the richest wines and the finest fruit – as they honoured the Chamberlain for saving the town from being burnt and captured. He'd saved it indeed, for the Constable and his men had left it to be sacked when they'd so shamefully run off. The court rang with merry, jubilant talk as all described what they'd seen that day, the mighty blows and valiant deeds and who it was who'd done them. They declared that the Marshal had stood firm against all comers; he'd plunged into the thick of the fray, sending them reeling, tumbling, battering some and capturing others. But he'd given no thought to personal gain – only to saving the town; and William de Mandeville, so good and worthy (though he was not yet an earl),[34] said to him:

'Marshal, grant me a boon by way of friendship; it'll be well repaid in future.'

'Gladly; what's your wish?'

'A crupper, or at least a spare halter.'

The honest, guileless, modest Marshal answered: 'God bless me, I've never had a spare in all my life.'

'What? Marshal, would you refuse me such a small request? You must have had forty today, or even sixty – I saw it with my own eyes! And you really mean to refuse me?'

Everyone laughed at this – they could see what Mandeville was getting at: as the saying goes, God, when He chooses, rings rapid changes.[35]

Marshal's First Tournaments

And affairs now took a different turn: order was restored as the barons intervened and managed to secure a truce between the two kings,[36] a truce willingly observed by both parties. The Chamberlain and his household then returned to Tancarville.

With peace prevailing tournaments now were held throughout the land, attended by any knight who sought to win renown and had the wherewithal. This was most frustrating for the Marshal, who was in a quandary: all he had was his palfrey, his destrier having died from its wounds – since then he'd had to take his squire's mount, so that he was accompanied by only one mounted squire. But the Chamberlain didn't help him, showing him little regard and leaving him humiliated; as we all know, many a noble man has been undone by poverty, and so it was with the Marshal: he hadn't a penny to his name and was forced to sell the mantle he'd worn at his knighting – and all he could get for it was twenty-two Angevin shillings.[37] And he soon blew that: he spent it on a rouncey* that proved

---

[34] See note 32, above, p. 36.

[35] i.e. Marshal could have won any amount of harness from all the knights he'd beaten, but had been too intent on battle to bother with spoils; he would have to learn quickly and change his ways if he was going to make a living!

[36] This is presumably a reference to the one-year truce agreed by Henry and Louis in August 1167.

[37] '*sols de deniers de la moneie as Angevins*'. I've translated as the rough English equivalent, inasmuch as the *sol* (sou) equalled twelve deniers, as a shilling did twelve pennies, and was a twentieth of a livre as a shilling was of a pound. 'Angevin' denotes the currency's origin, the exact value varying according to where it was minted.

to be only any good for carrying his arms – it was in fact the first time that a rouncey had been used as a packhorse.[38]

It was now that word spread far and wide that a tournament was to be held in a fortnight's time between Sainte-Jamme-sur-Sarthe and Valennes,[39] and everyone was astir, busily preparing and equipping for the event. And to avoid any bickering, a fortnight's notice was given that the knights of Anjou, Maine, Poitou and Brittany would tourney that day against the French,[40] Normans and English. News of this reached Tancarville, and the Chamberlain, eager to take part, prepared with a will. His hall filled with knights, all ready to go to the tournament; but the Marshal sat sullenly, making no move. The Chamberlain addressed him, saying:

'What's the matter, Marshal?'

'I'm in no position to go, my lord – I haven't a horse!'

'Don't worry, Marshal, there's no need to fret! I'll see you mounted sure enough!'

The Marshal thanked him, trusting his word completely.

All night long the knights had their hauberks sanded,[41] their chausses* furbished and their weaponry, caparisons and harness prepared: saddles, bridles, breast-straps, saddle-straps, stout stirrups and girths. Others tried on their helms, making sure they'd fit well when the time came. And:

'Bring me my shield!' one would call. 'I want the neck-strap to be strong and the handle to fit my arm just right!'

On every side you'd have seen mail hoods and ventails* readied, laces threaded through mail, and everything was done with all possible care. They were at it all night, sleeping little, awake for hours.

In the morning they set off early and pressed on till they reached the tourney-ground. The Chamberlain had brought a train of fine steeds to be presented to his knights; but when they'd all been given out the Marshal was forgotten! He watched them being handed round and came straight out with:

'The horses are all allotted, but you've not included me!'

The Chamberlain replied: 'Oh Marshal, you really should have been among the first! But come what may you'll have a good one; you'll not go without, regardless of the cost.'

Someone pointed out that there was one horse left – a good one: big, strong, spirited and swift. This destrier was led forward, a handsome, costly steed indeed – but with one unfortunate trait: he was so averse to having a bit that he was quite untamable! But the Marshal leapt straight in the saddle and thrust in his spurs. The horse bounded forward, flying faster than a merlin. When it came to reining him in, no horse had ever resisted so: he'd have pulled no less hard against the finest horseman equipped with fifteen bridles! Then the Marshal hit

---

[38] See 'rouncey' in the Glossary. Evidently the rouncey bought by William with his twenty-two shillings was less than impressive.
[39] '*entre Sent James e Valeines*': villages near Le Mans.
[40] Knights from 'France' – i.e. the king of France's own domain, as opposed to the duchies of Normandy and Brittany and the counties of Anjou, Maine and Poitou.
[41] Literally 'rolled': rolled in sand to clean and brighten, removing rust from the mail.

on a brilliant ploy: he lengthened the headstall by several inches,[42] loosening the reins, so the bit dropped on to the horse's teeth instead of sitting hard back in his mouth. Nothing normally would have induced him to set it so, but it worked a treat! So much happier now was the horse with the bit that the Marshal could turn him in tight circles like the tamest in the world!

On the morning of the tournament the knights appeared and stood before their refuges[43] and took their time while they were carefully, splendidly armed. Then forth they rode in tight, well ordered companies; and I can assure you there were no private jousts before the tourney ground, or any special conditions discussed – only the challenge to win or lose all! The Chamberlain brought up the rear, with forty knights or more following his banner that day, and a grander company was never seen. In fine array they rode to the tournament. On the other side the king of Scotland[44] advanced in splendid order with an impressive body of knights almost beyond count. But to come straight to the point: Sir Philip de Valognes[45] was so elegantly, superbly armed – a more handsome figure than anyone, sleeker than a bird – that many a knight set his sights on him. The Marshal certainly did, and broke swiftly forward, spurring Blancart, and charged into the opposing lines and seized Philip by the reins; Philip did all he could to fight him off, but in vain: the Marshal overpowered him and pulled him from the fray; he pledged himself his prisoner, and the Marshal took him at his word and let him go. Once he'd gone, the Marshal charged back into the mêlée and instantly felled a knight with a lance he'd salvaged, and threatened him so with the broken stump that he yielded as his captive. Now he had two valuable prisoners, won fair and square. He set about taking a third, and in no time forced him to submit; but just as he was making him dismount another knight rode up and said:

'Since I'm present at the capture, I should have a share in the horse!'

'Very well,' said the Marshal. 'If you want to claim a share, be there at the division of spoils.'

He said this and later regretted it, but he never went back on his word.

One thing's certain, sirs, and it's no lie: God is good and kind and always quick to come to the aid of those who trust in Him. That morning the Marshal had been poor both in money and in horses; now – thanks be to God – he'd won four destriers (and a half-share in another), and fine and handsome they were, along with rounceys, palfreys, a string of packhorses and a fine array of gear.

The tournament broke up and the Chamberlain and his company departed. They honoured the Marshal highly now, regarding him with far more respect than they'd shown him before. As the saying goes: how much you've got is how much you're worth – and how much we care about you!

---

[42] Literally 'the length of three fingers'.
[43] '*recez*': their bases at the tournament, usually fenced, protected by barriers, to which convention allowed them to retire if needed, free from attack.
[44] William I ('the Lion').
[45] Chamberlain of Scotland at this time.

It wasn't long before word arrived that there was to be another tourney, between Saint-Brice and Bouère,[46] a fine chance for a knight to prove his prowess and enhance his reputation. The Chamberlain prepared to go, but for some reason – illness or ill counsel – he never did. But the Marshal made ready, keener than ever. He asked his lord's leave, but the Chamberlain said at once:

'You'll never make it: it's a journey of three long days – you won't be there in time.'

But the Marshal wasn't to be deterred and said: 'Yes I will, God willing.'

'Well I'm not going to stop you. Go, then, and God guide you! I shan't stand in your way!'

So the Marshal set off, joyfully following his heart. Day and night he rode, following signs and directions, and arrived just as all the knights were arming – many were armed already. He jumped down and was swiftly armed, then mounted his fine charger, a steed of many qualities indeed. The opposing companies sighted one another; some charged wildly forward, some advanced at a measured pace in good, tight order. The Marshal knew his business and went about it, and before he joined the fray he'd already unhorsed a knight; but as he paused a moment over him, five knights charged up and seized his bridle, determined to take him captive. But they couldn't do it – he was too hot to handle: however keen they were to take him, he was even keener to resist! They showered him with mighty blows, but he wasn't soft with his – or mean: he paid their generosity back in full! Not that anyone was keeping count! One of them tried to drag him down, another to tear off his helm, others hauled him back on to his horse's crupper; they pummelled and they struck at him but still he broke free and dealt them wild and awesome blows, repaying their service liberally! For all their striking and beating they couldn't unseat him. On they strove till at last they gave up and he fought his way free and escaped them – but they left him in a tricky state: his helmet was twisted back to front, and no matter how hard he tried he couldn't pull it round and had to rip off one of the laces,[47] hurting his fingers badly in the process. With the greatest effort and difficulty he hauled the helmet from his head and let some cooling air get to his face.

Two eminent knights were passing by who'd seen what he'd just been through: Sir Bon-Abbé de Rougé[48] and Sir John of Subligny.[49] Sir John recognised the Marshal, but Bon-Abbé did not and, very impressed, said:

'Who's that knight, Sir John? He certainly knows how to handle himself! No quarter asked or given! See how his horse is sweating!'

'He's William the Marshal,' replied Sir John. 'And I don't think you'll ever have come across a trustier young knight. He bears the shield of Tancarville.'

Then, truly, Sir Bon-Abbé said: 'Any company with the Marshal at its head would be sure to gain in strength and courage.'

---

[46] South-west of Le Mans.
[47] A helm was laced to the ventail to hold it in position.
[48] Bonabes de Rougé was a member of a noble family from Brittany. He acquired the sobriquet 'Bon-Abbé' (Good Abbot) after founding the Breton abbey of La Meilleraye in 1180.
[49] A knight from the west of Normandy, Jean de Subligny was a long-standing member of Henry II's retinue.

The Marshal heard this loud and clear and his heart was filled with joy; and truly, joy and happiness are the due reward and stimulus for aptitude and prowess. He donned his helm once more and – regardless of who might suffer or grieve – he charged back into the tourney, where he performed so outstandingly that all marvelled at his strength and might as he drove right through the press. Everyone steered well clear and gave way before him; on both sides the company trembled! The fearsome blows he dealt and took gave them no choice but to declare him the outright winner of the tournament. He wasn't concerned with booty, but when he reached for one Lombard horse its rider didn't have the nerve to resist – though he didn't want to be captured, either, and dropped down to the ground! So the Marshal, not wanting to leave the horse, grasped its reins and led it from the fray and handed it over to his squire. But enough of that – let's move on!

War in Poitou

The Marshal enjoyed such a fine career in tournaments and wars that he was the envy of many. He made his way to every land where a knight should wish to win renown: through France, the Low Countries, Hainault, Flanders, word of his deeds resounded; every worthy man in Brittany and Normandy sang his praises; his valour was known to all in Anjou, Maine and the duchy of Aquitaine.

He yearned now to come to England, for it was the land of his birth and he wanted to see his good kinsmen, and as soon as there was a favourable wind he asked gracious leave of the Chamberlain and his household. The Chamberlain granted it, but earnestly entreated him to return as soon as he could and not to stay in England, for it was a land suited only to vavasors[50] and men with no ambition;[51] anyone eager to venture forth and test himself and tourney would be sent to Brittany or Normandy – everywhere tournaments were being held – to mix with knightly company: that should be the way of any knight who seeks to enhance his reputation in arms. The Marshal could clearly see that the Chamberlain was right.

With the wind set fair he crossed the sea, and passed through Surrey and into Hampshire. He asked everywhere for news of the good Earl Patrick, and happily heard he'd returned from court and was now at Salisbury. So there he went to join him; and to come straight to the point the earl gave him a joyful welcome, and since the Marshal was a good and worthy knight (and his sister's son) he gave him an honoured place in his household.

I don't know how long he stayed there; but suddenly King Henry prepared to cross the sea, urgently needing to rescue his land which was under attack,

---

[50] This implies noblemen of lesser note and worth. The insinuation is subtle and hard to convey: see 'vavasor' in the Glossary.
[51] Literally 'with no urge to roam'.

being wasted and ravaged by the men of Poitou:[52] they were mounting wild raids throughout his domains and plundering and destroying all they found outside his castles. You've only to look at the past to see that the Poitevins have always been rebellious towards their lords – there are many instances still.[53] So the king sent letters to his earls, barons, sheriffs, castellans, bidding them guard his land and castles and cities, which they promised to do and faithfully did, being ever true to their word, while he set off with his wife and a chosen company of lords. Among them was Earl Patrick – and it was to prove a fateful venture, leading to a grave and woeful loss lamented by all his kinsmen to this day. And William the worthy Marshal, so brave, astute and trusty, much loved by his uncle, returned across the sea with him.

The king and his companions made the crossing in high spirits. What more should I tell you? He landed at Barfleur in Normandy and went by way of Caen, Lisieux and Rouen, visiting all the castles and cities in his rich inheritance, before heading down through Maine and Anjou till he reached Poitou, where he swept through the land in search of the foes who'd been ravaging and wreaking havoc.

It was now that he summoned Earl Patrick and bade him and his knights escort the queen.

'Very gladly,' the earl replied.

But alas that it should fall to him, for no safe conduct had been granted and they were caught in an ambush by the Poitevins. Geoffrey of Lusignan, without a doubt, was the head of this crew, a man who'd never shown faith or loyalty to a lord – never wanting to be under the yoke, he was ever inclined to lupine treachery.[54] Earl Patrick looked at this band, all armed, and then at his men, unprepared for battle, and knew he was up against it; but come what may, he sent the queen to the safety of a castle but wouldn't dream of fleeing. He called urgently for his charger – but it was too far away: in this moment of dire need there wasn't time; nor was there time to arm. Without any armour he prepared to attack the foe, still mounted on his palfrey. At that very moment his horse arrived – but his companions weren't ready to follow him: they were busy arming. What happened then is dreadful to relate: while he was trying to mount his proper horse, before he was even in the saddle, a murderous, treacherous villain speared him through the back, killing him instantly, to the utter dismay of his men. Seeing his uncle mortally stricken, the Marshal was almost crazed with grief that he hadn't been able to stop his killer. He was desperate to take revenge. Not waiting to arm fully, clad only in a hauberk, he rode straight to the attack. Clutching a lance he dealt with the first he met, sending him crashing to the

---

[52] Details are confused here: Henry launched a campaign in Poitou in the early part of 1168, but was already in France, having been there since 1166.

[53] It was a widely held view in the late twelfth and early thirteenth centuries that Aquitaine, and Poitou in particular, were ungovernable: see John Gillingham's paper 'Events and Opinions: Norman and English Views of Aquitaine' in *The World of Eleanor of Aquitaine*, ed. Marcus Bull and Catherine Léglu (Woodbridge, 2005), pp. 57–81.

[54] Geoffrey of Lusignan was a warrior of great renown, and one 'completely unhampered by any delicate feeling about feudal propriety' (Sidney Painter, 'The Lords of Lusignan in the 11th and 12th Centuries', *Speculum* 32, 1 [1957], p. 41). Henry II had dispossessed him and his brothers of their estates in Poitou.

ground. Burning to avenge his uncle, no ravening lion was ever so savage with its prey: anyone who got in his way he put to a painful, dismal end. He would have avenged the earl indeed if he hadn't run into their lances and had his horse killed beneath him. But being unsaddled didn't slow him down! He could see no possible way of escape – a band of more than sixty attacked him all together, all bent on overwhelming him and taking him captive – but he showed not the slightest sign of fear; setting his back to a hedge so that he had only to defend the front, he cried:

'Anyone who fancies testing his strength, step forward!'

All of them strove with might and main to kill or capture him, but he fought back even harder, defending himself with such resolve that he slew six of their horses. Confronted by a riotous clamour, the Marshal made a stand like a boar against a pack of hounds. They would never have taken him – they couldn't lay a hand on him, not daring to go near! – and he would never have been theirs had it not been for a sly attack: one knight jumped the hedge and straightway aimed a spear-thrust through it to strike him from behind, sending at least a yard of the shaft clean through his legs. To his utter anguish now they seized him; and if they'd realised who he was they'd have butchered him for sure: had he had a hundred lives he'd have lost the lot!

Once they had him captive they drew the spear from his legs; as they did so, blood poured from the wounds through his chausses and through his braies,* soaking the ground, leaving a vivid trail behind him. They put him on a trotting donkey – they were such wicked rogues they didn't care about his pain: they preferred to see him suffer. Why? There's no mystery there: it was to make him more inclined to pay a ransom. That's how prisoners are treated when they fall into base hands. They gave him nothing to bind his wounds, so he did as best he could with the cords from his braies – and no one dared to help, and why? Because of his captor's arrant wickedness. He managed to get hold of some wadding to bung his wounds, but once it was saturated with the blood that kept pouring from his veins and down his braies,[55] still no one would give him any help and he had to wash it out and use it again. How base and mean of spirit they were, seeing him suffer so and showing no pity.

No one took any care of him, and they led him, jolting and bumping, into hidden, wooded country – for they were very fearful: they had nowhere safe to stay at night and were on the move at the crack of dawn, knowing that if King Henry tracked them down and caught them, all the gold in the world wouldn't stop him exacting punishment, for so he'd promised.

One night they sheltered at the house of one of their closest allies, which was hardly a comfort to the Marshal, in pain from his wounds and with little hope of treatment. But a lady kept looking at him and asked one of the knights who he was. He told her what had befallen Earl Patrick, just as I've recounted, and how this prisoner was in a bad way but no one cared about seeing him suffer. She asked the knight what the captive needed most.

---

[55] *'plaies'* ('wounds') is repeated here in the MS, but *'braies'* makes a better reading.

'Proper bandages, by God,' he said. 'But it's not our fault if he's poorly tended – we don't dare even look at him! But I don't think there's a finer knight here: he's better than them all – there's none to compare. His prowess is such that in a tight spot he'd be the equal of the lot of them put together!'

That kind and noble lady did as a good lady should: she went to her chamber and found a loaf of bread, removed the crumb and stuffed the crust with wads of linen and sent it to the Marshal. He returned a thousand grateful thanks: now he had what he needed most. And so – with no Hippocrates or Galen, masters of the poultice, to see to him – the Marshal made himself a surgeon!

For a long while they dragged him round, their prisoner, till at last his painful wounds were almost healed. One night they stayed at a place where a great band of knights, squires and pages had gathered. They were playing various games; some were pitching a stone, wanting to show off their strength. One gave a mighty throw and launched it fully two feet further than any. They all declared:

'He's won!'

'He's the finest pitcher of the age!' said one knight.

But another said: 'I'd say there's someone here who could throw it even further if he wished.'

'Rubbish!' said the first. 'Impossible! No one can beat this man!'

The other knight turned to the Marshal and asked him to go and throw the stone.

'Ah, leave me be, sir, please,' the Marshal said. 'That's too much – ask something else of me: you know I've been in a bad way.'

'By all the saints of France,' the knight replied, 'and by whatever you hold most dear, if you've ever granted a request, grant mine!'

'Since you ask so charmingly! I'm not really up to it but I'll do my best.'

So the Marshal threw off his cloak and hitched up his sleeves. Then he launched the stone a good foot and a half further than the best.

'Oh my word! It's gone well past!' said the knight.

'You're right, by God! It's the biggest throw ever!' So said they all, in utter amazement: they'd never seen the like.

But it's often the case that a man of strength will overdo it and damage himself: the harder he strains, the greater the harm. The Marshal put so much into the throw that he split and tore open his newly healed wounds: that's what happens if you try too hard. He couldn't recall being in such pain, anywhere at any time.

And the healing now was all the harder because they kept him endlessly on the move, night and day, never giving him a chance to rest: he was in the clutches of wicked men indeed. And he was all the worse for having no mount that he'd ever have chosen: they put him first on a mare and then on an ass and then on a mangy nag. Hither and yon they led him till at last he recovered and was healed.

It hadn't really taken all that long; but it would take me all year to recount the war waged by Geoffrey of Lusignan against the king, and the king against him. It would be tiresome to relate – it would go on forever! But when at last she could Queen Eleanor ransomed the Marshal, who'd suffered so much at the hands of his vile captors: it was an outrage, a disgrace. When he was freed and delivered to the queen, the Marshal was relieved indeed: I tell you truly, never since the days of Abel had any man escaped such cruel clutches. But now he thought he was in clover, as Queen Eleanor provided him with everything befitting such a fine young knight: worthy, gracious lady that she was, she would brook no objection and insisted that he be supplied with horses, arms, money and fine clothes.

And he wasn't idle now – never since he'd been a knight had he given way to Sloth: he'd followed always the call of Prowess, who advances all Her followers as long as they stay worthy. And let me say this: no one who seeks to win renown will be happy sitting still for long – and the Marshal could never bear it; rather he journeyed far and wide in search of fame and adventure. He often came back rich, but was never mean or careful with his money, spending freely – so generously indeed that all who came to serve him were more than satisfied. He grew so in prowess, goodness and largesse that he was held in high regard by kings, queens, dukes and counts.

Henry the Young King

It was at this time that that most able king brought his war in Poitou to an end, and returned to England with a lordly company and a mighty train.[56] It was his wish and resolve to have his son now crowned; the queen and all his counsellors agreed that it was the right course of action.[57] I don't want to lengthen my story by listing all the earls, barons and vavasors* who attended the coronation in London that day,[58] or by describing the rich pageantry or the fine and costly gifts that were given: I'll say no more – it's not relevant to my subject. I would add only this: in my view it was a bad move by the king to make all his barons pay homage to his son. How many times he wished he'd never done it! But it must be said, we often rush into doing things we then regret: hindsight's a wonderful thing.

So keen was King Henry to promote his son that he selected the finest knights in the realm to be his companions. The Marshal was summoned – so valiant and loyal, endowed with every quality, lacking none – and the king placed him with his son, promising he would be rewarded well for guarding and instructing him.

'There's no need to discuss that now,' was the Marshal's reply. 'I'll do my very utmost.'

And so he gave his word. And thanks to his guidance and instruction the Young King grew in honour, nobility and esteem; Prowess was his constant companion; and in view of his many virtues he was deemed the finest of all princes on earth, Christian and Saracen alike.

---

[56] Henry II returned to England in March 1170. He had been in France for four years, though the war in Poitou had ended earlier (and indecisively) in 1168 as he moved on to deal with matters in Brittany and Normandy.
[57] The custom of crowning a king during his father's lifetime had been practised by the French Capetian dynasty and was adopted now by Henry II.
[58] His eldest son, the fifteen-year-old Henry, was crowned at Westminster on 14 June 1170.

There was no war at that time, so the Marshal – the best possible guide – escorted the Young King to many lands, wherever tournaments were being held, giving him the finest instruction in arms that any youth could have. Young Henry loved this life – which suited his tutor! – and he travelled a lot and spent a lot, too, wanting to conduct this lofty venture in a manner befitting a king, the son of a king. So when he was almost out of money he let his father know; but his father, hearing this, thought he was being profligate, and there were plenty of people around him saying:

'Sire, this is typical of the men you've made his guardians – it's all their fault! He had five hundred pounds just the other day – a thousand not that long before! He's gone through it in a flash! He'll ruin you if he goes on like this – he'll clean you out! He's taking you for a ride: you don't realise!'

The father believed the malicious, base back-biters who abound in so many courts: they twist their lords round their little fingers and ply them with all manner of ill advice – may they come to a dismal end! The king sent word to the Young King and his entourage, making it quite clear that he'd have to get by as best he could – his largesse couldn't continue! He was spending far too lavishly! The Young King was more than a little peeved, and there were plenty of voices around him saying he should confront his father and sort him out – make him do what he wanted, whether he liked it or not! Others, who'd been with King Henry man and boy, had no time for this and tried to talk the Young King out of it, saying it was a bad idea. Anyone stirring trouble between father and son deserves to pay the price. It's a long story, but in short the Devil, ever lurking, sowed many a harsh and bitter word between son and father till they came to open war, which cost the lives of many worthy men and the ruin of many a [castle][59] and many a land.[60]

A great number of counts and barons sided with the Young King, having paid him liege homage; but the father was determined to put an end to this, and both sides went too far. The father advanced on the son with a mighty army, riding swiftly till he reached Tours. There he heard a stream of reports about who had sided against him and who had not: from Bayonne to Chinon, he was told, all the nobles had turned against him, and the people, too, were hostile. He was enraged by this, and little wonder! He asked where his son was now, and was reliably informed that he was on the border of Anjou, either at Vendôme or at Trôo,[61] I'm not sure.

The Young King soon received reports that his father was heading straight his way, riding night and day, aiming to surprise him: he would attack that very night. On hearing this he acted with propriety and sense, seeking advice from his good counsellors. He told them the exact position and asked what he should

---

[59] A word is missing from the MS; 'castle' (or perhaps 'region') seems probable in the context.

[60] The rift began in March 1173, when the Young King parted company with his father at Chinon.

[61] i.e. not far to the north of Tours. Henry II attacked and took Vendôme at the end of November 1173, which may possibly help to date the event that follows (though the author is about to say that 'the father ... never arrived').

do. The craven told him he should flee, but the worthy among them disagreed, insisting that wasn't the way.

'Damn the eyes and balls of any man who'd urge his lord toward shame and dishonour! Flee when no one's chasing you? Never! God forbid! How shameful to have it said of us that we'd fled without receiving a blow! Exquisite shame! There are at least four hundred knights among us here, outstanding warriors all: those who think of fleeing are not worth counting. God forsake anyone who'd rather be elsewhere! But we won't force you to join us – we'd rather sell our lives dearly. We'll stand and face them, indeed we will! That's the proper course, I'd say!'

And all of them agreed.

'But one thing, my lord: you're not yet knighted. Not everyone's happy with that.[62] We'd be all the more effective a force if your sword were rightly girded: your retinue would be all the braver, prouder, in better, happier heart!'

'Very gladly,' the Young King replied. 'And truly, if it please God, the finest knight who ever was and is and will be, who has done and will do more deeds than any, shall gird my sword.'

So his sword was brought before him; and taking it in his hand he strode up to the Marshal, bold and valiant man that he was, and said:

'I wish to receive this honour, good sir, from God and from you.'

The Marshal had no wish to refuse; he gladly girded his sword, and kissed him; so the Young King was now a knight. And the Marshal prayed that God might keep him in great prowess, honour and nobility – as indeed He did: his prayer was to be answered. And so it was, sirs, that God granted the Marshal a great honour that day: in the presence of counts and barons and men of such high rank, he girded the sword of the king of England. Yet the Marshal owned not a single strip of land: all that he had was his chivalry. Many men were jealous of him, though they kept quiet, not daring to say a word.

In any event, King Henry the father never arrived. The son now went to the king of France and told him of his plight, as he'd done before.[63] (By the way, if any thinking person is wondering why he'd been made king before he'd been knighted, I'll gladly explain: his father had wanted to elevate and enhance his son's honour and prestige by having the king of France be the first to gird his sword and make him a knight.) Anyway, when the French king learned of the trouble between father and son, he sent the Young King some of the finest knights of France, and counts and barons too. Many of them I can name: foremost among them were the very worthy count of Clermont[64] and the king of France's brother Peter of Courtenay[65] – from Paris to Parthenay there was no knight as powerful as he; among them too was William des Barres,[66] the epitome of prowess and

---

[62] King Henry had delivered arms to his son immediately before his coronation in 1170, but the Young King's retinue may have felt inclined to claim that this had not constituted the conferring of knighthood.
[63] He had met King Louis at Chartres in March 1173.
[64] Raoul (Ralph) I, Constable of France since 1164.
[65] Peter I of Courtenay, the youngest son of Louis VI.
[66] 'le buen Barrois': William II des Barres. His son, William III des Barres, is to feature later.

courage; also the lord of Montmorency[67] – from Clermont to Beaugency there was no knight of any degree more committed to noble deeds. It would be tiresome to name them all, but let me explain why I've mentioned the illustrious knights involved in this affair: it's because they were among those who were deeply jealous of the high honour that had befallen the Marshal that day.

But going back a moment, I forgot – a grave omission! – to mention the action of the count of Nantes,[68] who was endowed with more fine qualities than anyone could say, so it's good to put on record his prowess and his courage, his intelligence and conduct: on hearing the unwelcome news that the father was on his way to seize the son, the Young King's forces didn't want to be taken unprepared and went to arm; but the good count leapt straight on his horse, quite unarmed, and while all the other knights were carefully arming, the count, without any fuss or any help, threw on his hauberk while sitting in the saddle! Someone said:

'Please tell us, good sir, why you mounted unarmed and are arming on horseback!'

'I'll tell you,' he said, 'indeed I will. It's all very well being armed when you're in danger, but if your horse is too far away when your enemy attack, they'll capture you in no time – you'll be in much less trouble if you're mounted. In a crisis you'll quickly come unstuck if you don't have your horse to hand. I've seen men caught out like that – killed or shamefully captured. I think that answers your question.'

I'm glad I've filled you in on this: I shouldn't have forgotten the noble duke of Brittany,[69] the wellspring of many great deeds.

But let me now return to the story, to what I'd begun to say. The war between the father and son was so bitter and savage that it was grievously baneful and damaging to all; and it was disastrous and shameful for those who'd sided with the Young King, for they were stripped of their inheritances. The war led to many a castle and many a town being razed to the ground; many worthy men, blameless and uninvolved, were killed or ruined, reduced to wretched poverty by the dreadful conflict. Curse the day that those treacherous tongues created the division between father and son: what a wicked game they played. And there are many places where the war's scars can still be seen: in Normandy, in England, in Anjou, Poitou and Maine, and in the duchy of Aquitaine, lie the ruins of many castles which were never rebuilt and never will be. Sic transit gloria mundi.[70]

---

[67] Bouchard V.

[68] This is the Young King's younger brother Geoffrey (Henry II's third surviving son), who was betrothed to Constance, duchess of Brittany and might appropriately have held the title 'count of Nantes' between his betrothal and much later marriage (Constance was only five years old at the time of their betrothal and he was only eight). He is not referred to as count of Nantes elsewhere, though the title had previously been held by his uncle Geoffrey FitzEmpress.

[69] Another way of referring to Geoffrey: see previous note; he was to become duke of Brittany through his marriage to Constance in 1181. At the time of this event (1173) he was only fifteen.

[70] 'Esi dechiet l'orguil del munt': literally 'thus falls the pride of the world'.

The war was the fiercest ever seen, involving as it did three kings, for the son was supported by the full power of the king of France as well as by those who'd turned against the father and sided with him. But no matter how hard they fought – and they strove with all their might – and for all their bluster and boasts and claims, they never won a foot of ground from the king of England. And let me tell you: in the end, when it came to it, many of the rebels were in such a state that they didn't have a penny to give a minstrel![71] Nor could they get credit, pledge what they might and try as they did without a moment's rest:[72] they were in debt beyond any hope of repaying. How deflating it must have been: when money goes, pride goes with it! The higher that men are borne by wealth, the more shameful is their fall through poverty. And the rebels, now quite penniless, had to pawn or sell their arms, their rounceys, packhorses, palfreys, destriers – they had to give up the lot. They had no choice, no other recourse; and even their closest friends wouldn't lodge them for a single night, not daring to harbour them. And let me tell you, the most eminent lords of France very readily turned their backs on them to seek their own advantage: the king of England greased their palms and won them over with well-tuned words to secure his own position. And it was plainly apparent that the king of France, on whom the son depended, was far from happy about the expense he'd incurred and resources he'd committed and, in short, he wasn't keen to carry on. That became clear to many. His ear was bent in no uncertain manner, as everyone kept deploring what he'd spent and done, and telling him he was risking his own position: the enterprise was doing nothing for the crown of France, advancing and enhancing it not a whit. They reproached him for the lavish expense of his grand campaigns: he'd gone and besieged Rouen to no avail; Verneuil likewise he'd left with nothing – no homage, no ransom:[73] it had all been fruitless.

'And it isn't right or proper setting father against son,' they told him. 'No good will come of it. It'll be disastrous for the son – and for you: you'll earn the blame unless you extricate yourself! You can see he's coming unstuck, and you're gaining nothing. When carrying on is bound to lead to losses and disgrace, heed wise and trusty counsel, so that people don't reproach you and your honour is preserved.'

He courteously replied: 'I'll do exactly as you say: it makes absolute sense.'

The archbishops, bishops and barons advised that this be put before the Young King and his supporters; and the Young King was persuaded – he didn't object at all: but then, there's a lot in the saying 'when needs must'! So they sent the archbishop of Reims with a bishop, an abbot and a Knight Templar to confer with the old King Henry.

---

[71] I take the '*menor*' in the MS, which might be interpreted as 'the least [person]' or as '[Friar] Minor' (a Franciscan), to be a spelling of '*menour*', a roving minstrel.

[72] This is an attempt to explain the possibly corrupt line '*Que il ne cloïssent lor iels*' ('that they might not close their eyes').

[73] '*tensement*': payment made to buy off an attacker (effectively protection money). Henry II had relieved both cities: in August 1173 he had seen off Louis's army from Verneuil and given his rearguard a battering, and in August 1174 Louis and the Young King decided to retreat from Rouen when Henry arrived.

This able deputation duly set out and found the king between Conches[74] and Verneuil. As soon as he set eyes on them he knew exactly who they were and what had brought them. He went to meet them and welcomed them warmly, for he was courteous and wise indeed, and they greeted him most fittingly, for they, too, were wise and cultured men. They quickly told him why they'd come; and when King Henry had heard them out he gave a bitter laugh and asked, very reasonably:

'Who's going to repair the damage and the losses my lands have suffered, ravaged in the war they've waged on me?'

'Good sire,' they replied, 'your anger shouldn't be directed at your son or those who sided with him but at those who egged him on: those who urged him to turn against you are the ones who should be punished and despised.'

'And so they will be, by my life!' said the king. 'Every hour of every day to come, they and their issue will feel my wrath!'

With that their negotiations began, the king calling only a few advisors.[75] I don't know exactly what was said, or what further news was brought from the French, but peace was made; the war ceased and the son was reconciled with the father, returning to him without any ill will. It was agreed that his supporters would be pardoned, but they were ruined. Ruined? Yes, that's the only word! They were destitute: they could engage in lawsuits as much as they liked, having nothing to lose! They didn't know which way to turn; they were utterly confounded. 'The winner takes all, the loser's finished' might well have been their refrain; those who'd stirred up all the trouble could now boast they'd got exactly what they'd sought! They no longer had any standing at court; if any business brought them there they found themselves powerless and shunned.

With the war brought to an end, the king, his son and his men returned to England.[76] And a pleasant time they spent there, indulging in all manner of sport in forest and on river. They stayed in England for almost a year, involved in no business but jousting, tourneying and hunting.

But this wasn't to the Young King's liking – far from it; his companions, too, found it deeply frustrating – they wanted to be travelling, not staying put. Let's be honest: being sedentary is shameful to the young. Unamused at being stuck like this in England, Henry the Young King, prompted by his companions, came to his father – who loved him dearly – and said:

'If you wouldn't mind, I'd like to venture abroad again: it's doing me no good, lingering so long in England – it's tiresome! I'm not a moulting hawk to be kept mewed up! A young man who stays put can come to no good – and will earn no respect.'

---

[74] Conches-en-Ouche.
[75] The peace negotiations lasted most of September 1174 and were held in several places, with a first meeting at Gisors and final agreement being reached at Montlouis-sur-Loire just east of Tours.
[76] In May 1175.

His father could see his point and thoroughly approved; he gave him fond leave and provided his companions with ample money and fine gifts, bidding them, whatever they did, look after his son. And he especially entreated and commanded William the Marshal, whom he deemed most worthy and loyal, to take care of him: he trusted him more than anyone.

'I shall do all in my power,' he replied, 'truly.'

So they all promised. Then they headed straight for Dover and put to sea at once and landed at Wissant.[77] They slept in the town that night, and their stay was a bother to no one as they paid their dues in full. They asked for news of the count of Flanders, and were told they would find him at Arras without a doubt. They pressed on with their planned journey and found him there indeed; and when he heard of the Young King's coming he was far from indifferent: he was delighted, and went at once to welcome him, and as they met they greeted each other with equal warmth, exchanging kisses in happy meeting. Such amity was only right: they were cousins, close allies indeed. And without question, no king of England was ever made so welcome in Flanders or shown such love and honour: Count Philip of Flanders, so mightily renowned, personally escorted him to all his castles and all his cities, and ensured that he was honoured like a king.

They now heard word that a great tournament was to be held between Gournay and Ressons:[78] it was the subject of much excitement. The Young King was thrilled by the news, and said that if he could only get hold of arms and horses he'd be very glad to go.

'We can't let that stop you, my good, dear sir!' said the count. 'Anything you need you'll have. I'm only too delighted that you should go, indeed I am!'

He and his companions were promptly and lavishly supplied with the most splendid gear imaginable, and when he arrived at the tourney ground the king looked quite magnificent: his harness and trappings and show were beyond all price – and no one could have guessed that they were borrowed. His side drew up in good and serried order, but their opponents scorned to do so: oozing proud confidence because of their mighty numbers, they charged in disarray to meet them before their lists.[79] There were no preliminaries or warm-up jousts! They went straight at it with all their might, storming in disorder at the Young King's battalion, who met them fiercely, fired to fight well. You'd have seen maces smashing down on heads, swords cutting through heads and arms. And the over-confident came off worse: charging as they were with no formation, not keeping together at all, they were quickly routed and sent reeling back, the first to arrive the first to leave. The Marshal left the king and rode after a troop who were trundling off in retreat; he charged into their midst with such force that he brought a knight crashing down, but he didn't stop to take him captive:

---

[77] The Young King sailed in fact from Portsmouth (in April 1176) and landed at Barfleur. The author may well have assumed a Dover to Wissant crossing because of the coming meeting with the count of Flanders.

[78] Gournay-sur-Aronde and Ressons-sur-Matz, north-west of Compiègne.

[79] '*lor lices*': the '*lices*' ('lists') were the barriers, sometimes further fortified with a bank and ditch, marking each side's base and refuge (see note 43 above, p. 41).

he was bent on giving such an account of himself that all who saw him would have to bear true witness! He drove them back and sent them packing, showing them the way with fearsome blows. Another troop now fell on him in numbers, forcing him back to the Young King's lines; but with that they left the combat, in which the Marshal's display had won him mighty esteem that day from all who'd witnessed it.

The king, seeing him return, said: 'Ah, you're back, Marshal – I should think so, too! Leaving your lord's side at such a time, it's not right – but you couldn't resist! I don't mean to teach you lessons, but you must understand that you shouldn't have left me at a time like this: it wasn't right; it was very wrong.'

The Marshal replied with good-natured humour, saying: 'So help me God, sire, I did ride off, it's true. But when I left I didn't realise you wanted to surpass your forebears in chivalry! If you're aspiring to such excellence, I'll be with you all the way!'

For a year and a half the Young King and his retinue, fiercely ambitious to perform great deeds, went from tourney to tourney. But from every event he came away battered and bruised; his men were captured and given a sound beating and sent packing. That's how it was; and yet he had an exceptional company, all hungry to excel. Everyone was very struck by this and mightily puzzled.

One day he and his men came to a tournament where Normans and English were ranged against French. As they surveyed the opposition the French were celebrating as if they'd already won and taken the whole lot prisoner – for that's what they were used to! The Young King's company gathered to discuss this. One said:

'Why are we losing all respect? We're made of flesh and bone just like the French! God bring shame on anyone who lets himself be captured and doesn't have the spirit for a fight!'

At the Marshal's urging they all agreed: without exception they pledged to stand by all that the man had said. I can't tell you exactly where this tourney was; nor can I be bothered to list the names of the French involved – who were expecting rich booty, so brimming with confidence that in their lodgings, the night before the tournament, they'd already agreed a division of the money and the gear they'd win from the English: rich spoils, yes, but not yet won!

Ever since the rebuke he'd had from the king, the Marshal had stayed at his side wherever they went (regardless of personal consequence), ever ready to aid, defend and rescue him. And that day no one dared try to catch the king or seize his reins for fear of the Marshal's mighty blows, which were weighty and wicked indeed; and the Young King's company fought so well that they lost nothing to the French: they rather won spoils from them – along with victory in the tourney.

So splendidly did they perform there that thenceforth every tournament they entered saw them repel and defeat all opposition: from every fray and every mêlée they emerged with booty! Bless the Marshal for inspiring them with his brave heart!

For a long while now he was the presiding influence over his lord – and rightly so, by God, when he was so intent on raising him in prowess. I promise you, the good, handsome, courtly Young King behaved in such fine fashion that he revived the spirit of knighthood, which was then in terminal decline: he was the portal, the door, the gateway through which that spirit returned; he was its standard-bearer. Its standard-bearer? Yes indeed! How so? Because at that time the greatest lords did nothing for budding knights, but the Young King was the flower, the epitome of knighthood, attracting good knights to him: he wanted all knights of quality to join his company. And when the great lords – who at that time were achieving nothing of note – saw what he was doing, they realised how wise the Young King was: for without able support, no king or count can prosper. As I understand it, it was now that the great lords began to select good knights for their retinues, establishing Chivalry in its rightful state – in which it hadn't been before; to compete with the Young King, these lords took good knights under their wing and maintained and nurtured them. Truly, it was to vie with the Young King that the good count of Flanders, so valiant and wise, set out to prove his prowess to the world – his heart brimmed with it; the Young King had learnt how to attract and retain good young knights of worth – Prowess and Wisdom giving him an eye for valour – and the count did likewise. Then the great lords of the land, eager to win honour, sought out and retained the good young knights they knew, and happily provided them with horses, arms and money, or land or a source of healthy revenue. But now the great lords have fettered Chivalry once more: overcome by Sloth, in thrall to Avarice, they've shut Largesse away out of sight! The life of the knight errant, travelling from tournament to mighty tournament, has been replaced by tame and regulated jousts. But if it please God, King Henry[80] will restore exuberance, joy and laughter to the world – and God confound all those who've advised him otherwise! Through him we hope to see Largesse freed from its shameful prison. And God grant that in time to come we see Merlin's prophecies fulfilled – his prophecies about the kings of Britain, that is, which I've found in the *Brut*:[81] God grant indeed that the king of England may recover what is rightfully his, which through sheer greed and treachery was sold![82] If it please God, it will not be lost forever.

But let's return to the story. I've more to tell about the worthy Count Philip of Flanders, who in shrewd intelligence surpassed all men of his time. Great prowess needs to be combined with guile! And whenever the Young King went to a tournament with his mighty company, fierce and bold, following his banner, the count of Flanders would bide his time, joining the tourney only when all were flagging and had lost their shape! Then, seeing his advantage, the count, shrewd as well as valiant, would charge in from the flank! Many a saddle was

---

[80] i.e. the young Henry III, in the early years of whose reign the poet is writing.
[81] The poet is presumably referring to the *Roman de Brut* by Wace (c. 1155), a history of the kings of Britain, written in French and in verse, based closely on Geoffrey of Monmouth's Latin *Historia Regum Britannie* (c. 1135). However, most MSS of the *Brut* in fact omit Merlin's prophecies (Book VII of Geoffrey's *Historia*), so 'the Brut' may simply be a shorthand way of referring to Geoffrey's hugely influential work or to its matter.
[82] i.e. the lands lost in France by King John.

emptied then, many a knight unhorsed, beaten and battered, taken prisoner and ransomed – the same knights who at the outset had been the first to enter the fray. It's foolish to break ranks too soon. That's how the count dealt with the Young King: he attacked when he saw his men disordered, tiring and sore from blows; that was his tactic every time!

The king realised the damage the count was doing, and that he wasn't going to spare him, so he looked for a way to respond. One day he gave the impression that he wasn't coming to a tourney; he gave no sign of bearing arms or taking part. Then suddenly, taking everyone unawares, he cried:

'At them! God is with us!'

And the king's men charged Count Philip's men when they were in no state to put up a fight and didn't dare to face them! So many banners and pennons then were toppled and dragged through the mud! So many horses of every hue roamed riderless over the field, to be seized and captured by all who could. The king's men put the count's to flight and won spoils a-plenty. And this devastating ploy had been prompted by the Marshal. That's what happened; and from that time forth whenever the Young King went to a tourney, in field or town, he used the same ruse and trick!

Then, in the spring, a grand tournament was to be held between Anet and Sorel.[83] Every knight errant who heard of it made eager preparations to attend: no knight in France,[84] Flanders, Brie or Champagne was going to miss it. To face them came the Normans and the Bretons who sided with them, and knights from England, Maine, Anjou and Poitou with their lord the Young King, who now had them so well trained and confident that, wherever they fought, they were convinced that provided they kept together they would put paid to anyone they met and come out on top, with ample spoils to share.

The tournament duly assembled, and it was great indeed, to the delight of experienced tourneyers. The French entered in wild disorder, in such reckless disarray that their squadrons were colliding, impeding one another. Seeing this, the king's men let them carry on and then spurred into a charge, meeting them so fearsomely that they drove them apart and sent them reeling, unable to resist for an instant: when the king's own company arrived, the French were already in flight. Whenever anyone gives chase there are many who flee – and on the other hand, it's often the case in tournaments that when anyone flees there are many who give chase! It was an utter rout; and the king's men, losing all discipline, set off in such wild pursuit, so intent on winning booty, that they left the king behind, all alone except for the Marshal! These two headed after them, and found themselves riding down the main street in Anet. There were no knights to be seen – they'd all gone rushing on; but glancing to their right they saw a great crowd down another street: Sir Simon de Neauphle[85] was there – he'd mustered three

---

[83] Anet and the village of Sorel are just north of Dreux, west of Paris.
[84] i.e. the king of France's own domain, essentially the Île de France.
[85] Simon IV, castellan of Neauphle-le-Château to the west of Versailles. He was a figure of some notoriety: just a year before this tournament, in 1176–7, he'd had to make reparations at King Louis's court for murdering one Simon de Maurepas.

hundred foot soldiers armed with bows and spears and gisarmes, and they were blocking the way.

'We'll not get through,' said the king, 'but there's no question of turning back.'

The Marshal's reply was: 'There's only one thing for it, by God: attack!'

And when the soldiers saw them charging they were off! They didn't dare stand and face them! The Marshal rode up and reached for Sir Simon's bridle; the moment he seized it, that was it: he had such fast hold that Simon couldn't break free, and he led him off, the king following behind. Now, the Marshal didn't notice, but there was a gutter hanging low above the street, within Sir Simon's reach; he grabbed hold and stayed swinging there while the Marshal, unaware, carried on without a backward glance! The king had seen, but preferred not to say; so on down the street rode the Marshal, leaving Sir Simon hanging from the gutter! Back he came to the baggage train leading the horse by the reins and said to a squire:

'Take charge of this knight.'

'Which knight would that be?' said the jovial, witty king.

'Which knight? The one I've captured!'

'You can keep his horse and harness,' said the king, 'but I think you'll find you've lost the knight!'

'What!' said the Marshal. 'Where's he gone?'

'He decided to hang around back there – suspended from a gutter!'

When the Marshal looked round he roared with laughter and thought it a splendid joke! They left the town then, but the story of this caper was often told thereafter.

The Tournament at Pleurs

Word spreads fast, and soon everyone was talking about a tournament to be held three weeks later at Pleurs,[86] featuring the most illustrious lords. It was too far to travel with much of a train so the Young King didn't go, but the Marshal didn't want to miss it – he was keen to enhance his reputation, eager to win honour. He asked his lord's leave which was readily given, for he was a devoted friend: the king wished him nothing but fortune and honour, knowing that he wished him the same – he had tested him on many occasions and found him always true. So the Marshal left his lord, taking with him just one knight – I don't know who he was: no one's ever told me.

They went swiftly on their way, pressing ever on till they reached the tournament site. Every banner-bearing lord from there to the heights of Mont-Joux[87] had come with a will, as had every knight who frequented tournaments. Of the great counts and barons who attended I know the names of many. The duke of Burgundy,[88] a great lover of tournaments, was present, truly, as was the

---

[86] *'Pleierre'*. Pleurs is east of Paris and north of Troyes.
[87] *'Mongeu'*: Mont-Joux was the medieval name for the Great Saint Bernard Pass.
[88] Hugh (Hugues) III.

good Count Philip of Flanders; the counts of Clermont and Beaumont[89] were there, too, and the worthy Jacques d'Avesnes,[90] held in the highest regard by all, and the bold and courtly Count Theobald,[91] and the courtly, valiant William des Barres[92] and Sir Guy de Châtillon.[93] But there's no point trying to name them all: in short, every knight in all France, Flanders and the Low Countries with any desire to win a reputation came to that tournament if he could. So many came from all directions that the country round about was teeming, thronging; on every side they were arming with fierce attention, all who were set on doing great deeds, and mighty steeds from Spain, from Lombardy and Sicily, were being spurred across the field. Any man would struggle to describe the magnificence of the gear and apparel, the rich display and trappings of the knights on both sides as they armed.

When both camps were armed and in proper array they made their way into the field. There were so many handsome companies of fine, outstanding knights! And a fair amount of noise there was as they bawled their battle cries! And I don't think it was long before there were lances shattered, shields smashed and sword-blows rained on helms. Enter William the Marshal, finely armed and tall and strong, a mighty figure; he charged into their ranks like a lion into a herd, and helm, coif* and ventail were of no avail to anyone he met: he clove and hewed like a woodsman felling oaks! All around they were saying:

'Who's this wild warrior[94] who's savaging our men?'

They tried their utmost to wound or capture him, but couldn't cope with his blows: many recoiled and got out of his way! But others landed blows with sword and mace on the Marshal William, stoving his helm right down to his head. But he dealt them like for like, in no way second best! And he seemed to have two pairs of hands as he sent them tumbling, crashing before him. Many of them stared in awe, not recognising him; how keen they were to fell or seize him, but he made it very clear they'd got no chance!

'He's faultless!' they were saying. 'I don't know how or where he learned to fight like this, but he knows what he's about!'

It was a splendid tournament, both sides giving their all for their companions, striving to strike and capture, defend and rescue: many a mêlée raged on and on, ending only when decided with great profit and great loss. So many displays there were that day of shining prowess; the finest knights showed their valour indeed. As for the Marshal, who'd come from another land to build his reputation, he performed so many feats of arms, in short, that every great lord at the tournament, every count and baron and knight, yearned to match him. He was the focus of all attention. And what a hard time he gave his jealous rivals! But

---

[89] The Constable of France (as noted above, p. 49) and Matthew III of Beaumont.
[90] One of the most noted lords of Picardy and Hainault, he was to lead a French and Flemish contingent on the Third Crusade, where he died at the Battle of Arsuf in 1191.
[91] Theobald (Thibaut) V, count of Blois and seneschal of France; he, too, was to die (along with Philip of Flanders) during the Third Crusade.
[92] '*li buens Barreis*': see note 66, above, p. 49.
[93] Like Count Philip and Count Theobald, he was to die at Acre in 1191.
[94] '*Qui est cist Sesnes*': literally 'Who is this Saxon'.

he wasn't concerned with spoils: he was so intent on fighting well that he gave no thought to booty; he won something of far more value, for the man who wins honour has made a rich profit indeed.

The tournament lasted till late afternoon,[95] by which time many were exhausted. They parted then, but didn't leave, for their business wasn't done; they all had work to do: a mighty throng, bigger than at a fair, swarmed about seeking friends taken prisoner in the fray, or hunting for lost equipment; many were asking on every side for news of friends or kinsmen and who their captors were, while the captured were seeking bail or ransom from friends or acquaintances. It's always the same after tournaments: everyone mills about, trying to sort out his losses! That's why the lords were still thronging there, as I say, either on their own account or to attend to their friends.

It was now, I understand, that an illustrious lady of the highest degree made a gracious presentation to the duke of Burgundy, who'd taken part in the tourney. A splendid pike it was, more than two and a half feet long and in perfect, prime condition. The duke responded courteously, saying that for the greater honour of the lady, so worthy and bright and charming in body and soul, he would present it in turn to another, and he sent it to the count of Flanders; the good count, the most honourable of men, insisted it should go to the count of Clermont; he for his part sent it at once to Count Theobald: everyone who received it passed it on! Then the good count of Flanders, the most affable, courteous and judicious of them all, said most agreeably:

'I've a proposal to make, if you'd welcome my advice.' They all did so, so he said: 'Then let me say what would be best: let's make this pike a noble prize[96] and send it to the worthiest, the most deserving, the one whose weapons[97] have been used to the best effect today!'

They gladly agreed, but wanted to know in that case who should have the award.

'Sirs,' replied the count, 'a knight who fights with outstanding valour and skill wherever he appears; he comes from the Young King's household and is valiant and courteous and loyal indeed: he is William the Marshal.'

'It's only right and proper,' said they all, 'that it should go to the one who performed best.'

They appointed two knights, with a squire carrying the pike before them, who searched up and down until they found the Marshal's lodging. But he wasn't there; they asked the ones they met there where he was, and they told them that he'd ridden to the forge.

'We're not expecting him to come back here,' they said. 'We don't know where he's heading next.'

So they left the Marshal's lodging and hurried to the forge – and found him with his head laid on the anvil! It was no joke: the smith, with his hammers and pliers and tongs, was trying to prise off his helm, cutting through the joints where

---

[95] 'After none' – i.e. after the ninth canonical hour, around 3 p.m.
[96] Literally 'let's make this pike a swan'.
[97] Literally 'iron and wood'.

they were buckled and battered in – it was so tight about his neck that it was a struggle to loosen it. But when at last the helm was free and heaved off with a mighty effort, the knights who'd come to find him greeted him warmly and said:

'We're sent by counts and other great lords who've come from far-off lands to win honour and fame. They've made this pike a noble prize[98] and declare you its worthy winner; they've sent it to you, deeming you the most deserving of all knights here today. You should be delighted!'

His reply was eloquent – he'd many times been called upon to act and speak with grace. 'God reward their kindness, sirs,' he said. 'There are others far more deserving than I, but since they've chosen to send it to me I thank them heartily – and you, too, sirs. It's no merit of mine but their noble generosity that has moved their hearts to grant me this great honour.'

'Good, dear sir,' they replied, 'you may say what you please, but in contests like today's, fine deeds speak for themselves.'

I don't know all the words that passed, but they took their leave and returned to the lords and reported what had happened at their meeting. They all crossed themselves in astonishment! Now they were sure they'd made the right decision with the prize: they knew no one more deserving than he – they thought him peerless; his equal in speech and deed could not be found, nor one more modest in word and action.

And so it was that the Marshal received the pike, awarded at Pleurs as a prize to the knight deemed the finest of all those present.

The Tournament at Eu

This history of the Marshal isn't easy to relate: no one in the world has a memory good enough to recall it all, however hard he tried – in fact ten men between them couldn't recount all the fine deeds the Marshal accomplished as he built his reputation – it's impossible! And I don't claim to be all-knowing: I'm just relating what I've been told. But I don't set any store by some of the crazy stuff that's blurted out about him: some men swallow bellyfuls of nonsense till they bloat and spew it out – the malicious and the envious can't keep it down.

Let me tell you now about a splendid tournament held at Eu in Normandy. Word of it resounded far and wide, through France, Hainault, Flanders, Burgundy, Poitou, Touraine, Anjou, Normandy and Brittany: no man of worth was going to miss it; no knight who heard of it and wished to win renown would fail to be there – it was obligatory for any knight with chivalrous ambition. And the Young King was there at Eu with a company of at least a hundred knights – and the finest, I swear, you could hope to find: he spared no expense to attract any good, brave, experienced knight to his side – he'd surpassed all other princes in largesse, as he had in bold enterprise and all other qualities.

---

[98] See note 96 above, p. 59.

Once both sides had all arrived they duly armed. The opposition comprised French, Burgundians, Flemings and Hainaulters. Some couldn't wait to begin, and Sir Matthew de Walincourt[99] rode eagerly forward on a swift charger seeking a first engagement; the Marshal smartly galloped to meet him, with such force that he sent him crashing from his horse. He seized the reins immediately and rode straight back to rejoin his company – how well he knew his business! Sir Matthew came at once to where the Young King was arming, and asked him outright to have his horse returned. Never one to refuse a request, the king replied:

'Gladly, good sir. Who's got it?'

'The Marshal, truly.'

'Marshal, let him have it.'

'Certainly, my lord. Far be it from me to refuse.'

So the horse was returned and away Sir Matthew rode; but he needn't have bothered: he lost it again that day – to the same man!

The great tournament now engaged outside the castle, close to each side's lists.[100] It was a splendid tournament indeed; and truly, the count of Flanders, so canny and astute, had gathered to his side dukes, counts, barons, castellans, viscounts and a fine body of knights and soldiers who would have given the king's men a battering if they hadn't had their refuge[101] close at hand and known how to take care of themselves. What a tournament it was: I don't think any king or count ever saw one better contested. And it wasn't long before Sir Matthew de Walincourt reappeared, with far more display and flourish than before – and found himself confronted by the same man as at the start! And the Marshal didn't hang about! He struck him in the chest with a force that sent him tumbling over his horse's crupper to the ground. Seeing him flat out he didn't go to help him up but didn't want to hurt him more, so he took his horse – which was bad enough: the knight had done himself no favours in his quest for revenge! But the Marshal had done good business: he'd won the same horse twice in one day! Away he led it – nothing would induce him to leave it there, no matter who objected, and he'd no intention of giving it back again that week! He led the horse from the fray and handed it to the squires to keep. Then back he went to the fighting, where many great feats of arms were seen that day: fearsome mêlées formed in numerous places; you'd have seen charge after charge, men captured and rescued, some fleeing, others giving chase. Anyone less than fully fit[102] would have had no fun at all: he'd have been on his rear with his legs in the air in no time, trampled in an instant.

Play continued till they were tourneyed out. Then those who'd won sent their spoils back to their lodgings, while those who'd lost pledged securities or hostages, or settled their promised dues or sought a reprieve; so you must if you come unstuck.

---

[99] An experienced and respected knight from Hainault (Walincourt is just south of Cambrai).
[100] '*lices*': as noted above (p. 53), these are the barriers marking each side's refuge.
[101] '*recet*': as above, note 43, p. 41.
[102] Literally 'a man with a wooden leg'.

Once helms were off, all the nobles drew aside to talk together, the most eminent of them gathering about the king. They had many matters to discuss, as ever, but in the middle of their deliberations up came Sir Matthew de Walincourt, who'd had the worse of those two encounters with the Marshal, parting company with his charger. He stepped up to the king and hailed him, and the gracious king gave him his full attention; Sir Matthew set his case before him and entreated him to have his horse returned.

'Who's got it?' asked the king.

'Sire,' he said, 'the Marshal.'

The king called for him at once, and insisted he return the horse: he was most displeased that he'd waited so long to do it.

'My lord,' said the Marshal, 'I returned it early this morning, before prime*: the knight can vouch for that himself.'

'Indeed you did,' Sir Matthew said, 'but you unseated me a second time and led my horse away and have it still!'

'Sir,' the Marshal replied, 'you don't know whether I have it or have given it away. And now you're being repaid for your behaviour towards me at a tournament when you refused the pleas of several worthy men. Listen: at that tourney you won a horse from me and kept it; some gentlemen asked you to oblige them by returning it to me, but you ignored their request and refused to give it back. Now I'm repaying you in kind!'

Sir Matthew said: 'You weren't as respected then as you are now (and doubtless will be even more) – that's why I wouldn't return it!'

'Well then, sir,' replied the Marshal, 'if my standing was lesser then, yours is lesser now! So following your own fine reasoning I shouldn't give it back!'

There was much delight at this apt riposte: everyone roared with laughter. And the Marshal duly led the horse away. And that was the least of it: at that day's tournament he took ten knights prisoner; worthy, valiant knight that he was, he delivered telling blows indeed, and won twelve horses with their saddles and their harness – one of them twice over! Believe me, there was much talk about his deeds from all who witnessed or heard of them. His reputation for prowess and valour was beginning to soar, his status ever rising.

Now, there was another knight, much respected as a warrior, valiant, bold and daring – wily, too – though with an eye a little too much on profit. His name was Roger de Gaugy,[103] and from Dieppe to Baugé[104] there was no braver knight or one more adept at winning booty save William the Marshal, and his prowess had earned him a place in the Young King's household. When he heard about the spoils and prestige that the Marshal was winning, his heart – typically – was gripped and fired by Greed; it urged him to seek to be the Marshal's companion, for the company of a fine knight can be only to one's benefit. Two hands, after all, are better than one – if one fails to strike, the other will land a blow and success comes all the sooner. So he asked to be the Marshal's companion, and the

---

[103] A Flemish knight who had joined the Young King's retinue and was later to be a counsellor to King John.

[104] '*Baugies*' (to make a rhyme with Gaugy): this is probably Baugé in Anjou.

Marshal gladly agreed: knowing how fine a knight he was, he was sure he had nothing to lose.

They were companions for two years, and at every tournament they attended they won richer spoils than six or eight others put together. That's not a wild and naïve guess: it's exactly what was recorded by the clerks of the court who kept accounts – Wigan, the clerk of the kitchen, and others indeed, recorded that between Pentecost and Lent they captured precisely one hundred and three knights; and that's not to mention the horses and equipment they won, of which the clerks kept no account. So that's how they fared.

The Tournament at Joigny

And it wasn't long before word spread – swiftly, as it ever does – that a number of great, illustrious lords were planning a tournament at Joigny,[105] and all who loved competing flocked there. The Young King and most of his company didn't, but the Marshal prepared to go nonetheless. He and those who went with him pressed on till they reached the castle of Joigny, where they were given the warmest welcome. Once all had arrived the knights in the castle armed and rode forth. They dismounted in a fine, delightful stretch of ground outside the town, and there they waited; they'd been reliably informed that their opponents' numbers were great, far greater than their own, so they'd no wish to venture on and seek them out: that's why they'd dismounted; they stood before the barriers of their refuge, fully armed, and waited for the others to arrive.[106]

It was now that the countess[107] – in face and body as perfect, I understand, as Nature could fashion – came to join them with a company of ladies and damsels of flawless beauty and gorgeous attire and the utmost wit and charm. The knights quite properly broke their ranks and came to greet them, and felt all the better for the ladies' arrival – as indeed they were: the ladies redoubled the strength, the spirit, the courage and the heart of every knight present. Then someone said:

'Let's dance while we're waiting! That'll pass the time more agreeably!'

And knights and ladies joined hands. Then someone asked:

'Who'll be so kind as to sing for us?'

The Marshal, who had a fine voice (though he would never have said so), began a song, most soft and dulcet, which charmed them all and they happily joined in. When he'd finished his delightful song, a young singer – a novice herald of arms, he was – struck up one not heard before. I don't know whose idea it had been, but part of the refrain was:

'Give me a good horse, Marshal!'

As soon as he'd heard this song Marshal slipped away from the dancing without a word to anyone; a squire brought him his horse and he beckoned the

---

[105] In Burgundy, between Sens and Auxerre.
[106] The implication is that the opposing side had made their camp some distance from the castle.
[107] i.e. the countess of Joigny, Alice of Courtenay, mother of King John's wife Isabella.

young herald who saw this and raced after him. At this point, tourneyers from the opposing side who were keen to get some jousting started were coming that way; the Marshal – never one to mess about! – headed straight for one of them, and trusting in his prowess and in the strength of his stout and sturdy lance he brought him crashing from his horse without the slightest fuss. He bade the young herald mount the horse, and without another word the herald rode straight back to the dancing and called to them all:

'Look! Look! What a horse! The Marshal gave it to me!'

Imagining the Marshal had been still there dancing, they were amazed! It created a mighty stir, and knights, maidens, ladies, damsels all declared it was the finest deed ever seen at a tournament.

Now they saw the opposing battalions advancing; they laced ventails and helms and promptly mounted, the presence of the ladies inspiring even the least daring with the will to win the contest! But they rode to meet them steadily in good, close formation, no one going ahead of the rest. From the other side, lance levelled, a knight came charging into their midst, but he didn't escape: he was instantly seized by the reins. Everyone eager to win honour was fired, determined to fight well, and the tournament began with splendid vigour, locked together in a dense mêlée. And those who'd been dancing with the ladies put their all into it – body, heart and soul – and performed so magnificently that their opponents were in awe. The din and dust-cloud were immense, for as a thunderbolt smashes and crushes all it strikes, sparing nothing in its path, so the knights inspired by the ladies fell on all before them. It was a brilliant contest, with many fine deeds of arms that day, but the knights who'd enjoyed the company of the ladies overcame all opposition. They won great spoils, as was witnessed by all, but it was clear to winners and losers alike that the prize should go to the Marshal. He'd won his fair share of booty, too, but he generously shared out much of it among captives and crusaders,[108] and released many of the knights he'd taken, an action much admired. I can't recount his every deed – even with all my faculties I'd need my whole life over again and still I wouldn't manage it! There's no man alive who could! But that's what happened that day.

The Tournament between Maintenon and Nogent

He now returned to his lord the Young King, who had no peer in prowess and largesse. Neither Arthur nor Alexander, who devoted their lives to prowess, achieved so much in so little time; had God granted him longer life he would have surpassed them both in prowess and fine deeds. And he gathered about him such a splendid company of knights that no emperor or king or count ever had so many of their quality; the like was never seen: he had the pick of all the best young knights of France and Flanders and Champagne. And it wasn't because he did deals with them: his deeds were such that good knights couldn't

---

[108] '*croisés*': knights sporting a cross on their surcoats.

wait to join him. Not that I'm going to name them all – it would be quite a job to list all their names! And it would get in the way of telling my story. But names will emerge in due course.[109]

The Young King's deeds were such that all the good yearned to have his intelligence, prowess, integrity and largesse: they all aspired to emulate him. And whenever he appeared in combat he made the opposition tremble! Many times in tournaments he'd launch a charge with all his troops, with such force that his opponents – even though often they'd greater numbers – couldn't withstand them, and were scattered in moments by the power of their charge. When they all came spurring onward no one would face them, no one would raise a hand against them, no one would dare engage with any; indeed, the Young King often charged in vain – knights galloping ahead of him had swept all foes away, leaving no one for him to attack! So he would often be left with a handful of men, decide to charge against another force and find himself in trouble! But whenever he made these rash attacks the Marshal would always rescue him, ever ready and swiftly to hand to haul him from the fray just as he was on the brink of capture. The Marshal, who was doing so much to build the Young King's reputation, was constantly saving him, sending the enemy packing! He had him ever under his wing; and through actions such as these, and others, he won the Young King's love and affection, more than any other knight from any land who was ever in his company.

For a long while thus the Young King roved the lands, exceeding all in Christendom in valour, courtesy and largesse, surpassing all princes on earth in perfect honour and loyalty, his standing such that wherever he went his reputation outshone everyone's. And how could it be otherwise? For his tutor in arms was the finest in his time or at any time since, so I find in my sources. It's the Marshal I mean, who without the slightest doubt gave him unfailing, devoted attention. And it wasn't wasted, for the Young King with all his prowess was wedded to Largesse – it was no fleeting attachment but a lasting marriage: as long as he lived he loved Her faithfully, and She was his true and constant partner.

Blind Forgetfulness is apt to lead a man and his thoughts astray, but Memory has happily put me back on track! Bless Memory for giving me timely guidance, reminding me of a splendid part of my story which Forgetfulness has led me to omit! On Trinity Sunday[110] a great tournament was held between Maintenon and Nogent.[111] Those delighting in chivalry went in mighty numbers: the Young King was there, as was Philip, the most courteous and celebrated count of Flanders ever born; so too was the count of Boulogne,[112] who always seized a chance to test his prowess – he was devoted to tourneying; with the Young King, too, was the count of Clermont, one of the finest knights in the world. But I can't name

[109] Literally 'but I shall yet detail their names for you', which the author never exactly does.
[110] Literally 'the octave [the eighth day] after Pentecost'. The probable date of this tournament is therefore 27 May 1179.
[111] Maintenon and Nogent-le-Roi, north of Chartres.
[112] This will be one of the first three husbands of Countess Ida of Boulogne, none of whom lived long.

everyone – I wouldn't want to try: it would be quite a task! And it's hardly wise to spoil a story with pointless detail. Let me simply say that no worthy knight in the kingdom and the Empire[113] who knew of the tournament failed to be there if he could.

When the young among them duly arrived they began the vespers[114] with the utmost vigour. All were eager to prove themselves, which led to so many fine deeds of arms that all those watching declared they were inspired by Chivalry indeed. But I can tell you for sure that the barons and great lords didn't take part in the vespers, though they sent some of their men; and, according to my source,[115] Sir Renaud de Nevers[116] took two of the king's company captive and led them off with him that night. And that evening, in their lodgings, knights discussed this and said to the king:

'Dear lord, hear us: two of our companions have been taken prisoner and led away by their captor, Sir Renaud de Nevers.'

'If I ask for their return,' said the king, 'he'll be obdurate, so I'll not make the request. He's asked to join my retinue several times and I've always rejected him.'

'But you must,' they said. 'Don't be too high-handed – ask at least. And if he refuses, you'll owe him no favour at all: it'll prove he neither loves nor respects you.'

He followed their advice and made the request; but Renaud, urged by others to refuse, did so, returning word that if he had the chance he'd take whatever he could from the king – and the king could keep whatever he had of his! The Young King was enraged by this and said to his knights:

'Listen to Sir Renaud's answer, sirs: he swears he'll take and keep all he can from me – and if I take anything of his I should do the same, whatever I like! I pray you, sirs, for love of me, in tomorrow's tournament do all in your power to capture him! If he were my prisoner he'd at least return those men of mine. I've nothing more to say on the matter.'

Many knights stepped forward, undertaking and vowing to deliver Renaud captive next day; some who'd yet to win a reputation said that if they could capture him they'd hand him over there and then!

'And what do *you* say, Marshal?' said the king. 'Is he going to get away with this?'

'Sire,' he replied, 'I'll be happy if I stop him taking my horse and my gear, since he says he'll keep all he wins from us.'

It was a measured response from one who never made boastful claims: he wasn't going to commit himself further.

---

[113] i.e. the Holy Roman Empire.

[114] Not the church service but a preliminary part of the tournament: see 'vespers' in the Glossary, p. 230.

[115] '*li vers*': literally 'the verse'. If this is to be taken literally, rather than as a filler line giving a convenient rhyme for 'Nevers', it seems to imply that the author's source at this point was itself a poem.

[116] Renaud, one of the younger sons of William III, count of Nevers. Like Philip of Flanders and so many others, he was to die at the siege of Acre in 1191.

The tournament next day was great and splendid and finely contested. In the course of it the count of Clermont was unhorsed in a mighty, fierce mêlée, as some fought to capture him and others strove to aid, defend and rescue him. The king ordered them to back off, fearing they'd destroy the count before they pulled him free! They did then manage to rescue him, but it was hardly a painless process: caps[117] and helms took a battering from blows of sword and mace, till those who'd unhorsed the count fell back in ignominious retreat. And when the count, endowed with so many fine qualities, was remounted, he and his men withdrew behind a ditch to rally and recover.

The fighting you'd have seen then! So many horses seized and won! There was no time wasted in bargaining – they'd too much else on their hands, some more than others, as the tournament was joined once more, and fiercely indeed, with everyone striving to excel: they wouldn't have fought more keenly if they'd staked their eyes on winning! All were fighting with might and main, seizing horses, plunging into mêlées: there was turmoil as they locked in fevered combat, no one budging, intent as flies upon a sore. There were thronging mêlées all over the field, each company yelling its battle cry. The Marshal charged amongst them, hunting through the press, here and there and high and low, till he found Sir Renaud de Nevers – and his effort wasn't wasted: he seized Sir Renaud's bridle and hauled him over his horse's neck, and for all his struggling, whether he liked it or not, he carried him off to the king.

'Sire,' he said, 'behold: I give you Sir Renaud!'

'Thanks indeed!' the king replied. 'A delightful gift, so help me God! Now I needn't worry about recovering my men or capturing his! You've done me great service – now and very often, by my life!'

The tournament raged on in no uncertain manner; without a word of a lie, in absolute truth, they charged and clashed with all their force, heedless of their safety, raining sword-blows on each other like a carpenter hewing and cleaving wood.

Now remounted, the good count of Clermont, that lord endowed with so many qualities, called his brother Sir Simon – his marshal, he was[118] – and said: 'Simon, I swear I'll consider you no brother if we don't go and give them a seeing-to! No refuge[119] will be any good to them!'

With that they donned their helms, and heedless of all danger they charged full tilt, striking and hammering at heads and arms till they put the foe to flight. There was no recourse or refuge – the king and his men drove many back into the town, and sent the others scattering in wild disorder, battered and decisively defeated; the scale of the rout was astonishing, as was the might of the king and the good count of Clermont who'd scored this tremendous victory and crushed the opposition, with the help of the Marshal.

---

[117] '*testieres*': this usually means the head-harness of a horse, and may do so here; but it may also refer to another kind of head-armour, iron caps like the 'cervellieres' used by many crusaders unable to afford more expensive helms.
[118] i.e. a key member of his retinue. See 'mareschal' in the Glossary.
[119] '*lices*': see note 79, above, p. 53.

The Tournament between Anet and Sorel

Now let me tell you something else. This history has a lot more yet to say about the Young King and the Marshal, but it's reminded me of something I saw myself and remember vividly; I was about to overlook, inexplicably, a tournament that took place between Anet and Sorel,[120] the greatest, I think, there had ever been. The competitors came from far and wide: unless prevented by dire emergency, no knight between Poitou and the Low Countries wishing to win a reputation would have missed it at any price. I don't know how it happened but the Young King wasn't there,[121] but his fine household were, and they surpassed all the rest – which is saying something, for the very best knights, the most experienced to be found, were at that tournament. And not the least of them was the Marshal, who made his presence well and truly felt in every clash and mêlée that he entered; and his presence made the company all the more daring and courageous.

From all around they thronged to the tourney-ground in vast numbers: it was no quiet, private affair – how could it be, when word of it had spread so far, and for so long? They duly armed and advanced and went about their business. The French, I assure you, were fighting ferociously – until the Young King's men arrived! Then I don't think they were there for long! They were too hard-pressed by the new arrivals who charged them with all their might, not letting them off the hook and giving them no respite – they were forced to turn tail. The rout was total: nothing would have possessed them to stop and make a stand – but there was nowhere to take refuge. None of them knew what to do – except that there was an old motte, poorly fortified with no more than a spiked stockade. Some of the fleeing knights climbed up it, pulling their horses after them and tethering them to the spikes; but fearing for their own skins they didn't have time to get the horses in – they had to leave them outside. The Marshal now came galloping up, eager for more deeds of prowess, and undertook a daring feat indeed: he dismounted at once and, waiting for no help save from the man who held his horse, he climbed the motte, seized two fine horses by the reins and led them back down, one in each hand, into the ditch below. This wasn't exactly advisable – the counterscarp was very high! Any man from there to Dover would have struggled to climb out! But he, without more ado, clambered up and strained and strove till he hauled the horses out behind him! He was worn out then, and little wonder – it had been quite an effort, climbing up the motte and down again to win those horses. And now two knights appeared and thought they'd struck it lucky, finding him alone, on foot and clearly tired. They did him no favours, grabbing both horses from him. He made little attempt to resist; he knew for sure

---

[120] Evidently a regular tournament site, as they were the scene of a previous tourney – above, pp. 56–7.

[121] This tournament was probably held in the summer of 1179, when the Young King had returned temporarily to England.

he'd recover them soon enough: they wouldn't stop him! So he didn't put up a fight just then, for he knew exactly who they were and whose company they were in, and their names and surnames, too. One was Peter de Leschans;[122] the Marshal would have had him panting with terror if only he'd been mounted (he'd have made him fulfil his every demand and hand him whatever he wanted!); I'm not sure of the other's name, but before the day was done he'd take them on – and they wouldn't come out of it well!

Once he was back in the saddle, he longed to catch them up and make good his losses and give them fitting payment – they'd have struggled to put a brave face on it! In fact there wouldn't be any brave faces around if he got his hands on them! So on he galloped, and suddenly came upon a barn where a band of knights were under siege – and in real trouble: it was hardly an even contest, their fierce attackers outnumbering them four to one. They weren't afraid to defend themselves but were on the point of capture when one of them peered between two planks that barred the entrance (not that it would have stayed barred much longer) and boldly cried:

'Ah, Marshal! Marshal! Gracious knight! Help us!'

'Who are you?' he called back.

'A company of knights,' was the reply, 'who'll surrender to you alone.'

'What are your names? Tell me.'

'My name's Florent de Hangest[123] – Louis d'Arcelles[124] is here with me. We're very glad to see you! Take us – we're your prisoners – there are fifteen of us altogether. We'd rather our possessions went to you – since it's come to this! – than to the knights who're attacking us and bent upon our capture.'

The Marshal agreed, and they surrendered to him. But their besiegers didn't go along with this! They swore by their lives the knights wouldn't escape – they'd leave only as *their* prisoners – and said the Marshal was taking a liberty! They weren't best pleased!

'By my life!' the Marshal cried. 'I'll take on the lot of you! They've surrendered to me so I'll defend them, come what may! Go and tell Count Theobald and Sir William des Barres! You'll have a fight on your hands before I let you take them, since they choose to yield to me – there'll be broken heads before we're done! They've surrendered to me – you'll have your work cut out before you haul them off! Damn anyone who lays a hand on them!'

When they heard these threats they all trooped off in twos and threes and fours, not fancying a fight! So the besiegers left, and the knights emerged from the barn without further harm or mishap, thanks be to God – and thanks to the Marshal, who saw them safely on their way. Once they were safe they offered again, quite

---

[122] William des Barres's nephew, who is listed (as 'Petrus Lieschans') among the prisoners taken by Richard Lionheart at Gisors in 1198. He appears at that time to have changed his allegiance from Richard (who had earlier retained him in his service) to Philip of France, thus explaining, perhaps, the disdain the author shows for him in the following passage.

[123] Hangest-en-Santerre, in Picardy.

[124] A Louis d'Arcelles ('*Arcelles*' may well be Aizelles, also in Picardy) was a vassal of the count of Champagne. Like his companion Florent de Hangest, he was to die during the Third Crusade.

properly, to surrender themselves to him – but he declined to take anything from them and declared them completely free. This earned their warmest thanks and admiration, and they promised to be his knights wherever they met in future; he asked for nothing more, and commended them to God.

They parted then, and that was that. The Marshal returned to his lodging and had himself quickly disarmed. But then he called for a palfrey straight away: he was still vexed about the horses taken from him by the churlish knights. He rode to the lodging of the good and courteous William des Barres: he was a knight endowed with all good graces, lacking none, and was the uncle of that Peter de Leschans who'd so offended and wronged the Marshal by taking his horse. They flocked to hold his stirrup when he came to dismount, and as he went inside he was recognised by many and they all cried:

'Welcome, Sir Marshal!'

Sir William des Barres himself was the first to step forward, and he gave him a joyful welcome. The Marshal immediately told him why he'd come, and how his nephew had wickedly stolen his horse: he told him the whole story, just as you've heard it; and when Sir William heard he crossed himself in amazement, outraged.

'Who would have treated you so?' he said. 'Only an arrant scoundrel! If anyone else had told me this I'd never have believed him! But your word I trust. It's a wretched way to repay the support and many favours he's had from you.'

Peter de Leschans was promptly called for; he'd gladly have ignored the summons if he could – if only he'd had an excuse! And when he arrived his uncle said:

'How could you behave so badly towards my lord the Marshal? To wrong him so, taking his horse! How did you dare lay a hand on it? You should be punished like a thief caught red-handed: you've acted shamefully!'

He claimed he hadn't done it.

'Indeed you did! You took the horse and have it still! How little regard you show for all his favours and services to you! A man reveals himself by his actions!'[125] Return the horse at once, I command you!'

At this Peter sent for a packhorse of his; it was iron grey, the same colour as the horse he'd taken, but it had seen a good few years, so many that it was wizened and worn, broken-backed and slashed by spurs – in fact half its hide was missing. It was a wretched, clapped-out nag.

'Sir Marshal,' said des Barres, 'is this the one? Do you recognise it?'

'Indeed I do,' the Marshal said, 'but it's nothing to do with me. You know it well enough: it's a run-down packhorse he's had for five years or more.'

'Do you take us for infants, Peter?' said des Barres. 'This is hardly polite: it seems you mean to treat us as fools. I promise you this – and you can guess what I'm about to say: if you don't bring the proper horse – and sharpish! – you and I will be parting company!'

At that, Peter sent for the Marshal's horse, not daring to keep it longer, and des Barres had it returned at once. But some of those present, who were friends of Peter, suggested to the Marshal that it would be good to go halves with him

---

[125] Literally 'from a wicked man, wicked tricks'.

on the horse, as a token of peace and friendship. The Marshal, with his perfect manners, replied:

'Very well: if that's your judgement I'll not oppose it.'

But another knight said: 'Let the horse go wholly to whoever rolls the highest with three dice! How about that?'

'Fine by me!' said the Marshal. 'I've no objection!'

'Nor have I,' said Peter. 'I'll not be churlish.'

So dice were brought, and they promptly shook and threw. Sir Peter stepped up and rolled nine; then the Marshal rolled eleven.

'The horse is the Marshal's!' everyone said. 'He wins!'

'Again, you mean!' said des Barres. 'He wins *again*! That's more to the point, by God: he's won it twice!'

Des Barres returned the horse and the Marshal passed it to his page. They pressed him to stay, but he was determined to recover his other horse, in return for payment if not polite request. So he sent the first horse to his lodging and headed to where he knew he'd find the knight who'd taken the other. This knight was in the household of one of the greatest lords of France, an illustrious baron of high renown, though I don't know his name. All who saw the Marshal coming gave him a joyful welcome, the lord and everyone – everyone, that is, except the knight who knew what was in the wind: he had the Marshal's horse and feared he was about to lose it. As everyone came thronging to greet him, the lord said:

'Welcome, Marshal! Here! Come here!'

And he seated him at his side, greeting him with joy and honour. Without more ado the Marshal told him why he'd come: how his knight had robbed him of his horse despite the fact that he'd never, to his knowledge, wronged him in any way.

'I'm not impressed!' the lord replied. 'By my life, I'll have the horse returned to you, whatever anyone says.'

So the horse was brought – the knight dared not refuse. It was a strong, swift, handsome steed, worth a good deal more than thirty pounds, and it was returned to the Marshal.

But listen now: as is often said, a man frequently seeks his own advantage and ends up profiting another. What happened was this: the Marshal was pressed to share ownership of the horse, or roll dice for it again. He said he'd do whatever they said if it sounded reasonable. 'Since you ask so politely I'll go halves on the horse – or if he prefers, we'll leave it to chance: let's roll dice for the whole!'

All was ready for play; but then the knight heard how the Marshal had won the other horse, and said: 'It's crazy to lose it on a dice-roll! I'll not risk it, by God!'

'You won't?'

'No indeed!'

'We'll have to call him Half-cut,[126] then!' said the Marshal. 'He'll need to be sawn in two!'

'Would you rather I put a price on him?' said the knight.

---

[126] Literally 'piebald'; 'Half-cut' is an attempt at a modern equivalent to the humorous word-play that would have been grasped by the medieval audience.

'Yes – let's get it settled.'

'He'd sell for fourteen pounds, I reckon – on credit or bought outright. I'll buy up your half shortly.'

'Done! But better still, he's mine right now! Here's your seven pounds – I don't need a loan or time to pay!'

The knight thought he'd been clever, undervaluing the horse! Now, seeing the Marshal with cash in hand, he realised he'd come unstuck! He didn't expect him to have ready money! That's why he'd been sharp with the valuation – the horse was worth a good forty pounds! People often get what they deserve, and those who covet all lose all. So the Marshal paid him and led the horse away; he'd come out right on top: now he'd recovered both the horses he'd lost, despite the best efforts of the knights who'd tried to rob him – and who certainly hadn't earned the Marshal's favour: like many men they thought they'd profit from their work but in the process only lost. Those at court who earn the ill will of worthy men are fools: they always lose more than they gain.

The Tournament at Épernon

After this, another truly mighty tournament was held at Épernon.[127] Word was sent to great lords in many lands, and those who attended tournaments came flocking – for anyone intent on enhancing his reputation through fine deeds seizes every opportunity, and those who strive the hardest earn most praise, esteem and credit. Great lords duly came from far and wide, for as I've said before, the Young King's example of prowess and valour had inspired everyone to uphold chivalry, which now is very nearly dead – there's too much competition from hawking and hunting and tame, formal jousts! And Avarice holds sway now, inducing men to be careful with their wealth: no one wants to spend or risk what he owns! I'd better not say too much, but if King Henry of England[128] can hold his land in peace, I believe we'll yet see the time when Chivalry and Prowess and Largesse and Noble-heartedness will sally forth once more, and Avarice will be put to death.

The great knights assembled at Épernon, and a mighty gathering it was, it seems. The Young King wasn't there, nor were many of his men except the Marshal, but he was only too keen to attend. If there were any others of the household I don't know who – I can't find any recorded.

The nobles had taken lodging throughout the town. Now, it's their custom to visit one another in their lodgings in the evening – a good and civilised custom, too: it's a chance to converse and chat and discuss their various affairs. So the Marshal, always courteous and sensible, never one to put on airs, rode to the

---

[127] West of Paris, north-east of Chartres. This probably took place soon after the previous tournament between Anet and Sorel, in the summer of 1179, as we are about to be told that the Young King (in England that year from June to September) was once again not present.

[128] i.e. Henry III, still young at the time of writing.

house of Count Theobald.[129] He was mounted on a splendid horse, but had taken no one with him to look after it, and seeing a lad among the rabble in the street, he gave his horse to him to tend. He dismounted and the young lad climbed up in his place.

As the Marshal entered the house he was warmly welcomed by many, and when he came before the count all attention was on him – no notice was taken of anyone else: his deeds had won him such renown that he was fêted to the exclusion of them all! The servants duly brought the wine. But while all this was going on, some rogue ever given to thievery, who'd seen the Marshal leave his horse, came up to the lad who was in the saddle, grabbed him by the hair and dragged him down and dealt him a fearful blow. The boy yelled:

'Ah! Marshal! Marshal! Someone's stealing your horse!'

The Marshal heard his cries and was less than pleased; he leapt up, and without taking leave or waiting for anyone else he raced to where he'd left his horse. But the rogue was galloping off right down the street. It was impossible to see a thing – the night was very dark – but the hooves were clattering loudly on the stones. The Marshal didn't dally; he set off in pursuit, but all alone and blindly in the darkness. The thieving rogue turned away down a side street to avoid the cobbles, and hid behind a timber-laden cart that was parked in front of a kiln. With the horse standing still and making no noise, the Marshal didn't know which way to go or what to do. But then, as he stood in a quandary, the horse started gently tapping its hooves and the Marshal headed straight that way. Making as little noise as he could, he crept up to the horse, who gave a loud snort; at this the rogue hunched over and made to slip down off the saddle, but the Marshal grabbed a stick and gave him such a whack across the brow that the rogue had made his last blink with that eye – it went flying from his head. Well, they do say "an eye for an eye"![130]

'Mercy, sir!' the scoundrel cried. 'I'm done for!'

'Don't blame me,' the Marshal said. 'You brought it on yourself.'

The count and all the others now came running after the Marshal as fast as they could, but by the time they reached him he'd already seized the rogue. They admired his speed and efficiency, and greatly praised his prowess. They gave orders for the thief to be taken to the gibbet and hanged, but the Marshal said:

'By my life, my horse won't cost him his neck – he has troubles enough: his brow's split open and his head's an eye short. He'll suffer no more on my account.'

That's all I'll say about that tournament – the one who gave me the information told me nothing else. And I've a weighty matter resting on me now that needs lengthy, detailed treatment – much as I prefer not to spin things out; that's why I sometimes move on briskly to avoid wearying the listener. But now the story demands it: I think any clerk from here to Montoire[131] would find it a daunting

---

[129] Theobald (Thibaut), count of Blois (see note 91 above, p. 58).
[130] Literally 'an appropriate feast-day for such a saint': a saint's feast day often marks the day of his martyrdom.
[131] Chosen, it would seem, simply because it provides a rhyme ('*Montorie*' with '*estorie*'), Montoire is a small town north of Tours.

challenge to put into verse all the many people who need to be named at this point. It's daunting me! And feeling the burden, I fear it may tax impatient listeners who don't enjoy long stories and prefer to move on swiftly.

The Tournament at Lagny

According to my source, the tournament that now took place at Lagny-sur-Marne[132] was the greatest ever seen before or since, and the Young King attended with a splendid company as you're about to hear – I'm going to tell you and no one's going to stop me! The count of Flanders came, too, bringing knights from Flanders, Hainault, the Low Countries and Germany: he'd sought to enlist every good knight as far as the heights of Mont-Joux![133] But the Young King had all his household at his side, and their reputation now was soaring. Hear now the names of those involved, which were given to me by eye-witnesses, men who were present, for knowledge so reliable should be given full respect.

I'll name the French first – it's only right to give them pride of place, on account of their rank and reputation and the high honour of their country. Let me describe the conduct and the qualities of those who bore banners[134] – I'll not skate over this! Count Robert of Dreux[135] was there: from Orléans to Évreux there was none more valiant than he – no one came near; he was the equal of them all together – and his valour had earned him a place at the Young King's side. Sir Simon de Rochefort[136] had every right to bear a banner: he was a fine knight, good and skilled indeed, his courage known to all; likewise William, the first of the des Barres, a good, sagacious knight who surpassed in his deeds all the finest knights of France. Those were the ones who bore banners. With des Barres was William his son, who followed in his footsteps in terms of deeds and conduct, as did his brother Simon,[137] endowed with prowess, largesse and *franchise*;[138] then there were Sir Peter de Leschans and Sir Amaury de Meulan[139] (not one to shirk in the field of combat), Sir Miles de Châlons and his brother Macaire, Sir Adam de Melun, rated among the very finest, Sir Odo du Plessis[140] who should certainly not be omitted, and Theobald de Vallangoujard, a worthy competitor indeed; William de Boury was there, too, a most cultured knight,

---

[132] Not far to the east of Paris. This famous tournament may well have followed the festivities surrounding Philip Augustus's coronation at Reims in early November 1179.
[133] See note 87 above, p. 57.
[134] i.e. commanded their own companies of knights.
[135] Not yet in fact count, this Robert is probably Robert II, the son of the elderly Count Robert I of Dreux (who was the third son of King Louis VI).
[136] Rochefort-en-Yvelines, between Paris and Chartres. Simon was a younger son of the count of Évreux.
[137] It is not clear whether this is his half-brother Simon de Montfort, later to be earl of Leicester and leader of the Albigensian Crusade.
[138] This important but not easily translatable concept – though 'frankness' of course comes close – is one of the central qualities of a good knight, implying openness, honesty, integrity.
[139] The third son of the count of Meulan in Normandy.
[140] The last named four were all vassals of the count of Champagne.

and Sir Herman de Brie, his chivalry held in high esteem; Stephen de la Tour, of the highest standing and most impressive show; Wauchier, who'd started poor but proved more than able to improve his lot; Sir Corin of Saint Servin; Sir Geoffrey de Vienne, committed to fine deeds; and Sir Robert de Bouvresse, endowed with many qualities.[141] The count of Soissons[142] was present, too: it would be very wrong to leave him out, as he bore a banner there, but I've added his name later because that's where I found him listed – he should really have appeared at the start. So those were the French, named in order; now here are the knights of Flanders.

There was Sir Baldwin de Béthune,[143] whose banner had appeared so often, so far and wide, that it was familiar to all; Sir William de Cayeux[144] – from there to Eu there was no bolder knight when called upon; Sir Aleaume de Fontaine, who had made prowess his very own; Sir Eustace de Neuville, whose reputation in every city and town could not be bettered; Eustace de Canteleu, of no mean esteem; and Sir Engerran de Fiennes – from Arras to Fresquiennes, far and wide in every direction, there was no knight more admired in his day.[145] Those were the ones who bore banners; the others, less prominent, I shall name one by one: Sir Hugh de Malaunay, another worthy man indeed; Sir Ralph de Plomquet, a fine, upright, good-hearted knight; Sir Baldwin de Caron,[146] respected above many of his degree – few struck better with lance and sword; Hugh de Hamelincourt, a handful for any knight who engaged with him – he knew how to deal with anyone; Sir Cardon de Fressenneville, a worthy knight of complete integrity, free of guile; Sir Eustace de Campagne,[147] one of the finest of the whole company; and Sir Roger de Gaugy[148] – from there to Baugé[149] there were few knights who won so much from tourneying (and he had no qualms about doing so);[150] Sir Robert de Beaurain,[151] who never held back in any mêlée, his mind always set on excelling; Sir Baldwin de Strépy, full of vigour, always prominent in the hottest battle; Baldwin de Wartenbeke, ever ready to draw his sword when the time came, experienced fighter that he was; Roger de Hardencort, a well known figure at court; William de Poternes, unbeatable at dice and a master at chess;[152] and

---

[141] Little is known about the last named knights, but the place-names suggest they were from the Vexin, Picardy or Champagne.
[142] This may be Count Conon, who died quite young in 1180, but is more probably his brother Count Ralph (Raoul) I.
[143] Baldwin (Baudouin) was later to accompany Richard Lionheart on the Third Crusade, and was imprisoned with him in Germany.
[144] A baron from the county of Ponthieu, he was another of Richard's companions on the Third Crusade.
[145] The last named four were all from Picardy, Artois or the Pas-de-Calais, as are those about to be named.
[146] Another who fought on the Third Crusade with Richard.
[147] Campagne-lès-Guines, south of Calais.
[148] Mentioned above, p. 62.
[149] See note 104, above, p. 62.
[150] Literally 'he never went to confession about it'.
[151] Another to die on the Third Crusade.
[152] I take this to be the implication of a line which literally (and somewhat eccentrically) means 'who would often throw a triple when he wanted to take the queen'.

Guizelin de Wartenbeke, equally adept on the board and as bold an adversary as you could find.[153]

So there we have the Flemings and the French; now I shall name the English,[154] and William the Marshal first of all, for his presence made those in his company worth far more than the rest – he'd have enhanced a whole army, by God! That's a claim I'm willing to make and stand by! Then there was Sir Robert FitzWalter,[155] a worthy knight indeed, as a good knight should be, and his worth shouldn't go unrecognised; Earl David[156] was there and bearing a banner, an impressive figure indeed; also present were Robert of London (there were few finer warriors than he), and Simon de Mares, brave and bold and valiant, and Sir Robert de Wanchy, worthy and ever ready for battle. Sir Walter of Ely was present, too, who graced and enhanced any company, being a valiant knight of great worth; and William FitzRoger, a good and proven knight, and Sir Robert de la Borne who could be counted on to do his duty, and Sir William Revel, who always made a fine show in combat, and Sir Ansel the Marshal,[157] a trusty, charming, loyal, worthy knight. Sir Richard of Berkeley[158] was with them, I know that for sure, as were Sir John of Saint-Michel and Sir Robert le Breton. There are no more names of English knights recorded.[159]

Now I shall list the Normans, who certainly weren't idle in the days of the Young King:[160] then they were grain – now they are chaff! Since King Richard died they have lacked all help and leadership from an overlord – there has been no one to inspire them. But it's only right to mention first those who bore banners at this tourney. One was Count Henry of Eu, who sadly did not live long;[161] then Robert d'Estouteville, who ranked among the finest – his banner was recognised wherever it was seen, for he was a good and worthy knight indeed. Then there was Sir John de Préaux, a bear of a man[162] when receiving blows, and anyone who took him on received a few himself! He always showed what he was made of! A skilled fighter he was indeed: he rightly bore a banner. With Peter and Roger de Préaux (a good, courageous knight), and William and Enguerrand, there were no five finer brothers (or even as good) between Rouen and Le Mans – and that includes kings and counts. Reinaud de Vassonville was there, a fine and worthy

---

[153] The last six named were from the county of Hainault or in the service of the count.
[154] Little is known about some of the following (and one or two are hard to identify), but the majority are known to have supported the Young King in his conflict with his father in 1173–4.
[155] Later to be a major figure in the Barons' War against King John.
[156] David, earl of Huntingdon, brother of William I ('the Lion'), king of Scotland.
[157] William's brother.
[158] No Richard of Berkeley is known at this time, and this is probably an error for Roger of Berkeley, lord of Dursley.
[159] This sentence more than any other strongly suggests that the author was working from a tournament roll.
[160] As with the English knights, some of the knights from Normandy and Anjou who follow in the next two lists are unidentifiable, but many are known to have supported the Young King in his conflict with Henry II in 1173–4 and to have been members of his retinue.
[161] Count Henry II of Eu was probably in his forties when he died, but that was in 1183, only a few years after this tournament at Lagny.
[162] 'cil ki fu ors': 'ors' could mean either 'bear' or 'gold', the latter implying an outstanding ability to defend himself, the former being more graphic.

fighter, and Sir Gerard Talbot, whose prowess, in short, was such that he was worthy to be a king. And there were the two brothers William and Robert de Thibouville, truly good and able knights, as their descendants are still. And Adam d'Yquebeuf, whom I shall neither praise nor censure. Why? Because I didn't know him, and know nothing about his abilities as a knight.[163] Another bearing a banner was John Maleherbe, as his high, redoubtable prowess entitled him to do; and there was Sir Robert de Tresgoz, a brave and most eloquent knight, and Henry de Longchamp, who could always find a worthy lord to serve; and Thomas and Hugh de Coulonces, of great worth indeed, and Ralph de Hamars, highly renowned, and Sir Robert Chaperon, and Sir William de Dives, more courtly than any man alive, and Sir Robert de Buisson – none more valiant or courtly, I think, was to be found, though he was never one to flaunt it; and Robert de la Mare, who captured horses with ease, and once he had them there was no chance of winning them back! And we shouldn't forget Sir William le Gras, ever worthy, and liberal, too – though inclined to be confrontational; and Sir Roger de Boudeville, and [his kinsman] Peter who was no discredit to him; then there was Alexander de Arsic – I shouldn't omit him: he was so good and charming and worthy that he earned the love of all.[164] And Alexander Malconduit, who would fiercely engage with anyone single-handed, in full view of all, and perform most valiantly.

So now I've named the Normans; next come the men of Anjou: Sir Jaquelin de Maillé, a knight of unfailing prowess, a true master of arms; Harduin de Fougeré, endowed with great prowess; Sir Geoffrey de Brûlon, who never held back when the need arose – his fighting qualities should certainly be recorded; Sir Robert de Bloc, who always gave as good as he got, fighting with might and main in the thickest press; William de Tinténiac, who was never one to be taken in – he was a keen judge of a knight's true worth; and Sir Geoffrey FitzHamo deserves fond mention, devoted as he was to all good men.

Of the Young King's company competing with him at Lagny I've named four score knights of outstanding quality – the select of the select. Why should they be so called? Because the most discriminating had chosen them as the very best; that's how it should be understood. But there were a great deal more than eighty altogether – seven times that number, in fact, for I should explain that every banner-bearing knight in the Young King's company was paid twenty shillings[165] per day (both while travelling and while there at Lagny, from the moment they left their lands) for each knight he brought with him. It was a wonder where all the money came from! But God bestowed such wealth on the Young King and he dispensed it freely. And since there were fifteen bearing banners, I assure you there were well over two hundred, as I say,[166] who were the Young King's knights and took their living from him.

---

[163] The reason for this sudden non-commitment may be Adam's part in causing a rift between Marshal and the Young King, as will shortly be seen.
[164] Son of a sheriff of Oxford, he was to be a member of King Richard's household and was with him on the Third Crusade (and visited him while imprisoned in Germany).
[165] 'Shillings' is again a translation of 'sous': see note 37, above p. 39.
[166] Referring back to 'seven times that number [eighty]'; either the scribe has made an error with numbers or the arithmetic is odd.

But that's not all: besides the Young King there were no fewer than nineteen counts at this tournament, not to mention the duke of Burgundy; in short, it was reckoned there were more than three thousand knights at Lagny, in the company of either king or count.

But let's move on! They armed, advanced and set about their business. There were so many different banners unfurled that they couldn't be distinguished well enough to describe them in any detail. The plain was seething, completely filled – there wasn't an inch of empty ground. And then the two sides charged.

There was nothing restrained about the clash: the noise was deafening! All were bent on landing mighty blows; what a shattering of lances you'd have heard, the stumps and shards so littering the ground that the horses were stopped in their tracks. In the heaving throng that filled the plain the companies bawled their battle cries. There was plenty to be learnt about fighting there! You'd have seen knights' bridles being seized, other knights being rescued, horses running in all directions, pouring sweat. All were striving with might and main, seizing the chance to prove their prowess. There were fearsome clashes all over the field and many great feats of arms that day; it was a splendid tournament indeed, even before the king and count[167] entered the fray.

But then you'd have seen the earth tremble as the king cried: 'This is getting tiresome! I'll not wait a moment longer! Charge!'

And he thrust in his spurs; but the count cannily held back, not joining the fray till he saw the time was right – though then he charged at once. The king's men surged forward so audaciously that they left the king behind, and with such ferocity that their opponents took to flight – and it was a shambles: they found themselves driven among vines and ditches, floundering over thick-laid vinestocks where horses fell by the dozen, and thrown riders were dreadfully trampled, mangled, battered. Now Count Geoffrey led a furious charge with his company, and soon the whole battalion who should have been with the king were far ahead, in hot pursuit of the fleeing foe – some intent on a fine display, others intent on booty – leaving the king stranded, and mightily frustrated at being so, with the enemy out of his reach. But then he spotted a band of them away to his right – at least forty knights there must have been. Clutching his lance he charged at them and smashed into their midst, with such force that his lance shattered like glass, and he was overwhelmed by numbers and they seized him by the reins. They were swarming round on every side, and he found himself entirely alone except for the Marshal, who was right behind – he always stayed close to the king in any combat. There he was, near at hand, along with William de Préaux, who'd just been made a prisoner that day and withdrawn from the contest:[168] he had a hauberk hidden under his surcoat and an iron cap on his head, but was otherwise unarmed. The enemy had the Young King in their clutches and were bent on tearing the helm from his head. The Marshal

---

[167] As will become clear in a moment, this is Geoffrey of Brittany (Henry II's youngest son, the Young King's brother), earlier referred to as 'the count of Nantes' (above, p. 50), who has strangely not yet been named.

[168] Presumably he had been captured and released on parole.

charged and plunged amongst them, striking out to right and left: he showed them what he was made of! Then he seized the headstall of the king's horse and hauled and heaved till he dragged it off, along with the bridle, and William de Préaux grabbed the horse by the neck and did all he could to escape from the fray while their enemies pressed about him, trying to keep hold of the king. They aimed blow after blow at de Préaux; the king deftly covered him with his shield, warding off the blows and protecting him from harm; but they'd managed to rip the helm from the king's head, much to his vexation. On and on the combat raged, but the Marshal had the best of it, raining mighty blows upon the foe.

Meanwhile the count of Flanders was thrilled to hear that the Young King's banner had appeared in the mêlée – it had been there now for quite some time. There was no stopping him: he confronted them with a mighty charge, scattering the king's men, weary from their long contest, and the pursuit that followed was hell for leather. Count Geoffrey was dismayed and distraught; several times he turned to face the pursuers, but he was the only one who did and he couldn't keep it up – though when he laid into them they found him quite a handful! He left a good few unhorsed.

But before this rout there was another incident I really should have mentioned; I'll describe it exactly as I find recorded – not that it's possible to relate every action and blow in a tournament. While the king was trying to escape from the fray as I explained, standing apart was Sir Herlin de Wavrin, seneschal of Flanders,[169] with a company of at least thirty knights. One of them came racing up to him and said:

'In God's name, sir, look there! The king is on the brink of being captured! Go and grab him and take the credit! He's already lost his helm: he's in real trouble!'

Sir Herlin was overjoyed and replied: 'I'd say he's ours!'

And he and his company thrust in their spurs and went galloping after the king. But the Marshal didn't hesitate: he charged to meet them, with such force that he smashed his lance to pieces; [he was nearly knocked from his saddle, his head][170] right down by his horse's hocks. But he hauled himself upright instantly; then battle raged about him, they attacking and he defending, hewing and cleaving everything in sight, splitting shields and staving helms: that was William the Marshal's way! They'd completely lost track of the king, who declared – as did all who witnessed it, or heard it recounted later – that no single knight was ever seen to deal finer blows than the Marshal did that day. The most illustrious knights heaped praise upon him.

I don't know the details of every tournament: that's well nigh impossible – I'm sure nobody knows them all, for there was a tourney somewhere nearly every fortnight! But I do know about one held after this at Épernon:[171] I can give a

---

[169] '*Herlins de Vanci*': Wavrin is west of Lille; Herlin appears not to have been as high-ranking as a seneschal, but Paul Meyer identified him as Count Philip's *dapifer*, the steward who served the meat in a noble household.
[170] Unresolved rhymes indicate at least two missing lines.
[171] This is the second to be held at Épernon (see above, pp. 72–4). If it took place not long after the tournament at Lagny, the probable date would be very late in 1179.

true and thorough account. There were Flemings and French, and knights from Burgundy, Champagne, Normandy, Brittany, Anjou and Poitou. The Young King wasn't present, but many of his retinue were. There was no shilly-shallying: as soon as they were in the field lances were levelled and off they went: horses charged, lances shattered, shields split and saddles emptied. The Marshal and Sir Peter de Préaux meant business, charging to take on the Burgundians who were there in force, and before they were done you'd have heard the clash of swords, hammering, parrying, and ringing blows on helms; some were seizing hold of reins, others striking out to defend themselves with sword and mace. One group were intent on capturing Sir Peter, and did so; others were doing all they could to unhorse and seize the Marshal: at least four there were around him, all bent upon his capture. But anyone stretching out a hand soon rued the day: he was doling out alms by the fistful – alms they didn't seem keen to receive! They kept striking at his mount, but despite their blows the horse wouldn't budge an inch: he'd respond only to the Marshal's spurs. Sir William Mauvoisin,[172] who'd been a prisoner since the morning,[173] came riding by and called to them:

'You haven't a chance, by Christ! Forget it – you'll never take him! Why get in a lather? If you're hoping for booty you're wasting your time! You're mad – he'll fight you off all year: you'll be at it till Saint John's Day!'

Sir Peter de Préaux, weaponless now, was crying out for help for the Marshal, and a troop of Normans charged and fell on the Burgundians – and I'm not sorry to say the Burgundians lost! Aid came to the Marshal, and some of his would-be captors were given such a thrashing that they left their mounts there in the field.

'There! You've come unstuck!' cried Mauvoisin. 'I told you you'd gain nothing. It's cost you – and rightly so: you've got what you deserve!'

The tournament broke up and the Marshal departed, returning to his lord who loved him very dearly: he kept him ever close, finding him a true and loyal friend.

Rift with the Young King

The Young King now travelled to many lands in search of honour and renown – and won a good deal with his inexhaustible generosity, always eager as he was to answer the demands of fools and the wise alike: he couldn't help himself – he was unable to refuse a request! He was possessed indeed of every noble quality, for Nobility is born of a good heart and flourishes therein, fulfilling every command of Largesse – for it is in the house of Largesse that Nobility is nurtured. And where did Largesse reside? Tell me: where? In the heart of the Young King. She resided there as long as he lived – but was left bereft when he died, I've heard: now She's a widow without a dower. The truth is that, in castle and city, wherever he went, the Young King was so free and lavish with his spending

---

[172] Probably a member of a prominent noble family, the lords of Rosny-sur-Seine (near Mantes, north-west of Paris).
[173] And therefore would have given his word to participate no further.

that, when he came to leave, he struggled to settle his dues! At the end of his stay they'd come flocking, all those he owed for horses, clothing, food.

'You owe this man three hundred pounds,' they'd say.

'A hundred to him.'

'And two hundred to him.'

'That makes six hundred,' said the clerks.

'Who's going to pay?' one of the agents said.

'My lord hasn't the money on him, but you'll have it within the month,' said the Marshal.

'Truly,' said the burghers, 'if the Marshal gives his guarantee we're not worried at all – it's as good as being paid!'

Now you can see the honour and grace that God in His goodness bestowed upon the Marshal: in cases such as this no respect or credit was shown to barons, counts or vavasors, but the Marshal, with no revenue or land behind him, was entirely trusted simply on account of his character, known to all. God! What a great thing it is, I'd say, when prowess, goodness, largesse and wisdom are all found together in one man!

But as you know, this life is blighted by Envy: there are many men so riddled with it that it's close to killing them. Envy will happily burn its own house down to set fire to its neighbour's – anything to hurt another! Yes, it sets its own house ablaze and lets the flame and smoke engulf its neighbour's. A curse upon it! Envy drove Adam from his God-given place in Paradise; false, bitter Envy made Cain kill his brother Abel – and all who commit acts of treachery are of the line of Cain. And men diseased with envy were jealous at seeing the Marshal thrive and prosper and so cherished by his lord. They seethed with resentment, almost bursting with frustration at finding no way to do him down: night and day they brooded over how to bring him into conflict with his lord. The very men he'd helped the most, the very men he'd brought to court, were now plotting deadly treachery, causing the Young King to conceive a deep and bitter hatred of the Marshal. You've never heard of the like. I know exactly who they were, the men who hatched this treacherous plan, but it wouldn't do to name them all: they have kinsmen who wouldn't thank me! So I'll do the wise thing and restrain myself. But the truth is that Adam d'Yquebeuf[174] concocted in his heart the false, outrageous scheme which hardly bears recalling: a foul brew in a foul vessel. And Sir Thomas de Coulonces[175] added his two ounces of salt – stirring trouble[176] was all he was good for. Five were involved in cooking it up,[177] but I'll keep quiet about the other three for now – though their names will emerge well enough in time.[178] None of them dared voice the base charge they'd concocted. Why? Because they knew it would never have been believed. So they looked for someone else

---

[174] Listed among the Norman knights above, p. 77.
[175] Likewise in the list of Normans, above, p. 77.
[176] Literally 'making such sauces'.
[177] Literally 'were involved in this mustard'.
[178] If the author means in the course of his work, this doesn't in fact happen.

to be their cover: they'd reveal to him their shameful fabrication and have him convince others that it was true.

'By God,' said one of them, 'I know how we can get people to swallow this. Let's not hang about till March! Sir Ralph de Hamars,[179] he's the man: he's often in close contact with the king – he could soon drop this potion in his ear! And he'd be on our side for sure: he's not on the best of terms with the Marshal, any more than we are.'

'You're right – let's fetch him!'

So they called Sir Ralph to join their huddle, and charmed and plied him with endless tales to talk him round. It's always the way: when someone wants to recruit a crony, he softens him up with flattering words, as infants are dazzled and pacified with baubles. The one with the readiest way with words began:

'Listen, Sir Ralph. We can't stop thinking, worrying, fretting about something quite extraordinary – it staggers us all. William the Marshal makes out that he's so brave and worthy, is so confident in his every quality, that he's assumed pride of place over all in this household: no baron or count can match him, and the king pays no heed to anyone but him, regardless of their valour! It's humiliating for us all to be outshone by an Englishman! We count for nothing: all you ever hear about are his mighty exploits![180] In France, in Normandy, wherever you go, all the talk is of him alone! And do you want to know how it started? Let me tell you: the fact is that the moment the Young King enters a tourney, as he goes charging up and down, Henry the Northerner[181] starts yelling "This way! Over here! God save the Marshal!" That's Henry's cry, and then everyone goes rushing, and there's such a heaving press around the Marshal that no one can move, and all he has to do is reach out and grab whatever's in front of him – horses, knights. Everyone forgets the king once Henry the Northerner starts his bawling – all attention's on the Marshal! I tell you, that's how he comes to look so great; that's how he comes to win all the loot that gains him so many friends! And we're all pushed into the background! But there's something that upsets us even more: without a shadow of a doubt, he's having it off with the queen![182] It's appalling, an utter disgrace! If the king knew of it we'd all be avenged on the Marshal! And we know of no one better placed to tell him than you. So we beg you, good sir, let him know of this foul outrage: we're as shamed by it as the king's dishonoured and duped!'

When Sir Ralph realised where this was leading he replied at once: 'You may try to turn my wits, but God preserve me in my right mind and forbid I ever turn traitor! What you're suggesting is wicked!'

'It's no wickedness, in faith!' they cried.

'Indeed it is! It's foul and flagrant treachery! To accuse a man without cause – and without warning, unexpected! A man who contemplates such action is a traitor indeed: treachery has his heart in thrall! I tell you the Marshal is worthy,

---

[179] Another Norman knight listed above, p. 77.
[180] Literally 'his great chivalry'.
[181] '*Henri li Norreis*': i.e. Henry from the north of England, 'Norreis' being a common soubriquet for a northern Englishman.
[182] In 1160, when only five, the Young King had married Margaret, the three-year-old daughter of Louis VII of France; she would now be about twenty-five.

courtly, loyal and has been a boon to us all! But as the saying goes: "stick your neck out for some men and they'll break it!"[183] People can say or do what they will, but I'll have no part in this.'

Hearing his words they assumed feigned smiles and tried to mollify him with: 'There's a big gap between words and deeds! We bear the Marshal no ill will, and none of us has any desire to commit any wrong or treachery. One often says things to please a man – and to test him! – with no intention of doing them! So we pray you, don't tell him any of this! We don't want you passing it on! Keep it to yourself!'

'Damn anyone who breathes a word of it!' said Ralph; and with that he left.

But it wasn't the end of the wretched affair. Sir Peter de Préaux, noble, good and true,[184] got wind of the business, and he wasn't best pleased: he was very concerned that shame and harm were intended towards the Marshal. As soon as he could he told the Marshal what was afoot; he didn't and wouldn't give him the names of those involved, but he couldn't conceal the treacherous plan, inspired by mortal hatred, to bring the Marshal into conflict with his lord. He told him to take the utmost care, for every word he said was true, and advised him in all good faith to reveal the hateful, treacherous details to the king, to protect himself from the king's wrath, and to forestall any allegations they might make.

'I, sir?' said the Marshal. 'God desert me if I raise the subject of something I've not done! It would be shameful to refute a charge that hasn't yet been made! I'd be ashamed even to speak of it! I'll not say a word till I hear an allegation; then I'll trust my fate to God. Treason is a heinous crime, but the truth will always out. And when the treachery comes to light, the hatchers of the foul plot will be revealed in all their shame!'

Sir Peter said nothing more. But the plotters pressed on with their plan, seeking a way to make their insinuations to the king: treachery it was, despised by God. One of them said he knew a young man who was in very great favour with the king: he was sure they could make their charges known through him.

'And if the king doesn't believe it, the youth can urge him to ask *us*! Then when we come before the king we can all bear witness, each of us in turn; and a matter known to several should surely have more credence than an assertion made by one. This is the way to get to the king!'

'You're right! Let's arrange for the youth to come and meet us.'

'Leave it to me,' he said. 'He's a close relative of mine. I'll ask him to come to me – I'm sure he'll come at once – and we'll sort it out! Before the hour of compline* the king will know our mind – and someone we know is going to suffer!'

They thought it was a perfect plan. So the youth, much favoured by the king, was sent for and he duly came – curse him that he did so! His name was Ralph Farci – and he'd be well and truly *farci* before he left: stuffed with the foulest

---

[183] '*de bien fait, col frait*': literally 'from good done, neck broken'.
[184] The Norman knight Peter de Préaux was a loyal servant to the Angevin kings in turn – Henry II, Richard and John – and with his brother William (mentioned above, pp. 76–80, and like him a renowned figure on the tournament circuit) he was to accompany Richard on the Third Crusade.

filth; and may his gullet roast in hellfire along with the heart that put the words in his mouth! Never in our time, before or since, has a traitor conceived such utter falsehood. To them he came, and they all rose as one before him as if to greet an emir,[185] each of them showing him the utmost reverence and honour! Then, to inveigle him into their Devil-prompted plan, they plied him with drink: Sir Wassail's tricks were instrumental in enticing him on board! What they said doesn't bear repetition, and I can assure you, no decent man hearing their treacherous slanders would ever say a prayer for them again! But that wretched youth, far from balking at their lies, said:

'By my life, I can believe it! The Marshal's so high and mighty! Don't worry, sirs,' he said, 'the king shall hear of it this very night! But he won't want to believe it – he'll say it's all nonsense – so I'll need you to back me up and testify: I'll call on you.'

And each of them replied: 'Go ahead – you can tell him all: we'll assure him it's the truth.'

So off the scoundrel went, God curse him, and came before the Young King and told him he knew the Marshal was wronging him – and in what way.

'By Saint Denis!' the king replied. 'I don't believe it! Don't start spouting wicked lies! What an allegation! Unless you've witnesses to back it up you're for it!'

'By the faith I owe you, sire,' he said, 'I can bring five knights who'll gladly testify!'

They were summoned and they duly came and endorsed the lie, claiming it was common knowledge: eyes and ears, they said, bore witness! The king was deeply shocked, and turned so against the Marshal that he would no longer speak to him and forbade him audience. The Marshal now realised that Sir Peter had been right: the king made it clear – and publicly, not in private – that he hated him with all his heart; and his position at court was not as it had been: his influence with the king was gone along with the king's affection. But no one except the king and those who'd caused the rift could understand the cause of this disfavour: all who witnessed it were baffled – they could see no reason for it and thought it most unjust, knowing well enough the effort and fine service that the Marshal had devoted to the king. The worthy men who saw this were far from pleased and lost much confidence in the king, and the Marshal himself was most aggrieved that he should be treated so when he'd done the king no offence or wrong.

But he took comfort in his innocence and trusted in God who always saves those who are wrongly afflicted and accused; this helped him to endure the hurt, and lessened the distress and pain. He thought of Saint Susanna,[186] abandoned to treacherous accusers but promptly rescued by God; and likewise of Daniel, unjustly thrown – and without a trial – into the lions' den. What more can I say? God is most powerful and kind. And he remembered, too, the Three Kings,

---

[185] *'almazor'*: a high-ranking title from the East.
[186] In the book of Daniel, Susanna is falsely accused of adultery; in the Middle Ages she was considered a saint.

THE YOUNG KING BELIEVES THE SLANDERS

guided by God to steer well clear of the hands of the wicked King Herod, who committed the appalling massacre of the Innocents, having them slaughtered in their hundreds and thousands in an attempt to ambush God; but God is not one to be outsmarted.[187]

The Marshal railed against Fortune's spite in so cruelly rewarding all his service and good deeds. He begrudged it very much, and distanced himself from his lord the Young King, staying well clear of his presence. But thanks be to God, things turned out well: he found a welcome elsewhere from men who greeted him with joy and honour. And rightly so, by God! Such a man he was that those lucky enough to have him in their house or retinue were only too pleased – they thought themselves well repaid!

And then the time came when news spread far and wide that a tournament was to be held between Gournay and Ressons.[188] Word reached the Young King and the dukes and the counts and, to come straight to the point, the Young King made ready to go and wondered where the Marshal could be – he'd always been his friend and guide in many a tournament. Now he'd no idea where he was, or in which land. But he sent in search of him with a summons to come without delay and join him at Gournay. He was duly found and he came without demur: he let nothing get in the way – the moment he heard the king's summons he considered it a command.

The tournament was held just before Advent. Great nobles and knights flocked from many lands and countries in the hope of winning renown. They didn't hold back: skirmishes began at once; and it would take some doing to record all the fine deeds that were done! And then, when the great companies advanced, the whole valley rang – for the fact is, truly, that the barons and counts and noble men had come with all the forces they could muster. The Young King and his company were a little to the rear, further down the valley, just outside the lists,[189] when he saw the Marshal coming, fully armed and helmet laced; and he looked anything but cowed or inclined to flee: he rather looked like a man prepared to perform great deeds in any contest – and by my life that's what he did that day according to my source, as you're about to hear.

The tournament was joined, and the like had never been seen before; so many lances had never been put to use in a single day! And when the Young King joined the fray the combat focused around him, as well it might, for he performed so splendidly that many thrilled to witness his courage and prowess and dexterity; and his men were superb, forcing all the rest to cower in tightly huddled packs before them. All the same, it was the Marshal who was deemed a wonder: everyone marvelled at his amazing feats, to the delight of all his friends – and to the dismay of those jealous men who'd created the rift between him

---

[187] Literally 'God had nothing to learn from him'.
[188] The second tournament to be mentioned there: see above, p. 53. The probable date is late November 1182, as we are about to be told of Henry II's Christmas court at Caen, which is known to have been held that year.
[189] '*lices*': see note 79 above, p. 53.

and the king. He gave no thought that day to booty or taking prisoners; he was paying such attention to his lord that twice that day he rescued him from men who'd seized him by the bridle. They couldn't get away fast enough when he appeared in the fray! He soon sent them scattering!

It was a fine tournament indeed, and truly, the king and his men performed so many feats of arms that they won the day. The Flemings won and lost in equal measure, and the Burgundians and Normans and French and English excelled, and happily no party was put to rout and the contest was ended by mutual agreement. All had fought so well that those who'd witnessed it declared that never in their lives had they seen such a great display of chivalry at any tourney, when so much was to be won and lost, without one party being forced to a crushing defeat. And there was unanimous praise for the Marshal's mighty prowess – so much so that everyone from both sides awarded him the prize. It was everywhere reported that he'd never performed such deeds of arms and chivalry in his life.

Before they parted the magnates came and spoke together – rightly so, it seems to me; and the good count of Flanders said to the Young King, who in all Christendom was the image and flower of nobility and valour and the fountain of largesse:

'Dear cousin, if you have the wherewithal to secure the service of a knight as fine as the Marshal here, it's neither wise nor laudable to let him go!'

That's what he said, but the king made no response: he still harboured a dark and bitter hatred – an enmity for which no one could see a cause. But seeing that it was so, the count, inexplicable though he found it, dropped the subject and said no more: he was aware that the king was flushing with shame – and the Marshal was flushing, too, with embarrassment and anger. The talking stopped and they parted, returning to their lodgings or to where their business took them.

The king left the town, and I tell you, at his leaving the Marshal made no attempt to speak to him and didn't escort him very far – and the king addressed not a word to him. The Marshal took leave of his companions and headed elsewhere, accompanied by just one of those friends who were very distressed about his troubles. As for his enemies who'd been at the tournament, when they saw that the king had called for him, they said he clearly didn't know what to do without him!

'Well, he'll be doing without him soon enough,' said one, particularly cunning, deceitful and malicious. 'I'm a master of this craft, so trust me:[190] his name'll be mud once word of this reaches the father![191] So damn us all if we don't let him know!'

'True enough! True enough!' they all cried. 'That's the way to do it! He'll never be seen at court again! Neither of the kings[192] will want to know him!'

---

[190] Literally 'if ever I knew anything about the goldsmith's craft' – i.e. 'I'm the best in the business!'
[191] i.e. the Young King's father, King Henry.
[192] i.e. neither King Henry nor his son the Young King.

They couldn't go fast enough. Off they went to find the Young King's father at Rouen. As one they blurted out the details, explaining why his son had good reason to feel ill will towards the Marshal. When King Henry heard this he was little bothered, apart from the shame involved, for in his eyes his son's entourage were dreadfully profligate, squandering his wealth, and he was only too pleased to see the best among them leave!

With their false and baseless slanders they thought the Marshal would come no more to court, and would no longer be welcome there or loved, esteemed or trusted. They thought they'd nailed it – but they would come unstuck yet! Despite their efforts the truth would come to light and be known to all – and they would be disgraced and humbled. For the Marshal would return indeed, and achieve the pre-eminence that such a worthy man deserved, and rightly earn the love and favour of both father and son; for when the truth was brought to light and the slanders exposed he would be loved and exalted and acclaimed all the more, an even greater pleasure to his friends, just as gold, the more it is exposed to the fire, is ever brighter, more lustrous and more fine.

Shortly after their meeting, at Christmas,[193] the old King Henry held at Caen the most magnificent and sumptuous feast, truly, that he ever held in Normandy. Many men arrived as summoned – and many more unsummoned! – from far and wide; a plenary court it was indeed, so grand that men of every degree and every trade came flocking. I've heard it said that from Saint-Mathieu to the Empire,[194] from Aix-la-Chapelle to Gascony, from the Mediterranean[195] to Cologne, the holding of the court had been announced and proclaimed. Many of those who came were well rewarded – though, as is always the way, there were many, too, whose attendance was less fruitful.

The Marshal came, for sure: no wrong he'd suffered, no wrangling or resentment – nor anything anyone said – would stop him going and finding out if the truth was known or the slanders given credence, if his lord now realised he'd been deceived by the arrant traitors and would be willing to forgive him. He was given a joyous welcome by the great lords present, but his enemies were dismayed and aghast when he arrived, fearing he might be reconciled with the king and that their treacherous plot would be uncovered and exposed. They stayed well away from him, but sent someone to keep a close eye and ear, to find out what the Marshal would say to the king and if he'd vindicate himself; for one thing's for sure: if it came to trial by combat, they'd be hard pressed to find any one of them who'd be keen to take him on and defend their cause!

When the Marshal realised they'd laid their foul, treacherous accusations before the old king, and that the tale these faithless men had concocted was now known to all, he dearly wanted a trial to prove to everyone whether it was true

---

[193] The Christmas of 1182.
[194] From Pointe Saint-Mathieu in Finisterre, the furthest tip of Brittany, to the Holy Roman Empire.
[195] The text says simply 'the sea'.

or a lie. He couldn't wait to rebut the charge. Raging, furious, he came before his lord the Young King and said:

'Hear me, sire: a moment, please. Base, bitter calumnies have been told to you about me. My lord your father is here with you, and barons, counts, vavasors, castellans, viscounts, all of them men of reason; and in the presence of all I'm willing to prove I've never wronged or betrayed you in any way, whatever you may have been told. And this is how I'll contest the charge: let my accusers come forward, and with God's help I swear that if they're willing to prove their claim, I'll defend myself alone against their finest three! The battle will last three days; if I'm beaten by the first of them, hang me on the spot! But if I defeat him, I'll face the second next day – again, if I lose, let me be hanged at once. And if I lose to the third, have me hanged and drawn.'

'Truly, Marshal,' the Young King replied, 'I don't care for this; I'll not have you defend yourself this way.'

'My lord, the men who've spread these calumnies are here! Why does none of them speak? They've heard my offer well enough! So here's another, since there's clearly nothing else for it: have a finger cut from my right hand – whichever one you choose – then let the best of them step forward and challenge me! And if he can defeat me, deal with me as befits a proven traitor! It's clear now, is it not, good sire, that a wicked tongue dares utter what it dares not prove! And it's clear to me, since you won't show me mercy even now, when I've offered more than reason demands, that you're merely looking for a chance to be rid of me. In the presence of this noble assembly I must take my leave of you. I've no wish to stay a moment longer.' Then he turned to King Henry the father and said: 'I pray you, sire, show me the gracious spirit I believe you possess and grant me safe conduct from your land. That's all I ask of you, for you've made it clear that your court is prejudiced against me, contrary to reason and the law of the land. I must go elsewhere and make my way and live where best I can, since here I cannot clear myself of these false charges when none of my accusers dares show his face. This is evidently allowed, to do me down! But if I'm to be denied justice, I'm glad it's in the presence of such an illustrious company!'

The old king saw he was in earnest, not mincing his words, and to put a quick end to the matter he granted him and his companions safe conduct as far as Mortagne in Perche.[196] So off he set, and may God be with him! But he didn't go like a fugitive or a man in fear of any knight; he would take present blows and buffets on the chin, confident that those responsible would be brought to shame – they'd get their just reward for their fervent efforts.

The slanderers were now at ease, as happy as could be, convinced that there was no way back for the one they'd manoeuvred out of court. The lying rogues said:

'What will he do now, the one who'd outdone us all? His prestige will be much reduced! He won't be so well off now – the booty won't go all his way! No longer will we hear Henry the Northerner[197] yelling up and down the field: "This

---

[196] Mortagne-au-Perche is a little to the east of Alençon.
[197] See above, p. 82.

way! This way! God save the Marshal!" That cry's a thing of the past! So are the stacks of spoils he used to win – which he always took for granted. He lorded it over the whole court – night and day there was no talk of anyone but him: it's caused us grief and embarrassment many a time! But now his proud bubble's pricked! We've brought him down a good few notches!'

In the hearing of everyone, at every opportunity, these villains bragged of how they'd knocked the Marshal off his perch.

Sir Baldwin de Béthune, who despised the clique, heard all about this behaviour of theirs and their conceited boasts, and saw how they were carrying on, crowing and swaggering, openly rejoicing about their wicked, shameful deeds until their treachery was clear to all, and how they mocked and abused Henry the Northerner, in the hearing of anyone inclined to listen. Sir Baldwin was deeply aggrieved; he raged in his heart; he was speechless with anger, inconsolable. So he had everything they said, word for word, set down in a letter, along with details of their bearing and behaviour, just as you've heard. Then he sent a boy to take the letter to the Marshal, under his seal. The boy set off at once and pressed on, hardly stopping day or night, and searched hither and thither till he found him. He gave the Marshal warm and loving greetings from his master with prayers for God's protection wherever he might go, and straightway handed him the letter. The Marshal had it read at once, and the clerk read every detail loud and clear, just as you've heard, omitting nothing. The Marshal was pleased to receive the good knight's message, but the smile with which he greeted it belied what was in his heart.

Meanwhile the great lords of France had heard about this sorry affair, and news of it flew through Champagne and Flanders, for Rumour is ever swift, and those at court soon spread word of the wicked, baseless way the traitors had created a rift between the Marshal and his lord and forced him to leave – they'd seen him go; and they reported, too, how he'd offered to defend himself against the charge of betrayal and any other wrong but the king had refused to listen or accept his rebuttal. And let me tell you, in brief, that every duke and count and great lord in the kingdom of France yearned to have the Marshal in his household! They searched for him high and low! The count of Flanders was the first to send for him – he longed more than anything to have the Marshal at his side, aware as he was of his honour, goodness and prowess, so often displayed. The duke of Burgundy likewise sought his services, as did the Advocate of Béthune.[198] I promise you all, and have no doubt, that there was hardly a single magnate in France who didn't send men to scour the land for him.

Meanwhile the Marshal had been to the fair at Lagny[199] and bought a splendid horse; he thought it an excellent buy at only thirty pounds: he wouldn't have considered selling it on for forty or even fifty, I understand. He now had two fine

---

[198] Robert V of Béthune; the lords of the town and castle of Béthune were traditionally the Advocates of the Abbey of Saint Vaast at Arras.
[199] Lagny-sur-Marne, to the east of Paris (the site of the tournament described earlier); the great fair at Lagny was held in January, so the date is now January 1183.

and valuable steeds, and with them he could happily present himself anywhere as a man of worth.

To come straight to the point: twenty days after Christmas another tourney was promptly held between Ressons and Gournay, with many a duke and count and magnate coming from far and wide in the hope of winning honour and prestige. But I can't name them all: I saw far too many there to list in full. Now, the great lords who'd sent people in search of the Marshal had failed to find him – they'd hunted everywhere but found no trace; but he turned up at the tournament in superb array: it would have been hard to put a price on his gear and apparel – no knight ever had finer (he always took great care of his appearance). By happy chance the count of Saint-Pol[200] caught up with him: he'd spotted him from afar and recognised his shield at once, and galloped ahead to meet him. Up he rode and greeted him, and the Marshal came to join him and met him with an embrace and kiss. The count was delighted, thinking himself lucky to have found the Marshal after sending men in search of him, and said:

'I pray you, if I may be so bold, let me be on your side in the tournament, come what may!'

'I assure you, my dear sir,' the Marshal replied, 'you won't be on my side; rather, I shall be on yours – for as long as my strength holds out – and I'll not let you down.'

'A thousand thanks, sir!' said the count. 'I couldn't have wished for more!'

And with that – and no doubt to the dismay of some – they headed to the tourney ground.

The Flemish arrived in force with the good count of Flanders, and the Picards joined them along with Germans and the knights of Brabant and Lorraine; and the duke of Burgundy came, not just with Burgundians but, for the first time ever, joining forces with the knights of Champagne, France, Normandy, Poitou, Brittany and Anjou. When all parties had arrived they set about their business. The count of Saint-Pol was first to arm, along with thirty knights, but he'd distributed his horses to his companions and had no mount left for himself! The Marshal heard what had happened and said:

'I've two fine horses, sir. I pray you kindly, tourney this day on whichever you think best.'

'Thank you, Marshal!' said the count. 'I'll do so gladly!'

The two mounts were promptly brought forward, and the count was spot-on with his choice, I can tell you: he mounted the very best, as became plain in the course of the day.

The tournament began, and its like had never been seen before: never were so many lances used and spent in a single day, as all vied intently with each other in the quest for honour. The preliminary jousts were brief; then the great squadrons and companies advanced in all their might and splendour, fearing each other not a jot. And they clashed in a splintering storm so great that in an instant the ground was littered with shards and stumps of lance, leaving no space

---

[200] Hugh (Hugues) IV of Saint-Pol, a county centred on Saint-Pol-sur-Ternoise, north-west of Arras.

for a horse to charge unhindered. The combat was intense – and none finer was ever seen, with mêlées on all sides. The shattering of lances and the ringing of mighty blows of swords on helms filled all the surrounding land: God's thunder would have made no impression at all, or been heard by anyone. It was no place for the timorous! The count of Saint-Pol was seized by the bridle, but the good Marshal valiantly came to his aid, rescuing him from more than seven who were striving to wound him and lead him off. The cowardly stayed well clear! You'd have seen many a banner dragged and trampled in the mud – along with many a toppled knight; but it's always been said that the gallant and brave are often to be found under horses' hooves, for the cowardly never end up there: they hold their lives too dear to venture into a fray and risk any loss or injury! You'd have seen knights being taken prisoner and horses won and lost: anyone who could seize a bridle did all in his power to keep fast hold, while the other strove to seize it back, defend himself and fight him off – there was no chance of bidding them compromise! Anyway, to cut things short, so many feats of arms were performed that day that it was a marvel to behold: everyone wondered where such outstanding knights had come from, to sustain quite such a contest.

And one thing above all was clear, for it was witnessed by all: the Marshal performed more feats of arms that day than anyone, by far. No matter how thick the press, when he charged in he delivered such an array of blows that all went reeling back; they couldn't resist him in the least, and were filled with utter awe.

The count of Saint-Pol was seized again, and again the Marshal rescued him; and it wasn't straightforward: the count was taken by a great body of men, and the count's men couldn't see what had become of him, but the Marshal came in the nick of time, charging in and driving the captors apart. He gave them a handsome battering and they had no choice but to let the count go; they resisted with all their might, but their best wasn't good enough and they were forced to give him up.

The companies now parted and the tournament drew to a close. It had been quite magnificent: no one present, no king, duke, count or anyone else, could claim to have seen its equal. Before leaving, the great lords met to confer on the tourney-ground. The count of Flanders and the duke of Burgundy sent for the Marshal, and roundly declared that he'd outfought everyone that day. All longed to have him in their service! No amount of money was too much: in the hearing of all, the count of Flanders made him a serious offer of an income of five hundred pounds simply to stay with him. The duke matched the offer! The Advocate of Béthune, no less admiring, was willing to give him a town and land with a revenue of five hundred pounds: with that he solicited his service. The worthy Jacques d'Avesnes[201] offered him three hundred and lordship of all he possessed! The Marshal thanked them all, but said he'd accept no lands or pay in exchange for his service – he'd another mission to accomplish first if he could: he wished to go on a pilgrimage to the Three Kings at Cologne[202] – his heart was

---

[201] See note 90 above, p. 58.
[202] The Shrine of the Three Kings is a huge reliquary, supposedly containing the bones of the Biblical Magi, placed behind the altar of Cologne Cathedral.

set on it. Jacques d'Avesnes cherished his company and offered to go with him, and the Marshal said:

'Thank you, dear sir: there's no one I'd rather have.'

Sir Jacques escorted the Marshal through his own lands and was a splendid companion – no better knight ever climbed in a saddle, or was more eager for the company of worthy men – and together they made their way most happily, it seems, to the Three Kings.

Word travels swiftly, and reports now reached the Young King's court of the mighty tournament at Ressons. 'Never,' he was told, 'did king or count see one so great, or anything like! So many bold and worthy knights all gathered there together!'

'Which of them did best of all?' asked Baldwin de Béthune.

'Which?' said one young knight. 'Everyone to a man agreed that the Marshal was supreme.'

'I don't believe you, knight!' said Baldwin. 'Are you saying the Marshal – ?'[203]

'Yes, I swear! He made such a fine show that he outfought everyone! The verdict was unanimous!'

'Nonsense!' said Baldwin. 'It can't have been the Marshal! Did you see him yourself?'

'Indeed I did! I was there that day and assure you he surpassed everyone on both sides, absolutely!'

'Really?'

'Truly, by my life!'

'Do me a favour, friend, and tell me if you please: did you see Henry the Northerner running around after him and yelling his battle-cry hither and yon: "This way! Over here! God save the Marshal!"?'

'No, sir – he wasn't there.'

'Then you're having us on!' said Baldwin. 'Are you trying to tell us, friend, in all honesty, that the Marshal can manage, all by himself, to perform any feat of chivalry?'

'What do you mean by that, sir? You surely can't deny he's one of the finest knights in the whole wide world!'

Baldwin was delighted by this, and summoned a number of knights who were present, notably those ill disposed towards the Marshal, and had the youth repeat all he'd said, so pleasing to his ears. Thereupon another knight stepped forward; he'd been at the tournament, too, and he stood before them now and told them all:

'Every word this young man's said is true! I was there and can vouch for it – I saw it myself; and I'm thrilled to report that the Marshal was the outright winner of the tourney: he won so comprehensively, so stunningly, that no one would believe it unless he'd seen it with his own eyes! And don't doubt what I heard with my own ears – a hundred heard it and so did I: the count

---

[203] This rather naturalistic interruption is unusual; there may be an accidental omission here. If so, the missing lines would presumably have been as ironic as Baldwin's following protestations.

of Flanders offered the Marshal land worth five hundred pounds a year – he had numerous men implore him to be a permanent member of his retinue. The duke of Burgundy did likewise, and the Advocate of Béthune[204] made a greater offer still: revenue of a thousand pounds and his beautiful daughter's hand in marriage if he wished! I heard the Marshal thank him warmly, but he said he wasn't yet inclined to marry. And then Sir Jacques d'Avesnes offered him three hundred if he'd join his household, along with lordship and mastery of all his estates, outright! Again the Marshal thanked him graciously, but insisted that he'd accept no one's offer – castle, manor or payment – for his services, for he'd other business to attend to first.'

Then Sir Baldwin, a true and loyal friend to the Marshal, said: 'God! What an honour it would have been for my sister to marry him! He's a warrior indeed![205] May God, ever supporter of the good, take revenge upon those who've wronged him so when he's done them no offence!'

So he said, in the clear hearing of those who were less than pleased, fearing as they did that the Marshal's prowess and shrewd intelligence would win him power, honour and eminence once more.

War between King Henry's Sons

The Marshal now resided in France enjoying great prosperity and prestige: the noble and the mighty deemed themselves most fortunate when they could have him in their company; he was joyously welcomed by them all. But lest I incur anyone's impatience let me return now to my story.

What happened was this: the following Lent saw conflict between the three brothers.[206] The Young King and his brother Count Geoffrey, lord of Brittany, angrily left their father, offended and enraged that their brother the count of Poitiers,[207] with their father's backing, had made so bold as to wage war on the highest nobles of that land[208] and to treat them most unjustly. They'd complained to the Young King and declared that they would sooner serve him than their lord who wronged them so – indeed, they were his liegemen, having paid him homage, and would no longer acknowledge Count Richard of Poitiers as their lord when he wilfully mistreated them. The Young King and his brother Count Geoffrey protested to their father about the count of Poitiers's abuse of his men, but their father said:

'What's it to do with you? I've given him the land. If any of them wage war on him I hope he takes them on and teaches them a lesson!'[209]

---

[204] The 'Advocate' was Baldwin's father.
[205] Literally 'he bears a shield and lance well'.
[206] i.e. Henry II's three eldest sons: Henry, Richard and Geoffrey.
[207] Richard.
[208] i.e. Poitou. Richard's offensive treatment of his barons had begun to cause problems in the summer of 1182, but came to open warfare early in 1183 (hence the author's reference to Lent).
[209] i.e. because Henry saw the Poitevins as a constant cause of trouble: see above, p. 44.

The Young King replied, in short: 'They've long been my liegemen: it would be wrong of me to fail them and let them be so abused! It's only right that I go to their aid!'

'Very well!' said his father. 'Off you go and help them!'

With that they left, and a conflict started that wasn't resolved till all parties had thoroughly suffered, as everyone knows, and you'll hear exactly how in what follows.

It was a bitter parting, the two brothers leaving their father in a fearful rage. I don't know what more to tell you, other than that they made their way to Limoges and mustered a force of knights and soldiers, mercenaries, crossbowmen, archers and infantry of quality. The nobles of those parts, whom the count had treated so high-handedly and who hated him so bitterly, came in great numbers, all eager to do battle, yearning to crush Count Richard's haughty pride if they could get the better of him.

But the brothers soon had their father moving against them:[210] old King Henry swiftly assembled a mighty army – men of Normandy, Anjou, Flanders, Ponthieu and Poitou, as well as all manner of mercenaries: what an array there was of pennons and banners shimmering in the wind – and he advanced with furious speed against his sons at Limoges. Tents and pavilions there were beyond count: it was a truly colossal host.

But before their father arrived the Young King sent for his brother Count Geoffrey of Brittany who came with a splendid company of fine, valiant knights; and he appealed to his knights throughout France and Normandy, Anjou and the Low Countries and all of Flanders, and they responded to his call without demur. Duty and love for their lord having brought them to Limoges, they withdrew with him inside the castle. Seeing this, the old king's forces encircled them, with strong blockades at every approach, determined to keep them fast besieged.

Inside the castle they sat down to dine – but I shan't pretend it was a cheery feast; you'd hardly believe me if I did: idle fancy that would seem, or an outright lie. And when they rose from the table the Young King retired to a chamber to consult with his chief counsellors. Just three of them there were: his brother Count Geoffrey, Geoffrey of Lusignan and Roger de Gaugy. The Young King said to his brother:

'You realise our father's out there, besieging and blockading us with his host? How do you think we should respond?'

'I'd say, my dear sir,' Count Geoffrey replied, 'that you've lost your best advisor. By giving credence to false counsel, you've driven from your side the worthiest man from here to Rome. It was shameful and reprehensible: you believed lying, treacherous, malicious tongues, inspired by envy to slander him. I swear there's no man alive who could have given better guidance and assistance in your hour of need: how poorly you've repaid him!'

'Indeed, count,' said Geoffrey of Lusignan, 'you couldn't have said a truer word. God grant me honour, it was purely the work of men who'd taken against

---

[210] i.e. in support of Richard.

him out of envy. They wouldn't expect me to say this, but upon my soul, I'll defend both him and my lady the queen from the allegation against them – a fiction spawned by envy, treachery and wicked malice. I want to see it disproved, and I'm ready to do combat and quash this treacherous charge against the worthiest man in the world! God confound these traitors of yours! I know the Marshal was never base or false! Though truly, he feels no love towards me, for he suspects me of a wrong of which I'm innocent: I never killed his uncle.'[211]

Now hear a true wonder: how God, who ever watches over the good, swiftly exposes treachery – for nothing can be hidden from Him. The one who'd first conceived the plot, its instigator and prime mover, was at that time seneschal and master of the Young King's household.[212] Wily as ever, he interrupted their discussions without being summoned and addressed the king, saying:

'Hear me, my lord: I see your father has besieged you here in this castle. I'm his liegeman – I've paid him homage; I can stay with you no longer, and crave your leave to go and join the king your father as duty bids me.'

When the Young King heard this he cried: 'Hark at him, the traitor! Now he shows his true colours! How wickedly he slandered the Marshal, the worthiest man I had!'

He strode in fury to the head of his bed and snatched up his sword; blazing with rage he was about to attack and kill him, but Sir Geoffrey restrained him and said:

'Stop, my lord! Never let it be said you soiled your hands with this traitor's blood! Just get rid of him!'

'You're right,' said the king. 'Absolutely. Throw him out, the treacherous villain – and all his gear and belongings, too! Get him out of my sight – I want nothing more to do with him!'

Delighted by this turn of events, the count of Brittany, whose watchword was Prowess, said: 'That's the way – be rid of him! His faithlessness is revealed: it couldn't be more plain!'

So he was cast out in shame. And that's the last I'll say of him.

Then the Young King said to the three: 'I pray you, sirs, for the love of God, give me guidance now: tell me what to do.'

Sir Geoffrey of Lusignan replied: 'Our advice is simple, truly: send for the worthy Marshal! He has so often given you sound, wise counsel: he can guide you better than anyone.'

'You're right,' said the king. 'I'll do as you say.'

So he called for Ralph FitzGodfrey – he was his chamberlain, and he loved him dearly and trusted him entirely: he was indeed the most courtly and worthy servant in his household – and said:

'Ralph, search every land for the Marshal till you find him, and do all you can to beseech him in good faith to come to me without fail. And make it clear – be it in public or in private – that I bear him no ill will at all; on the contrary, I'd have him be lord and master of my household, just as he was before – and more so!

---

[211] Earl Patrick of Salisbury: see above, pp. 44–5.
[212] The author – perhaps deliberately – gives no name, and this 'seneschal' is unidentifiable.

Let no one think otherwise! And assure him that I realise now he was a victim of slander, bred from the malice and envy of traitors – God curse and shame them for their wicked lies!'

Like the good and trusty servant he was, Ralph set off on his mission. He scoured many lands and many places, but could find no sure news of the Marshal. He searched and searched to the point of exhaustion – and then met him on the way back! The moment he caught sight of him he raced joyfully to join him; they were both delighted to find each other and kissed and embraced. I can't tell you all that was said between them, but I can assure you of this much: the trusty Ralph greeted him on the Young King's behalf as his true liegeman for whom his love was whole-hearted and unswerving, and he delivered his message perfectly, just as you've heard, omitting nothing. The Marshal was overjoyed to hear that the plot against him had been recognised and the traitors exposed; thrilled by the news, he thanked the Lord and His father and holy Mary, His mother, for this turn of events, that the foul treachery was revealed. Then he said:

'I've been to Cologne, on a holy pilgrimage to the Three Kings, in the hope that through their intercession God might prove me innocent, clean and blameless of the charges made against me. I've never entertained the slightest thought of committing the shameful wrong alleged by those treacherous villains!'

Then he told Ralph FitzGodfrey to be on his way, promising in all good faith that he'd follow as soon as he could. So while Ralph set off and returned to court, the Marshal made full preparations. Shrewd man that he was, he decided to go first to the king of France and discuss the affair, explaining how his lord had sent a messenger bidding him return to him with all speed, without delay, for he'd discovered the truth about the shocking, wicked, unprecedented slander levelled against him – but I shan't repeat all that: you've heard the allegations made. The king of France was delighted by the news, and said that if the Marshal needed anything from him it would be granted without fail: great words indeed, from a king of France.

'A thousand thanks, sire,' the Marshal said. 'I'd gladly ask that you provide me with a letter to the Young King's father, asking his permission to return to my lord his son without incurring his displeasure.'

'Most certainly,' said the French king. 'As a truly loyal knight you shall have it. It shall be a letter patent. And the king should understand this: if he chooses not to respect my letter, it'll be assumed that he was behind the plot to malign you and create the rift between you and his son!'

The Marshal was duly given the letter, just as he prescribed in every detail – and another, likewise according to his stipulation, from the archbishop of Reims. This was considered a very shrewd move. Count Robert[213] happily gave him another, as did Count Theobald,[214] who considered the Marshal a staunch friend. And when King Henry heard these pleas on the Marshal's behalf he gladly complied,

---

[213] Robert, count of Dreux: see above, p. 74.
[214] Theobald (Thibaut), count of Blois – see above, p. 58 – who was brother of the archbishop of Reims.

and sent greetings and assurances of his love and approved his return to his lord the Young King. Indeed, I understand King Henry went further, giving the Marshal full leave to wage war against him with fire and sword, to do all in his power – such grace would he be granted by the king that he would bear him no ill will for opposing him at all: he was to have it in letters patent, plain and clear.

The Young King's men gathered to his side from all parts, near and far, in response to his call.[215] The Marshal, that fine knight Baldwin de Béthune and Hugh de Hamelincourt,[216] a model of prowess, agreed to meet one another at Montmirail-en-Brie.[217] One Wednesday, it was. Now, as the Marshal made his way there he was overcome with the need to sleep and gave in to it. Eustace de Bertrimont was with him, no one else, and the Marshal, so sleepy, dismounted at the roadside and lay down to rest while his squire Eustace unharnessed their horses and left them free to graze in the open country. While the Marshal slumbered, a tall, fine figure of a man appeared with a beautiful woman – whether married or not I don't know. They were mounted on a pair of big, handsome palfreys, sleek and well-fed. They were riding at quite a pace, though heavily laden, and were swathed in fine brown cloaks of Flemish cloth. And as they drew near to where the Marshal lay sleeping, the woman murmured:

'God, how tired I am!'

Eustace heard this, as did the Marshal and it woke him; he said: 'Who was that, Eustace?'

'A man and a woman, sir,' he replied. 'I can see them riding past. The woman says she's weary, but they're riding fast enough. They've handsome baggage, that's for sure.'

'Harness my horse,' the Marshal said. 'I want to find out where they're from and where they're headed, and about their business and who they are.'

Then he mounted as fast as he could, but in his haste he forgot his sword. He spurred ahead and caught up with them, and taking the man by the sleeve of his cloak he said:

'Tell me truly, sir, who are you? I'd like to know.'

Annoyed at being bothered, he answered: 'I'm a man, sir!'

'I'm aware of that much!' the Marshal said. 'You're clearly not a beast!'

The man snatched his cloak away, freeing himself from the Marshal's grip, and laid his hand on his sword.

'Are you looking for a fight?' the Marshal said. 'If you are, you'll have it sure enough!' And he loudly called: 'Eustace! My sword! Give it to me! Now!'

The man recoiled in alarm and let his cloak fall back, covering his sword – he'd hitched it up as if to draw it; and the Marshal spurred forward and grabbed his cloak and pulled with such force that one of his fingers caught in the hood and tore it back – to reveal, quite simply, the most handsome monk from there to Cologne! With his head now bared, there was no hiding it! Then the Marshal said:

---

[215] i.e. to support him in his war against his father and his brother Richard.
[216] See above, p. 75.
[217] Between Reims and Paris.

'I knew there was something up! Tell me, who are you, and who's this woman here?'

Embarrassed and afraid, wrong-footed and distressed, he replied: 'Have pity, sir, in God's name! We're at your mercy! I'm a monk, as you can plainly see.'

'So what are you up to? Come on – don't try to hide it.'

'This woman's my sweetheart, sir; I've taken her from her homeland – we're heading for foreign parts.'

Then the Marshal asked the damsel: 'Tell me, my dear: who are you? Of what family?'

Filled with shame, weeping in distress, she replied: 'I'm from Flanders, sir – I'm the sister of Sir Ralph de Lens.'

'You're not being very sensible, my dear,' the Marshal said. 'Not at all. In all good faith I advise you to stop this foolishness; I'll settle things with your brother – I know him well.'

Mortified, the damsel replied: 'Please God, sir, I'll never be seen again where anyone knows me!'

The Marshal said to the monk: 'Be honest now and tell me: if you're serious about this, have you any money to live on and support yourselves?'

The monk hitched up his cloak and produced a bulging money-belt. 'Indeed I have, sir! Look at this: we've forty-eight pounds in here!'

'My dear man,' said the Marshal, 'how do you propose to live on that? What are you going to do with it?'

'I'll tell you! I've no intention of spending it: I'm going to loan it out in some foreign town and we'll live off the interest!'

'Usury!' cried the Marshal. 'By the Holy Lance I can't abide it! We're not having that – God forbid! Take the money, Eustace! If you won't turn back or act decently but are set upon such a sorry path, be off with you! The Devil take you!'

With that, the Marshal headed off to the rendezvous – and told Eustace on no account to breathe a word to anyone!

So, to continue, he came to the arranged meeting-place where he found Sir Baldwin, to whom he was very close, and Hugh de Hamelincourt. They ran to greet him joyfully, crying out together:

'We've been starving, Marshal, waiting for you!'

'Don't worry, sirs – the delay's been worth it! You'll each have a share: Eustace, the money!'

Eustace gleefully showered the coins before them, and the Marshal said: 'This should settle a debt or two!'

'Marshal,' they began to ask, 'where did you get all this?'

'Hold your horses!' he said. 'I'll tell you later!'

They ate and drank very merrily, and when they rose from the table they counted the cash, the Marshal thinking that the money-lending monk might have got it wrong. But once it had been counted they found it all there – forty-eight pounds in good coin!

'It seems our lender friend was right!' the Marshal said; and he told them the story from start to finish, in every detail, just as you've heard. Sir Hugh, let me tell you, wasn't happy at all. His response was:

'God's teeth, I swear you were much too kind! You let them off with their palfreys and baggage! Quick! Get my horse! I want a word with those two!'

'For God's sake, calm down, good sir! My story's done and so's this business!'

The Death of the Young King

They pressed on day by day till they reached their lord's court, where they were highly honoured by the king and all his company.

But Fortune, ever capricious, ever fickle, was soon to turn Her back on them in no uncertain manner. Chivalry gave way to indolence, inaction; Largesse was abandoned; Fortune cast the whole world into shadow. And there's no avoiding it – I have to tell you the reason: it was because of the death of the Young King. He fell ill;[218] and then what pain and affliction he suffered – and how admirably he repented as his death approached. But Fortune, ever keen to topple and cast down the good, was determined to put paid to him, and turned the world's joy to utter woe.

And when it came to the reading of his will, which he made wisely and well, he said: 'Marshal, Marshal, you have always been loyal to me, whole-hearted in your faithfulness. So I bequeath my cross[219] to you, that you may bear it to the Holy Sepulchre on my behalf, to fulfil my vow to God.'

'Thank you, my lord,' the Marshal said. 'Since you see fit to bestow this task upon me I'll fulfil it gladly, indeed I will: no true friend fails to give help in the hour of urgent need. But Death is harsh and cruel indeed, allowing you to live no longer.'

'Marshal, dear guide and mentor,' said the king, 'when God wills it, it must be so. It seems I'm now to die.'

And as he said this his face paled; his complexion, once so delightfully bright and fresh, turned dull, sallow and wan. Grieving broke out in the hall, as anguished as could ever be; for God never gave life to any knight whose loss was more worthy to be mourned – if weeping could ever bring him back. But it was no use: death is a bow that never misses, cruel and without scruple, oblivious to the ruin it leaves in its wake – what woe it brings us, God confound it! And the woe and the grieving for the Young King that day were piteous indeed. How they wrung their hands, how they wailed and railed against Death.

'Ah, Death, wretched, insatiable!' they cried. 'What are you doing? Are you blind? No indeed, it's wilful: without cause you take the life of the finest, fairest man ever born since the days of Abel. It's a grievous shame! He was filled with largesse and every other virtue, lacking none. Ah, God, what will become of Largesse, Chivalry, Prowess, who all had their home in him? Where will they dwell now? He was their castle, their mansion! They'll never find another to compare!'

---

[218] With dysentery, in the last days of May 1183.
[219] i.e. his cloak emblazoned with the crusader's cross.

Such was their lament. But Death, so harsh and cruel, was heedless of their every word, impervious to their curses, and racked and beset the king with agonies till he collapsed unconscious in their arms. They thought he was dead. But wicked, hateful, torturing Death was not yet done with him. The king, so wise and courtly, recovered from his swoon with a cry of pain, and the barons around him, overcome by grief, distress and woe, said:

'Speak to us if you can, dear lord, in God's name.'

'Gladly,' he said, 'but I can't for long. I pray you, take care of my will and testament – and of my soul. And when my soul is gone, carry my body to the church of Notre Dame at Rouen. I pray and bid you also crave my father's mercy, that he may forgive me his ill will and give me his blessing.' Then he said: 'I commend you to glorious God. I can say no more: Death has such a cruel, insistent grip on me that I no longer have feeling in heart or limb. Now in God's name, remember me!'

And as he said that, his soul departed. May God receive him at His side!

He died at Martel, I understand,[220] that embodiment of courtesy, prowess, kindness and largesse. The barons who were with him prepared to carry him to his father – who, needless to say, was distressed at the news of his son's death, and little wonder: it's only right, for the heart cannot lie; Nature will not allow it; had he been otherwise he would rightly have been reproached.

Once the body was embalmed and anointed and shrouded he was carried from the castle[221] amid loud cries of lamentation: all those who'd been his companions were beside themselves with grief at their dreadful loss.

Now, there was a prominent mercenary named Sancho[222] who was owed a great deal of money by the Young King. He felt very hard done by, and realised he'd have to resort to some devious ploy if he was ever to recover his due. So, knowing the Young King had loved the Marshal and trusted in him more than anyone, he charged up and seized him by the reins, crying:

'You're my prisoner, Marshal! You're coming with me!'

The Marshal asked him why.

'Why? I'll tell you right enough: I want you to cough up the money your lord owed me!'

The Marshal saw fighting would do no good and didn't resist.

'I'm not going to lose that money!' Sancho said. 'I'm holding you responsible! But I've decided to be generous: I'll let you off in return for a hundred marks.'*

'What are you saying, sir? That would be tough for me! I'm a poor knight – I don't yet have a scrap of land! I wouldn't know where to get that kind of money. But I'll tell you what I'll do: I faithfully swear to surrender as your prisoner on whatever day you set.'

'Fair enough,' said Sancho. 'It's a deal – you're a trustworthy knight.'

---

[220] On 11 June 1183. Martel is between Brive and Cahors, on the bank of the Dordogne. The poet has not made it clear that the Young King had at this point, after campaigning in the Limousin against his father and Richard, been ravaging Aquitaine.

[221] i.e. from Martel.

[222] 'Seinces': Sancho de Savannac, who had been engaged with his company of Basque mercenaries to support the Young King's campaign in the Limousin.

So the pledge was made, and the Marshal set off with the body to the Young King's father, who was distraught when he saw that the news was true: his son had been dearer to him than anyone. But such was his strength that he never betrayed his feelings, no matter what befell him. The Marshal, filled with deepest sorrow, told him all that had happened: how his son had fallen ill and suffered much pain, but how he'd made full confession and borne his sickness and his suffering without complaint.

'Now God grant that he be safe.' That was all the father said. His heart was more afflicted than he showed: he suffered in silence.

Then the Marshal said: 'What shall I do, sire?'

'That's obvious, Marshal. Go with your lord and take him to Rouen. You will be in charge of the escort.'

'I can't, sire,' he replied. 'I've promised to surrender as a prisoner to Sancho: he was owed a lot of money by your son, my lord, and that's the truth, though he says he'll release me for a hundred marks.'

The king summoned Joubert de Pressigny, a most influential courtier, and said: 'Go to Sancho on my behalf and bid him defer the Marshal's debt of a hundred marks.'

'Sire,' said Joubert, 'if that's your command there's no refusal: I'll do so willingly.'

There wasn't far to go: Sancho was found nearby. But on the way the Marshal was downcast, and Sir Joubert said:

'Marshal my friend, why are you so troubled?'

'I've reason enough,' he replied. 'If only I could worry away my woes! The pain of my lord's death, and the bother of this debt – it weighs heavily indeed, for I've no way of paying: I've good cause to fret!'

'You'd be grateful, then, to the man who could release you from the demand of the hundred marks, and free you of the debt?'

'Dear sir,' replied the Marshal, 'I'd be grateful indeed to anyone who could clear my debt – if it were possible!'

'Then leave it to me,' Sir Joubert said. 'When you've never had the money, it's not right that you should pay it! Let me handle this – don't worry: I'm sure I can sort it out.'

So they tracked down Sancho and greeted him on the king's behalf, and Sir Joubert said straight out that the king had taken on the debt he'd imposed upon the Marshal.

'That's fine by me! The king himself has said so?'

'Yes indeed.'

'I'm happy with that!'

They didn't dally but took their leave and were gone.

It wasn't long before Sancho came before the king and asked for his hundred marks. The king thought he'd lost the plot.

'What hundred marks, dear man?' he said.

'The debt you've taken up from the Marshal.'

'Someone's been having you on!' said the king. 'I said nothing of the sort. I never assumed the debt; I simply asked for a deferral.'

This didn't go down well with Sancho, and he swore by glorious God: 'Joubert spoke on your behalf and assured me you'd taken the debt in hand!'

Sir Joubert was told to come at once, and the king addressed him, saying: 'Why is this man asking me for the money?'

'I'll gladly explain. I told him straight that you'd assumed the debt. That's what I understood so that's what I said, I admit it!'

'Oh, so be it!' said the king. 'My son has cost me more than that – and if I had my way he'd be here to cost me still.'

His eyes were filled with sorrow: he seemed to be slightly weeping. It's best to say no more.

As the party carrying the Young King made their way to Rouen they came to Le Mans, where the canons chose to take charge of the body and buried it in their cathedral; but after a lawsuit and much trouble and wrangling the canons of Rouen managed to reclaim it.[223] And in the high church at Rouen it was honoured with a glorious service[224] befitting such a good, handsome, gracious, courteous, generous and valiant king, so much loved by all. His death, quite rightly, was deeply mourned, bitterly lamented by many a man and woman; and the count of Flanders, filled with grief and sorrow, said:

'Ah! Ah! Chivalry now is dead and finished and Largesse cast into the shade! Just so: their guiding light in the world has been snuffed out! Poor knights will have to seek their living elsewhere. They'll never find anyone to give them horses, arms and money as readily as he.'

But that's how the world is. The ambitious young knights of the Young King's court now had to roam the land in search of honour and renown, and that was that. They came at last to some out-of-the-way place in Normandy between Saint-Pierre-sur-Dives and Caen[225] where they heard a tournament was preparing. The Marshal, Sir Baldwin de Béthune (a very close companion) and Hugh de Hamelincourt, whose renown endures to this day, rode into the town, and as soon as they dismounted they sat down to dine without delay. But they hadn't been sitting long before the knights outside began to joust, and the opposition charged with such force that they drove the Normans and the English back into the town. Inside the gate one of the opposing knights, about to withdraw, turned so abruptly that he had a dreadful fall and couldn't move. He lay there helpless, with broken limbs, in agony. The cries from the street were so loud that they were heard by the knights eating inside – not that they were troubled. The Marshal went out and saw the knight lying there; he ran to him and swept him up and carried him, fully armed, into the house. What a fine fellow he is who brings such a gift! That bright and courteous knight said to his companions:

'Here – this should help to pay your dues!'

---

[223] i.e. to fulfil the Young King's own wishes. There was indeed much acrimony, and the king had to intervene.
[224] On 22 July 1183.
[225] The second place-name is accidentally omitted in the manuscript: it might be Caen; it could be Falaise; it could be a village closer to Saint-Pierre-sur-Dives.

'Oh,' said Sir Hugh, 'well done, that man! I'll happily take your promise of ransom, sir – while I fill my mouth with fresh herrings! Come on – give us your oath!'

And the captive duly gave his word of honour.

The Holy Land

Now, the Marshal had taken the crusader's cross,[226] and wherever he went people gave fine gifts and horses and money more liberally to him than to anyone else – and rightly so, given the cause. And the Marshal was keen to embark upon his pilgrimage. Chafing at the delay, he made preparations with all speed, not wanting to wait longer. He went to take his leave of King Henry. The king duly gave him leave, but implored him to come back soon, being eager to retain him in his household; and by way of guarantee he took from him two splendid horses.

'Very well, sire,' the Marshal said. 'I'll not refuse.'

The king gave him in return a hundred Angevin pounds[227] to support him on his pilgrimage. It was a costly deal for the Marshal: each one of the horses had been worth that much! But the Marshal didn't mind.

He came now to England to take leave of his friends, his sisters, his family – all his relations – as was right and proper. When he came to the house of Sir Robert de Pont-de-l'Arche, far away in the Marches,[228] his sister[229] spoke out, saying:

'Ah, God, what will they do now, my five unmarried daughters? Who will give them guidance and support? There's no one capable left!'

'Sister,' replied the Marshal, 'if I didn't care for them and the others dear to me, I wouldn't have bothered to come back.'[230]

And so it was that the Marshal left and was gone for two years. In Syria he performed more feats of prowess, more acts of daring and largesse, more fine deeds than anyone else had achieved in seven! Their renown endures, and they'll continue to be recounted far and wide, in many a noble household. I refer to them only briefly because I wasn't there to witness them and have never found anyone who could tell me even the half of it – it's a big subject!

---

[226] Bestowed upon him by the Young King, above, p. 99.

[227] i.e. from Anjou, different duchies at this time minting their own currency. But pounds (*livres*) did not exist as coins – the pound was used simply as a sum in accounting.

[228] '*de la outre, qu'il est en marche*'. This awkward phrase may well be corrupt, but the Pont-de-l'Arche family did hold lands, if not in the Welsh Marches, then at least as far west as Gloucestershire.

[229] The poet doesn't make it clear (perhaps because his family audience would have instantly understood), but Robert de Pont-de-l'Arche was Marshal's brother-in-law: Robert had married his sister Maud in 1179.

[230] This is another possibly corrupt passage, or there is an accidental omission that blurs the sense. Marshal appears to be saying that his sister needn't worry: the fact that he's returned shows his commitment to his family and intention to take care of them in time. And there was no immediate hurry to arrange marriages for these five nieces: if 'five' is correct they must have been born in very quick succession and the eldest can have been barely five years old.

When he left the Holy Land he went to take his leave of King Guy[231] and all the king's men and the Templars and the Hospitallers, all of whom loved him dearly for the great qualities they had found in him: they were very upset to see him go. I can't record his journey or where he stayed – no one's been able to tell me – and it's not really what concerns me so I'll pass on; there's no point spending time on what's not relevant.

He found King Henry at Lyons[232] with his barons and his court. The king was overjoyed to have William the Marshal back with him safe and sound, and held him very dear, retaining him as a member of his household and making him chief among his privy counsellors – and rightly so: he repaid his trust in proper fashion.[233] The king also gave him wardship of the young lady of Lancaster, a damsel of great estate;[234] for a long while he guarded her honour admirably, protecting her from all disgrace and harm and treating her as his dear friend, but he didn't marry her.

War between King Henry and King Philip

It wasn't long after the Marshal's return that the news reached France and spread everywhere that the True Cross had been lost[235] along with all the land in which God became incarnate of a virgin good and wise to save mankind. The two kings met to confer, I understand,[236] and after exchanging kisses as a mark of peace they took the cross to confront this crisis.

The crusade that now began was so great that in France and Normandy, Brittany and England, Flanders and the Low Countries, Burgundy and Poitou, Gascony and Anjou, every last man who aspired to valour abandoned his wife and children to take the cross and avenge the offence against God.

When the kings and all who were resolved to go to the Holy Land had taken the cross, King Henry sailed back to England to prepare, committed to fighting in God's service in Syria. But Treachery and Envy, ever striving for dominion in the world, intervened, for the king of France promptly made moves to do King Henry harm and wrong. I don't want to prolong my story here, only to say that he seized Châteauroux,[237] ever bent as he was, insatiably, on inflicting all the

---

[231] Guy of Lusignan, king of the crusader state of Jerusalem from 1186 to 1192. But this leave-taking of the king, if it took place, must have been with the young Baldwin V, not Guy, as Guy did not become king until August 1186 and Marshal was almost certainly home by April of that year.

[232] Lyons-la-Forêt in Normandy, between Rouen and Gisors; it was the castle in which Henry I is famously said to have died of a surfeit of lampreys.

[233] Literally 'he didn't repay him by lounging by the hearth'.

[234] Heloise, daughter of William of Lancaster, Henry's seneschal, who had died without a male heir in 1184. A wealthy ward was a valuable gift to the guardian, who could manage and exploit the ward's lands for his own benefit.

[235] Captured by Saladin in the devastating defeat of the Crusaders at the Battle of Hattin, 4 July 1187.

[236] Henry II and Philip Augustus met between Gisors and Trie-Château on 22 January 1188.

[237] On 16 June. Châteauroux was no ordinary target. John Gillingham quotes the chronicler Robert of Torigni's comment that "some say it is worth as much as the revenues of the whole of Normandy", and adds that 'by the late 1180s there was no place in Aquitaine that

damage that he could upon King Henry – a fact of which his descendants remain all too conscious.

When old King Henry heard this news he was far from happy. Very troubled and aggrieved, he summoned a great number of lords and a massive army and crossed the sea to Normandy.[238] Fierce warfare followed, and it ravaged and laid waste the land. At last they came to parley outside Gisors,[239] the king of France backed by a mighty force and King Henry by many of the finest of his land. The kings and their most trusted privy counsellors convened and there were long discussions. I don't know all that was said – they didn't invite me to join them! – but as I understand it, they couldn't agree any terms of peace because pride had an unshakeable hold on them, of that you can be sure; both parties were so stubbornly haughty – urged on by poor advice and guidance – that they were about to part, declaring that, regardless of who was in the wrong, they should carry on the war and see who came off best. In the nick of time a knight of great wisdom intervened and said:

'My lords, why should all these men die when they're not to blame for the conflict and wish it would end? It's wrong that they should die because of your pride! Since our masters insist it can be settled only by battle, I suggest that each side selects four champions to engage at once to defend their cause: winner takes all.'

The idea was accepted – and those most full of fighting talk went very quiet! They didn't say a word! But just as this was happening, an ill-mannered French knight decided to start hurling mockery at the Welsh.[240] The Welsh took offence, and with only the river between them and him, one of the Welsh, who'd had enough, loosed an arrow at him and hit him in the head. The knight's joke had rebounded and he wasn't amused; crestfallen, humiliated, he came before the king of France and showed him what had happened – the arrow was still in his head.

'Look what they've done to me, sire!' he said. 'The king of England's men have no respect for the peace declared in God's name and your own! A fine way to behave! They hold you and all your forces in contempt!'

The king of France thought it an outrageous slight and cried: 'What! What! God's eyes, I'm not having this!'

He withdrew in fury with all his men to Chaumont,[241] as angry as could be. The very next day he returned to Gisors in force, with his lords and counts and viscounts and castellans and all his common soldiery in almost countless numbers. Helmeted and armed for battle, his knights arrived outside Gisors in all their pride and pomp and raring to go. But who knows what they were planning? The French are wily customers! And they know how to get out of trouble if things don't go their way: they know what they're about!

was more headline news than Châteauroux'. Gillingham, 'Norman and English Views of Aquitaine', in *The World of Eleanor of Aquitaine* (Woodbridge, 2005), pp. 58–9.

[238] Henry landed at Barfleur on 11 July.
[239] In early October. The castle of Gisors was a major fortress on the Norman border with the kingdom of France.
[240] Henry had a good number of Welsh mercenaries in his army.
[241] Chaumont-en-Vexin, a little to the east of Gisors.

Word reached King Henry that they'd arrived with helms and ventails laced, in order of battle. Then the good king of England, eminently able to defend his land, ordered his troops inside Gisors to arm and marched boldly out of the town with all his men – they numbered more than twenty thousand – leaving the town and castle with a fine, strong guard, needing to fear no one: he alone would be able to enter. He and his forces drew up on one side of the river;[242] the French confronted them on the other bank: only the river lay between them. When the two armies saw each other so close, there were some who were raring to show what they could do if given leave. The king of France now commanded Sir William de Garlande and Sir Dreux de Mello, always judicious of speech,[243] to go to the barbican and ask the men there for permission to speak to King Henry.

'He's wronged and offended me in so many ways. But he'll wish he'd let sleeping dogs lie![244] I'll have revenge if I can – I'll not rest till I do! And make it clear I mean to settle it by combat as proposed: that's the advice of my barons. Spell out the conditions and come straight back.'

So the knights set off and told the men at the barbican that they'd a message for the king; then they rode through the town and found King Henry amid his army. They didn't mince words, bright, bold knights that they were; they said:

'Sire, our king sends word that he wishes to do battle, and will brook no refusal or delay. We wish to inform you which four of our knights will do combat with yours. We'll name each in turn: one will be the count of Flanders; the second to be chosen was the count of Clermont; then Count Robert of Dreux. Of those three you can be certain; and finally, to make up the four, there'll be myself, Dreux de Mello. And now I'll name the four of yours who'll face them: Sir William FitzRalph, who never stops bellyaching; Sir William de la Mare – he loves a fight (for what he pockets from it!) so he'll be handy; Sir Richard de Villequier – he's always full of it (when he's playing chess!); and that mealy-mouthed Sir Richard d'Argences.'

When King Henry heard that the king of France was behaving so high-handedly, I can assure you he was not amused. But he showed his usual wise composure and replied thus to the messengers:

'Sirs, I'll discuss this with my barons and do as they advise; we may decide quite differently.' Then he summoned his foremost men and said: 'Sirs, we've heard with what disdain the king of France addresses us! How do you advise me to respond?'

There were counts and other great lords among them but they didn't say a word.

'He's slighting us all!' King Henry said. 'What do you think we should do?'

None of the counsellors uttered a sound – they might have been deaf or dumb. The king couldn't help but be annoyed, and angrily cried:

'God's eyes! I've never seen the like! What's the point of you being here? You're my counsellors and give no counsel!'

---

[242] The Epte.
[243] Literally 'he spoke neither too much nor too little'.
[244] Literally 'he shouldn't have goaded the ass'.

The Marshal saw at once that the king was annoyed and troubled at heart, and politely interjected, saying: 'If it please you, sire, and if the noble lords here present will permit, I'll tell you what I'd do if it were left to me.'

'Speak up, Marshal,' said the king. 'And say what you like! They don't want to commit themselves or tax their brains!'

'Gladly, sire,' the Marshal said. 'It's clear to me – but I trust that you and your lords approve – that since the king of France demands such a combat it would be wrong of us to refuse. But he's trying to push you into a corner. Ask him this: at whose court is this combat to be fought and right upheld? If it's at yours, and we see our men in need of aid we'll not fail to intervene. The same will be true if it's fought at his: if they saw their men in trouble, all the kinsmen and friends of the high nobility of France would rush to their support. That'll put paid to a just decision! So let it take place at the Emperor's court, or the court of Navarre or Aragon. And the king of France has no business choosing your knights; it's for you to choose them, sire, as he chose his. He can't have it all his own way! William FitzRalph is a worthy and experienced knight, but he's too old now for fighting: we should rule him out; de la Mare is in poor health and de Villequier's suffering from gout; and d'Argences isn't up to it: he has a recurring fever. In any case, it's for you to select your champions – he shouldn't take it upon himself to choose them for you! Your first choice should be that good and guileless count, William de Mandeville;[245] next, if it please you, myself; and I don't think we can fail to include Sir John de Seeneis and Sir Osbert de Rouvray.'[246]

'Well said, Marshal!' said the king. 'No one will argue with that!'

But Count Richard of Poitiers protested. 'Sir Marshal,' he said, 'that's a foul snub to me, excluding me from your choice of knights! In all my father's land I'm counted one of his finest defenders! You seem to be suggesting otherwise!'

'Oh, my lord!' the Marshal replied. 'God bless me, that's not why I excluded you! I'm very mindful, as are we all, that you're our lord the king's most direct heir: it would be a shameful mistake to risk you in this – that was my reasoning.'

'He's right, Richard,' said the king. 'He's spoken most courteously. Count William[247] is a man of judgement; you and he, Marshal, will be my messengers and tell the king of France what we've decided. You know how to handle this.'

'Sire,' said the Marshal, 'if these envoys of his will conduct us safely and unharmed, we'll deliver your message perfectly.'

The two who'd come from the king of France promised to do all they could to escort them safely there and back. So they rode through the town and came to the barbican, where Sir Dreux de Mello said they should wait a little while they spoke to their king and found out if he was willing to receive them. So they rode to the king and told him who the messengers were and asked if he would see them, for they were eager to speak with him and deliver their message. But the king refused to let them come and address him, and sent

---

[245] Earl of Essex and also count of Aumale, as noted above, p. 36.
[246] The former is unidentifiable; the latter is a Norman knight, Rouvray (Rouvray-Catillon) being north-east of Rouen.
[247] De Mandeville.

Count Theobald,[248] along with the count of Dreux and the count of Flanders, too, to talk to them and find out what they wanted. So off they went, and told them that the king had no wish to see them, but that they'd come to hear their message which they would relay to the king.

'Sirs,' replied the Marshal, 'we're not going to tell you our private message: that would hardly be deemed wise. We weren't sent to you but to the king.'

But the good and worthy Count William de Mandeville spoke, saying: 'Marshal, give them the message entrusted to us – we don't want further delay.'

So the Marshal spoke exactly as instructed by their lord the king, avoiding offence or disrespect and not exceeding his commission (you've heard it already so I shan't repeat it – it's rightly said that a man makes a story tiresome by telling the same thing twice). When the count of Flanders heard this he gave a jovial smile and showed his good sense by replying thus:

'God's teeth, Marshal, you won't find me fool enough to take you on – I don't care what anyone says! Champion I'm not!'

'Sir,' said the Marshal, 'I'd like to hear the king's response to our message, and what we're to report to our lord.'

So the counts rode back to King Philip and told him what had been said; and the king, nettled, irate and full of spite, swore by Saint James's arm:[249]

'I've had enough of this! It's maddening! Why couldn't I have had my way?'

The count and the Marshal returned smartly to King Henry and told him how they'd fared; and meanwhile the king of France in his fury ordered his forces to advance on the barbican and drive its defenders, audaciously ranged before it, back inside – and to give them a good battering. The wise, astute Count Robert[250] realised the king was in earnest, and with levelled lance he charged daringly[251] with the French into the defenders' midst. But they didn't flinch; stout, brave soldiers that they were, the men at the barbican met them with their lances' heads and the rash charge came to grief, many of the attackers losing their mounts. A fine, ferocious fight there was, and Sir William des Barres was seized by the bridle and held for quite some time. He was finally rescued by his men, but I tell you, there were a good few swaggering rogues who'd charged full of confidence and were left there battered, bruised and broken. They launched two attacks, but our men behaved superbly, defending with such resolve that they suffered no losses at all.

The king of France and all his troops withdrew, incensed. Now, outside the town there was a lovely, verdant, spreading elm, offering delightful shade in the summer months; and the French, in their mad fury, chopped it to pieces: what a display of their prowess that was![252] When the king of France heard this he

---

[248] The count of Blois.
[249] This is presumably a reference to Saint James 'Intercisus' ('the Mutilated'), so called because he was martyred by being cut into twenty-eight pieces. A curious oath, but given King Philip's mood it is aptly chosen.
[250] i.e. Robert of Dreux, chosen as one of the four French champions.
[251] Literally 'exposing his body'.
[252] In his *Philippide,* King Philip's chaplain and biographer Guillaume le Breton explains that the English had been taunting the French from the shade of the elm while the French had

was far from pleased, and angrily and publicly declared that it was the greatest shame ever to befall the French crown: all he'd achieved at Gisors was the felling of the tree!

'Is that why I came here? To chop wood?'

So he set off back to France[253] and disbanded his great, fine army. The news reached the Marshal who went at once to speak to King Henry, saying:

'Hear me, sire: the king of France has dismissed his army: they've gone their various ways. I suggest you do the same, but secretly tell your men to return to us without fail on a specified day. Then launch a campaign into the king of France's domain, so bold, concerted and fierce that he suffers far more damage than we have with our elm! It'll be fine revenge indeed!'

'God's eyes!' said the king. 'That's splendid advice from a worthy counsellor! We'll do just that!'

And so King Henry did, commanding his men to meet him at Pacy[254] without fail on a day he specified, but he kept the purpose secret. To come straight to the point, they all arrived at Pacy on the appointed day, and King Henry promptly set out with a mighty force of knights and good and valiant soldiers, many of them bent on wreaking havoc – it certainly looked that way, as they made a great show of burning all the land as far as Mantes, with the king's full will and approval. The king of France was there at Mantes, distraught and enraged to see his land laid waste. Nothing could have distressed him more, but he had only a small force with him. They went out all the same and had a fine engagement, giving it their all; some were taken prisoner and some unhorsed, and others battered and bruised, but I don't want to crow about which French knights were captured or came to grief – that would be unseemly.

King Henry now advanced upon Bréval,[255] burning and destroying all in his path, unsparingly. All day long they carried on, and took a handsome amount of booty.

He went to spend the night at Ivry,[256] and next morning spoke with his men and with his son Richard, the redoubtable count of Poitiers, and said:

'Richard, we've well and truly avenged our elm! We've more than paid them back!'

'I'm delighted, sire!' said the count.

'Before God, dear son, it was the Marshal's idea, good and trusty knight that he is.'

'My dear lord,' said the count to his father then, 'if you'll take my advice, stay here while I head towards Poitiers. I've a mind to go to Châteauroux and do such

---

      been baking in the heat, and that King Henry had placed a provocative inscription upon it declaring that, just as this great elm was impossible to fell, so the French were incapable of inflicting losses on the English.

[253] i.e. (as noted above, p. 40) the king of France's personal domain – effectively the Île-de-France – as opposed to the duchy of Normandy.

[254] Pacy-sur-Eure, in Normandy between Évreux and Mantes.

[255] South-west of Mantes.

[256] Not Ivry-sur-Seine near Paris but Ivry-la-Bataille (so named after the 1590 battle during the French Wars of Religion), south-west of Bréval.

damage thereabouts that the king of France will follow with all his forces. Then while I keep him occupied, you can wage war all the better here!'

'True enough – an excellent plan!' the king replied. 'That's what we'll do.'

They did as agreed: the count set off, and – rightly or wrongly, whether justified or inspired by pride – they carried on the war all season long till the approach of winter when cold descends: the French hate fighting then!

The king of England now went to Chinon, which takes its name from Kay.[257] And there he fell ill. I don't know what more to say, except that he remained so for a long while. Then he summoned his chief seneschal[258] and William the Marshal and said to them:

'Take some of my men and ride straight and swift to Montmirail:[259] the French there are giving us grief and we need to sort them out! Burn and destroy the whole country – be ruthless: no good comes of sparing wicked men! They need to be made to suffer! Do your utmost; if you can take them in the town – having captured it first, that is! – you'll have achieved a valiant feat indeed! And if you do take the town, be sure to burn and destroy it utterly!'

So the Marshal set out with the seneschal. They made straight for Montmirail, looting, burning and pillaging on the way, and reached there in a single day and night; they rode through the land, ravaging and plundering everything in sight, sparing nothing, till they came before the town and laid siege to the place with a force of nearly two thousand knights and good soldiers. There was a mighty body of knights inside who mounted a stout defence, but they were powerless to stop them entering the town and giving them a cruel battering. They fell back to the castle, and then, like the brave and worthy knights they were, they mounted and launched a fierce attack and drove the besiegers back in no time, winning great credit by capturing two knights. One knight ran down and unlocked the lower gate and they charged out to do battle. One of our knights rode to meet him in a mighty clash; our other mounted knights charged likewise to meet the foe, and there was a fine, grand mêlée in the street. Ours were gaining the upper hand when Sir Richard Clifford[260] came to the Marshal and said:

'What are you doing here, good sir? There's a fine contest going on in there! You shouldn't be keeping out of it: they're fighting like fury in the streets!'

The Marshal's reply was: 'Bring me my shield.'

John of Earley,[261] his squire at this time, brought it swiftly and gladly; then the Marshal thrust in his spurs, his true and guileless heart bidding him show his

---

[257] According to Geoffrey of Monmouth in his *History of the Kings of Britain*, King Arthur's seneschal Kay, mortally wounded at the battle of Saussy, was buried at Chinon, 'the town which he himself had built'. Following Geoffrey, Wace in his *Roman de Brut* (vv. 13403–6) adds that Kay in building it had given his name to the place.
[258] Stephen de Marçay, seneschal of Anjou.
[259] Montmirail (Sarthe), to the east of Le Mans.
[260] Brother of 'Fair Rosamund', Henry II's famous mistress.
[261] 'Johan d'Erlee'. This is the first mention of Marshal's squire, the source of much of the information on which this *History* was based. He was the son of William of Earley, a chamberlain to Henry II. In 1186, when John was fourteen and his father dead, Henry gave wardship of the boy to William Marshal (Earley is near Reading in Berkshire, close to the

valour, and into the town he rode. When he arrived their men had withdrawn and retreated to the castle. But on the bridge, which sloped steeply at both ends, ten of their knights made a stand on foot along with one on horseback. Without a second thought the Marshal charged up the steep incline of the bridge, which spanned a yawning ditch – the drop to the bottom was perilous: the ditch had been dug more than sixty feet deep; no one on earth would have fallen in more than once! But the Marshal gave it no thought or heed; he didn't care; he spurred up the slope as fast as his horse could go. The knights on the bridge met him with a solid, fearful body of lances, thrusting out at his horse's chest; but God in His might saw to it that the horse kept its feet and turned smartly back down the slope unscathed. Those watching in the street rejoiced: had the horse veered inches in either direction he'd have plummeted from the bridge to the ditch's bottom, hewn sixty feet deep from the solid rock. They accused the Marshal of recklessness: Sir Hugh de Hamelincourt and Baldwin de Béthune ran to him – they loved him dearly and had been horrified by his daring venture, fearing it would prove calamitous – and scolded and chid him for what he'd done. They asked him why he'd acted so: they thought it needlessly rash.

'Can't you see,' he said, 'why I made that charge? Don't think it wrong of me: there was a mounted knight among them, and if I'd caught him by the bridle I'd have brought him back with me for sure: he couldn't have pulled back on a bridge that steep!'

'So help me Christ,' said Baldwin, 'I'm sure Sir Stephen de Marçay, the seneschal of Anjou, wouldn't have attacked with so little at stake! There was no point in a gamble like that!'

'No!' said Hugh de Hamelincourt. 'He wouldn't have risked it for the fief of Angers!'

But a number now charged to the top of the bridge – though the defenders repelled them, and a good few of our side were wounded, horses and knights; but, thanks be to God, the Marshal suffered no harm or hurt at all.

That night they stayed at Châteaudun.[262] John of Earley was in charge of the Marshal's horse, and when he took off his caparison he saw the cuts and stab-wounds inflicted by the lances.

'Your horse is hurt, sir,' he told his lord the Marshal. The Marshal came up and they counted seven wounds from steel lance-heads: the horse was wounded in the shoulders, neck and chest. But the Marshal wasn't worried: he saw they would quickly heal.

They returned then to the king, who thought the mission a great success and said they'd all done well.

I can't record all the exploits they undertook – it could get tiresome – but the fact is that they agreed a winter-long truce. The Marshal strove hard to secure a lasting peace, but for all his efforts neither he nor the others involved succeeded.

Marshal estates). At the time of this attack on Montmirail John would have been about sixteen.
[262] To the east of Montmirail.

Such was the ill feeling between us and the French and so deep the grievances, that pride, envy and offence, ever the promoters of conflict, barred any chance of concord.

King Henry was ill, I understand, all that winter, and stayed a long while at Le Mans until, on the Tuesday after Easter,[263] the two sides met to parley between Moulins and Soligny.[264] At the same time, dark and dismal Covetousness, inciter of every other vice, blinding its prey to wisdom and honour (for which it has no care or respect at all), inspired the king of France to a pernicious scheme which proved harmful to the line of English kings, robbing them of land. Let me reveal the words that passed, and explain what's said in this book of how the grubby, wickedly planted shoot of treachery came to sprout: I'll rake up the muck for all to see. It was thus: the king of France convinced Count Richard of Poitiers that if he became a good friend and sided with him, he would straightway give him Touraine, Maine and Anjou, and confirm them absolutely as his own. Sadly for Count Richard he believed the king, and came to him in private and paid him homage for these lands. But the king broke his promise – as he did to each of King Henry's sons in turn: it always turned out badly for them all! This isn't the time or place to recount his dealings, but I can assure you he cheated and deceived them one by one: his trickery led to the deaths of the father and three of his sons and finally to the death of the fourth. But now's not the time to speak of it: it'll become clear in what follows, as I deal in detail with each in turn, omitting nothing.

The pressing matter now is the conference held between Soligny and Moulins, right by Bonsmoulins. On the date agreed the king of France arrived there in great splendour: he'd taken every care in his preparation. Then came the king of England with the high nobility of his land and all his retinue. But the moment he arrived, King Henry clearly saw his son beside the king of France, and realised at once he'd been betrayed. He was shocked and enraged, though he didn't show it; but seething with anger he said to his son the count:

'Where have you come from, Richard?'

'My dear lord,' he replied, 'I'll gladly tell you: yesterday I ran into the king of France along the way, and having seen him I didn't think it right to snub him, not when we were so close. For the sake of peace and concord I accompanied him here.'

'Very good, Richard – if it's true!' his father said. 'But I don't believe it! Make sure you're not up to something!'

The two kings and their counsellors negotiated reasonably and calmly. They were on the brink of peace – terms had been drawn up and approved – and they were about to be as one, I believe, with everything agreed, when the king of France drew our king aside, in strictest confidence, and said:

'I've a fine idea to put to you – I'm sure you'll approve. To come straight to the point, your son the count of Poitiers is deemed by all a worthy man but has very

---

[263] The author's dating is incorrect. He is about to refer to a conference held at Bonsmoulins on 18 November 1188.
[264] Moulins-la-Marche and Soligny-la-Trappe, north-east of Alençon.

little land. I would ask you to give him – in addition to Poitou – Touraine, Anjou and Maine. They'll be perfectly safe in his hands.'

'That's your advice, is it?' King Henry said.

'Indeed it is!'

'Then you're clearly set on his advancement; but unless I lose my wits you'll not see me agree to that, not today!'

And the two kings parted without another word, much to the dismay and distress of some, but to the delight and satisfaction of those who hated peace and relished war. And so it was that the wasting of the land began. The king of France departed and the conference, convened on the Tuesday as I explained, came to a bitter end and a conflict began which could never be resolved and saw excesses and atrocities that led to dreadful damage and loss. And Richard count of Poitiers, only too pleased by it all, rudely set off without taking leave, leaving his father as soon as he could. King Henry was quite unaware, and when he was told he was furious and deeply troubled.

'Ah!' he said, 'I knew it! My children are incapable of doing good: all they'll do is ruin me – and themselves! They've always caused me trouble and harm!'

Then he summoned the Marshal and his other close, most trusted advisers and sought their guidance, asking what he could do about his son who'd gone over to the king of France and was bent on doing him harm and shame. He could see what was afoot: the king of France, with his scheming and presumption, was out to rob Count Richard of the lands that his father had inherited – for unless the king of France died first he'd take them from the count: that's what he was planning.

'My dear lord,' the Marshal said, 'the best advice I can give is that you send after the count if he's already gone, and order him to come to you at once or send an explanation of why he's left you without reason.'

'You shall be my messenger, Marshal – I want you to go with Sir Bertrand de Verdun. Tell him he's making a big mistake by leaving me: if he's done the deal I think he has, he may find he comes unstuck before the game is done!'

So the Marshal set out with Sir Bertrand, who was never false in word or deed but upright and ever loyal, and rode straight after Count Richard. They came to Amboise where he'd lain the night before, but they were too late – it was already noon, and their host told them the count and his men had left early, at the crack of dawn, and there was no point going on: they were wasting their time – they'd never catch him. He told them, too, that the previous night the count had dictated hundreds of letters: no one had ever seen him so fervently summon his men from all over his land, along with those who'd joined his side and supported him.

When the Marshal realised what the count was doing, he immediately sent word to his father the king, reporting the false, cruel treachery planned by his son, who was showing no love or respect for him. Then they rode to Tours to wait for the king. He arrived there at speed: anyone fired by anger and resentment has itchy feet, is irritable and restless. He raged to his barons and his men about his son, saying – and how true it was! – that he'd raised a terrible brood of sons. Indeed he had; he had to admit it! Then he sent to England for support and help, with a letter commanding Ranulf de Glanville, justiciar of England, to summon by name – and urgently, without delay – his great lords and barons to join him in France at once and without fail; and he was to come, too, if he could, with all the royal treasury.

King Henry now made an arduous, wearying journey as far as Le Dorat;[265] there he stopped but didn't stay long and it was fruitless and he turned back, heading first to Chinon and from Chinon back to Le Mans. And in the course of this he fell ill; I don't know the details, but the sickness gripped him, I think, right through Lent.

All his great barons and supporters now came to him as summoned, as did Hubert Walter, Ranulf de Glanville's clerk,[266] who came in his place, Ranulf being unwell at the time. It was now that the king promised the Marshal, in return for his service, the good and beautiful damsel of Striguil.[267] Having made the promise, he instructed Hubert Walter to see that the Marshal was given both the damsel and her lands as soon as he arrived back in England.

When the king had recovered from his illness, which had been serious, affecting several parts of his body, he called the Marshal to him along with the archdeacon of Hereford and bade them both go to the king of France, to ask and enquire if he'd agree to peace in return for payment. The two envoys rode to France,[268] to Paris, and found the king; but the count of Poitiers scuppered their mission, sending skilled and wily agents to ensure they could make no headway. William Longchamp,[269] a cunning man indeed, was one of those involved, and so thwarted their efforts that they were forced to give up and leave. They returned to King Henry and reported what had happened, and the king of England realised then that there was nothing for it but war. He asked the advice of his barons, saying:

'Well, sirs? What do we do now?'

No one really knew, so the king saw to the strengthening of Le Mans's defences, having ditches repaired or newly dug and houses demolished that were too close to the gates or prevented the ditches' construction. This carried on till Pentecost.[270]

Then the king of France, bent on deceiving King Henry and inflicting harm, called a parley between La Ferté and Nogent.[271] Both sides went there armed and

---

[265] North-west of Limoges.
[266] i.e. clerk of the Exchequer. Walter was later to be archbishop of Canterbury and Lord Chancellor.
[267] Striguil was the medieval name for Chepstow, or more precisely the castle and surrounding fiefdom, deriving as it does from Ystrad Gwy, the Welsh for the Wye Valley. The 'damsel of Striguil' was Isabel de Clare (1172–1220), eldest surviving child of Richard, earl of Pembroke (known as 'Strongbow'), who had died in 1176. On the death of her brother in 1185 she had become countess of Pembroke in her own right, and marriage to her would make Marshal one of the wealthiest men in the kingdom.
[268] See note 253 above, p. 109.
[269] Richard had made him chancellor of the duchy of Aquitaine and on his accession was to make him Chancellor of England (and bishop of Ely); as we shall see, he was to govern England while Richard was away on the Third Crusade.
[270] The end of May 1189.
[271] La Ferté-Bernard and Nogent-le-Rotrou, not far to the north-east of Le Mans.

mounted, the French strutting around very haughtily; and the count of Poitiers arrived with all his forces, siding with the king of France against his father. And the conference didn't go well: they parted on bad terms, King Henry riding from La Ferté in a rage. Leaving Roger Thorel, a very worthy man, as constable[272] he made his way to Ballon,[273] and the king of France came straight back to La Ferté and besieged it. The fact is he took it by storm; Roger Thorel resisted stoutly, defending it with all his might, but in the end he was forced to surrender and was taken prisoner – though he had earned great honour.

King Henry now left Ballon; the king of France followed hard on his heels and besieged and took the place without resistance. He stayed there for four days and then advanced to Montfort-le-Rotrou,[274] which was barely fortified and quickly surrendered, undefended.

The king of England, inside Le Mans, was aghast at this loss of his land. He summoned William the Marshal, who was distressed to see the king's wrath and anguish, along with Sir Geoffrey de Brûlon and his brother and Sir Peter FitzGuy and Sir Robert de Souville (who was in charge of the king's stables, but all I can say is that he was happier dealing with business in town than in the field).[275] The king bade them rise early next morning and reconnoitre, to see which way the French army would march. Ever ready to do as he wished, they rose early and donned light armour so that they could ride more swiftly, be it to harry the foe or to rescue their own men. So, armed early, and in buoyant, high spirits, they crossed the River Huisne. There was thick fog that morning which hampered their task, but as they pressed on they suddenly caught a glimpse of the French outriders. The odds weren't in their favour; but they mounted their horses and took up their lances and shields and headed cautiously onward. Robert de Souville said to the Marshal:

'By Christ, sir, if you'll heed my advice I suggest I go and tell the king that the French king's thundering towards him!'

'You'll not tell him anything of the kind, sir!' said the Marshal. 'That'll do no good. I'll go with Sir Geoffrey de Brûlon and see what sort of men those riders are and what they're up to.'

So they rode to the top of a little hill; and from there they beheld the king of France's whole army on the move in all its might, close enough to hit with a crossbow if they'd had one to hand.

'Let's go, Geoffrey,' the Marshal said. 'We'd better not hang around!'

And they rode back to their companions and told them the news. Again Robert de Souville said:

'Marshal, I'd better go and tell the king.'

'Not if I have anything to do with it, sir,' the Marshal replied, 'by the Holy Lance!'

---

[272] i.e. in command of the castle of La Ferté. Roger Thorel was a minor noble, lord of La Bucaille, a castle and small estate near Guiseniers in the Norman Vexin.
[273] North of Le Mans.
[274] East of Le Mans.
[275] He was *mareschal de l'ostel* (see Glossary), an important post, and so, the author implies, might have been expected to behave more impressively in action in the field.

And Sir Geoffrey said: 'Sir Robert, it's a shame Emenidus didn't have a messenger like you in his hour of need – what a pity you weren't there: he could have done with you!'[276] All the knights laughed at this. Then Sir Geoffrey said to the Marshal: 'Since those scouts are so close and suspecting nothing, I say we attack them! Before anyone can come to their aid there'll be some saddles emptied! We'll sort them out – if we can catch their bridles they'll lose a good few nags!'

'Oh yes,' replied the Marshal, 'we could easily win twenty or thirty of their wretched mounts. But it's proper horses we're in need of – never more so than today, by God! The king of France is heading straight for Le Mans; if we mount a charge as you suggest our horses would be blown before we got to safety.'

With that they turned back and reached Le Mans and told the king the certain news: they'd seen it for themselves. When the good King Henry realised that the king of France, with all his guile, was rampaging through his land, he rode out from the town with his barons and, to prepare for the coming onslaught, had the bridge over the Huisne demolished and the fords planted with stakes so that no man could safely cross on foot or horseback; and he had further ditches dug to make the approach impassable, no matter what the enemy tried: he was sure there was now no way of crossing. While they were discussing this they looked across the river and saw, on the other bank, the king of France advancing with all his forces. He planned to camp there for the night, and had his tents pitched beside a wood called Le Parc, within a bowshot of the river. The Marshal said to the king:

'Hear me, my good lord. The enemy have made camp. I say we go and rest our horses, in faith; then tomorrow we'll venture out and see what their intentions are and what they're up to.'

'By God, Marshal,' the king replied, 'that's good and worthy advice.'

So saying they returned to the city, where they agreed that if the king of France made a move towards the town they'd set fire to all the suburbs outside the walls.[277] And that's what happened indeed. Next morning,[278] with little delay, they arranged for mass to be sung very early, worried as they were about the vast French army. The Marshal armed at once, but the king went out through a lower gate towards the Maison Dieu,[279] mounted but quite unarmed; the Marshal didn't follow his example, and how wise he was: it would have been risking serious injury. The king said:

'Take off your armour, Marshal: why are you armed?'

---

[276] This ironic quip refers to a memorable episode in the *Roman d'Alexandre*, in which Alexander's general Emenidus, faced by overwhelming numbers, can't find anyone to take a message to Alexander to call for reinforcements, as (unlike Sir Robert!) they all think it shameful to leave the battlefield. See *The Medieval Romance of Alexander*, trans. Bryant (Woodbridge, 2012), p. 63.

[277] By the late twelfth century Le Mans had extensive suburbs.

[278] 12 June 1189.

[279] It is not quite clear, but Henry is unarmed presumably because he planned to attend mass here, in the imposing church-hospital called the 'Maison-Dieu de Coëffort', just outside the walls of Le Mans, which he'd had built around 1180 in atonement for the murder of Thomas Becket.

'I prefer it this way, if it please you, sire,' the Marshal replied. 'My armour doesn't bother me. I shan't disarm till I know what we've to deal with! An unarmed man won't last in a serious clash or crisis, and we've no idea what the French are going to do.'

'In faith!' said the king. 'You won't be coming with me, then!'

And so saying, the king told his son – Count John,[280] that is, whom he loved and fully trusted – to disarm, as he did Sir Gerard Talbot, Sir Robert de Tresgoz and Geoffrey de Brûlon; indeed all who rode from the city with him disarmed before they did so. They rode as far as the Maison Dieu, and then all his loyal men stopped to take counsel, whereupon they saw the king of France's vanguard coming, many men abreast, right up to the deliberately demolished bridge. They didn't think there'd be any ford but they tested the depth with their lances and found the most perfect ford in the world! Ten knights ventured into the river and made their way across. Our side had been mistaken! Robert Tresgoz saw what was happening and said to the king:

'Look, my lord! Their knights are coming!'

Gerard Talbot, able knight that he was, took up his shield and a lance; one of the French came galloping well ahead of the rest and Sir Gerard charged and met him with such a blow to the shield that he smashed his lance and it flew into a thousand pieces. Sir Richard FitzHerbert saw Sir Gerard's fine and well delivered blow, and likewise took up his shield and grabbed a lance and charged full tilt to meet another advancing knight, and struck him so fiercely on the shield that his lance broke and shattered right down to his fist.

The good Marshal, positioned by the city gate, now called to John of Earley for his helm; he bade him lace it, and said that those who'd disarmed would be rightly sorry now and wishing they had their armour! John of Earley brought him his helm and quickly had it laced; and the Marshal made his stand before the gate, all alone, without support or aid of any kind, and defended himself as a good knight should in such a case. The French charged up and delivered mighty blows, but he mounted such a stout defence that they made no impression at all. The men on the wall above the gate and on the brattice* cried aloud, in all directions:

'Over here! God be with the Marshal!'

Baldwin de Béthune heard and wasn't going to shirk: he was an established member of his company and was devoted to him as he'd demonstrated many times; and Sir Hugh de Malaunay joined him, I understand, and Sir Renaud de Dammartin (a knight as fine as any, who later became count of Boulogne) came charging without a second thought; Hugh de Hamelincourt couldn't come fast enough, and Sir Eustace de Neuville galloped down through the town and Eustace de Canteleu came at no mean speed, as did Ralph de Plomquet and Sir Pierre Mauvoisin. Out through the gate they charged, and a fine and mighty combat followed, undertaken in no playful spirit. Up came Sir Andrew de Chauvigny, one of the count of Poitiers's men, renowned for the highest

---

[280] His youngest son, later to be king of England after Richard.

prowess; he charged straight at our knights, and what a shattering of lances and clash of swords on helms you'd have seen then! No time was wasted on threats or taunts – they had far more pressing business! In a fierce and mighty fray they drove ours back – they attacked with fearful force. Sir Hugh de Malaunay fought splendidly but was knocked into the moat, I understand, he and his horse together. Then the Marshal, with Baldwin and Renaud de Dammartin, launched a fierce counter-charge, repulsing them in no time, so that our side recovered ground, driving them back down the road[281] almost the length of a bowshot. There was ferocious fighting all the way. The Marshal reached out and seized Sir Andrew de Chauvigny's bridle and led him off; he hauled him back as far as the gate, and the horse, moving at speed, already had its head inside the gate when someone on the brattice flung down a massive stone that struck Sir Andrew on the arm, doing him no good at all – it broke his arm in two. Another man hurled a big, weighty lump that caught the horse on the head and made him rear so violently that the reins came loose in the Marshal's hand and he was left there while the horse shot away; so Sir Andrew was free and managed to escape, though he was sorely wounded. The Marshal dumped the bridle in the gateway to be collected by a boy; then he returned to the fray – it was still raging, no one wanting to abandon it, determined as they all were to excel. In the course of the fighting the Marshal took two more knights by the reins, holding both bridles in one hand! But they slipped the bridles loose to escape him and left the fray. John of Earley, to whom, I think, the bridles were given, attests to this – and being the recipient, we can surely trust that he saw and heard all that happened.

There was splintered debris – stumps and broken lance-heads – strewn the whole length of the road, and the Marshal's horse fell foul of one and hurt his hind hoof. The Marshal reached out instantly and seized the bridle of a fine knight from the count of Poitiers's side – Aimery Odart by name, a native of Loudun – and decisively, keeping fast hold and hauling him back to the gate against his will. It was now that the king rode up to him, still quite unarmed, and as they met he said:

'I tell you, Marshal, your indulging in these chivalrous feats could be our downfall here! None of our other gates is as well defended as this![282] It could cost us, truly!'

'Sire,' said the Marshal, 'it would be disastrous if they entered the city, it has to be said. Let it be as you wish. But here, sire: accept this knight I've captured – I give him to you.'

'See to him yourself,' the king replied. 'You deal with him. Have him disarmed.'

Then the Marshal dismounted, his horse being injured, and mounted the destrier he'd won; the knight he'd captured with it he sent straight back to his lodgings. Then he set off with King Henry, who in all honesty went much too far and rashly ordered the burning of the suburbs outside the walls. As soon as the king of France – who'd no intention of leaving yet – saw this, he had his pavilions

---

[281] i.e. the road that leads away from the city gate.
[282] i.e. Marshal has seen off the threat at that gate and is now busy capturing knights; he would be better employed elsewhere!

pitched beyond the river, on the further bank. And then, when he saw the flames now spread to the town, he was delighted! But King Henry, distraught, rode with the Marshal up and down the town, a lost part of his inheritance that day. They saw a woman, weeping bitterly, in terrible distress, carrying her belongings from her house which had just caught fire. The Marshal, ever compassionate, was filled with sorrow and pity, and bade his squires dismount and go to her aid at once; he dismounted himself and gladly gave her all the help he could, eager as ever to repair the harm done – it was in his nature. He took hold of a feather mattress that was smouldering beneath: there was so much smoke that it got inside his helm and choked him and he was forced to take it off.

And then, as the king returned to the city's heart, the fire made its way there with him! In three or four places the blaze took hold; the king's men could do nothing to check it – they had to give up and beat a retreat. He sent down to the town to find the count of Mandeville; the ever good and loyal Marshal was already with him, and a number of other barons had gathered to his side, and they speedily agreed to quit the town as one. With all their gear they set off with the king and made for Fresnay.[283]

As they were leaving the town the Marshal was quite unarmed, his doublet his only protection; and he was on his own.[284] When the French saw King Henry's men abandoning Le Mans they were jubilant and set off in eager pursuit: whenever people flee there are plenty to give chase! The count of Poitiers mounted, too, clad in no more armour than a doublet and an iron cap for his head, and charged swiftly after. He soon caught up, but others were even quicker: at the head of them all was Philip de Colombières,[285] one of his retinue and highly esteemed in arms, who charged at a knight and struck him a ferocious blow upon the shield. Seeing the commotion to his rear, William des Roches,[286] one of those retreating with the king, turned about, and went and met Colombières with a blow that made his stout, strong lance smash and shatter to his fist. Up then came the count of Poitiers, spurring furiously, and cried to des Roches:

'William! You're mad to hang about – a big mistake! You're wasting your time – you're deluded! I'd shift if I were you!'

The Marshal was less than pleased to see the pursuers gaining on them; alert and ready as ever, he promptly took his lance and shield and spurred straight towards the approaching Count Richard. Seeing him coming, the count roared:

'God's legs, Marshal, don't kill me! It wouldn't be right – I'm quite unarmed!'

'No,' replied the Marshal, 'I won't kill you – I'll leave that to the Devil!'

And he drove his lance clean through Count Richard's horse, killing it on the spot: it didn't move another step – it fell dead and the count fell with it. It was a fine blow indeed, and proved the saving of the party in retreat – without it they'd have been slain or captured: their pursuers had been bent on nothing less, and

---

[283] Fresnay-sur-Sarthe, north of Le Mans, near Alençon.
[284] Bringing up the rear, as will become clear.
[285] Probably the son of the knight of the same name mentioned above, p. 29.
[286] Later to be seneschal of Anjou, Maine and Touraine under King John.

would have achieved it but for the Marshal's feat. Knights and soldiers were swarming forward, but Count Richard leapt up and cried:

'Go no further! You're mad, you're crazy – you'll be undone!'

And the moment he said this they stopped in their tracks. I'm told Sir Philip de Colombières was taken prisoner during this pursuit – it was clearly witnessed: he was captured by Baldwin de Vernon, one of King Henry's men.

It's my firm belief that no single lance-blow achieved so great a rescue, saving men doomed to loss and pain and woe, since God in His Passion allowed Himself to be stricken with the lance.

King Henry pressed on to Fresnay, while the king of France entered Le Mans and took the town and besieged the tower, capturing Sir William de Sillé there; he mounted a valiant and vigorous defence but in vain: he was taken in the tower, though he'd done much to enhance his reputation.

King Henry lay that night at Fresnay and stayed there, but his men, fearful and dismayed (not without reason), hurried on, hell for leather, to Alençon. The Marshal, too, with the knights at his command (he had, for sure, fully fifty with him), was ordered to leave and join them there. And there he found the barons of Normandy dithering, to be honest, fearful to go on: they'd been on their way to join King Henry, but were so alarmed by the size and fierce advance of the French army that they dared go no further.

The Death of King Henry

King Henry, ever more troubled and pained by his illness which was worsening by the day, went and stayed at Sainte-Suzanne[287] and from there made his way to Chinon. News now reached him that the king of France was at Tours and had taken possession of the city and its towers; he immediately sent a letter to the Marshal ordering him to come at once with all his company and those under his banner but to leave the rest behind. He did as bidden without demur and arrived to a joyous welcome from the king and all who saw him: the whole court and household were greatly cheered and heartened by his coming.

'Oh, Marshal!' said the king. 'Have you heard the news? The king of France is at Tours and has taken the city and the castle: he controls all its defences.'

'Yes, it's true,' the Marshal said. 'The presumption of the French is doing you damage indeed.'

It was at this point that a messenger arrived from the count of Flanders, the archbishop of Reims and other friends of King Henry in the French camp, secretly informing him that the king of France wished to meet and parley, as soon as could be, between Tours and Azay;[288] they urged him to go without delay. He discussed this with the Marshal, who said he should consult his barons, and if they counselled him to go he should do so. And so he did: all his men advised him to go, and with his friends' backing he went on the day proposed – and

[287] A walled town south-west of Fresnay and west of Le Mans.
[288] Azay-le-Rideau, half way between Tours and Chinon.

promptly, arriving before the king of France: he dismounted at the Templars' house[289] and waited for him. And there's no avoiding it: it was now that sickness struck – he was seized with insupportable pain; he had to prop himself against a wall, in agony, and he called for the Marshal and said:

'Marshal, dear sir, I have to tell you: a dreadful pain has taken hold of me – it started in the heels and has spread right through my feet and legs; they're burning, front and back, and now my whole body's afire – I've never known such torturing pain: my body, heart and limbs are lost to me.'

The Marshal was filled with grief to see the king in such a state, first blazing red and then turning black.[290] 'I beg you, sire,' he said to him, 'please rest a little.'

And they laid him in a bed.

The king of France had now arrived and asked what had happened to King Henry: wasn't he going to come?

'He already has,' they told him, 'but he's terribly ill; his heart's so weak that he can neither stand nor sit – he has to stay lying down.'

Count Richard was quite unmoved and told the king of France it was all feigned. King Henry's friends, in person and by letter, urged him again to go and parley, no matter what; and with a great struggle and much pain he went to the appointed place. On the way he said:

'Listen, Marshal: if you can get me away from here, do so at all costs! I'll concede just about anything, regardless, if it means I get out of here. But this I swear: if I can live long enough I'll batter them till they can take no more and the land will remain mine!'

And the Marshal promised him: 'I'll do all I can, sire.'

So the two kings met to confer. All the great lords present could see King Henry was in a sorry state: it was clear from his colour that he was suffering grievously. The king of France saw this, too – he could hardly fail to – and said:

'We realise, sire, you can't stay standing.'

And he called for a cloak.[291] But King Henry countermanded this, saying he didn't want to sit: he simply wished to see and hear what they wanted of him and why they were robbing him of land. I don't know exactly the words exchanged, but they parted and left with a truce agreed; it was the last time they would ever meet. Nor do I know exactly what was decided about those who'd switched their allegiance; but the two kings promised to send each other, in secret, lists of the turncoats who were now their sworn supporters.

King Henry made his way to Chinon, but his health was now so woeful that he was quite beyond recovery and never rose from his bed again. He lay sick upon his death-bed, and those who loved and attended him were filled with grief and anguish. But he was still desperate to know the names of those who'd sided against him – he wanted a written list. He told Master Roger Malchael, then bearer of his seal, to go at once to Tours and ask the king of France to set down in writing, as he'd promised, the names of all who'd sworn to support

---

[289] The Templars had a hunting lodge at Ballan-Miré, a little to the south-west of Tours.
[290] This is possibly a description of dry gangrene.
[291] For want of seats, he evidently intends Henry to sit on a folded cloak.

him. Master Roger duly did just that: he went to Tours and made a record of all who'd pledged their aid to the king of France in his war against the king of England. Having done as bidden, Master Roger left the French king and returned straight to King Henry, who bade him tell him privately the names of those who'd given the king of France written assurances of support against him. He replied with a sigh:

'Christ help me, sire, the first name written here is that of your son, Count John.'

When King Henry heard that the one he most trusted to do good, the one he loved most dearly, had betrayed him, he uttered not a word except: 'You've said enough.' And he turned over in bed, his body burning, his blood boiling, his skin growing ever blacker, darker. In his ever-worsening state he lost his faculties, his sight, his hearing. He suffered so till the third day; he spoke, but no one could really understand a word. Then the blood stopped in his heart, and finally, inevitably, Death took his heart in an agonising grip: clots of blood burst from his nose and mouth. No man can live when Death strikes so cruelly as She did the king. It was a grievous blow and loss to all who loved and attended him.

And let me tell you straight: what befell him at his death had never befallen a man as great as he, for they had nothing with which to cover his body, neither wool nor linen, and he had to lie there poor, bereft. Such is Fortune, alas, alas! From such a height She brought so great a man so low – a king of such might, so honoured and so feared! It's well worth asking how a lofty prince, possessed of such a vast domain, could have fallen so soon into poverty. Once Fortune turned against him, rightly or wrongly, She wouldn't let him be till She'd delivered him to Death; and once Death had him in Her clutches She stripped him of all power, of everything.

And as they always say, a dead man has few friends. When those around him – who should have looked after his body – saw that the king was dead, they all hung on to everything he'd entrusted to their care. Anyone feeling the approach of Death is foolish to trust scoundrels to look after his estate: he does better to apportion it (giving God a share) before Death takes hold of him. By the time those thieving rogues had finished stripping him of his clothes, his jewels, his money, of all they could lay their hands on, the king of England was left as naked as the day he came into the world, save for his shirt and braies. He was given next to no protection – it was done quite openly.

As news spread that the king had died, great lords gathered round him from far and wide; they came with the Marshal, and were distraught at his death and filled with shame to see him lie disgracefully exposed – for they'd left him exposed indeed, those false, heartless, wicked men who'd robbed him even of his blanket. One of the first to arrive, for certain, was Sir William Trihan who, shocked and mortified, realising thieves had stripped his body the moment they'd seen he was dead, covered the king with the light woollen mantle he was wearing. Then the Marshal summoned the worthy and the loyal lords and churchmen, and the king was wrapped in his shroud in proper, royal fashion. He lay in state that night, given all due honour and a noble service.

Next day all his barons came from the lands they'd held from him. A great crowd of poor folk had gathered at the foot of the bridge[292] in the hope of receiving alms, but there was no money to be had. The Marshal promptly said to Stephen de Marçay:

'Seneschal,[293] we must find some money. The king of England lies here, Death's victim, newly added to Her list, and in honour of so great a man these poor folk should be given some of his wealth – it's the last service he needs from us, and it's only right.'

But Stephen insisted: 'My good, dear sir, I haven't a single penny of his, truly.'

'Sir,' the Marshal rightly replied, 'you may not have any money of his, but you've plenty of your own, amassed in his service! What gifts you've had from him – in cash and land alike – and for so long!'

'Nonsense! I've nothing at all of his or mine, not that I can think of – you can be quite sure of that!'

There was nothing to be done about the money: Stephen, who'd made this deft reply, had seen to it and concealed it all in his own estate and affairs! That's how this wealthy man treated the one to whom he owed it all, refusing to acknowledge his debt, even before God.[294] And the expectant poor from numerous towns – a good four thousand, there were – waited in vain; their hopes were dashed: it had always been the custom to distribute generous alms on the death of a king.

But when the barons duly came to their lord they paid him high respect and honour, dressing him in his regalia as befitted a king anointed and consecrated according to law and holy decree. Then the Marshal and the barons bore him on their shoulders from Chinon to Fontevrault. And God omnipotent gives reward, each according to his efforts, to those who strive to act well and honourably: you'll hear the relevance of this statement in due course.[295]

On their arrival at Fontevrault the ladies of the convent came in a long and reverent procession to greet their lord who had bestowed great riches and honour upon them. And when the body reached the church they received it with song and service befitting such a lord and noble king. The nuns held vigil over the body that night, reciting verses from their psalters, many of them weeping bitter tears and praying to almighty God to have mercy on King Henry.

Meanwhile the Marshal and the others present sent word to Count Richard that his father the king was dead. I don't know – and I haven't asked – whether he was sad or glad. The barons who were with the king gathered and said:

---

[292] i.e. outside the castle.
[293] He is the seneschal of Anjou – see above, p. 110.
[294] This is an attempt to reconstruct a badly garbled sentence in the MS. Its original meaning is very unclear; the subject may instead have been King Henry (saying he'd had all he could wish for in life but was now left bereft in death), but that is rather less appropriate (and interesting) in context. One thing is certain: Stephen de Marçay was held in such suspicion that Richard had him arrested a few days after Henry's death, though he was later released from imprisonment.
[295] i.e. in terms of the rewards that were to come to Marshal.

'The count will be here soon, and who knows whether it'll be good or bad for us? We've sided with his father against him, have we not? He might hold it against us!'

'He'll do as he chooses,' several said, 'but God, defender of the good, won't fail us. And the whole world isn't his – we can move from his domain. If we must switch our allegiance to a different lord, God will be our guide; we've no need to fear on that score. But we do fear for the Marshal! He slew Count Richard's horse beneath him with a thrust of his lance! He wasn't best pleased! But the Marshal can be assured we'll gladly provide him with all he needs: horses, arms, money, clothes – all at our disposal will be his.'

'Sirs,' said the Marshal, 'it's true I killed his horse and took its life – and I'm unrepentant. I'm grateful for your offers but, God grant me grace, I'd be uneasy taking from you what I couldn't be sure to repay. Ever since I was first a knight, God in His great mercy has granted me so many blessings that I trust in Him entirely for the future: it will be as He pleases.'

It was while they were discussing this that they saw the count of Poitiers arrive. And truly, as he came he gave no sign of grief or joy: no one could tell if he was feeling sadness or glee, distress or elation. He stood awhile before the body, motionless, then stepped up to the head where he remained lost in thought for quite some time, uttering not a word of any kind. Then he asked for the Marshal to come at once, along with Sir Maurice de Craon,[296] but no one else, it seems, from those who'd sided with the king – I don't know which of his own supporters were there. The Marshal and Sir Maurice came as soon as they were called, not tarrying an instant. They joined him beside the body, and he said:

'Come with me – let's go outside.'

Those summoned did as he said without demur, and accompanied him willingly. They gathered outside, and the count's first words, it seems, were:

'Marshal, my good sir, the other day you tried to kill me, and would have done so for sure if I hadn't turned your lance away with my arm. It would have been a black day indeed!'

'Sir,' replied the Marshal, 'I'd no intention of killing you and didn't try. I'm quite strong enough to direct a lance, whether I'm armed or not – even more so when I'm not, and I wasn't at the time – and if I'd wanted I'd have buried it in your body as I buried it in your horse. I don't think I was wrong to kill your mount and I'm not sorry I did.'

Those were his very words. And the count replied, most decently: 'You're forgiven, Marshal: I shan't hold it against you.'

'Thank you, my dear lord,' the Marshal said. 'I have never wished to see you dead.' So replied the Marshal, one never inclined to treachery.

Then the count said: 'I want you and Gilbert Pipard[297] to go at once to England. Take charge of my land and my affairs; do whatever's necessary, and see that

---

[296] One of the great lords of Anjou.
[297] A notable man, he had been Sheriff in turn of Essex, Gloucester, Hereford and Chester, and High Sheriff of Lancashire from 1185 to 1188.

we've reason to be satisfied on our arrival, whenever that may be. I'm going now, but I'll be back in the morning early, and the king my father will be buried with the honour and majesty due to such a noble man.'

'My lord,' said the Chancellor,[298] 'I hope you'll not object: I wish to remind you that the king gave the Marshal the damsel of Striguil.'

'God's legs, no, he didn't!' said the count. 'He merely promised to! But I do give her to him absolutely – the young lady and her estate. I know they'll be well and truly safe in his hands.'

They all thanked him. But the Chancellor hadn't finished; he added: 'Forgive me, my lord, but the king also gave, graciously and gladly, the fair maid of Châteauroux to Sir Baldwin de Béthune; nor, I promise you, did he treat Gilbert FitzReinfried as a lesser son – he gave him the maiden of Lancaster, the Marshal's ward (and a fine guardian he has been indeed);[299] and Gilbert FitzReinfried's ward, along with her estate, he gave to Reginald FitzHerbert; and finally he gave Lillebonne[300] to Renaud de Dammartin.'

The count replied: 'The truth is I've given Châteauroux and its heiress to Andrew de Chauvigny; but I'll see to it that Baldwin has no reason to complain – in time I'll endow him to his satisfaction.[301] And here and now I freely grant to Sir Renaud de Dammartin and Gilbert FitzReinfried what my father gave them, just as he promised; likewise Reginald FitzHerbert – I vouchsafe the maiden to him, and will grant him greater favours yet than my father did.'

With that they parted. And when they reconvened next day, they saw the king of England buried with great honour. But in the event, and what a shame it was, when he was dressed in his regalia he hadn't a crown of the splendour befitting such a noble king; nor were his men happy to find that, for all his wealth, he hadn't a ring to put on his finger as they'd have dearly wished: many of them were very upset. Then Hugh of Sandford, the king's page at the time,[302] came hurrying with a precious, handsome ring and said to them all:

'Truly, sirs, my lord entrusted this to me the other night, thank God! I've been keeping it safely all the while – but, God preserve me, I've nothing else of his at all.'

After burying the body in the finest service that they could – one worthy of an anointed king – they all returned homeward or to where their business took them, while the Marshal and Gilbert Pipard went to spend the night at Mouliherne[303] before making the long journey across the land as they headed for England. The count of Poitiers, on leaving, stayed overnight at Saumur; but I don't want to recount the journeys made by the count and the others when they left Fontevrault – there's little point.

---

[298] Henry's illegitimate son, Geoffrey Plantagenet.
[299] See above, p. 104.
[300] A substantial castle on the Seine just east of Le Havre.
[301] Richard was later, in 1195, to grant to Baldwin the twice-widowed Hawise, heiress of the county of Aumale.
[302] Hugh came to be a member of Marshal's household, and William granted him land at Wittenham in Berkshire.
[303] To the north of Chinon and Saumur.

Marshal's Marriage

The Marshal and his companion rode on with all speed through Maine and Normandy. I don't know what more to tell you, except that they came to Caux[304] to claim the land of[305] the young heiress given to him by the king. (The marriage proved to be much to her benefit, too, as she grew in status and dignity, thanks be to God and to the Marshal, for he was so good and so loyal that she and all those close to her gained much.)

With the land now in his possession, the Marshal took chosen companions to stay at Équiqueville,[306] and sent men ahead to Dieppe to arrange his passage to England, not wanting to tarry longer. Once they'd dined they rode swiftly to Dieppe to embark, impatient of all delay. In their eagerness to board they all piled on to the deck together, and the crowd was so great that the deck collapsed beneath their heaving weight. Many were hurt in their crashing fall: arms and legs were broken. Sir Gilbert Pipard didn't go unscathed: he was battered and bruised and broke an arm, and many others suffered likewise as they fell. The Marshal had leapt aside and managed to grab hold of a broken strut, but he hurt his leg badly: it was to cause him pain for a very long time. Anyway, he stayed hanging there, clinging on, till a crowd of men came rushing to his aid; and to come straight to the point, the Marshal carried on to England but Gilbert had to stay behind, downcast at being injured and unable to make the journey.

By all accounts, once in England the Marshal carried out Count Richard's instructions admirably; and he found Queen Eleanor (whose name encompasses 'gold' and 'pure')[307] at Winchester, now at liberty[308] and much happier than before.

Having ably and efficiently fulfilled his various duties, he went to take possession of the good and beautiful damsel of Striguil, who was in the city of London under the protection of Ranulf de Glanville[309] – though she was handed

---

[304] The Pays de Caux is the area of Normandy stretching east from Le Havre to Fécamp and Dieppe. The heiress Isabel de Clare, promised to Marshal, also held lands here, at Longueville.

[305] The MS reads 'and', but this is not consistent with what will shortly follow: the young lady herself is clearly not there but in London. The 'e' ('and') is easily corrected to 'a' ('belonging to').

[306] Saint-Vaast-d'Équiqueville, south-east of Dieppe.

[307] 'qui out le nom d'ali et d'or'. There are two possible meanings to this obscure derivation of the name Alienor, and they interestingly conflict. 'Ali' could mean either 'pure, fine, unblemished' and be therefore unreserved praise of Eleanor, or it could mean 'alloy', in which case the author's intention is the exact opposite, implying that Eleanor's golden qualities were not unalloyed. There is, however, nothing in the History to suggest that the author might have wished to insinuate the latter; on the contrary, she appears to be on excellent terms with Marshal: we are told below (p. 131) that 'Queen Eleanor, the king's mother, who was devoted to him and never wished him ill, received the Marshal joyfully'.

[308] She had previously been held captive there by King Henry; it is likely that part of the mission entrusted to Marshal by Richard had been to see that his mother was freed.

[309] Justiciar of England (see above, p. 113); Isabel de Clare, the 'damsel of Striguil', was residing under his protection in the White Tower.

over with reluctance.³¹⁰ Then he didn't dally long: as soon as he'd claimed the damsel he didn't want to lose her and said he'd go to her lands and wed her there. His host, Richard FitzReinier,³¹¹ who loved him dearly, said:

'By my life, sir, no you won't! You'll marry her nowhere but here! The wedding will take place here in this house – and it'll be splendid: you'll want for nothing befitting a worthy man!'

'But I haven't the wherewithal!' the Marshal said.

'*I* have!' replied his host. 'More than enough! By God's grace I have wealth enough that we needn't call on yours at all!'

And so without further delay, the auspicious marriage took place of that good, fair, sagacious, courtly damsel of high lineage, whose issue have been blessed and elevated by God, as has been clearly seen and is seen still. And after the fittingly splendid wedding, the Marshal took the lady to the house of Sir Engelram d'Abernon at Stoke,³¹² a peaceful, calm, delightful spot.

But I want to move on now and tell you about Count Richard, who made his way to Normandy and, to come straight to the point, was girded with the ducal sword at Rouen before an illustrious assembly of great barons and counts.³¹³ But it would be tiresome to recount every detail, and I've many more important matters to relate. Duke Richard crossed the sea to England where he was received with pomp and honour befitting so great a man – England hasn't had such a fine lord since. He was crowned king on the day of the Assumption,³¹⁴ being received at Saint Paul's in a glorious procession – while the Jews, I understand, were treated as mad deviants and put to the slaughter.³¹⁵

The king of England spent the whole of the following winter in his land. He showered his brother John with far more favours than he was ever to repay: he gave him four counties and other lands, too, until he said he had enough.

And meanwhile the Marshal came to the king and requested him to ask his brother John to give him back his land in Ireland – and a very reasonable request it was, I'd say, for it had been conquered by his forebear.³¹⁶ The king did ask this of his brother, but he didn't warm to the idea at all; he wouldn't consider it.

---

³¹⁰ Glanville at first resisted, perhaps because Richard, yet to be crowned, hadn't the authority to overrule his guardianship. And, being a close ally of Richard's brother John, who was then Lord of Ireland, he was far from keen to lose his ward when she was heiress to Leinster.

³¹¹ A prominent cloth merchant, he had been joint sheriff of London in 1188.

³¹² Stoke d'Abernon, Surrey.

³¹³ On 20 July 1189.

³¹⁴ 15 August, but this is incorrect: Richard's coronation took place on 3 September; he was received at St Paul's on 1 September and crowned at Westminster two days later.

³¹⁵ During Richard's coronation banquet wealthy Jews tried to bring gifts to the newly crowned king, but a crowd decided this was a blasphemous affront and a serious riot broke out that led to deaths, destruction and looting.

³¹⁶ Henry II had made John 'Lord of Ireland' in 1177 (though eight years later, on his first visit, John had managed to alienate all parties and lost real power there). Leinster had earlier, in 1169–71, been won and held by Richard 'Strongbow' de Clare – father of Marshal's new wife and therefore 'his forebear' – but when Strongbow died without a male heir, Leinster had come under royal wardship and been entrusted by King Henry to John.

'What?' said the king. 'God's legs! John! You surely don't mean to withhold what's rightfully his? He can't expect any favours from you if you won't even give him what he owns! But you shall indeed, for God's legs, that's my will!'

'I'll do so, gladly,' John replied, 'on condition that the gifts of land I've made to my men are allowed to stand.'

'That's not possible,' said the king. 'What would he be left with? You've given it all to your followers, every bit!'

'In that case, sire, if you insist, I ask merely, by your grace, that he leaves Theobald my butler the land I placed in his possession.'

'Very well,' the king replied, 'provided he holds it as the Marshal's vassal – otherwise it'll be a grievous loss to him. But he's not to acknowledge any other gift of land you've made – only that one.'

When all this had been settled and agreed, the Marshal sent to Ireland Reginald de Quetteville. He was a treacherous man: it was apt that he came from Quetteville, for in his service to the Marshal he was never straight;[317] but the Marshal commanded him to go to Ireland to secure his estates and possessions. He didn't decline the mission, but God help him if he did the Marshal any favours!

In King Richard's Absence

But I'll say no more about that – I've much more worthy matters to address, for I must devote proper time, care and attention in telling the perfect truth of how King Richard, during his stay in England, prepared his great fleet for the journey to the Holy Land. I'd be hard pressed to record how splendidly he equipped his ships with everything a man could need. A mighty host of great, fortified ships there were, superbly rigged and manned by such fine bodies of troops that they feared no enemy galleys or attack from any foe: they were more than ready to defend themselves. And such a store he placed aboard of gold and silver, fur and plate, rich and costly robes and arms of every kind that no one who beheld them could describe them adequately. And no provisions were lacking: there was ample bacon, wine and grain and flour and biscuit, more supplies stockpiled than tongue could tell; they had pepper, cumin, wax, all kinds of spice, the finest electuaries* and galantines,* and every variety of drink and sweet beverage; and there were bows, crossbows, bolts and arrows, swift and razor-sharp. It's worth recording that Sir Robert de Sablé[318] and Sir Gerard de Canville were in charge of this fleet.

When all his ships were fitted, but before they put to sea, King Richard sent word to the king of France that he would come in full force and with all speed to

---

[317] There is an obscure play on words here, made all the harder to penetrate because the place-name, given as '*Kedevile*' in the manuscript, is uncertain. There is a Quetteville in Normandy, just south of Honfleur. The pun might possibly be based on '*queue*' (tail/arse) and '*vil*' (base, contemptible).

[318] Later to become Grand Master of the Knights Templar, 1191–3.

meet him at Vézelay[319] to arrange matters and to plan their journey. Meanwhile he appointed – wisely or not – William Longchamp as Justiciar of England, commissioning him to hold the reins of power with the assistance of the Marshal and other lords I'll now name: Sir Geoffrey FitzPeter, Sir Hugh Bardolf and Sir William Brewer; by the king's command they were to remain in England to give loyal guidance to the Chancellor[320] – but this wasn't to his liking and he wouldn't be counselled by them. I understand that the last-named three had all taken the cross but the Marshal had not, having already made the journey to the Holy Land to seek God's mercy, faithfully taking there his lord the Young King's cross[321] and, thanks be to God, fulfilling his mission admirably and to the letter. Whatever anyone else may tell you, that's how it was. King Richard also left William FitzRalph as seneschal of Normandy, who by general consensus surpassed in wisdom all his successors. The same could not be said of the Chancellor: from the moment the king departed he ignored all the advice of the Marshal and the other lords I named. His arrogant high-handedness was all too apparent.

The kings met at Vézelay on the appointed day[322] and duly made their plans. I'm not going to recount every detail of their venture or their journey – it's not relevant to my story and would be quite a task! But the king of England arrived in Marseille where he awaited his fleet as it sailed gloriously and nobly over the sea; from there they sailed to Messina, where King Richard stayed all winter.[323] The king of France joined him there; he was very poor company, but it's not the place to go into that – I'll return to my main theme.

The Chancellor, now Justiciar of England, had the loftiest pretensions, and started spending wildly and surrounding himself with foreigners. He squandered the king's money on fripperies, his sole aim in life being to be recognised as lord. He was loved by no one, and a number of the king's loyal barons gathered and made plain their dismay at his conduct and his reckless spending of the royal treasury.

'You're wasting your time, sirs!' he replied. 'By glorious God, I'll not be guided by you!'

Count John took deep offence at his disdainful, mocking tone and would have nothing more to do with him.

When the barons returned from escorting King Richard to Vézelay, it didn't take them long to realise how outrageously the Chancellor was behaving, acting as he was as chancellor, chief judge, legate and king: he was enforcing his own rule everywhere, and emptying the royal treasury, leaving it devoid of gold and silver, and ruining the abbeys where he lorded it about. The barons sent a letter to the king at Messina, reporting all that was happening; but the Chancellor had spies among the barons and was fully aware of this, and sent word to the king

---

[319] In Burgundy, between Auxerre and Dijon.
[320] i.e. Longchamp: see above, p. 114, footnote 269.
[321] Above, pp. 99, 103–4.
[322] 2 July 1190.
[323] Richard arrived in Messina in the middle of September 1190; he didn't continue his journey until 10 April 1191.

that his brother John, abetted by the barons who had rallied to his side, presumed to plan foul treachery and intended to usurp him.

The following year the two kings set out on the voyage to Syria, but the king of France, without a doubt, was first to arrive at Acre, while the king of England was taking Cyprus, conquering the land.[324] After the fall of Acre – won only with great difficulty – the king of France fell ill, so ill indeed that he had to return home;[325] but it's thought his departure was a sly, malicious move: that he was deserting King Richard to leave him in a fix. Nonetheless, if left to it, that daring and resourceful king would have conquered the Holy Land for sure and the Saracens would have been crushed, had it not been that his mother and the Chancellor sent word that his brother John was conspiring with the king of France against him, and if he didn't return home quickly he would lose his land. And so it was that, in response to this message and many more, King Richard concluded a truce and left the Holy Land to go and secure his own. But in the course of his journey he was disgracefully taken captive.[326] News reached England that the king was a prisoner in a foreign land; his mother was distraught but it didn't worry his brother.

But I've forgotten to mention what I meant to say – and it really should be told: while the king was in Syria, the Chancellor sent word insisting that his land was undoubtedly lost unless he changed course, for Count John was wickedly bent on taking it and all the barons were fully behind him; and the king said:

'What? Have they all turned to him? I'm sure there are some still good and true. Abbot, bearer of this message, you are honest and wise: give me the names of the most notable of those who've sided with my brother.'

'Sire, the Marshal, they say, and many more have become his allies.'

'The Marshal! God's legs! Lord abbot, I truly believed the Marshal was the most loyal knight in my kingdom today – or ever born in my land! On your honour, is this true?'

'I take back what I told you, sire. I'll be honest: I said it only because I was ordered to!'

'God's legs, I thought as much!' said the king. 'The Marshal was never wicked or false!'

Meanwhile, it seems, the noble lords of England, by common consent, had driven the Chancellor from the land,[327] and with equal unanimity had replaced him with Archbishop Walter of Rouen – a wise choice. As Justiciar of England he governed the land more properly than the Chancellor had done, never abusing his power and always careful to do the right. He acted well and wisely, responding to the guidance of the Marshal and the barons – and the queen, who was in England at that time.

---

[324] Philip of France arrived in April 1191, Richard not until June, having first won Cyprus in a rapid campaign in May against Isaac Comnenos, who had taken Richard's wife-to-be and his sister captive after their ship and others had been wrecked there.
[325] Early in August.
[326] By Duke Leopold V of Austria, on 20 December 1192.
[327] In October 1191.

Count John wanted the archbishop to follow *his* counsel, too, but he took no notice of a word John said – and why? Because he didn't trust him – he knew where his ambitions lay: he knew what he was up to. Anyway, Count John learned that his brother the king was a prisoner in Germany,[328] and his counsellors urged him to take control of the land and become lord of England. And he did all in his power: he'd already taken Nottingham, as is common knowledge, and we all know how he fortified and garrisoned Windsor. The archbishop and the loyal barons who were at hand took speedy action and laid siege to Windsor,[329] and sent word to the Marshal to join the siege without delay – which he did in no mean fashion, I assure you, bringing with him all the lords of the Welsh Marches who loved the king and were loyal to him. The Justiciar and all the barons came to welcome him in jubilant procession: it was a joyous meeting indeed, the whole army greatly cheered by his arrival. Queen Eleanor, too, the king's mother, who was devoted to him and never wished him ill, received the Marshal joyfully. Then they met in council and all of them together said to the Marshal:

'We have sworn to maintain this siege: we've vowed not to abandon it at any price until the castle is taken or surrendered; we'd like you and your men to make the same oath – with you beside us we'll be all the more feared.'

But the Marshal replied: 'I'm not sure that's a good idea. If Count John knew for certain that we'd no intention of moving, he'd ride across the country and wreak havoc – he'd lay waste all the king's land. Would you like my advice? I think it's best if those of us who've just arrived stay here and maintain the siege – we won't leave till the castle's taken or surrendered, that we promise; but you meanwhile will go after the count, and if he's causing trouble and you choose to do battle, you'll be more than able to humble his pride! He'll be in no position to defend himself – he hasn't enough men to confront you, and all the local levies will be on your side. Or if you prefer, I and my men will go, and if I find him I promise I'll do battle – and give him such a hiding he'll be forced to leave the land!'

And so it was agreed; but in the meantime, let me tell you, the men of the castle had chosen to surrender on terms guaranteeing their safety: they were only too pleased. With the castle now in their hands, the king's men appointed a constable of whom they all approved and considered good and able, and from there they went and laid siege to Marlborough, but the men of the castle offered little resistance and quickly surrendered.[330]

Meanwhile word had spread through every land that King Richard would be released if ransomed – unwelcome news to his enemies, but a cause of rejoicing for his friends, who duly set to work to raise the money: it was to cost more than a hundred thousand pounds to free him. His loyal liegemen were elated at hearing that a ransom would release their king so courteous, wise, valiant and mighty

---

[328] In the spring of 1193 the duke of Austria handed Richard over to the Holy Roman Emperor, Henry VI, who imprisoned him in Trifels Castle in south-west Germany.
[329] On 29 March 1193.
[330] The chronology is awry; this refers to the taking of Marlborough nearly a year later, in February 1194.

that he'd surpassed all others in his deeds in Syria – kings, dukes, barons, counts: none had matched him in any way; it was envy of his eminence that had caused him to be so wickedly taken captive. The nobility assumed a heavy burden in raising the ransom, but almost all of them did so. Throughout his lands, and particularly in England, a fifth of all chattels were taken, so pressing was the need, and likewise chalices of gold and silver. And how devoted they were to releasing the king, those who willingly sent their children as hostages! They committed all at their disposal and thereby earned his deepest gratitude. He sent letters throughout his lands in Normandy and England, to all his subjects and especially to the Marshal, expressing his thanks and loving greetings for having defended his realm; and he sent instructions to the archbishop of Rouen[331] to appoint as bishop of Exeter, and rightly so, Henry, brother of the worthy Marshal who had been so loyal to him.

When the Emperor's envoys arrived, the hostages were sent with half the ransom. Then home came the king[332] as his people so desired: he was dearly loved by them. The nobles and his supporters came to receive him with the utmost joy, tears of happiness streaming from many an eye.

King Richard's Return

At the moment of the king's return the Marshal was at Striguil.[333] And let me explain what happened. He'd received the bitter news that his brother John had died, and was so overcome with grief that his heart was close to breaking: it might have proved fatal had he not had other news, thank God, that made his heart rejoice, as a messenger, fluent, bright and courteous, arrived and said that the king of England was home again, completely free and in good health and spirits. Had he been given ten thousand pounds the Marshal wouldn't have been so relieved of the sorrow that had beset him.

'Oh, God be praised!' he said. 'I've never felt such grief as this for my brother's death, but nothing could have brought such comfort as my lord's return. I thank God for bringing me so swiftly both suffering and elation: my joy at the king's return gives me the strength to overcome the grief I thought would crush me.'

He sent his knights to Marlborough to collect his brother's body, which gave him more sorrow than he could express. They made their way back with all the speed they could and on the third day arrived with the body at Cirencester. There they met the Marshal, who was so distraught that he almost collapsed, and no one can blame him for that. He was truly in a sorry state. His brother's wife, daughter of Sir Adam de Port,[334] accompanied the body, grieving deeply. It was carried into the church[335] to a glorious service. But then the royal messengers arrived to

---

[331] i.e. Archbishop Walter, who had been acting as Justiciar.
[332] In the middle of March 1194.
[333] Chepstow: see note 267, above p. 114.
[334] Port-en-Bessin, near Bayeux.
[335] Cirencester Abbey.

hasten the Marshal's coming to the king, so preventing him accompanying his brother's body to its burial-place.[336] So all his people set out and bore the body in state to Bradenstoke[337] where they interred him with great dignity, laying him to rest most honourably alongside his ancestors.

Meanwhile the Marshal went to join the king, taking with him just three knights, as the rest of his men had stayed with his brother's body. He met his lord at Huntingdon; the king honoured him highly, giving him a more joyous greeting than he'd given anyone, no matter how close or dearly loved, since his return to the land. And after dinner, as the barons attended the king in his chamber, in high spirits, happy and rejoicing that he was back, the king spoke thus:

'Marshal, I thank you for your service to me. I'm reliably informed that you've served me nobly and I thank you deeply, as I do my other men present thanks to whom I'm here – I thank you all! You've striven to defend my land from those who would have robbed me of my inheritance, and through your great enterprise you've freed me from captivity from which I would never have escaped, sirs, but for God and your good selves. You've proved your loyalty indeed!'

'Sire,' said the Marshal, 'we merely did our duty. All good and honest men should suffer hardship and pain for their rightful lord.'

Each of the nobles in turn expressed gratitude to the king for acknowledging how much they'd done for him. Then the king said:

'Marshal, sir, I say this to you and to all lords present: all, of every degree, should know truly, without doubt, that of all men living in this world it is my good friend Baldwin de Béthune, whom I see here, who did most for me all the while I was imprisoned, and he secured my release: I would never have been freed had it not been for him.'

'Sire,' the Marshal said, 'Sir Baldwin is loyal indeed, devoted to doing good; he will forever be your true, unfailing servant – on that I'll stake my life.'

Sir William de l'Étang wasn't slow to stand and declare: 'Marshal, Marshal, you're right to put your life on the line for him: he has many times done the same for you, vouching for you and your loyalty against those who slandered you. When they came to malign you before my lord[338] he always swore upon his life that their words were false. He did so a hundred times! So I'd surely say you should do so once for him!'

When Count John heard the certain news that his brother was free and safe and sound and returning to the land, he didn't dare confront him. He needed another plan. He made sure his castles were well garrisoned and provisioned –

---

[336] The somewhat evasive character of the author's account of William's brother's death may well be connected to his body having been collected (without authorial explanation) from Marlborough, which had been taken, as mentioned above, by the king's supporters that February. 'Though William's biographer tried to conceal it, John Marshal seems to have declared for the count [Prince John] in 1193, holding Marlborough Castle in his name ... It is quite likely that [he] had been seriously injured when royalist forces recaptured Marlborough ... and died as a result of his wounds.' Asbridge, *op. cit.*, pp. 234, 236–7.

[337] Bradenstoke Priory in Wiltshire.

[338] i.e. Henry the Young King, above pp. 84–9.

afraid as he was of losing them – and then went to the king of France, who took him under his wing but couldn't and wouldn't make any guarantees: he cared little for his plight, and had no intention of supporting him – he'd no real interest at all, and was playing him for a fool, taking him for a ride. But I'll say no more of him for now; I want to return to my subject – which is far more appealing and enjoyable to hear: things of little consequence should be swiftly dealt with!

The king set out from Cheleberge[339] with a great army and baggage train and made straight for Nottingham to join the Northern lords who were besieging it.[340] They had barely begun their siege when they heard the great news that the king was coming; they went to receive him joyfully, and when they met he kissed them all in turn. They were greatly cheered by his arrival.

The king, not wanting to dally, gave orders for his lodgings to be arranged in the closest house to the castle – and rightly so. Why? Because the men in the castle would be all the more daunted! And as soon as the king had dined he wouldn't allow the defenders any respite: donning just a light hauberk, as was often his way, and with a simple iron cap upon his head, he advanced towards the gate behind a large body of men bearing thick, broad, hefty shields. Seeing this, all the king's most ardent supporters rushed to arms and charged boldly forward and took control of the outer bailey. The king and the barons entered the bailey, covering themselves with shields against crossbow bolts; the king's own crossbowmen then replied and did their level best, and the upshot was that the barbican was taken amid fierce fighting, the defenders suffering heavy casualties – much to the attackers' delight. It was a finely delivered assault indeed, but nightfall brought it to an end. As the attack broke up and they all withdrew, that night the defenders set fire to the gate and burnt down the barbican beyond. What a waste of time! Next morning, when the king heard this, he burst out laughing and said:

'If you ask me, that suits us fine!'

The next day our besiegers went to parley with the defenders; they said they were mad to hold the castle against the king of England, the lord of the land. But the defenders were sure this was a trick, a fantasy: they refused to believe that the king was free and had returned, and asked for safe conduct to the camp so that they could see him for themselves. This was relayed to the king who had no objection: he very readily agreed. So the defenders sent a knight, Sir Fulcher of Grendon,[341] accompanied by Henry Russell; they came and stood before the king and recognised him by his face and bearing.

'Am I he?' said the king. 'What do you think?'

---

[339] It is hard to interpret this place-name: '*Cheleberge*' appears in a Patent Roll of 1204 as a spelling of Charborough in Dorset, or it may be a misreading by the scribe of '*Meleberge*' (Marlborough), but both are highly unlikely: there is no reason for Richard to have gone to either place from Huntingdon, nor is either an obvious starting-point for an advance on Nottingham.

[340] Nottingham, secured by John as mentioned above, p. 131, was besieged by David, brother of the king of Scotland, Ranulf, earl of Chester and William, earl of Ferrers, in March 1194.

[341] Member of a minor noble family from Grendon in Warwickshire; Fulcher's companion Henry Russell is unknown.

And they said: 'You are.'

'You're free to go back,' he said. 'That's only right. And do as best you can.'

So they took their leave and returned and reported what they'd found. They thought it over and put an end to the matter by placing themselves at the king's mercy – a wise move: they made it a great deal easier on themselves! And so it was that the king took possession of the castle, to the delight of all his followers. And the captured defenders found their fate much less harsh than they'd expected: they'd been fearing for their lives. But no one should be in any doubt that when a worthy man has the upper hand he should always refrain from cruelty and malice – though I tell you, when the wicked prevail, cruelty and shameful treatment are in store. I shan't go on, but the king was so compassionate and cordial and merciful that he held them to fair ransom without dispute or recrimination.

I'll move on now. Next morning after mass the king was in the castle hall, and around him at the table were his barons and all his men; the hall was very crowded. Then the Chancellor,[342] an impressive and eloquent man, stepped forward and in the hearing of everyone addressed Sir Walter de Lacy, saying:

'The king wishes and commands you to pay him homage forthwith for your land in Ireland.[343] Do so: it is only right.'

Sir Walter did, without demur. Then the Chancellor said to the king:

'Hear me, my good lord. The Marshal is here; you should tell him to do as Sir Walter has done.'

'That's hardly unreasonable!' said the king. 'Come: do so!'

But the Marshal replied: 'I'll do no such thing, so help me God! I'll not be so base: no one will see me do wrong! I paid homage to your brother for what I hold from him.[344] No one will accuse me of falseness.'

'God save me,' said the king, 'that's well spoken!'

All the barons present approved and praised him for his words and said he was a worthy man indeed. But the Chancellor looked thunderous and said:

'You're planting a vineyard.'[345]

The Marshal replied, quite frankly: 'You can plant a vineyard or a garden if you wish, sir, but I'm not going to break my word. I tell you straight: if any man alive tried to take Ireland, I'd do all in my power to aid the lord to whom I've paid homage. You'll have no blandishments from me; I stand before our lord the king whom I've served in all good faith for what I hold as *his* vassal, so I've nothing to fear.'

---

[342] This is now Hubert Walter, archbishop of Canterbury, who had replaced Walter of Rouen as Justiciar, the latter having gone as hostage to the Emperor as surety for the outstanding portion of Richard's ransom.

[343] Walter de Lacy held land in the Welsh Marches and also in Meath in Ireland.

[344] John had been Lord of Ireland since 1177 (see note 316 above, p. 127), and Marshal had therefore owed him homage for his lands in Leinster, as Lacy had for Meath.

[345] The archbishop is implying with this phrase that Marshal is being devious and preparing the ground for his future gain (with a possible reference to 1 Corinthians 9:7: 'Who ever goes to war at his own expense? Who plants a vineyard and does not eat its fruit?'). In his frank reply Marshal shows that he understands this and (perhaps scornfully) suggests that he doesn't share the archbishop's *modus operandi*.

King Richard's War in Normandy

From there the king went to Winchester where he wished to be crowned, and prepared for his coronation; he wanted to bear the crown to hearten his people, who'd truly endured great anxiety and woe.[346]

Then he fitted his fleet to cross at once to Normandy, brooking no delay; he set sail from Portsmouth and landed one morning at Barfleur on the Cotentin. He made for Caen by way of Bayeux, pressing on with all speed, anxious as he was to reach Verneuil which had long been under siege from his enemy the king of France, who was bent on doing him harm and had done a good deal – though he hadn't managed to deter him from returning to confront him, and there were to be some very fine encounters.

We know King Richard stopped at Lisieux to dine and lodge for the night with Jehan d'Alençon,[347] but he was very unsettled all the while, worried as he was about Verneuil. His heart wouldn't rest and he couldn't get a wink of sleep, knowing that the king of France was besieging the town. He wanted to rest a little after dinner, as was his custom, but he was too much on edge. It was then that Jehan d'Alençon appeared looking tearful and distracted, downcast and anguished. The king asked him straightway:

'Whatever's the matter, Jehan? Ah, you've seen my brother John – don't lie! He's no reason to be afraid – let him come before me. He's my brother; in all good faith he shouldn't fear me: he may have been acting foolishly but I'll not hold it against him. But those who put him up to it have had their just deserts – or will do soon enough. I'll say no more for now.'

So Jehan, much cheered, set off at once and said to John: 'You're safe to come – it's quite all right! The king's gracious and compassionate – much more generous to you than you meant to be to him! Your counsellors gave you bad advice – and it'll be their loss: they'll have their comeuppance. Come – the king awaits you.'

Very apprehensively, John came before the king and fell at his feet. But all was well; the king took his brother by the hand and raised him up and kissed him and said:

'Don't worry, John: you're a child and have been led astray. Those who gave you ill counsel will rue the day! Up you get now, and go and dine. Jehan,' he said to Jehan d'Alençon, 'what shall he have to eat?'

Thereupon a salmon was presented: this was most acceptable, and the king bade that it be cooked for his brother at once. Kindness and generosity rightly emerge when a man's heart is infused with them; but no good, I tell you, will come from the heart of a wicked man. That's why the bad are not included in accounts of notable deeds: it's best to make no mention.

But there's one thing I've forgotten to tell you and really should: when the king arrived in Normandy all the people, the moment they saw him, showered him

---

[346] Richard's second coronation took place at Winchester on 17 April 1194.
[347] Archdeacon of Lisieux and vice-chancellor of Normandy.

with gifts and words of welcome. Wherever he went, on road, in field, whichever way he turned he was surrounded by joyous dancing and jubilant crowds, so dense that you couldn't have thrown an apple without it hitting someone before the ground! So great was the celebration. And the bells rang everywhere, and old and young came in great processions, singing:

'God is come in all His might! Now the king of France will have to go!'

With a fine escort and train King Richard came to Chambreis[348] and dined at the house of Jean le Roux. But he'd no wish to dally; without more ado he mounted once more and said:

'Let no one give in to idleness! Come, all of you who would follow me – I'm going to camp right next to the king of France, and no one will stand in my way!'

He reached Laigle that very night and Tuboeuf[349] next day. Showing not a jot of respect for the overweening king of France, he sent knights and troops and crossbowmen straight through the besieging lines and into Verneuil, where they mounted a superb defence, as the besiegers soon discovered. Until then the town had been defended better than words could tell: William de Mortemer had been on the battlements night and day, ordering a rain of burning crossbow bolts to keep the attackers at bay, letting them nowhere near. And Sir Peter de la Rivière, a fine knight indeed, made frequent sorties on a Lombard steed, regardless of all opposition, without ever being caught; he rode to the king at Tuboeuf but had a ready plan for getting back into the castle.

King Richard acted shrewdly, blocking all supply routes to the besieging army; so the king of France was forced to withdraw,[350] and no sooner had the besiegers left than King Richard rode into Verneuil with lance held high. No eyes ever beheld such joy as the defenders of the castle showed him then – and the king met them with even greater joy: he couldn't stop kissing them, one by one! And he promised and delivered such rich reward for their defence of the castle that they were more than satisfied.

Then so many flocked to him, and his army grew so great, that more than twenty thousand had to make camp outside the town. He divided his forces into two; he made his way to Beaumont-le-Roger[351] while Count John went and set up camp around Évreux, besieging it. The king took Beaumont and Évreux was quickly taken, too, the day after the siege began. After capturing Beaumont, which had risen against him, the king had the tower burnt and destroyed. Then without more ado he moved on to Évreux and garrisoned the poorly defended castle to make it the strongest in that borderland. From there he went straight to Pont-de-l'Arche, where he had the bridge, part of which was broken, quickly repaired. Then, downriver from Elbeuf, he fortified the rock of Orival.

And now let me tell you this: he arrived at Le Vaudreuil from one direction and the king of France with all his forces from another; they arranged a parley,

---

[348] The medieval name of the town now known as Broglie, midway between Lisieux and Verneuil.
[349] Saint-Michel-Tuboeuf, to the west of Verneuil; Laigle (now L'Aigle) was an important castle.
[350] On 28 May 1194.
[351] North-west of Évreux.

but the French behaved disgracefully: while the kings were discussing peace they carried on undermining the castle till they brought it down. It was a craven, treacherous act. When King Richard heard it falling he wasn't pleased; he swore:

'God's legs! This is flagrant treason! There'll be saddles emptied yet – they'll rue the day!'

The king of France departed, and as soon as he'd gone King Richard – who knew about fortifications – set about repairing the damage. 'It's a nuisance, but a castle half-ruined is a castle half-built! I'll have it repaired despite their efforts. And I'll make them pay, since they're so keen to fight: I'll track them down, no matter where.'

Fine reinforcements flooded in from England, Gascony, Poitou, Maine, Anjou, Brittany and elsewhere. Then the great war began; the French had their hands full and came thoroughly to grief! With his prowess and shrewd strategy King Richard soon won back the majority of his castles; I shan't name them all: it would be quite a job to list which he recaptured and when and how. But it's only right that you should hear how he built the bridge at Porte-Joie[352] to allow his whole army to cross, and then fortified the isle of Andelys[353] to secure the whole of that borderland. And also how the king of France advanced on Vendôme and King Richard went to meet him,[354] and their two armies confronted each other for a long while, unmoving. Then the king of France was told that the king of England was set upon driving him from his land forthwith; the moment he heard this he set off without more ado – and without informing any of his men! The first they knew of it was seeing him ride away! It was a disaster for them: they left likewise, in such disorder that they abandoned all their gear. As soon as our side saw them go they sprang into action. The Marshal and his men armed swiftly, preferring to be armed rather than disarmed in the chase, and the Marshal, fully armed, set off with his men in fine formation: a splendid company they were. The king came straight up to him and said:

'I pray you, Marshal, watch over me today.'

'I shall, sire, very gladly,' he replied.

'And my men, too: see that they don't lose discipline.'

'I will, sire,' said the Marshal.

Then the king charged off with his battalions. And no record or tally could keep count of the booty bequeathed by the French! They gave no thought to their riches: their intent was elsewhere! They left tents and pavilions, garments of silk and scarlet,* coin and plate, horses, palfreys, packhorses, handsome robes and money. Loot and drink the English won in abundance – and food! Gorgeous fish and meat a-plenty! But the Marshal and his men, let me tell you, gave no thought to booty, only to guarding the king's army.

---

[352] On the Seine close to Le Vaudreuil.

[353] In 1196. It was then that Richard, as well as fortifying the island at Les Andelys, began construction of the mighty Château-Gaillard on the heights above the river.

[354] The author is unclear about the order of events: he has jumped back to early July 1194, and is about to describe how Richard routed Philip's army at Fréteval, north-east of Vendôme.

The king came back and met his loyal Marshal and his company and said: 'God preserve you! You'd have been our only protection if they'd decided to attack us while looting! You can retire now – it's clear the French have no intention of turning back.'

'I'll not go yet, sire,' the Marshal said. 'I don't think that's a good idea while our men are still giving chase. If we were to retire now we might well come to grief: the French are none too fond of you – they might turn with a vengeance.'

'God bless me, you're right!' said the king. 'Stay, then: they're the wisest words I ever heard!'

So the Marshal stayed till the pursuit was done and everyone had returned; once he was sure there was no one left he sent them on ahead and followed behind, forming a rearguard with his company.

What more should I tell you? When they took to their lodgings that night they all boasted before the king about their spoils, displaying their winnings; but the king said:

'The Marshal's done better than any of you. In case you don't know, let me tell you: he'd have bailed us all out if we'd been in trouble. That's why I rate his actions higher than any of ours. No one with a good rearguard needs to fear his foe.'

I should tell you next how King Richard left Normandy, as is well known, to attempt an attack on Vierzon.[355] We know how he besieged and took it by force,[356] and how there was rich booty. And we know who was first to enter the town – no one should be in any doubt of that: the Marshal was there with him, guide to the king on many notable occasions.

King Richard then sent him on important missions to Count Baldwin of Flanders[357] (later to achieve high renown) and to Count Renaud of Boulogne, son of the count of Dammartin;[358] both became his allies because of the wrongs they'd suffered at the hands of the overweening king of France: they became the king of England's sworn liegemen. The king of France was none too pleased by this – in fact he was most aggrieved.[359] He met to confer with King Richard between Vernon and Boutavant[360] – he wouldn't go any further. On the appointed day, as they met for their parley as arranged, King Richard went in fine array and handsomely attended, taking with him, God save me, Count Renaud of Boulogne: I can assure you they went together hand in hand. The king of France was on one side of the river with his whole army; the king of England on the other, quite undaunted. To the parley, in fact, King Richard graciously led both counts,[361] one by each hand, for so he had promised; and when the king of France

---

[355] Vierzon, south of Orléans, was traditionally under the lordship of the counts of Blois.
[356] In July 1197.
[357] Baldwin IX, r. 1194–1205.
[358] See above, p. 117.
[359] Not least because, just a year before, both had undertaken to support him against anyone.
[360] A fortress on the Île aux Boeufs, an island in the Seine near Vernon. The date of this meeting is uncertain; it probably took place in late 1197 or early 1198.
[361] i.e. Renaud and Count Baldwin of Flanders.

saw them arrive together, he was far from pleased but most put out, and said to King Richard:

'Where are you going with those men, sire? My parley was with you alone – I'm not happy with this. I've nothing to say to them.'

'Sire,' replied the king of England, 'you've been taking their land as you've been taking mine, and they've become my allies. And let me tell you, I've given my word that you'll have war as long as you continue to rob the three of us.'

On hearing this the king of France was incensed and stormed away in fury. The parley was over, but neither King Richard nor the counts cared a jot about his anger. The two counts took their leave of King Richard, to whom they were very close, and returned to their own lands to prepare for war.

The king of England now arranged to send the finest, most highly regarded knights of his land to the two counts. They were duly chosen, and I'll tell you who they were: the first was William the Marshal – he needed little persuasion; he went very readily, as he always did: on any worthwhile mission he was prepared to go as soon as asked. With him went Sir Peter de Préaux, a fine and handsome knight, along with the good, trusty, upright knight Sir Alan Basset and the worthy, loyal, noble, open-hearted knight Sir John the Marshal.[362] They were the chosen party. It's always pleasing to recount the deeds of those committed to doing good. And they made their way straight to find the counts, who were delighted and gave them a joyous welcome.

The count of Flanders set out with an impressive, mighty army and a proud, committed force of levied troops to win back a castle[363] taken and garrisoned against him by the French king (adept at taking castles without having to exert himself).[364] With such a strong army he felt sure of satisfaction and of giving his foe a lesson. But the king of France swiftly raised a massive force to go to the castle's aid, confident he could save it. The count of Flanders heard what he was planning, and sought the counsel of the nobles there and of his barons; they were very fearful, and it showed in their advice (though each expressed a different view – such men, from my experience, are rarely of one accord: it's often the case that what some think best is anathema to the rest). The barons discussed among themselves making barricades of carts (the levies had brought them in great numbers), some proposing that the levies should be placed behind these barricades while the knights rode out and engaged the king of France, each trusting in God and Chance. But the Marshal rose, unimpressed by this, and said to the count of Flanders:

'If it please you, my lord, let me give you my view. I don't approve of building any such barricades: it would look like a loss of nerve and a lack of men. With your permission, I'll tell you what I'd do if it were left to me: I wouldn't depend

---

[362] William's nephew, illegitimate son of his elder brother John.
[363] This castle, presumably in Flanders, is sadly not identified.
[364] The implication seems to be that Philip of France was good at securing the surrender of towns and castles with bribes. And the author is about to observe that Philip 'always kept well clear of a fight!' (below, p. 141).

on the levies or barricades, but go and do battle in the open field and stand our ground, making no retreat, feigned or otherwise. I say we should set the carts to blockade the town, to prevent any sortie by the defenders to attack or surprise our men or do damage to our less disciplined levies. Go out tomorrow, fully armed and prepared for combat, ready to crush their presumptuous pride, with your squadrons ordered, your battalions arrayed, ready to face them and do battle. Foresight, good planning and judgement go hand in hand with prowess.'

After he'd spoken, all agreed with the Marshal's words, saying: 'Bless a worthy man's counsel!'

It was a great honour for the Marshal that day to win everyone's approval, and all the nobles praised him highly for his commitment to securing their rights when he wasn't from their land.

So forth they rode next morning, fully armed, following the advice of their fine counsellor! There were armoured knights in great numbers and a large body of levies, too: they looked a bold force to be sure, whatever anyone might say, resolved and fired for combat – anyone who attacked them would have a battle indeed! They were ready to confront them as bidden.

But I tell you, the king of France had spies in their camp who saw what they were planning, and they went and reported to the king that the Flemish were armed and drawn up, ready to confront him. He wasn't pleased, and he spoke to his council, one of whom said:

'I advise you to postpone your attack: they won't retreat – they'll stand and face you and give battle.'

That day passed; and the king of France then beat a retreat – wisely, for he could see nothing to be gained. How right he was: after all, no man will see his home unless he goes back – returning is a good idea! (In any case, he always kept well clear of a fight!) And when the Flemings saw the French so generously disappearing without giving them a look they were only too grateful, of course! And they all agreed they should send a messenger to King Richard to report what had happened. The council chose John the Marshal; they escorted him to the coast and sent him by sea to find the king, and he made his way over sea and land till he found the one he sought: King Richard, that is, who was on the border of France[365] where, on the previous day, he had captured Courcelles,[366] along with the lord of the castle and his men, and garrisoned it with a large force. This took place, for sure, on the feast of Saint Peter at the beginning of August;[367] it was then that Sir John the Marshal arrived with his report, and the king was delighted to hear the news of how the counts had fared: that the king of France had backed off without any plea or entreaty, and that his men couldn't get away fast enough!

And then, the day after Saint Peter's, King Richard heard news that thrilled and delighted him: the king of France was heading straight for Gisors with

---

[365] i.e. the border of the limited area – essentially the Île de France – that constituted the king of France's own domain.
[366] Courcelles-lès-Gisors, just to the west of Gisors.
[367] This is incorrect; the capture of Courcelles and the clash that follows at Gisors took place in the last days of September 1198.

considerable numbers. King Richard mounted at once with all his forces, and crossed the river below Dangu[368] with a strong, impressive company. He sent Mercadier[369] ahead to spy on the French army, along with Sir Hugh de Corny, a bold, shrewd knight who knew the country well, being a native of those parts. Mercadier took just a hurried glance and rode back to tell King Richard that the king of France had a massive army, a marvel to behold, and was heading straight for Gisors; but Sir Hugh de Corny said:

'Christ have mercy, sire, I made a careful count and there aren't that many, truly! Do battle with them and you'll win honour indeed – they'll be crushed or taken captive! Come, sire: enhance your prestige this day!'

King Richard knew in his heart that Sir Hugh was judicious, wise and worthy, being a knight of great experience in war, and turning his bold, fierce face to his men he said:

'Back to the ford! Things are looking promising!'

This went down well, it seems: they all turned and went straight back to the ford, among them Sir John de Préaux, a brave, courageous knight, eager to excel: back to the ford he headed. The good king, mounted on a Lombard horse, galloped ahead to the top of a rise from where he saw before him the king of France's army – and having seen them he was quite undaunted by their numbers. He called his men forward, pennons and banners unfurled; they were still a long way behind, but no men ever hastened to battle with such a will, so eager and fired to engage the foe. But King Richard, it seems, didn't wait for all his men! He rode on ahead, and as they raced to catch up as they rightly should, he said to John de Préaux:

'Now we'll see who's keen to charge this day!' And: 'God is with us!' he cried. 'At them!'

And with that he went charging as the ravening, famished lion falls upon its prey, its mind fixed on nothing but the catch. There couldn't fail to be a decisive outcome – one side was going to come unstuck – for the fray that followed was a heaving throng, more than I've ever seen at a fair or market! They charged like mad to be the first to engage! And no one was half-hearted – everyone who fought there did his duty. And the king, at the very forefront of it all, saw to it that the French were routed and took to flight. They weren't allowed to get off lightly; many were taken prisoner as King Richard's men seized all they overtook, and had it not been for the dust-clouds in the summer heat, the king of France himself might well have been captured. His prestige would have taken a blow indeed but for the dust and the confusion – and for Destiny, which allows nothing to happen that isn't meant. They pursued them hard to right and left, driving them back to the gates of Gisors. They captured many of the most eminent – for as you know, it's often the way that the bravest are at the rear when it comes to a rout: others, who don't fancy it, and want to save their skins, just take to headlong flight. The king of France did at least end up falling in a ford; he was hauled out by a clerk of his – quite a job,

---

[368] The river is the Epte; Dangu is just to the west of Courcelles and Gisors.
[369] A notable mercenary captain from the Limousin who had been in Richard's service since 1184.

when there was no other help at hand; the son of William de Mello,[370] he was. But others came running at last to rescue him. When they'd pulled the king from the water – in a terrible state of shock – he didn't stop at Gisors: strong castle though it was, he was so in awe of his enemies that he was afraid of being besieged and didn't want to find himself trapped. When a fox goes to ground there's a chance he'll never get out; that's why King Philip did all he could to escape – he didn't want to end up cornered. He headed back to France,[371] while King Richard with his mighty company made his way back to the rock of Les Andelys,[372] taking with him ninety-one of the French king's knights as prisoners, all captured in fair fight. I shan't labour the point by mentioning the others who were caught: there were so many that I won't bother with the number.

And let me tell you, the courage of their very bravest was so shaken that, in all the wars fought since, thirty of ours have always been ready to charge forty knights of theirs! That hadn't been the case before Gisors. I hope this shows that a fine lord is most heartening to his people, and enhances their prowess and their honour. The noble-hearted King Richard would never tolerate bad government – he had no time for it at all: it was ever his way to promote the good and crush the wicked. May God grant by His grace that King Henry does likewise,[373] that all his people may be inspired by his goodness to new courage and valour, that he may come to recover what is his and theirs!

The war raged on fiercely after the clash at Gisors. It lasted long – it hasn't finished yet! But I can't recount every incident: it's not my intention and it's irrelevant to my theme. If I can just deal with what matters, saying neither too much nor too little, I'll be well satisfied. I've often encountered wordy fellows straying off in endless digressions from their theme, when no one who wants to live by the pen should include in his work anything inappropriate or unrelated to the matter in hand.

But this much I will say for sure: King Richard was at Gournay,[374] where he secretly summoned men and provisions, a great host of knights, soldiers and mercenaries; quietly, without any fuss, they joined him at Gerberoy.[375] It was a mighty force indeed when they'd all assembled: they came from far and wide, eager to serve and please their lord. The king then rode towards Milly[376] while Mercadier made for Semilli[377] and on towards Beauvais. The people of those parts

---

[370] Brother of Dreux de Mello, mentioned above, pp. 106–7.
[371] i.e. his own royal domain, as noted previously.
[372] Richard had built extensive fortifications on the Seine at Les Andelys (above, p. 138), including his famous Château-Gaillard on the heights above.
[373] i.e. Henry III, the young king at the time of the poem's composition. I have opted to translate Paul Meyer's suggested emendation of a clearly corrupt line in the MS: '*Que sunt vencu le rei tel face*', which has no discernible meaning, to '*Que Henris li reis itel face*'.
[374] Gournay-en-Bray, west of Beauvais. The author is now returning to an event in May of the previous year, 1197.
[375] North-east of Gournay.
[376] Milly-sur-Thérain, north-west of Beauvais.
[377] An unidentifiable place-name. If the campaign is correctly reported here, Savignies would make geographical sense.

had acquired a fearsome neighbour, as became plain to many that day! King Richard descended on Milly with his great host, taking the garrison completely by surprise: he was on them before they knew it. He launched attacks from every side, with scaling-ladders borne forward and thrown against the walls. It was a fearsome assault: the defenders resisted as stoutly as they could, raining missiles; the daring attackers swarmed up the ladders, but the defenders fought back with crossbow bolts and beams of wood and pikes and flails and sharp pitchforks – anyone who witnessed it saw sterling work from both sides. So many knights and soldiers were mounting one ladder that they massively overloaded it, and they were thrust back and sent plummeting into the ditch. Almost to a man they were badly injured – or worse – in the fall; a knight from Wales, Sir Walter Scudamore,[378] came off worse than most, breaking his leg. Many of the attackers now beat a retreat – they'd quite lost their nerve. But a Flemish knight, Sir Guy de la Bruyère, was still up a ladder, fiercely at it, performing splendidly, till the town's defenders trapped him with pitchforks between chest and chin, pinning him so completely that he was helpless. The Marshal, on the edge of a ditch, was horrified to see the knight in such a fearful plight; he leapt, fully armed and sword in hand, down into the ditch and clambered, I swear, up the other side, and pressed on resolutely till he reached the ladder where the defenders had the knight pinioned and were about to kill him. He laid about them with his sword, paying them back in no uncertain manner for their treatment of Sir Guy; he dealt so many blows to right and left that they reeled back and abandoned the battlements to him: they didn't fancy taking him on and slung their hook and shifted! That was fine by the Marshal! The king, seeing him leap up the ladder and assail the foe, was rather put out – he wanted to do the same that instant! But the lords at his side dissuaded him and held him back. The Marshal having broken in, our men were all so cheered that they cried with one voice:

'The castle is taken! Let's go and aid the Marshal!'

The defenders were aghast as our men swarmed on to the battlements. Sir William de Monceaux, the constable of the castle, was none too pleased; he didn't hold back but went straight for the Marshal to inflict whatever damage he could – but in vain: he found him quite a handful! Having hewn at the others with his awesome blows the Marshal was out of breath and it had cost him a deal of effort; but though the constable attacked with all his might, raining blows upon him, the Marshal landed a blow in return that cut through helm and hood and into flesh. It stopped him in his tracks; shocked, stunned, knocked senseless by the blow, he fell and lay unmoving, unable to rise. The Marshal, weary now – he'd done more than his share! – sat on him to hold him fast, while the king's men, entry gained by his great effort, poured in: the town was taken thanks to the Marshal. The king and all his forces entered now: they won rich plunder, while those inside lost everything. A host of prisoners were taken, and the castle and all within it returned to the rightful possession of the king.

---

[378] *'Sire Valt. de Kidomore'*; Scudamore was from a family on the borders of Herefordshire.

The Marshal set off at once, and came to the king with the knight he'd captured, holding him by the hand, and said: 'Receive this prisoner: I deliver him to you.'

'Sir Marshal,' said the king, 'it's not right – it's very wrong – that a knight of such eminence and prowess as you should undertake such exploits! Leave that to the young knights who have yet to make their names! We all know you've pursued honour so long that you've securely caught and won it! This knight you've captured I give to you – as I would were his value a hundred times greater than it is. You've well deserved the prize, I say, and he's rightly yours: I declare you his master and keeper.'

The Marshal gave fulsome and gracious thanks.

Just then Mercadier arrived. The dice had landed well for him that day and he'd captured the bishop of Beauvais, along with Sir William de Mello. His fellow mercenaries brought with them a fair few prisoners, too, bound together with ropes round necks like hounds on leashes. The town was now so packed with them that no one could move a step in any direction! Mercadier presented his captive bishop to the king, and the king was delighted: the bishop had waged bitter war against him and ravaged his lands – I assure you, in all the world he was one of the men he hated most, as became plain when he condemned him to a harsh imprisonment.

What more should I tell you? The king's army were jubilant at the capture of the castle and the prisoners. Some said it was a mistake not to press on and take Beauvais, as it was poorly defended now; but the king said:

'Patience! It's enough for now that we've captured this castle and some of our most powerful enemies – though for all their might, we're in the right and they're in the wrong: God in time will show them how wrong they are to oppose us!'

The king didn't dally but went straight back to Gournay in high, triumphant spirits with all the booty he'd won, and made generous division of the spoils. But the prisoners, the defeated, had really struck it unlucky! Not that there was anything they could do about it. And that's how it goes in war – one man's gain is another man's loss.

The war lasted long – it continues still – and it was perilous and fierce. It lasted as long as King Richard lived, for the French were deeply envious of him; but their resentment was futile: none could ever get the better of him. Many times they tested him, but the more they tried the more daunted they became: they paid very dearly, as many of their most eminent and noble were taken prisoner. If they escaped his clutches they took care not to let it happen again, and on it went, the war, with no decisive end, till the king of France was sick of it: he was pouring his resources into it and all in vain. And the tireless King Richard had him on so tight a leash that he didn't know which way to turn – no matter where he went King Richard was there confronting him, giving fierce battle; and though fortunes were mixed, the king of France's men were not best pleased when they were on the end of a battering and stripped of gear as they often were.

Finally the French had had enough, and a good few went over to King Richard – I know that to be true: it was seen and heard by many – which was a great loss and vexation to the king of France. He called a privy council of his barons and magnates to discuss what he could do, and one of them declared outright:

'Unless you have recourse to the court of Rome, King Richard's going to wear you down: you'll never beat him off.'

The king of France was shrewd for sure, more cunning than a fox, and realised there was no other way. He summoned one of his clerks and supplied him with the relics he'd be needing in Rome: you get nowhere at the court of Rome without greasing palms – it's the only language they understand – and the relics of those martyrs Rufin and Albin,[379] revered in Rome, they always go down well; they count far more than law and principle. That's how things work there: if you've none of those holy relics you'll be hard pressed to get through the door.

It's down on record that the papal consistory decided to support the king of France, and sent a cardinal to settle matters for him without delay. His name was Master Peter,[380] a wily, sly, deceitful man: with his background he'd become adept at double-speak. When he arrived in France he was joyfully received by the king and all his barons: they sensed he was clever and cunning – just what they needed – and made a great fuss of him. The king drew him to his side and explained the whole situation and placed himself entirely in his hands (and lavished gifts and promises), confident that he knew how to handle matters and effect a favourable outcome. This cardinal, Master Peter, whose word was never to be trusted, told him he would broker peace or a lengthy truce, and the king accepted this, realising he had little choice: there was no other way forward. So he sent able, courteous envoys to King Richard, earnestly requesting that he should come and confer, without delay, between Le Goulet and Vernon; after delivering their message they specified the day when the two kings should meet and talk.

King Richard graciously agreed and, in brief, on the appointed day[381] he came to Le Goulet[382] with a great company of barons, seeking to make no presumptuous claims, truly, only to recover his own land. But the slippery King Philip, with his customary hauteur, treated the conference with contempt and didn't deign to appear; all high and mighty he stayed away. King Richard knew exactly what he was up to – there was no mystery to his little game; but patience, measure and moderation are valuable qualities, and he waited till it was clear that King Philip in his arrogance wouldn't attend the talks. But then the legate[383] came on his behalf – a man with an amazing talent for deviousness and shiftiness, for twisting words when it suited him. Sallower than a kite's foot,[384] he came before King Richard and played the saintly, pious hermit, oozing humility. He hailed the king in the name of God and the Curia, saying they cherished and respected him as the son of Holy Church, and King Richard greeted him in turn with

---

[379] There is a subtle play on words here: Rufin (red) and Albin (white) are to be understood as gold and silver.
[380] Peter of Capua, appointed legate to France by Innocent III in August 1198.
[381] 13 January 1199.
[382] A few miles down the Seine from Vernon.
[383] i.e. the cardinal, Peter of Capua.
[384] Kites do indeed have yellow feet, and the comparison with the talons of a bird of prey is of course carefully chosen.

great courtesy as a learned cleric and cardinal and spiritual father. The cardinal, thinking the time had come to say his piece, and confident that he could twist the king round his little finger, said:

'Sire, the king of France has sent me here; he is full of goodwill and would gladly make peace if you'll agree.'

'How,' the king asked, 'can we secure a lasting peace? I ask this as one deprived of what is rightfully his. When he returns my land and my possessions I shall serve him well. And I'll forgive him the wrongs and damage he's done me, and the broken oaths and pledges he made that when he returned to France[385] he'd leave my land and my people untroubled and untouched till forty days after my own return. I'll forgive him all this – I'll not say another word – if he's sincere about wanting peace. But otherwise, good sir, there can be none between us, truly.'

'Sire,' Master Peter replied, 'I wouldn't dare promise you that. No one could persuade him to give back all he's taken. His counsellors wouldn't approve and never will.'

'Then God be with you!' said the king. 'In that case there'll be no peace between us as long as I'm fit to ride a horse! You can tell him that from me!'

'Oh, sire!' said the cardinal. 'It's a wicked sin that you're locked in bitter war! If this carries on it'll cost us the holy land of Jerusalem! Seek compromise, in God's name, that the Holy Land may be recovered: it'll be in dire straits unless we take action! It'll soon be finished, taken, ruined, and Christendom's cause will be lost!'

The king leaned towards him and said: 'If my land had been left in peace, securely mine, so that I hadn't needed to return, all Syria would have been purged and cleared of infidels! They'd never have had dominion again! But the king of France has wronged me so, inflicted so much harm! He was behind my capture and my long imprisonment, and has striven long to rob me of my inheritance – and will carry on! But if it please God he'll never succeed!'

There was a moment's pause; then the cardinal changed tack and said to the king: 'Hear me, sire: if a lengthy truce could be agreed between the two of you, without loss to either party, it would be a blessing.'

'Good master Peter,' the king replied, 'if a truce could be secured without my suffering loss of land or status I'd welcome it – I'd settle it for good! State the conditions. I'll listen and you'll have my full attention, and if what you say is acceptable I'll gladly agree.'

'Truly, sire,' said the cardinal, 'neither party can have all he wants – that simply isn't possible. But let each of you keep what he holds, and on that basis let the oaths of peace be sworn.'

'A curse on such a truce!' cried the king. 'What are you saying? This goes against everything you've said so far! It's vile to see a gentleman go back on his word and deceive and lie! What do you take me for? He has my castles and my land, and you come here and ask me to leave him with them, free and clear?

---

[385] i.e. from the Third Crusade, which he left before Richard (above, p. 130).

There'll be no such truce as long as I live, please God! There's no chance of talking me into this! It's too much, far too much to ask!'

'I pray you, in God's name, dear lord,' the cardinal pleaded, 'be mindful of the plight of the Holy Land, left bereft!'

'I'd have rescued it in no time,' said the king, 'if he hadn't forced me to return by doing all he could to rob me! But listen: so you don't think me intransigent, I'll grant a truce for five years, on the understanding that he can keep my castles in pledge, but he'll not have a single foot of my rightful land outside them.'

'I accept that, sire,' said the cardinal then. 'That's as fair a proposal as I've ever heard. But the Curia requests that you return one of its men; you're holding him prisoner wrongly and unjustly.'

'Am I?' said the king. 'Indeed I'm not.'

'I tell you, sire, it's no use denying it. It's the bishop of Beauvais I mean; he's under Rome's protection, and it's wrong that you hold a man such as he, anointed, consecrated.'

'By my life, there's nothing holy about him! He's no true Christian! You've lost all credibility now! It wasn't as a bishop that I captured him but as a notable knight, fully armed and helmet laced! Is this what you've been angling towards? Listen, Master Silver-Tongue, you're not as clever as you think! If you weren't here as their envoy, your Curia wouldn't protect you from a hiding – you could take the marks back to the Pope, to show him what I can do! Does he take me for a fool? That's how he treated me when I sent to him for help from far away, telling him I'd been captured while on God's service. I implored him to do as he should and send me aid, but he didn't want to know – he didn't lift a finger! And now he appeals to me on behalf of a war-mongering, thieving, arsonist tyrant who's been ravaging and pillaging my land both day and night! Get out of here, Master Traitor, you false, lying, deceitful agent of a simoniacal church! Make sure I never catch sight of you in street or field!'

The legate was gone that instant – he couldn't leave fast enough. Nothing would have induced him to go back (even if he'd left his crucifix) – he feared it would cost him his balls! He jumped on his horse and didn't draw rein till he reached the king of France, in a terrible lather, like a frightened deer. The French were alarmed to see him arrive in such a state. He said to King Philip:

'That king you're at odds with is hardly a charmer! He's no lamb, that's for sure – he's fiercer than a lion! All the same, I'd brought him round as you asked me to, and he'd agreed to a five-year truce – it was all settled and we were about to shake on it; but then I asked him to release the bishop of Beauvais and he flew into a rage and turned on me, glowering and blazing red – I thought he was about to attack me!'

Some of the French started laughing at this and whispered to each other: 'This legate's nearly sick with fear! King Richard's no chicken[386] – he doesn't scare easily; he clearly thinks he can avenge the wrongs he's suffered.'

---

[386] Literally 'nanny-goat'.

King Richard meanwhile was still speechless with anger: he stormed off to his chamber, snorting and fuming like a wounded boar; he had the doors shut fast behind him and flung himself down on his bed. Not a soul[387] dared enter or even knock upon the door – till the Marshal arrived, staff of office in hand; he called loudly at the door and it was opened at once. He found the king lying there in a furious mood, and said to him:

'Sire, you've no reason for this anger. So help me God, my good dear lord, you should be laughing, not raging – you've won hands down! There's no way out for the king of France: he must either make peace or agree to a truce. So take the land that's rightly yours and leave him the castles in pledge till the next crusade. When he's getting nothing from the land and has to maintain the castles at his own expense he'll feel it's as costly as funding a war! That's what'll happen, I swear! I'm sure they'll be back in the morning.'

Meanwhile the legate was telling the king of France that he could secure a truce on condition that the castles would remain in pledge with him but King Richard would have the land; there was no alternative – unless he agreed to relinquish the land there would be war. The attendant barons of France advised him to accept these terms, since there was nothing else for it; so did the legate – though he swore he wouldn't go back to King Richard: they'd have to send someone else – he didn't want to die just yet!

So the good archbishop of Reims, never one to be confrontational or uncivil, went next day with a company of calm and level-headed souls. King Richard was in his chapel where the mass of the Holy Trinity was being gloriously sung. When he heard of their arrival he went to meet them at once, and he and the archbishop greeted each other with mutual pleasure and respect. And so it was, truly, that the archbishop of Reims saw the truce secured and signed on the terms outlined above, exactly so, and when he returned with the news it was to the satisfaction of the king of France and the relief of the French, who'd been waging war reluctantly.

On leaving there, King Richard summoned William le Queu and his band of retainers, and ordered them to keep close watch on the French garrisons of the castles and see that they took nothing from his lands and fiefs outside their walls. They did this so effectively that they stopped the French even daring to draw water from the well outside Beaudemont![388] And outside Gisors, le Queu and his men exacted all the usual tolls and dues, not caring a jot if it upset the garrison! That wasn't going to stop them!

The Death of King Richard

So that's the way things stood. But Fortune, ever casting down the good and elevating the wicked, wouldn't let it stay so for long – She's always quick to

---

[387] Literally 'neither monk nor novice', and the clerical allusion may be significant after Richard's fury with the papal legate.
[388] Near Les Andelys.

afflict and sink us all. King Richard, who had pressing matters in many places, left those parts and made for the Limousin,[389] where the viscount was robbing him of castles – alas that they were ever built, and would that the instigators had been flayed alive! He went and laid siege to Nontron;[390] but he hadn't been there long before a Satan, a traitor, a minister of the devil, loosed from the battlement a poisoned bolt, inflicting such a wound on the finest prince on earth that he was bound to die, to the grievous cost of all the world. It does not do to speak of his death: the grief of it, which still afflicts us all, will not permit it, so I shall say no more. The moment he felt the blow he was stunned and sapped of strength: he feared he would not survive. He immediately had letters written to the Marshal – with the royal seal attached and finely, forcibly worded – explaining what had befallen him and making him lord and master of the castle of Rouen and bidding him guard and take charge of his treasury and everything kept there; and he told the messenger to be sharp and sure he kept the instructions strictly secret, delivered only where intended.

The messenger was brisk and bright and prudent, and went straight to Le Vaudreuil, where the Marshal had been called along with a number of barons, I believe, to settle a dispute between two lords, Engelger de Bohun and Sir Ralph d'Arderne. The messenger arrived and found them there together. He didn't think it right to announce the grim news in the hearing of all, so he told only the Marshal and the archbishop.[391] They both heard the contents of the letter; they were dismayed and filled with sorrow, but set about doing as bidden, informing the barons that the king wished the Marshal to be guardian, constable and castellan of Rouen, keeper of the tower and the king's possessions thereabouts. This was done at once; but the grief and loss that will beset us forever occurred just three days later, with the death of the noble King Richard, valiant and courtly, generous and liberal, daring and all-conquering, who, had he lived, would have won world-wide fame and dominion, and honour and mastery and lordship over Saracens and Christians and all the peoples on earth. He would now be holding sway everywhere – except in the kingdom of France, which he never sought to crush but chose to leave in peace.

It was his kinsman Thierry[392] who brought the news, and he brought it all too soon. The date? That should indeed be told: it was the eve of Palm Sunday.[393] The Marshal was preparing for bed, and was having his boots removed when

---

[389] Richard, having spent a month or more at Chinon, set out for the Limousin in the middle of March 1199.

[390] 'Lautron'. Meyer suggested that this was Nontron. Nontron is south-west of Châlus, the castle where, according to most accounts, Richard was mortally wounded on 26 March 1199.

[391] The archbishop of Canterbury (Hubert Walter), who was in Normandy at the time of Richard's death and was present at the settlement made between the two lords at Le Vaudreuil on 7 April.

[392] 'Tiesri li neis'. I take the otherwise mysterious 'neis' to be a scribal slip for 'nies', an inexact medieval expression of kinship which can mean nephew, grandson or something slightly more distant, and Richard did have a relative named Thierry, the son of his cousin Count Philip of Flanders.

[393] 10 April 1199.

the heart-rending news arrived; he was terribly distressed. He pulled his boots back on and made ready with all speed, and left the tower of Rouen and went to find the archbishop who'd taken lodging at Le Pré.[394] He was on the very point of retiring, and was startled to see the Marshal arrive at such an hour – and then filled with dread at what he feared his coming meant.

'Come,' he said, 'give me your news.'

'Truly, dear sir, it's the worst,' said the Marshal. 'We are all plunged in grief and tears and woe this night. Thierry has brought us written word that my lord is dead. It is grim, dire news indeed.'

The archbishop was aghast and cried: 'Alas! Alas! Who can fail to be stricken with grief? All prowess now is dead! What comfort can there be if the king is gone? None, so help me God! I know of no one who can protect the realm or save us from any peril. The kingdom is doomed to disaster, grief and poverty! Before we know it the French will be attacking us and plundering and taking all, for no one will be able to resist!'

'We must decide, sir, and quickly,' said the Marshal, 'whom to make king.'

'It's clear to me,' the archbishop replied, 'that it should rightly be Arthur.'[395]

'Oh, sir,' said the Marshal, 'I don't think that would be wise. I don't advise it at all. He's surrounded by treacherous counsellors and he's arrogant and aloof. If we give him lordship over us he'll seek to do us down: he feels no love for the English.[396] I wouldn't go down that road. What about Count John? In all true conscience, I'd say he's the most immediate heir of his father's and his brother's land.'

'Is that your wish, then, Marshal?' the archbishop replied.

'It is, sir; I think it's only right. Without question, the son is the nearer heir to his father's land than the grandson.[397] We should see that that's observed.'

'And so it shall be, Marshal. But I tell you truly, you'll never have regretted anything you've done so much.'

'I hear you,' said the Marshal, 'but I still say it should be so.'

King John's Wars in France

The Marshal sent an envoy to England to take possession of the land, the castles and cities and all the royal fortresses; Sir John of Earley it was, I should tell you, who promptly carried out his commands in full. The archbishop stayed behind with the Marshal, who accepted his advice in all matters, having always

---

[394] i.e. the abbey of Notre-Dame-du-Pré on the opposite bank of the Seine.
[395] Richard's nephew Arthur I, duke of Brittany. In 1190 Richard had named him heir to the throne in preference to his brother John. He was only twelve years old at the time of Richard's death.
[396] Literally 'those of the land'.
[397] John was Henry II's son; Arthur was his grandson, being the son of his son Geoffrey. In fact, the rules of succession were far from clear: Norman law favoured John as the only surviving son of Henry II; Angevin law favoured Arthur as the heir of Geoffrey who had been older than John.

found him worthy of trust. Count John came to meet them, and what happened was this: as soon as they could they made him duke;[398] the Normans recognised him as such but the lords of Gascony and the Limousin, of Poitou, Anjou and Brittany did not – they had no wish to be ruled by him. Duke John, realising how opposed they were, made his way to those parts and made all manner of generous concessions to win them round, granting their every demand – and how he came to regret it! They respected him all the less! It won him neither their love nor their esteem, and they showed him no obedience but opposed him time and again.

In any event, he quickly crossed the sea and was crowned in London.[399] Liberal gifts were distributed there – or so they say: I wasn't there myself. But then he returned immediately, as soon as he could arrange passage. He paid homage to the king of France, duly becoming his liegeman;[400] but the king never respected this or behaved as a liege lord should – he rather worked against him all his life. That needs to be said but I shan't go on.

King John then headed straight to Poitou, making a grand return; the archbishop of Bordeaux and the barons in the region came to him there. And it was now that he separated from his wife,[401] a divorce which, it's said, proved to do him no favours, but I shan't go into that now.

He then led a great army into Gascony in a very successful campaign: he won a hoard of booty, and had he proceeded wisely he'd have been rich for a long, long time – his boasting about it was rich, for sure. The Marshal said:[402]

'I'm delighted about these spoils, my lord, even if I don't profit myself! However you decide to divide your gains, I'd have you share in mine: here are five hundred silver marks I've won in this land – I present them to you. God grant that the favour be returned!'

'Truly, Marshal,' the king replied, 'you're hardly greedy for riches if you're willing to give me all your winnings! You'll be well rewarded indeed!'

So he had thanks for his gift, but I don't know about the reward.

It was now, I understand, that the count of Angoulême had his daughter secretly taken from the count of La Marche.[403] News of this reached court: it was pleasing to some and not to others. And it wasn't a good move: the count of

---

[398] i.e. of Normandy. He was made duke at Rouen on 25 April 1199.
[399] At Westminster on 27 May.
[400] John returned to France about a month after his coronation, but did not pay homage to Philip until the following year: it was one of the terms of the Treaty of Le Goulet at the end of May 1200.
[401] Isabel, daughter of the earl of Gloucester. She was his second cousin, and their closeness in blood made the arrangement of the divorce straightforward.
[402] Marshal's appearance from out of the blue suggests there may be an accidental omission in the MS; but the author may simply have expected his audience to assume that Marshal stayed with the king throughout.
[403] Adémar (Aymer) III, count of Angoulême, had promised his daughter Isabelle to Hugh de Lusignan, count of La Marche, but then, before they were married, had her smuggled away to be given instead to King John, who was anxious to prevent a union which (since Isabelle was heir to the county of Angoulême) would have made Lusignan worryingly strong.

La Marche and his followers, enraged at the damsel's abduction, stormed away, knowing as they did that some of those who'd colluded in it were there at court. I can't explain in detail, but this was the initial cause of the disastrous war that was to cost the king his land. The king then took the damsel and married her; he had her acknowledged as lady and queen of England and she was crowned in London.[404]

He then returned with his barons, his queen and his court to Normandy, but it wasn't long before he was under attack from the one who was so keen to seize his land.[405] The war lasted a long while, until they finally met to parley and left on good terms, agreeing to suspend hostilities, and as a mark of concord and friendship King John promised to give his niece, the daughter of the king of Spain, in marriage to Louis.[406] This duly happened, but it did nothing to halt the king of France's excesses – he continued to pursue his every goal. It would take me forever to recount all the dealings between him and King John – they went on and on – but the more concessions King John made, the more King Philip did him down and turned all to his own advantage. No matter what land or money he had from him, he'd instantly be back on the attack. I can't tell you the huge sums – they'd be hard to calculate! – that King John gave him time and again; and King Philip paid him back by seeking every chance and pretext to attack him anew, seizing land and castles, inflicting all the harm he could. He advanced on Arques[407] and besieged it with a mighty army, assailing it with catapults and mangonels, bombarding the tower with missiles night and day; but they made no impression, for William de Mortemer[408] and the other defenders did their duty well. If I were to describe it in full I'd be digressing, which is never a virtue and you'd think me inept!

On the other hand it would be wrong not to tell how King John marched with a mighty force, outnumbering the enemy, to Mirebeau,[409] where his mother was being besieged: had he delayed she would soon have been captured, for the besieging force was great – it would have been disastrous: had she not been quickly rescued she'd have been in dire straits. It was quite a clash, and the besiegers really knew about it: they paid a hefty price; in the fierce battle that followed they were made to regret their presumption. To record the deeds of each man, one by one, would be taxing and exhausting – I'd never be done! The enemy, who had no choice but to fight, mounted a sterling defence, resisting capture with all their might. There were many blows dealt and returned in full, mail-rings dashed from many a hauberk, helms and ventails staved and split to

---

[404] At Westminster, on 8 October 1200.
[405] i.e. King Philip of France.
[406] John promised his niece, Blanche of Castile, to Louis, King Philip's eldest son, but the order of events given by the poet here is confused: this promise had been made at Le Goulet in May 1200, a year before the conflict just described.
[407] Now known as Arques-la-Bataille, near Dieppe; the ruins of its impressive castle still dominate the town. Philip's siege began in July 1202.
[408] Already mentioned as a defender of Verneuil (above, p. 137), this prominent officer of the dukes of Normandy had been constable of Arques since at least 1194.
[409] Between Chinon and Poitiers. John arrived, taking the enemy by surprise, during the night of 31 July–1 August 1202.

the skull, men hewing and hammering, pounding heads, seizing bridles, wielding maces. Many tried to flee the field, unable to endure: it was all too much. And the outcome of the day was that King John was victorious, and his bitterest foes were taken captive, whether they liked it or not. Arthur was among those captured in the battle: he'd been ill advised to go there,[410] and all his followers were rounded up and found themselves in harsh imprisonment. King John had won so much honour and prestige that day that his war would have been over and done had Destiny been kinder – and had it not been for his unfailing pride which was always his downfall. He was overjoyed by his success in taking such a rich haul; he'd surprised the proud Poitevins and Bretons and Angevins and trapped them so decisively that not a single one escaped.

A monk set off from Mirebeau and pressed on night and day till he found the Marshal. As chance would have it, the three earls worthy of high renown were all together: the good, valiant, upright, loyal Earl Marshal;[411] the good earl of Salisbury,[412] who counts Largesse as his mother and whose banner-bearer is high and perfect Prowess; and the good earl of Warenne[413] who, imbued with largesse, always aspires to prowess and honour, unfailingly. So this monk, spurring on from town to town, never stopping day or night, found them at Anglesqueville.[414] He eloquently delivered his message to the Marshal and his companions, who listened attentively. He said:

'I bring you good, true and welcome news that I've heard and witnessed myself – I can't wait to pass it on! I've come from Mirebeau, my lords, and if a word I say is idle or false you can abuse me as you wish! I promise you King John has captured Arthur, along with Sir Geoffrey of Lusignan! The count of La Marche is a prisoner, too! All the eminent barons who were siding with Arthur and supporting him in his war are now captives of the king – including Savari de Mauléon!'[415]

The Marshal was overjoyed at what he'd heard – as were the others: they hadn't had such welcome, heartening news for a very long while. And he said to the monk:

'You must take this news from Poitou straight to the French army besieging Arques – to the count of Eu![416] It'll cheer him up no end! Tell him all!'

'Have pity, sir!' the monk replied. 'If I tell him this he'll be so enraged he'll kill me on the spot! Send someone else!'

---

[410] By King Philip.
[411] John had elevated Marshal to the status of earl in May 1199.
[412] William 'Longsword', 3rd earl of Salisbury. The present tense used in the following phrase implies that this part of the poem was written before his death in March 1226.
[413] The present tense makes it clear that this is William de Warenne, 5th earl of Surrey (who was to marry Marshal's daughter Maud in 1225), and not his father Hamelin de Warenne, who died in the year of the events described, 1202.
[414] Probably Anglesqueville-sur-Saane, part of Marshal's fief of Longueville (-sur-Scie) south of Dieppe.
[415] Son of a prominent Poitevin lord, Savari was imprisoned at Corfe Castle but released in 1204, when John won him over and later made him seneschal of Poitou.
[416] This is Raoul (Ralph) d'Issoudun. Marshal directs the news specifically to him because he was a Lusignan, son of the defeated count of La Marche! He had acquired the county of Eu through marriage to the countess, Alix.

'By God, monk, no excuses! It's you who's going – no one else! It's not the custom in this land to kill messengers. So no dallying now – be off: you'll find him at the siege.'

So the monk set off at once – he had no choice! – and swiftly made his way to Arques where he managed to find the count of Eu. He told him the news from Poitou (saying he knew it to be true as he'd witnessed it himself), word for word and point by point, omitting nothing. The count had been expecting very different news, and when he heard the monk's report he turned dark as thunder and wouldn't utter a word. Stunned by what the monk had said, he went to lie down in his tent. He fell back and lay distraught, devastated, not knowing what to do or say, and not wanting to repeat to anyone the news that distressed him so.

While he lay in this anguished state, a letter was delivered to the king of France reporting the disastrous news – which didn't die down but spread, right through the French army, to the dismay of all. The king of France was beside himself: he said he'd never suffered such a blow (though his return from Jerusalem had been one such – it had earned him more reproach by far!). He didn't want to linger – he ordered his men to strike camp at once and dismantle their siege-engines. You'd have heard the carpenters at it then, battering and hammering, demolishing and breaking up, destroying in very little time what had taken an age to build. The defenders had never known such joy as they felt on seeing this: it was clear that the king whose presence had caused them so much grief intended to withdraw. Knights and soldiers armed and formed a strong rearguard, as if they had reason to fear pursuit and attack from an enemy force.

But never mind them! Spies, let me tell you, came to the three earls at once and reported the French withdrawal. They were delighted, of course, and said:

'Let's go and see what they're up to!'

Lightly armed, they hurried away and set off after the army that was marching in tight and strong formation – the French are very good at that when they think they're up against it: they always withdraw in prudent, well-ordered fashion. The three counts pressed on swiftly, and a large force with them; but when the French army saw them coming they were undaunted: they feared nothing with their strong rearguard. One of them went and told the king:

'By the faith I owe you, sire, there's a great force pursuing us.'

'Who are they?' asked the king. 'Are they very close?'

'On the ridge behind – look there.'

'It's the Marshal, sure enough, and the earl of Salisbury with him – and unless I'm much mistaken that's the earl of Warenne. They're intent on doing damage if they see the chance. They don't know my mind – but they will do soon enough if they don't back off!'

He summoned William des Barres and commanded him: 'Go quickly, good sir: take three hundred knights and head along that valley so they don't see you till you're upon them. If God grants that you capture one of those three earls, we may well recover one of our most valued friends – I'm confident we shall!'

Des Barres promptly did the king's bidding: he took three hundred knights and advanced down the valley, unseen by the three earls, and then confronted them, fully armed. Being unarmed the earls and their men fell back at once, knowing they'd have no chance against an armed attack; but truly, if they'd been properly armed they would never have retreated before some saddles had been emptied and the battle fought to a decisive end. But in serious combat men without their arms are inviting wounds and disaster. Des Barres went back to the king under no illusions: he knew the enemy had retreated because they were lightly clad, and would never have done so if they'd been armed.

So the king headed back to France[417] disconsolate, while the three earls made their way to Rouen with their knights and baggage train and all their men before them. The Marshal was eager to find lodgings as soon as could be. The burgesses and citizens of every degree heard of the earls' approach and were overjoyed; they mounted at once and rode out to meet them amid much rejoicing. The Marshal, seeing them coming, shared his thoughts with his dear companions, saying:

'Listen, sirs: if you fancy fine wines and luscious fruit tonight, and gifts and entertainment, leave the talking to me! I've an idea of what to say, and if it works I promise you'll have plenty!'

The others happily agreed. The citizens rode up to the Marshal and greeted him first and then the rest in turn as they arrived behind. They returned their greetings courteously, and were welcomed with great joy and honour.

'Sir,' said Matthew le Gros, then mayor of Rouen, 'where is the king of France headed? We feared he was planning to besiege our city.'

'He's not far away,' the Marshal replied. 'He's camped in the country nearby. If he's heading this way we wouldn't want to leave you undefended; that's why we've come with all our men and gear.'

The citizens were overjoyed by this and thanked the three earls and the others deeply, saying: 'That's splendid! You're doing your duty, sirs – the honourable and proper thing. Every living soul in the city we place at your command.'

Into the city they rode, and as the townsfolk saw them coming they hailed them with all joy and honour. The three earls, I understand, took lodging in the same house. Dinner was prepared for them, and when it was time to eat they washed at once and took their seats. The citizens went to great pains to provide for them, competing to present the finest gifts, to please and serve them best. Some gave clear, full-bodied wines, shining, sweet and fine indeed, others spiced or flavoured with cloves, the best they could seek out and find – and they took care to taste them before they sent them to the earls, to be sure they'd be acceptable! After the main dishes came the fruit, enough apples and pears and hazelnuts for all to have plenty. The streets were packed with people bringing it all, bustling and barging! The Marshal had been true to his word, and they laughed to see the heaving throng!

But I must return now and get back on track; a wise man will always retrace his steps to ensure he doesn't lose his way.

---

[417] As noted previously, this refers to his own domain as opposed to the duchy of Normandy.

It was William des Roches[418] who had urged King John to go to the relief of Mirebeau, and it was thanks to him that he'd triumphed there. How? That's well worth telling: nothing would have induced King John to go had it not been for William's great enterprise and daring (which were later to be the king's undoing). And let me tell you, no matter what anyone says, that of all the deeds of chivalrous prowess and courage and skill performed by both sides at Mirebeau, William des Roches's surpassed them all. He had three fine horses killed beneath him outside the gate; but still he tirelessly, tenaciously, relentlessly cleared the way before him – no one could resist his onslaught: he was no dove of peace![419] This I declare: it was thanks to him that all those enemies of King John, those supporters of Arthur, were taken prisoner. It should have been perfectly plain to King John that it was through William des Roches's energy and guidance that all was won, but he couldn't see it – or perhaps chose not to. Sir William came and spoke with him in private, saying:

'Sire, I would have you remember the promises you made me a while ago. You know what I mean; you should be mindful of what you said. King Philip, wily and persuasive as he is, promised my lady and her son[420] and their supporters – including me: I was with them at that time – that if we sided with him he would give my lord[421] Poitou, Gascony, Maine and Anjou. That was his promise, on the basis of which we joined him in a firm alliance. [He advanced on Ballon][422] and besieged it and eventually took it by force, but when the time came to hand it over to my lord he preferred to keep it for himself! I knew then that the pledges of the king of France, his words and his promises, weren't worth a jot! So that night – this is the perfect truth – I came to you at Bourg-le-Roi[423] where I found you in a poor way, short of good men. I told you I wished to talk in private, one to one, just the two of us; and there you promised me – you swore to me absolutely – that if I could return Anjou to you, and all Poitou and Maine, along with my lord and lady, too, so that we were all good friends, you would be guided by me in all matters.'

'Yes, I did say so,' the king replied, 'but my nephew has acted against me dreadfully, as you've seen.'

'Sire, you don't know if it was of his own volition or at the prompting of someone else. It would never have been the former, that's for certain. Let me handle this: I think I can resolve things to your satisfaction.'

'Very well. Granted. I agree. Come with me to Chinon.'

---

[418] Having been a prominent member of Henry II's household (see above, p. 119), William des Roches (originally from Château-du-Loir, between Le Mans and Tours) had acquired great holdings of land through marriage and was now seneschal of Anjou.
[419] Literally 'he had not sworn a peace treaty': a facetious phrase meaning 'he was thoroughly fired up'.
[420] i.e. Arthur (King John's nephew) and his mother Constance, widow of Geoffrey of Brittany.
[421] i.e. Arthur.
[422] In Maine, near Le Mans. This phrase is accidentally omitted in the MS, but Meyer's correction is highly plausible: as he notes, the incident in October 1199 is recorded by Roger of Howden (*Chronica*, IV, p. 96).
[423] The MS reads '*Bourg-la-Reine*', but this is surely mistaken; Bourg-le-Roi is just north of Ballon on the way to Alençon.

Sir William trusted him and went; but the king's conceit and pride, which blinded him to reason, were ever growing, and I can assure you that he lost the hearts of the barons of the land before he crossed to England. And when he reached Chinon[424] he kept his prisoners in such dire distress that all who witnessed their cruel treatment thought it base and shameful.

Sir William reminded him what he'd agreed; the king told him not to worry and to come with him to Le Mans. Sir William believed him, but the king's arrogance was growing still, and Pride makes its subjects blind to reason – and is their downfall. The king and his men made their way to Le Mans, but truly, he never kept his promise to the lord des Roches – and des Roches made him pay for it: upset at this treatment, he went and sided with the king of France. King John had made a big mistake in not keeping faith – it was a bad and unworthy move. It was through Sir William des Roches that he was to lose Anjou, Maine and Poitou.

The Poitevins took the king for a ride: they promised to support and serve him well – they gave him their word and hostages – but they didn't keep their pledges. And it didn't go well when the king took the word and hostages of Geoffrey of Lusignan – how little sense he showed then! Intoxicated by their sweet-talk, he ended up releasing the lot (except Savari de Mauléon: he kept him captive for a long time); and the moment the Poitevins were free they did what they were bound to do. And what would that be? Deceiving their lord and forging alliances with others! That's always been their way![425]

But moving on: the king now went to Normandy and found his land and its borders ever more beset by war, as the French, so hostile to him, ravaged it night and day, abetted by those who'd turned and sided with them. Anything that turns is rotten and makes everything turn that it touches. Turncoats likewise stink of rottenness – but God has kept our people[426] from such foul practice: we'll never be regarded so; no lousy song will be sung about them having ever turned. Anyway, the king made his way through Normandy – and don't let anyone tell you he took straight routes! He was in constant fear of harassment from the turncoats, and when he left Verneuil to go to Rouen, he went by way of Laigle or Breteuil and then Lisieux, Caen and Bonneville![427] If you want to know why, I'll tell you – and mark it well: if a man doesn't know who's his enemy, and is feeling ever vulnerable, he has to beware of everyone.

Meanwhile the queen[428] was at Chinon, too close for comfort to[429] the Poitevins, the Bretons and the Angevins who would gladly have dragged her from the castle given half a chance. The king was made well aware of this, and didn't

---

[424] In early August 1202.
[425] See the comment about rebellious Poitevins above, p. 44.
[426] '*les noz*': this may well mean specifically people associated with Marshal's family.
[427] The route becoming ever more circuitous! Laigle (now L'Aigle) is just to the west and Breteuil just to the north of Verneuil, but Lisieux, Caen and Bonneville (-sur-Touques) are many miles from Verneuil and Rouen.
[428] i.e. John's second wife, Isabelle of Angoulême.
[429] Literally 'on the border with', Chinon being close to the borders of the counties of Anjou and Poitou.

delay: taking a great force of knights and mercenaries he set off at once. But let me tell you first why the king failed to win the hearts of his men and draw them to his side. Why was it? Truly, it's because he let Louvrecaire[430] mistreat the people so, plundering the land of everything in his path as if it were enemy territory. And that's not all: if he abused their wives and daughters there'd not be a penny in compensation!

The king headed from Sées to Alençon, where he stopped only long enough to have dinner with Count Robert,[431] who acted shamefully: after the king had gifted him money and kissed him on the lips, he abandoned him that very day, switching sides in a base betrayal, allying with the king of France, paying him homage and handing the city over to the French. Shameful is the man who willingly acts dishonourably. Before King John even reached Le Mans came repeated reports that the count had defected to the king of France, and that the French had surer control of Alençon than he had ever had. He was shocked by the news and cried:

'Ah! Ah! What cruel treachery! How Robert has wronged me, betraying me so soon after taking my money!'

He was so upset that they struggled to calm him, and he would discuss no plans with anyone: he trusted no one now.

The road to Chinon and the surrounding country were solidly in the hands of foes who would have rejoiced to have him in their grasp – and wouldn't have dealt with him kindly. He wasn't inclined to carry on, and was on the point of turning back when Sir Peter de Préaux – a fine, upstanding, good-natured and spirited knight – daringly managed to bring the queen to safety in Le Mans: it must have caused some howling among the French, but the king was delighted and gave him warm and fulsome thanks.

The king now left Le Mans with a sense of achievement, in higher spirits than before, having got what he desired. But he didn't go via Alençon – he couldn't have got back to his land without a fight; he looked for a different route, by way of Mamers and the Bellêmois,[432] and so returned to his land and his castles and cities. It would still have been a rich inheritance indeed, if only he could have held it in peace, but it couldn't then be freely his – or his successor's since – for the one who wanted all for himself[433] would not allow it. A dearth of money and friends was King John's downfall – as it has been for many a man: we've often witnessed that.

And the one who was bent on having all proceeded to inflict as much damage as he could. The king of France now went to lay siege to Conches,[434] and King John sent the Marshal to him, asking him to have pity on his lord and make peace with him: he would agree to it at any price. But the insatiably greedy one

---

[430] A notorious and hated mercenary who enjoyed King John's protection.
[431] Robert III, count of Alençon. King John was with him on 19 January 1203.
[432] To the east of Alençon.
[433] i.e. the king of France.
[434] Conches-en-Ouche was an important castle west of Évreux and north of Verneuil. Philip besieged it in late April 1203.

raised all possible obstacles, till the Marshal realised there was no chance of peace. Then he said:

'Good sire, I'd appreciate it if you'd explain one thing: in France it's the custom for traitors to be treated as scum – burnt at the stake or pulled apart by horses! But now they're part of the establishment: they're all lords and masters!'

'That's fair enough,' the king replied. 'It's all a question of business now – and they're like shit-rags: once you've done your business, you chuck them down the privy.'

The Marshal left it at that. He took his leave and made his way to Falaise where King John was staying, and reported what had been said.

The king went next to Rouen.[435] It was now that the city was ravaged by a fire[436] that raged high and low on every side, reaching even the keep of the citadel, which would have been utterly destroyed but for Stephen Longchamp, then a prisoner there[437] – and what a fine prisoner! So manfully did he strive that he saved the tower from the flames! One of his friends reported this to the king, who was most grateful to him. His release from imprisonment was openly discussed; the Marshal said to the king:

'Hear me, sire: you're not well off for friends! If you weaken your position further you'll be strengthening your foe! And a man who boosts his enemy deserves to be attacked!'

'Anyone who's scared can run!' King John replied. 'You won't see *me* run, Marshal – ever! If others flee I could stand my ground as well as you would, anywhere!'

'I know that, sire – I don't doubt it,' said the Marshal. 'But you, sire, wise and powerful and of high lineage as you are, and meant to govern us all, you're ignoring the seeds of disaffection. It's better for us all that you take heed. It's only good sense, I'd say.'

When the king heard this he was so enraged that he was utterly speechless: he might as well have been skewered with a lance clean through the heart. He wouldn't stay a moment longer, and stormed off to a chamber. I don't know exactly what happened then, but next morning he jumped in a boat and sailed up the Seine to Le Pré, to the monks at Grandmont.[438] When his attendants didn't find him in the hall or in his chamber or his bed they were less than amused that he'd slipped away. As soon as they were all assembled they mounted and raced off over the bridge and out of the town and followed his route via Trianon towards Bonneville,[439] which he'd had newly fortified. (He'd have done better

---

[435] In August 1203.
[436] This terrible fire had in fact occurred earlier, in October 1200.
[437] Stephen was the brother of William Longchamp (Richard Lionheart's justiciar, above, pp. 129–30), and had accompanied Richard on the Third Crusade. It is not clear why he was in disgrace and in prison at this time; it was suggested by Maurice Powicke that he might have failed to defend his manor of Douville (-sur-Andelle, south-east of Rouen), which he'd been granted a licence to fortify. See Powicke, *The Loss of Normandy* (Manchester, 1913), pp. 245 n.3, 271.
[438] The chapel of Grandmont stands on the left bank of the Seine at Rouen.
[439] Trianon, a village near Pont-l'Évêque, and Bonneville-sur-Touques, where the remains of the castle still stand.

fortifying Beaumont or Brionne or Montfort:[440] that would have strengthened his land and shown he meant to defend himself.) He went then to Lisieux, but his route after that didn't make much sense: he went via Chambreis[441] to Breteuil, then dropped in at Verneuil again before heading back to Rouen: it was hardly the direct route, but he feared that would be too risky to take, watched as it was by hostile forces.

He didn't stay long at Rouen. As he made to leave he said he was going to England to seek the counsel and aid of his barons there but would soon return; but the fact is that, since he was taking the queen with him, many feared he would stay there rather too long. He was ready in no time: in secret, and quietly, he'd already sent his baggage train ahead.

When he left Rouen[442] his first stop was at Bonneville – lodging in the castle, not the town, for he was alarmed about a plot revealed to him: that most of his barons had vowed to deliver him to the king of France. He gave no sign that he knew, but decided to get well clear of them! He told the Marshal and those he trusted most not to lie abed but to be up next morning before dawn; this was promptly done, and he slipped away without taking leave, while most imagined he was still asleep. Someone or other alerted them, but by then he was seven leagues away; some of them went after him, but most turned back. He went to Bayeux by way of Caen, covering more than twenty leagues in a day – and they were Bessinais leagues, which are a good deal longer than French.[443] Then he headed straight for Barfleur, where some of those who'd escorted him took their leave and returned, commending him to God, most of them convinced he wouldn't be coming back.

From Barfleur he put to sea and landed at Portsmouth.[444] In England he was greeted by the people with the joy and honour due to their lord. But I'll leave it at that; I don't know exactly what happened then – I'll have to wait till I've heard more.

Crisis in Normandy

Before his hasty departure to England, he'd entrusted Rouen to Peter de Préaux and his other castles to those he chose; but he hadn't been in England long before these castellans in Normandy sent word that he needed to take action to defend his land, for the king of France was seizing every castle he approached. There was no time to lose; he had to move fast, and this is the move he made: he sent the archbishop of Canterbury, the Marshal and Earl

---

[440] Beaumont-le-Roger, Brionne and Montfort-sur-Risle are, like Bonneville and Trianon, to the west of Rouen but strategically more important.
[441] As noted above (p. 137), this is now called Broglie.
[442] On 12 November 1203.
[443] The league is a notoriously vague medieval unit of distance, varying from place to place and country to country, representing anything between two miles and three. 'Bessinais' means the measurement used in the area around Bayeux (the Bessin).
[444] Having reached Barfleur on 28 November, he sailed a week later, on 5 December.

Robert of Leicester, as fine a knight as ever could be. These envoys made their way to Rouen and from there to Le Bec[445] where they found the king of France. They courteously and judiciously delivered their message, but the king of France wasn't interested; he rejected every word. He declared instead that all who came and paid him homage by a certain date would keep their land as his vassals. Many a tear was shed by those who didn't make it in time: they'd never thereafter hold land from him.

When the earl of Leicester and the Marshal heard what the king of France had resolved – that unless they came by the set date they wouldn't keep their land – they (not wanting to be other than true) discussed the matter between them and agreed to offer, I understand, a generous sum of their own money to secure a respite, to give them time to find out if Normandy would be defended or lost. They decided to go and meet the king of France, and both of them gave him fully five hundred silver marks to secure a respite for a year and a day, on condition that, if within that time King John was unable to recover his land, they would come and pay him homage. With this matter of their lands settled, they made their way back to England.

The king of France now went and laid siege to Rouen from across the river – as you know, having seen it or heard about it.[446] Sir Peter de Préaux, wanting to act in a loyal manner, sent word to King John in England that unless he came to the aid of Normandy he would lose it utterly. He made it plain that from Bayeux to Anet every castle and city had promised to surrender to the king of France once he'd taken Rouen. So if Rouen was lost, he could count himself finished: he might as well stay in England – he'd have nothing left in Normandy.

King John reacted quickly. He ordered his army to go straight to Portsmouth, but many of those summoned were slow to respond and there were long delays when there was no time to lose. While the dog's intent on shitting and oblivious to all else, the wolf gets clean away! And so it was that Rouen was lost, and fell into the hands of the king of France.[447]

So matters stayed, I understand, till the following Lent. Then King John appointed envoys in secret, so that the archbishop [of Canterbury] wouldn't know the terms of peace proposed. The Marshal was entrusted with the mission. With him went Hugh of Wells,[448] I believe, bearing the king's seal. When the king had given them secret instructions of the agreement they were to seek, the Marshal said to him:

'Hear me, my good lord. I have no guarantee of peace, and the time has almost expired for my land in Normandy. What can I say? If I don't pay homage for it to the king of France it'll be disastrous for me – it'll be lost beyond recovery. What can I do?'

---

[445] Le Bec-Hellouin, between Rouen and Lisieux. Marshal and the others made this journey in April 1204.
[446] The siege began towards the end of May 1204.
[447] Rouen surrendered on 24 June.
[448] Hugh, archdeacon of Wells, who was to become bishop of Lincoln in 1209.

MARSHAL'S PEACE MISSION

'I know you to be so loyal,' the king replied, 'that you could never bring yourself to desert me at any price. I'm perfectly willing for you to pay him homage and avoid such loss – I don't want you to lose the capacity to serve me! I'm well aware that the more you own, the better service you can give!'

The messengers set off and rode to the coast and crossed the sea, and journeyed on till they found the king of France at Compiègne.[449] They delivered their message perfectly, able envoys that they were, and the king this time was amenable and agreed to meet them a week later at Anet, where he was mustering his forces to go and lay siege to Caen.

And he said: 'Marshal, you know the terms that you and I agreed. Your time is almost up: unless you pay me homage it could mean trouble for you.'

'If it please you, sire,' the Marshal replied, 'I don't deny it. I've no intention of going back on my word. I'm ready to do as I said whenever you wish.'

So pay homage he duly did.

From there they went to Anet on the day the king had appointed. But no agreement was reached – and this was thanks to senseless interference: by now the archbishop of Canterbury had got wind of the mission – he'd been told who had gone and what they'd proposed – and was furious, outraged that the king had cooked this up without consulting him, and in no time he undid all the work the others had done. It doesn't take long to wreak havoc. He promptly sent Ralph d'Arderne to tell the count of Boulogne[450] of the mission, insisting that those who'd gone had no authority to negotiate peace and were wasting time. Count Renaud immediately relayed this to the king of France, who confronted the Marshal when they met, saying:

'I'm amazed, Sir Marshal, that you've come here with these proposals: it's clear to me you've had no licence to make peace.'

So what they'd managed to achieve was now undone. Undone they felt, and undone they returned, more than a little frustrated, while the king of France went to lay siege to Caen,[451] to complete his conquest of Normandy.

And let me tell you, by the time they arrived back in England,[452] Ralph d'Arderne, who'd queered their pitch and scuppered their mission, had already got to work by going to King John before they returned and telling him they'd behaved appallingly in France: the Marshal, he said, had paid homage and sworn fealty to the king and was now allied against him! Oh, the injustice! The speaker of these treacherous words, the wrecker of the peace plan, had worked things so that he, through his cunning, was now the trusted one, while those who (but for his meddling) would have secured peace were now distrusted. It's always the way: liars and traitors are promoted at court and the worthy are disregarded. So when they arrived they weren't greeted as they should have been with favour by the king but with hostility, quite undeserved: it was hardly their fault that their

---

[449] In mid-April 1205.
[450] Renaud de Dammartin; see above, p. 117.
[451] The author is confused or misinformed here: Philip had captured Caen the previous June.
[452] At the beginning of June 1205.

mission had failed – others, adept at mischief, had seen to it that the path to peace was blocked, and it was a sinful and wicked deed. The king said to the Marshal:

'I know full well, Marshal, that you've sworn homage and fealty and allegiance to the king of France, in opposition to me and intending me ill!'

'My lord,' he replied, 'whoever told you that is no friend of mine! He lied, and the lie must be refuted here and now. Be assured, sire, that I have in no way acted against you – everything I did, if it please you, I did with your leave.'

'In faith, you did not!' cried the king.

'Indeed I did! You told me to pay him homage rather than lose my land!'

'By God,' said the king, 'I did nothing of the kind! I deny it absolutely, and I'll have my barons and my men pass judgement!'

'God bless me, I'll not object to that – I welcome it!' the Marshal said. 'I've never been disloyal, and a man who refuses honest judgement is offering a poor defence!'

And so it was that for a long while the Marshal was out of favour with the king, quite undeservedly: he'd done no wrong – nor was he ever so inclined.

It was very soon after this that the king mustered his army, summoning all who held land from him and owed him service. Those who responded to his bidding joined him at Portsmouth to go with him to Poitou, but many were far from keen. Meanwhile the archbishop, in his envious spite for the Marshal, was delighted to see the king's attitude towards him.

And then one day the king went down to the harbour with his barons, and a great crowd gathered about him. He sat down overlooking the sea, and as soon as he was seated he called for the Marshal to come before him, which he duly did. The king immediately bade him explain why he'd sided with the king of France against him.

'I assure you, my good lord,' the Marshal replied, 'I've never wronged you in any way. Truly, I did only as you instructed.'

'I deny that absolutely,' said the king. 'I'll have my barons pass judgement on the matter, indeed I will. And true judgement spares no man.'

The Marshal was deeply hurt; he took off his hat and said: 'I repeat, sire: I acted as you had given leave. And I call you as my witness that I went there as your envoy.'

'I'm not having that,' the king replied. 'You're wasting your breath. But I shan't rush. You'll come with me first to Poitou: I want you to fight against the king of France, to whom you paid homage, to win back my inheritance!'

'Ah, my lord!' said the Marshal. 'I crave your mercy, in God's name! It would be wrong of me to oppose him when I'm his liegeman!'

'Hear that, sirs!' said the king. 'Condemned by his own mouth! Now you can see the plain, vile truth: he says he's the king's man and won't come with me!'

'Not so, my lord!' the Marshal cried. 'I've never been disloyal! If the most valiant knight in your land wished to prove I meant to wrong you, I'd defend myself against him! I've no cause to hang my head for any treachery or offence, and shall commit none as long as I live; and I'll answer any slander or envious spite!'

'God's teeth, we're wasting time!' the king replied. 'I want my barons to pass judgement – and I mean it!'

'I've no objection to being tried,' the Marshal said. 'I never have and never will. I'll gladly hear their verdict.' Then he looked straight up and placed his finger to his forehead and said: 'Look at me, sirs, for by the faith I owe you, this day I am the mirror and the model of you all. And take good note of the king: what he plans to do with me he'll do with every man – or worse! – if he has the power.'

The king was enraged at hearing this, and roundly swore he wanted the judgement of the barons present. They looked at one another – and stepped back. Then the king said:

'Is that it, sirs? God's teeth! It's plain to see that none of my barons agrees with me! That's all too clear! There's only one thing for it: I'll have to consult my younger knights[453] about this shameful business!'

And off he strode across the field. The Marshal, very troubled, rose from his seat and went to seek advice on the best way forward. But I promise you, there was no lord, however strong and secure his position at court, who had the courage to talk to him, only Henry FitzGerald,[454] who would never let him down, and John of Earley; no one else – the rest stayed well away. The king saw this from where he was standing and was delighted.

'Excellent!' he said. 'It's good to see the Marshal so popular! None of those he'd like at his side will go near him! Only Henry FitzGerald and Peevish John – the rest don't want to know! Now tell me, sir knights, and don't hold back: what do you make of all this? Come on – out with it.'

Some of those present loftily said: 'If a man's to hold land as your vassal, we hardly think it appropriate that he refuses to come with you when he's needed on a mission. There's no excuse at all.'

Sir John of Bassingbourn wanted to have his pennyworth and said: 'I don't see how anyone can hold land from his lord when he lets him down in his hour of need.'

But then the good Baldwin,[455] so valiant and true, spoke up and expressed a thought of which many approved, saying: 'Enough of that, my landless friend![456] You've done your bit. It's not for you or me to judge in court a knight as fine as the Marshal. And I tell you, there's not a knight in this field brave enough to face the Marshal in a duel to prove he's wronged the king.'

The king realised it was useless: he couldn't have the Marshal denounced by his barons in court or challenged by his knights to a trial by combat; so off he went to eat.

---

[453] *'mes bachilers'*; the implication is that he means to seek support from more malleable, younger members of his court, eager for advancement and more eager to please.
[454] A member of Marshal's entourage since 1202, FitzGerald remained one of his closest friends till his death, when he was one of the executors of his will.
[455] Baldwin de Béthune.
[456] The MS reads *'uis de cité'*, which is meaningless; Meyer suggested the excellent emendation *'vuis d'erité'* ('devoid of inheritance'), implying the knight's unworthy motive.

After dinner he pondered long on how to take revenge and find a way to hurt the Marshal. That day and the next he spoke to a number of men, hoping to find someone who'd challenge him; but no one had the nerve to take him on.

On the talking rumbled, until the archbishop, I believe, declared that he wouldn't advise on any account that the king made the crossing to France: I'm not sure what was in his mind. Then, when the king saw that no matter what he tried he couldn't bring the Marshal down, he made overtures again, smiling upon him as though he'd never harboured any rancour or ill will. Mind you, he wanted to take his eldest, most beloved son as hostage; and the Marshal agreed to this willingly, having no animosity or ill intent – as the saying goes: if you bandage your finger when it's healthy, it's healthy when you take the bandage off.[457]

The following year, at Pentecost,[458] King John earnestly and briskly set about raising a mighty army; they all arrived and assembled at Portsmouth. Then, with little delay, he set sail for Poitou, leaving the land in the care of his finest knights including the Marshal, knowing him to be most loyal, and entrusting him with many of his knights and many of the other troops he'd mustered.

So the king made the crossing and landed in Poitou, and this time with success: he won back a good number of castles, towns and strongholds and exacted tribute. But it's a long story and I can't tell it all.

He returned at Michaelmas[459] and was well received by many in the land who loved and cherished him; they welcomed him with joy and honour. He spent a long while in England, travelling throughout the land, hunting his wide and well stocked forests and rivers.

Marshal in Ireland

The Marshal now asked leave to go to his fine, extensive land in Ireland: it had been his for quite a while but he'd never seen it.[460] The king gave permission reluctantly – the Marshal had asked several times and he'd always refused. Meanwhile Fortune dealt the king a blow that was heavier and more serious than he realised, as both the archbishop and the good earl of Leicester died;[461] they were to prove grievous losses to him indeed, but at the time he was indifferent, apparently untroubled: many men fail to see the obvious, seeing positive advantage in what prove to be disasters.

But let me tell you briefly that the Marshal at this point spoke to Earl Roger Bigod,[462] who was never slow to seize a chance of advantage and enhancing his

---

[457] i.e. 'take precautions in advance and you'll be fine'; but the implication is also of course that there's nothing wrong.
[458] Late May 1206.
[459] He didn't in fact return until December.
[460] He had acquired a great estate in Leinster by marrying Isabel de Clare. See notes 316 and 344 above, pp. 127 and 135.
[461] Hubert Walter, archbishop of Canterbury, died in July 1205, and Robert de Beaumont, 4th earl of Leicester, in October 1204.
[462] 2nd earl of Norfolk.

honour, and wisely proposed the excellent marriage of his daughter to the earl's son Hugh: he was a valiant, charming, noble youth, and she was young[463] and gracious and fair indeed. It was a fine match, and a joy to both families.

It must have been around Lent, I'd say,[464] that the Marshal, having arranged this marriage and his other affairs, followed the prompting of his will and made ready to head for Ireland. When the king realised he was going, he thought he'd made a mistake in giving him leave and tried to think of a way to stop him. He sent Thomas of Sandford[465] after the Marshal to order him on his behalf, before he sailed for Ireland, to give him his second son in pledge, because he wanted a guarantee.[466]

'Very well,' Thomas said, and he pressed on fast and found the Marshal at Chepstow. He greeted him in the king's name, and the Marshal rose to meet him. Then Thomas delivered his message, informing him that the king wanted his second son as a hostage before he left for Ireland. Hearing this, the Marshal courteously returned the greeting and welcomed him, saying:

'Wash and go and eat; I wish to discuss this with my barons and my household – then you'll have your answer.'

So Sir Thomas went and ate, while the Marshal took his countess and most trusted men aside and told them what had happened and asked for their advice. Most of them said he should do no such thing: they thought it a wicked demand and said he shouldn't send his son; but he responded wisely:

'No, by God, I shall! If the king so wishes I'll send him all my children!' He left it at that, and when Sir Thomas had finished eating he took him by the hand and told him: 'Truly, sir, whatever the king's intentions towards me, I'll gladly send him all my children if he wishes. But tell me, for the love of God, why is he taking this attitude?'

'I promise you, dear sir, he simply wants you not to go to Ireland – he greatly regrets having given you leave.'

'By God,' the Marshal said, 'come what may, be it good or ill, he gave me leave so I'm going!'

And he sent his son Richard to the king.

Next day he set out, having the fair wind that he needed for the crossing to Ireland, and sailed happily over the sea. When he reached his estate there, most of his people on seeing him welcomed him with great joy and honour. But some when they heard of his arrival were far from pleased: the worthy were delighted to see him, but his coming caused one of his liegemen, Meiler,[467] who at that time was Ireland's royal justiciar, greater anguish than he'd ever felt. Wishing to do

---

[463] Marshal's eldest daughter Maud (or Matilda) was born no earlier than 1192 and was therefore in her early teens.
[464] It was probably at the end of March 1207.
[465] Brother of Hugh of Sandford, a knight in Marshal's household (see note 302 above, p. 125).
[466] The author has confused two events: Marshal's second son Richard was demanded as a hostage the following year, 1208, when he was indeed handed over to Thomas of Sandford.
[467] Meiler (or Meilyr) FitzHenry was the son of Henry FitzHenry, an illegitimate son of Henry I. King John had appointed him Lord Chief Justice in Ireland in 1199. He was Marshal's liegeman because he had been granted part of Offaly by Isabel de Clare's father Earl Richard ('Strongbow'), and so now held it from Marshal.

him harm, Meiler sent word to King John in England that it wouldn't be in his interest to let the Marshal stay in Ireland for any length of time – royal power there would be lost; so the king sent an order to the Marshal to return without fail, come what may, and to bring Meiler the justiciar with him. Quite rightly, the Marshal discussed this with those he trusted, who said they greatly feared that the king was up to something and meant the Marshal more harm than good; this was said in the presence of the countess, who was troubled by their words of foreboding. It was clear to the Marshal that the king meant him ill, and he was certain, too, that when he was gone from Ireland there'd be friction and war between those of his liegemen left behind: they'd never see eye to eye, and he knew how devious they were. So he said to Jordan of Sauqueville:[468]

'I have to go to England; I want you to stay here, I pray you, and guard part of my estate: I'm entrusting you with a large swathe from Ballygowran[469] to Dublin, one of the furthest reaches of my land.' Then he said to John of Earley: 'Of my domain you're to be the guardian of Okencelath and Ossory[470] – they'll be in your keeping.'

John replied: 'Forgive me, my lord, in God's name, I can't do that – I wouldn't know how. Entrust it to whomever you wish – I promise I'll gladly support any man you choose and do all in my power to fulfil his commands, truly I will.'

'No, you'll take charge, I pray you,' the Marshal said. 'I'll leave my kinsman Stephen of Évreux[471] with you: he'll gladly assist you and be at your side – I'd have you follow his advice, for I know him to be trusty. As further support I'll leave Ralph FitzPayne,[472] and seven other knights I brought with me will stay to guard the land faithfully. In fact, of those I brought I'll take back none but Henry Hose.[473] I bid you follow the advice in all matters of Geoffrey FitzRobert, a good and loyal servant to me, and Walter Purcel, who'll give you full and fine assistance, unstintingly, as will Sir Thomas FitzAnthony. I'll have my banner-bearer Maillard[474] stay with you, too.'

'My lord,' John of Earley said, 'I'm very fearful of treachery. It would be wise to take hostages from your barons before you leave.'

'Hush!' replied the Marshal. 'I wouldn't have them know you'd said that for a hundred marks! It would be a black mark against us indeed! But I'll summon them to come to me, and bid them uphold the peace and honour of my land and avoid discord and war between themselves.'

---

[468] Jordan, who held land in Buckinghamshire, had been a member of Marshal's household for several years and was to remain a staunch supporter.
[469] Gowran, County Kilkenny.
[470] Okencelath (a transliteration of the Irish *Ui Ceinnsealaigh*) included all of County Wexford and parts of Carlow and Wicklow; Ossory (Irish *Osraige*) was an ancient kingdom covering most of present-day County Kilkenny and part of Laois. Jordan has thus been given guardianship of the north and east of Leinster and John of the south and west.
[471] Stephen d'Évreux (or Devereux), another of Marshal's household, hailed from the Welsh Marches. It is not clear how he was Marshal's kinsman. He was at this time about 17.
[472] '*Reinfrei Fils Paien*': he is unidentifiable.
[473] '*Henri Huesé*'. He was the holder of substantial estates in Southern England.
[474] FitzRobert, Purcel, FitzAnthony and William Maillard were established knights in Leinster and evidently loyal supporters of Marshal.

He called them and they came without demur. They gathered before him on the appointed day at Kilkenny, and when they'd all arrived the Marshal said:

'Here, sirs, is the countess; I bring her by the hand before you all. She is your lady by birth, daughter of the earl[475] who graciously bestowed your fiefs upon you after his conquest of this land. She will be staying here among you with child, so I pray you guard her well and as you should till my return – for she truly is your lady: all that I have here is mine through her.'

They replied that they would do so, absolutely. But some of those who promised broke their word – sooner or later the wicked always reveal themselves in word or deed.

The Marshal took leave of his people and swiftly put to sea, landing at Michaelmas and making his way back to England. Meiler, a man not to be trusted, made the crossing separately, having first told his followers, his kinsmen, his family, to cause havoc in the Marshal's land, to stir up mighty conflict as soon as they knew that he was gone. That's what he said and that's what they did – they didn't let him down! On the very first Sunday after Michaelmas they set fire to the Marshal's barns at Newtown,[476] reducing them to ashes, killed twenty of his men and carried off a pile of plunder. And so began fierce strife and conflict throughout the land.

But now we'll tell of the Marshal, who had yet to hear a word of Meiler's foul and wicked treachery. He came before the king – as did the treacherous Meiler. The king's attitude hadn't changed: he smiled on Meiler and looked on the Marshal with dark scowls of disapproval. Then came the fateful day when William of Briouze fell out badly with the king, having previously been a great favourite.[477] One day, after dinner, the king was in his chamber with Gerard d'Athée;[478] Meiler was there, too, along with his privy counsellors. They were discussing one thing and another till the subject turned to the Marshal and William of Briouze, who were very good friends, at which point Meiler stepped forward and said to the king in the hearing of all:

'They're against you, sire, you may be sure! But don't worry: let me go to Ireland and arrange things for you – between me and my allies we'll deliver them to you in London as your prisoners! I'll handle it all – it won't cost you a penny. If we can get all their cronies back from Ireland they'll be yours!'

---

[475] 'Strongbow', 2nd earl of Pembroke: see note 316, above, p. 127.
[476] Probably New Ross, County Wexford; Marshal had founded the port town on the River Barrow.
[477] Briouze had indeed been a favourite of King John. He had personally captured Arthur of Brittany at Mirebeau (above, p. 154), and John had granted him lordship over Limerick and possession of several Welsh castles.
[478] Formerly seneschal of Touraine and another of John's most favoured counsellors, he enjoyed a meteoric rise that earned the resentment of many other barons, to such an extent that he appears in Clause 50 of Magna Carta, which removed all his kinsmen 'and the whole of their brood' from their bailiwicks (even though he himself was by then dead). The plan that is about to be described was plotted at Woodstock in Oxfordshire – one of the great royal residences in the early thirteenth century – in the autumn of 1207.

'By God,' said Gerard d'Athée, 'you're a champion if you can pull this off – the Marshal's done for!'

Then Meiler continued: 'Wait, sire: there's a bit more to be done. Send letters to those who hold land as your vassals, bidding them come to England. I've no doubt at all – I know for sure – before the Marshal ever gets back to Leinster he'll have lost his land!'

The king said to his chancellor: 'See to this, quickly! Have letters written at once to all who hold land from me, making it clear that unless they come here and present themselves to me, they won't keep a single foot of land in all England! Tell John of Earley to come at once, and Stephen of Évreux likewise must come to me in England without delay; and tell Jordan of Sauqueville to try no tricks: unless he makes provision to come he'll never hold land from me again! In fact tell all my vassals that if they fail to come they'll regret it – they'll have lost their lands! They need to understand that if they're not with me – wherever I may be in England – within a fortnight of receiving their letters they'll be landless here! Unless wind or storm prevents them they'll find they've made a grave mistake!'

Then Meiler said to the king: 'Sire, give me leave to go now.' And the king granted it; but it was leave that Meiler would come to regret: it was bound to end badly, as it always must with traitors.

The letters were sealed and entrusted to Thomas Bloet.[479] Then the Marshal learned that Meiler had arranged matters just as he wished and been readily granted leave by the king to slip back to Ireland. So he didn't delay for an instant: he went straight to the king to take his leave in turn, very eager to be gone – but the king refused.

Meanwhile Meiler had a fair wind and made the crossing – and his proved to be the only ship that did so between Michaelmas and Candlemas: it's often the way that the wicked are more fortunate than the good. But when he arrived back in Ireland Meiler didn't find his allies or the land in the happy state he'd expected: to his great vexation and dismay, one of the men he loved and trusted most had got himself imprisoned for his crimes – he was a captive of the Earl Marshal's men, as were a good number of Meiler's other knights, seized and locked away for their misdeeds. Then Sir Meiler, rather too sure of his own cleverness, decided to call a meeting with the earl's knights and men outside Castledermot.[480] It proved to be a long and heated exchange. Thomas Bloet promptly delivered to each, in the presence of all, the letters written at the king's command; and when they'd been read, the various recipients withdrew to a corner of the field and had them read again and said:

'It's as plain as day: the king means to rob our lord of his inheritance! What a base reward for all that he's expended in his service!' They talked in secret and earnestly, saying: 'What shall we do, sirs? It's clear we're going to lose our lands.'

---

[479] A surprising choice, as Thomas was the younger brother of Ralph Bloet, one of Marshal's entourage.

[480] In County Kildare; this is a possible but not certain interpretation of the otherwise meaningless 'ceiste de mot'.

Then John of Earley said, most forcefully and wisely: 'It would be shameful of us to abandon the land entrusted to us by the earl. We must be mindful of honour and avoid reproach: shame lasts longer than penury! If this land is relinquished our honour is tarnished. And if we lose both land and honour – and our lord's love – the king will have beaten us game, set and match!'[481]

And Stephen of Évreux said: 'Christ forsake anyone who abandons the land! Let's do the right thing: God willing, we'll defend it well! The king may do as he pleases with our lands, but God curse any man who fails to defend our lord's land with all his might, whatever may befall him!'

And everyone spoke up instantly, saying: 'True enough! True enough!'

And Jordan of Sauqueville said: 'If you'll take my advice, I strongly suggest we send word at once to the earl of Ulster[482] and Ralph FitzPayne. When our lord is in such urgent need I say we should ask for their help.'

Everyone present agreed with this; then they returned from their discussions as calmly as they could. Thomas Bloet asked them:

'Well, sirs? What have you decided? Will you do as the king has bidden?'

'We'll do nothing to incur reproach,' was their reply.

They spoke together again and all chose Jordan, quite rightly, as their envoy to the earl of Ulster, to ask him to come to the Marshal's aid as his need was great. Jordan went at once; and the earl came with a splendid company of sixty-five knights, superbly armed and mounted, and two hundred men-at-arms, brave, valiant, experienced troops, as well as a thousand foot soldiers, all committed and ready for action, able archers and spearmen. I shan't recount all their impressive deeds, for it might seem like crowing, and they weren't ones to brag or boast; but what Meiler had planned to do to the Marshal's land, the earl's men did to his, devastating it!

The Marshal meanwhile was following the king as he travelled up and down England, unaware of the havoc being wrought by Meiler – as was the king, who all the while was treating the Marshal with the utmost disfavour, to the wonder of the court and the Marshal's detriment, for none of them would even speak to him in case the king noticed and they incurred his wrath.

One day the king was riding from Guildford with the Marshal in his train,[483] and he called the Marshal to him and said:

'Tell me, Marshal, have you had any good news from Ireland?'

'No, sire,' he replied.

'Well I've some for you!' said the king with a laugh. 'The countess was at Kilkenny, and John of Earley, hearing word of a clash somewhere, went dashing off with Stephen of Évreux and all the knights and troops in the castle, leaving behind only a handful of men. Now how about this for a ruse: once they were two leagues or so from town, up went Meiler and laid siege to the countess! She

---

[481] It's hard to avoid anachronism (though the earliest form of tennis was in existence by the 1220s!) in translating the phrase 'we'll have to "*querre la briche*"', a reference to being completely outdone in a medieval game for which there is no modern equivalent.

[482] Hugh de Lacy, 1st earl of Ulster.

[483] Marshal is known to have been with John at Guildford in January 1208.

was very afraid she'd be taken captive, and let a man down over the battlements to get word to John of Earley that she was besieged in Kilkenny and in fear of capture. They were alarmed by the news – as well they might be! – but it was almost dark so they said it was too late to make it back, and went to spend the night at Odo.[484] Not that they slept well! They armed at first light and went to take them on. Meiler was defeated and captured along with many of his knights, but Stephen of Évreux was killed, Ralph FitzPayne taken and slain, they tell me, and John of Earley was wounded and died that very day. But the honour of the field was yours!'

'Truly, good sire,' the Marshal said, 'that's dreadful news. Everyone here – even the dimmest! – knows those knights were your worthy vassals. That makes this sorry business all the worse.'

'I'll bear it in mind,' was the king's reply.

The Marshal drew back, enraged beyond description and brooding long; and as he did so, he thought: 'God almighty! How can this have happened without my being told?'

He found it hard to believe, but believe it he did because the king had asked him if he'd received any news from Ireland: the fact that he'd asked the question made him believe the king had true knowledge of what he'd told him.

No one could make the crossing with news from Ireland from then till Lent; but as soon as the crossing was possible the king heard the truth about what had befallen Meiler: that he'd been defeated and captured and had made peace with the countess and the earl's men, and given his son Henry as a hostage to save his land, and submitted to whatever punishment the Marshal's court thought fit for his wicked and misguided deeds. Philip of Prendergast,[485] too, had been forced to give his son as a hostage, and all the rest gave sons or brothers by way of guarantee: no other kind of pledge would be accepted. The king was far from happy at the news – he was sorely pained that it had turned out this way. But the Marshal had splendid tidings from his men, and rejoiced in his heart to hear the price his enemies had paid! He thanked God in His majesty! Then he came into the king's presence without giving any sign that he'd received this fair and joyous news; the king saw him and called him forward, but hiding his true feelings he smiled upon him, showing him far more favour than before, and asked him:

'Tell me, Marshal, truly: have you had any news from Ireland?'

'No, sire,' he replied, 'I've still heard nothing.'

'Well, I've some news for you,' said the king, 'and I hope it'll cheer you: your men are in good health and spirits, and so is the countess.' And he told him, point by point, how his men had won great honour in overcoming their foes.

The Marshal listened avidly, as if it were news to him; and then, with shrewd composure, he replied: 'Thanks be to Our Lord, sire; but when I left the land I didn't think I had any foes who'd want to wage war on me!'

---

[484] Meyer identified this as Idouch, north-east of Kilkenny.
[485] Prendergast had been a notable turncoat, having formerly been a member of Marshal's entourage since Richard's reign.

KING JOHN'S DUPLICITY

The king's attitude towards him now was changed, from hostility to favour; and all at court treated him with love and honour.

The Marshal followed the king and his court for quite a while. Then he came to him and asked permission to return to Ireland. The king graciously granted it, and the Marshal left in good spirits and without any bitterness or rancour. This was in the Lent of the year when England was placed under interdict,[486] which was a great vexation to the land.

The Marshal came ashore at Glascarrig,[487] a wild place. His men came to meet him there: his coming was a joy to some, though to others it was far from welcome but a cause of deep displeasure. But Sir John of Earley greeted him, head high – and clad in a hauberk. He kissed his lord, so happy to see him, but the Marshal said:

'What's this? Tell me straight – why are you wearing a hauberk, Sir John? Is this some joke? Are we not at peace?'

'Yes, my lord – but not everyone's observing it.' This was a very canny reply; they were the words of Reynard the Fox![488]

They set off with the Marshal, deep in conversation, and Jordan of Sauqueville and John of Earley told him all about the treachery that had taken place. Just then they saw two barons approaching; I can tell you exactly who they were, though it pains me even to mention them: Philip of Prendergast and David de la Roche[489] – I swear there was never such a pair. They promptly greeted the Marshal like the smooth-tongued men they were, and he returned their greetings, saying:

'God save you – if I'm right to say so.'

'Indeed you are, my lord! You're looking at two of your loyal men!'

'You've not shown that – it's common knowledge – and I'm hardly going to thank you for it!'

'No!' said Jordan of Sauqueville and John of Earley. 'They're proven traitors!'

'We've caused no harm or trouble anywhere!' said Philip of Prendergast. 'Truly!'

'Indeed you have!' John of Earley said. 'Grave harm! I recall at least nineteen empty horses – and a twentieth bringing up the rear with only a collar for a bridle – and I swear I could tell you exactly who their riders had been and where they were from. We should be shown no respect but much reproach if we said any different in a court of law – it would be shameful.'

Then Philip and David wept bitterly, saying: 'Mercy, sir, in God's name! Pardon us your anger! Kiss us – we'd rejoice if you'd forgive us our wrongs!'

---

[486] In 1208 Pope Innocent III placed England under interdict for five years (excluding the English from certain rites of the Church) after John's refusal to accept his appointee Stephen Langton as archbishop of Canterbury.

[487] *'Glaskant'*. Glascarrig is on the coast of County Wexford.

[488] In the *Roman de Renart* (Branch V, vv. 4575–8), Reynard says that 'the truce is agreed and pledged and sworn and we've absolute peace – except not everyone knows!'

[489] A prominent baron of Wexford, he was the son of one of the lords of Wales and the Marches who had conquered and colonised southern Ireland under Richard 'Strongbow' de Clare. His name refers to Roch Castle near Haverfordwest (Pembrokeshire), of which his father had been lord.

When the Marshal heard them speaking so, tears of pity flowed from his eyes and he said: 'Kiss you I shall – but only because you beg me.'

So he kissed them and that was that; then he made his way homeward.

The following day great hordes of people came flocking to meet him – some of them his former foes. And the countess came, overjoyed at their reunion. Just as they were about to dine in the hall, a prominent knight of those parts stepped forward; Haï del Val was his name,[490] and he'd done no end of mischief.

'My lord,' he said, 'I bid you welcome among us! Welcome to this land!'

The Marshal graciously replied: 'God grant you salvation.'

Then Haï began: 'I'm your loyal man and have served you well and faithfully in your absence.'

'Thank you, Sir Haï,' the Marshal said.

'The whole land will attest to my loyalty, as will Sir John of Earley – I bid him bear true witness by the faith he owes you. I pray you, Sir John, kindly state if this is the case.'

'It's no use, my good sir,' Sir John replied. 'I can safely say, if our lord cares to ask, that there's no worse traitor than you in all the land – nor has anyone striven so hard to do him wrong. You asked me to speak honestly, so I have to tell the truth.'

All the knights in the hall burst out laughing. And the Earl Marshal sat down to dine, saying to John of Earley: 'It was a bad move calling on you as his witness! It was clearly going to get him nowhere!'

The good, loyal Earl Marshal made his way to Kilkenny with the countess and the barons. There was jubilation in the country, for all who loved him were delighted at his coming – though some showed a cheerful front that belied their hearts. There is no fouler treason on earth than a smiling face with a wicked heart. As for those who'd wronged him most, when they heard the certain news that he'd returned they thought they were dead and done for. They came before him in deepest dread – they knew they'd done him grave offence – and wept and begged for mercy; and he, forgiving, generous, kind and compassionate, listened to the biddings of his noble, gracious heart and granted them due mercy, returning all their hostages who'd been held there on account of their wicked acts of treachery. Meiler alone was denied forgiveness, for he had aided and abetted all the traitors: he'd been the root of all the evils done. But the countess wasn't happy when she heard that they'd been pardoned, for they'd caused her so much trouble and grief – and truly, if the Marshal had followed her advice he'd have exacted cruel punishment.

Then the wise and courtly earl, knowing whom to value, duly thanked the good men who'd served him faithfully and praised them for what they'd done. He had every reason to be grateful, and so he was, truly, saying to them all:

'Sirs, I thank you for the great love and honour you've shown me. It is much to your credit: you've protected and defended my land and restored it to me, and I owe you my enduring love. Thanks to you all, from God and from me!'

---

[490] Lord of Rathtoe, County Carlow. As with David de la Roche, his father had come from Pembrokeshire.

WILLIAM OF BRIOUZE IS BANISHED

It wasn't long after this that the king arranged his own affairs: he sent the bishop of Norwich[491] to Ireland with his commission as governor and justiciar. That was his will, so it had to be. And finally Meiler, who'd been so savage and cruel, came and placed himself, weeping, at the earl's mercy, ashamed of his wicked deeds. He was forced to strike a deal: he ceded his fine castle of Dunamase[492] to the earl as an hereditary fief and made him heir to all his land after his death. The earl could hardly have asked for more! And Meiler was perfectly able to grant him this – he had no other certain heir, having never married. And so it was concluded.

It was after this that Fortune – never constant to those She favours but sooner or later callous and cruel – turned Her wheel full circle with Sir William of Briouze. She was harsh and hard on him indeed: the king, who for so long had favoured him with high position, changed his attitude utterly, clashing so fiercely that the rift was beyond repair; the worthy Briouze was banished, which was a great sorrow and a great wrong. I don't know the exact cause, and if I did it wouldn't be proper for me to meddle in telling.[493] The king turned against him savagely, launching attacks from every side. Briouze couldn't resist or cope with this campaign; he took refuge for a while in Wales, but his men were little good to him and he didn't dare depend on them, and he had to take a different course. Grim and daunting though it was, he put to sea in dreadful winter weather. For three days and nights he sailed with his wife and sons through a perilous storm. Off the Irish coast they were locked in a dire and fearful tempest, so battered and tossed by wind and wave that all on the shore, watching the ship approach, were convinced they were doomed to drown. But Ireland was that noble man's only resort: he planned to take refuge with Sir Walter de Lacy, his wife's father.[494] He feared the worst, but the sea's wild surge swept them ashore in Wicklow, where the Earl Marshal was then residing. After that terrible ordeal it was a God-sent providence. The earl was thrilled to hear of his arrival and came eagerly to meet him, and was delighted to give him and his wife and children the finest lodging, unstintingly for fully twenty days.

But when the bishop, now governor and justiciar,[495] heard certain reports that the earl was harbouring Sir William of Briouze and his wife and children, he sent furious protestations that he was sheltering a traitor to the king, and that it was a grave mistake and could bring him a deal of trouble; he commanded him in the king's name to send Sir William to him without demur. The Marshal replied to the messengers:

---

[491] John de Gray.
[492] 'Donmas'. The Rock of Dunamase, a substantial stone castle near Portlaoise, County Laois.
[493] Being Marshal's neighbour in the Welsh Marches and a fairly close friend, Briouze began to be distrusted by John during the crisis in Leinster, and John demanded Briouze's eldest son as a hostage. But when the king's men arrived to claim the son, Briouze's wife Matilda 'openly declared that she would never hand over her own sons to the man who had "murdered Arthur, his own nephew". When this desperately incautious remark was reported to John, a calamitous rift opened' (Asbridge, *op. cit.*, p. 312).
[494] Walter was brother of Hugh de Lacy, earl of Ulster.
[495] i.e. the bishop of Norwich, as mentioned above.

'I assure you I have no traitor here. I've given lodging to Sir William as I rightly should: I'd no idea the king was other than well disposed towards him. And since I've given him shelter I'd be betraying him if I placed him in your hands. I shall escort him safely till he's outside my domain. The bishop shouldn't ask me to do anything treacherous or worthy of reproach.'

Such was his reply to the messengers, wise and courtly man that he was and ever loyal. And he escorted Sir William safely to Sir Walter de Lacy. That's what happened, I promise you. The bishop was outraged that the Marshal didn't deign to do as bidden, and sent word to the king as soon as he could. The king was less than pleased: he went mad, quite wild with rage! And he promptly instructed the Marshal to come to him without delay. The Marshal realised what the king was up to, merely looking for a pretext to do him unjust harm. He quickly arranged his business and prepared for the journey back to England, to the king.

He'd hardly arrived before the king summoned his army, mustering a mighty force to cross to Ireland, with no expense spared. At Pentecost he came to Pembroke and they made the crossing shortly after; on Saint John's Day following[496] he and his forces arrived in Kilkenny to a lavish reception, the whole army, I swear, being lodged that day at the earl's expense. It cost him a fortune! And all the while no thought was given to defence or guarding the gate. From there the king made his way to Dublin, and then on to lay siege to Carrickfergus,[497] and so great was his army that the people were appalled to see themselves surrounded by such a host. And they didn't acquit themselves well: they weren't unprepared and the castle was strongly fortified, but giving in to fear and threats the disloyal men surrendered. When the castle was yielded without resistance, the king installed a huge garrison and then returned to Dublin.[498] And there, in the presence of the barons and the great lords of those parts, he accused the Marshal of intending him all manner of harm if he had the chance, and first and foremost of having harboured one he knew to be his mortal enemy and of seeing him to safety. The earl, standing before him, replied:

'I tell you, sire, I gave lodging to my lord,[499] who arrived in grave distress outside my castle. I was only too pleased to help him when he was in such a sorry state, and you shouldn't take it ill that I gave him shelter. I didn't think I was doing wrong – he was my friend and my lord and I'd no idea you'd fallen out with him! You were on good terms when I came here from England! If anyone but you thinks there's more to it than that, I'm willing to defend myself here and submit to the judgement of your court.'

No baron made a move; otherwise the king would gladly have made him face the charge – not that he'd committed any wrong. Seeing he could proceed no further the king was furious, harbouring deep resentment as he did, and demanded hostages of him.

---

[496] 24 June 1210.
[497] Earl Hugh de Lacy's main fortress in Ulster. When it fell in July, Walter de Lacy and Briouze fled to Scotland.
[498] In the middle of August 1210.
[499] This particular justification for having sheltered him is possibly a reference to Briouze being overlord of the Marshal manor of Speen, near Newbury in Berkshire.

'Very gladly,' said the earl. 'Who would you like?'

'Geoffrey FitzRobert, that's who! And Jordan of Sauqueville. Hugh of Sandford,[500] too, and John of Earley with him, and Walter Purcel. And I want your fine castle of Dunamase.'

Hearing this, the earl did not hold back; he said, very shrewdly: 'You have my sons as hostages, and all my castles in England. If you want my castles and strongholds here in Ireland I'll give them, along with many of my good vassals' sons. A man may do this with confidence when he's no intention of committing any wrong.'

When he heard these words the king retired to his chamber and spoke to his men, who made it clear that they thought the Marshal's offer great and a sign of his loyalty.

'No man making such an offer can be intending anything untoward! He's obeying your every command and offering more than you asked for! Don't brood any longer; tell him what you wish. You've no reason to be angry.'

Then he took aside the bishop of Norwich, the earl of Winchester,[501] the constable of Chester[502] and Peter FitzHerbert,[503] and sent them to make clear to the Marshal that he wanted no other hostages than the ones he'd cited. The earl replied that he'd only two of them with him, as was plain to see – Walter Purcel and John of Earley; but he'd go and ask them if they were willing to be hostages. The men sent by the king went with him, and were pleased to find them present. The earl was straight with John of Earley, saying:

'The king wants hostages from me, truly – you and Walter Purcel – and my fine castle of Dunamase.'

'In faith, my lord,' John of Earley said, 'I am the king's man and yours at all times and in all places. If that's the king's will I'll gladly accept, for he's no true friend who fails his lord in time of need, wherever he may be, near or far.'

And when Walter Purcel was told, he agreed likewise. So the earl returned to the king, who was satisfied. All was done quite openly: before the whole assembled court the earl placed his hostages and the castle of Dunamase in pledge. But it still wasn't enough for the king: he was tireless in his demands, asking now for substantial pledges from the earl's barons who were present. All of them acceded to the demands – except one, who roundly refused and said exactly why: David de la Roche[504] it was, who declared that the Marshal had done him so much wrong that he felt no obligation to him – either to offer a pledge on his behalf or to support him in any way. Then the Marshal said to the king:

'Hear me, sire, in God's name: ask the barons and the people here if I've ever wronged or abused Sir David who's refusing to offer a pledge for me.'

---

[500] The MS reads 'Thomas of Sandford', but it must surely be a reference to his brother Hugh, a member of Marshal's household (see above, p. 125).
[501] Saer de Quincy, 1st earl of Winchester.
[502] Roger de Lacy, a powerful Northern baron (not closely related to Hugh and Walter in Ulster).
[503] A lord of the Welsh Marches.
[504] See above, p. 173.

So the king asked all those present: 'What do you say, sirs? Has the Marshal done him wrong to justify his refusal?'

And they replied as one that they'd never seen or heard him commit any wrong or offence, any insult, affront or slight. Sir David was at a total loss: no one would endorse his claim.

You'll hear in a moment how each of the hostages was dealt with according to the king's command. But let me tell you first: Sir Peter FitzHerbert, a wise and able knight, stepped forward now to take a seat, and those sitting beside Sir David stood to make room for him;[505] but he said:

'God bless me, sirs, nothing would induce me to sit next to the traitor who has failed his lord!'

Most of those who heard this were delighted; they were grateful to him for rewarding the shameful knight with this cutting remark.

Now I'll explain how the king took the hostages back to England. The arrangements he made proved costly. Once they'd been chosen he made separate, careful disposal of each one: Jordan he sent to be held at Gloucester, Thomas at Winchester, John at Nottingham (where he endured a tough and wretched time), and Geoffrey at Hereford – which proved a grim captivity indeed: he fell ill in prison and didn't come out alive. But Walter Purcel was entrusted to a kinder keeper, Peter FitzHerbert: a worthy man is to be valued indeed when he merits praise for his actions, and Sir Peter certainly did so in this case.

The hostages were held for nearly a year – very wrongly, for the one on whose account they suffered was guilty of no offence. But then at last the war began between the king and Llywelyn.[506] The king now summoned the Marshal: he'd treated him so harshly, but he responded very prudently and came, whereupon the king returned the hostages quite readily. That was always his way: he kept his barons estranged from him until he had need of them. But tragically the hostage Geoffrey FitzRobert died just as he was about to be released. Once the war – which was fierce – was over,[507] the Marshal asked leave to return to Ireland, which was granted, and rightly so.

The Battles of Damme and Bouvines

It was while he was there in Ireland that a serious crisis arose which led to great trouble and suffering: the king of France, coveting the English crown, was preparing a fleet for an invasion of England, for the land had been promised to him.[508] When news of these preparations reached King John, he summoned all

---

[505] i.e. they are shifting away from Sir David: they would rather someone else sat there.
[506] Llywelyn ab Iorwerth, prince of Gwynedd.
[507] John had mounted a campaign in North Wales in May 1211 but had been forced to withdraw; it may well have been that initial failure which prompted his appeal to Marshal and his release of the hostages, and he led a successful second campaign against Llywelyn in August.
[508] By Pope Innocent III, following Stephen Langton's (see note 486, above, p. 173) protest at John's treatment of the English clergy. The invasion was being prepared in April and May 1213.

his barons and sought their advice about what he should do in response. Even the wisest had no idea; then someone said:

'Hear me, my dear lord – I'll be blunt: you're missing the worthiest man in all your land, and I strongly advise you to send for him. It's William the Marshal I mean: he's so worthy and loyal, so respected and loved and feared that in my view you'd do well to seek his guidance. The king of France isn't playing around![509] But it's long been said that a man with worthy guidance can rest easy. If you'll take our advice, sire, we all agree you should send for the Marshal.'

'Very well,' said the king, 'but first we'll return those two sons of his I've been holding as hostages.'

'That's a wise move,' said many. 'The Marshal will come more readily and be more committed in his friendship.'

And this was duly done. The king summoned John of Earley, who came to London without delay. The king told him:

'I've called you here, John, to deliver your lord's two sons to you: I'm sure you'll care for them better than anyone. I've decided to keep them hostage no more – such is my will. And I know you to be such a man that I shall make you marshal of my household before the day is out![510] And I wish you to receive on your lord's behalf confirmation of his rights, as guaranteed and as sure as they've ever been – and more so! Such is my will, by my eyes it is!'

'A thousand thanks, sire, for these words,' John of Earley said. 'But if it please you, it would take two worthy guardians to care for those boys with all due honour. To do it well they'd have their hands full!'

'I'll see to that,' the king replied. 'You've no need to worry.'

And the children were duly delivered, much to Sir John's delight. The king saw how young Richard was,[511] and not in the most robust health; he was unfit to suffer hardship at such an age – he wouldn't cope; so he said:

'It's clear to me, John, that Richard isn't ready to face the world – he'd struggle, and I want him to be safe. If you're in agreement, let him be entrusted to Sir Thomas of Sandford: he'll take good care of him.'

'Undoubtedly, so help me God!' said Sir John. 'He could have no better guardian.'

Then the king sent word to the Marshal in Ireland, bidding him come at once and let nothing detain him. The Marshal did so without demur, assuming the urgent call was prompted by a pressing need, and he came with all possible speed, as a worthy man should: devoted as he was to loyalty, he didn't stop to question the cause and he overlooked the king's past cruelties. It wasn't long before he reached the king, who was overjoyed to see him. He explained the situation and asked what he should do. The Marshal said:

---

[509] Literally 'this is no eve-game', which I take to be a reference to the 'vespers' of a tournament, a 'warm-up' before a tournament proper (see 'vespers' in the Glossary).
[510] Traditionally, the marshal (*mareschal*) was the officer in charge of the stables and horses in a noble household. There is no record of John of Earley in that position, though his father William had been a household chamberlain and it is possible that John was given that post.
[511] In fact Richard (Marshal's second son) was probably born in 1191, so was about 21.

180   THE HISTORY OF WILLIAM MARSHAL

'Have you summoned all your barons and nobles, all who hold land as your vassals?'

'Yes,' said the king. 'They've come.'

As he was advised, the king immediately, I understand, mustered his forces on Brandon Hill,[512] and found that he had a great army. Then he headed for Dover.[513] Following the advice of the Marshal – who'd always given him trusty counsel – and of the count of Boulogne[514] (a valuable man in such a crisis), of the earl of Salisbury and that most loyal justiciar Sir Geoffrey FitzPeter,[515] a bold plan was undertaken: with careful deliberation and much resolve he prepared his own ships to attack and maul the fleet assembled by the king of France at Damme.[516] And never since the days of Adam did a fleet come so to grief, thanks be to God – and to the good Earl William of Salisbury,[517] who gave the French king an unwelcome shock, setting his ships ablaze at Damme before his very eyes and plundering everything aboard.[518] What a bitter blow to the king of France, to see his fleet go up in flames and smoke – the sea itself seemed to be afire! And the earl and his men led off a host of ships laden with bacon, wheat and wine, in the face of the French and the men of Anjou and all their might: so much booty never came from France to England since King Arthur went and conquered! King Philip, in a mindless fit of rage and anguish, had the rest of his fleet burned to ash and left at once with all his mighty army, bested and shamefully humbled.

The earl of Salisbury meanwhile sailed back to England; but before he could reach land he was caught in a terrible gale and storm. None of the ships could make landfall together: they were driven apart by the force of the storm as far as Scotland and Northumberland; but thanks be to God they all came through it – no one drowned or perished.

When news of the triumph reached the king he was elated, and gave thanks to Our Lord for this God-sent, wondrous honour. It would have been good if he'd repaid Him by behaving well – but he didn't, more's the pity.

The English force disbanded, and the king spent the whole winter and summer in the land in greater joy and peace than he'd known before.

And then, the following Lent,[519] the Marshal and the other great lords urged him to lead an expedition to Poitou. It wasn't long before he'd assembled a mighty host, all able-bodied fighting men of every degree flocking in huge numbers, and he put to sea impressively with a great and splendid army. He left

---

[512] 'le mont de Brandone'. This is a difficult place-name to identify. David Crouch plausibly suggests that 'a possibility for such a muster might be the downs above Brabourne, Kent, a short march from … the principal Channel ports' (Vol. 3 of the ANTS edition of the *History*, p. 160).
[513] On 28 May 1213.
[514] Renaud de Dammartin: see above, p. 117.
[515] FitzPeter had been justiciar in the last year of Richard's reign; John had made him earl of Essex on his coronation day in 1199.
[516] In the Middle Ages Damme was the port of Bruges.
[517] 'Longsword': see note 412, above, p. 154.
[518] On 30 May 1213.
[519] February 1214.

England full of confidence that he would achieve his ends, his cause strengthened as it was by the backing of the counts of Flanders and Boulogne. He had them unite their forces,[520] and sent his good brother Earl William of Salisbury[521] to join them.

But I mustn't forget to mention that when the king put to sea he left the Marshal, along with other barons, to guard his cities, castles and all his land the length and breadth of England, while for his part the Marshal willingly gave him as many of his knights as he wished to take. But it has to be said, there's no hiding it, that a leopard doesn't change its spots:[522] the king informed the Marshal that he wanted to take his son Richard with him.

'My dear lord,' the Marshal replied, 'I think Richard's too young to be taken to a far-off land. But if you insist he'll not stay behind. I'll not oppose your will – I'll give you both my sons.'

The king did insist on taking him, but was later to be sorry, for Richard fell ill during the campaign: doctors had to be found and he very nearly died, which would have been a grievous pity and a cause of much reproach; but he finally recovered.

This isn't the place to discuss what the king achieved on his expedition; it didn't work out exactly as planned,[523] but that's not what concerns me. I shan't go into all that happened, but he returned to England – let that suffice. Meanwhile, as is well known, the three counts – the counts of Flanders and Boulogne and the king's friend and brother the earl of Salisbury – mounted a great campaign in which they would surely have triumphed had it not been for the error of someone other than themselves. As everyone knows, they were sorely misdirected. The fact is, they made great headway in Flanders[524] and went to join the emperor,[525] but he came in such haste that he hadn't even a quarter of his men with him. The king of France was dismayed by the news of his arrival, convinced that he was going to be outdone and killed or captured. The French had no appetite for battle and wanted to be gone – they'd gladly have fled that very night if they'd had the chance. A number who'd gone over to the emperor assured him of this: they'd seen for themselves and knew that the French were about to withdraw. The count of Boulogne spoke up, eager to see good sense prevail; he said:

'I'll be only too pleased to see them go! They'll be abandoning the land to us: it'll be easily conquered if it's undefended! And it'll be returned, if it please God, to the emperor and to our lord King John of England.'

---

[520] In Flanders, while he went to campaign in Poitou.
[521] 'Longsword' was John's half-brother, being the son of Henry II and his mistress Ida de Tosny.
[522] Literally 'the sack always smells of the herring and the good vessel of the good wine'.
[523] '*Ne sust lors chose qui ataigne*'. This line is corrupt, with no obvious original meaning; it may have been intended to convey the expedition's mixed fortunes.
[524] In March and April 1214.
[525] Otto IV, grandson of Henry II of England; he had been supported in his rivalry for the German crown by both his uncles Richard Lionheart and John; in conflict with Pope Innocent III, he had been excommunicated in 1210.

But Hugues de Boves[526] said: 'You're robbing them of honour and land alike, that's plain, refusing to let us do battle!'

'Deeds speak louder than words, good sir!' the count replied. 'You'll not mix with the best when it comes to battle, Hugues de Boves! You're sure to keep your head down – you'll stay well out of trouble, you scoundrel! You'll do nothing to enhance your honour, but I'll be killed or captured, I swear, sooner than leave in shame.'

Everyone knows the truth of the calamitous rout that followed – and so quickly: they attacked too soon, with too few men, disastrously. It was a grave mistake: the fact is, they hadn't a quarter as many as the French that day – the emperor's full forces weren't to hand; had he waited till the following day, when his whole army would have arrived, he would have won great honour. But that's as may be; the fact is, the counts and the earl were taken prisoner, and the emperor would have been killed or captured had it not been for the earl of Salisbury, who said:

'Be gone, my lord, for the love of God! If you're taken here it'll go from bad to worse! You may yet be able to have redress and avenge the king of France's arrogance!'

With great difficulty – and anguish – he made the emperor go. But he himself stayed and was captured, as were all the knights of worth – absolutely all, including Thomas Malesmains who fought most valiantly that day and earned unanimous praise.

I didn't mean to imply that the king had returned from Poitou before all this happened; and I'd forgotten to mention – though it's no grave omission – that Robert of Dreux was captured in an attack on the bridge at Nantes:[527] I should have added that. I don't want to go on too much, but after the dire defeat in Flanders[528] where the three counts and most illustrious lords were tragically, disastrously overcome and captured, the result was a truce the terms of which would never have been agreed had it not been for the dreadful day that had befallen the emperor. It was following this that King John returned to England;[529] and it was then that the war and bitter strife began between the king and his barons which, rightly or wrongly, went on endlessly till his death. He had wronged some of those who allied against him, but not all; some who followed their example were turning against him without cause. Almost all attacked him. But this is no place to speak of the whys and wherefores of what went on; the truth is that neither party was innocent – anyone who hadn't seen it for himself would struggle to believe the wickedness committed by both sides: everyone piled wrong on wrong.

---

[526] The lord of Boves, in Vermandois south-east of Amiens.
[527] Not the count but his son of the same name; he was captured by John's forces at Nantes in June 1214.
[528] i.e. at the battle of Bouvines, just described, on 27 July 1214.
[529] In early October 1214.

Marshal's Children

But now I wish to tell of the Marshal's fine children, descended from a worthy father and born of a worthy mother. I know I can claim with all confidence – those who came and saw them are my witnesses – that no finer children were ever born of a knight and lady, and if I'm lying let my soul answer for it! It's only fitting that I give you their names, and it's relevant to my theme.

The first son was named William, and I can assure you that in all this realm there was none so committed to great deeds – I've heard that said by everyone; and a man of whom such good is spoken must surely be destined for high honour and achievements. He became earl after his father, and was a truly splendid knight. Richard, the next born, was endowed with prowess, intelligence and handsome looks and good and noble manners; Charity, Honour and Largesse made him ever their host, and any man with whom they reside is a worthy man indeed. The third was named Gilbert: a cleric he was, renowned for his intelligence and character and good works, being open-hearted, gentle and compassionate. The fourth was named Walter; he was not yet a knight when I wrote this book, but it was said that if he lived he would prove to have many qualities: he was certainly so inclined. The fifth of the sons was named Ansel, a fine figure of a man in face and body and every limb: I remember him as impressive in all his deeds, and may God grant him a great future! So now I've named the five sons, but it's clear from all I've seen and heard that I could go on all day about the qualities and potential of each one – they'd be hard to encompass! Everything I've said is true and well worthy of credence: the evidence is abundant!

Now I shall tell of the five daughters in the order of their birth. The first was named Maud, favoured by God with wit, generosity, beauty, grace, charm and all the qualities, I tell you truly, that a noble woman should possess. Her good father, who loved her dearly, in his lifetime arranged for her the best, most illustrious marriage that he could: to Sir Hugh Bigod, of high lineage indeed, succeeding his father as earl.[530] To cut a long story short, he gave three of his daughters to the sons of earls – they were far from ill-matched! The one named Isabel (who could rightly have been called Vista Belle,[531] for she is a fair beauty indeed!) became the wife of the earl of Gloucester.[532] Then the father gave Sibyl, who should rightly be praised for her many virtues, to the son of Earl Ferrers.[533] And he gave Eva as wife to the son of the lord of Briouze – William by name, the son of Reginald. He is a wise, able, worthy man indeed whom God inspires to forge such noble bonds with his issue. Joan was unmarried at her father's death; it was left to her brother to see her wed – which he did most

---

[530] Hugh became 3rd earl of Norfolk on his father's death in 1221.
[531] This is an attempt, admittedly clumsy, to render the poet's rhyming pun *'vis a bel'* ('she has a fair face').
[532] Gilbert de Clare, earl of Hertford and of Gloucester.
[533] William de Ferrers, who became 5th earl of Derby on his father's death.

judiciously, arranging a splendid marriage indeed, a noble match well worthy of her, to Warin, lord of Munchensy; he was delighted to receive her, as was she to come to him.

From what I've said you can plainly see – and it's common knowledge – that from a good tree comes good fruit: children reflect the qualities of their father and their good mother. And this father, very astute in such matters, endowed with shrewd intelligence, turned his attention to arranging a marriage for his eldest son. He was aware that Count Baldwin of Aumale[534] had a beautiful daughter, and the damsel was his only child. He and Baldwin were very close friends, having been companions in arms, as they still were. They discussed the marriage, both welcoming the idea, and it was agreed; and the count bequeathed to his daughter all his land in England and elsewhere, subject to the king's permission. The worthy and the wise, on hearing of this planned union, all thoroughly approved, saying that no two children of such fine fathers and worthy mothers had ever been joined in marriage, and that it seemed good fruit was sure to come from them.

When the fathers had discussed the matter in full and reached agreement, they came together to the king to ask for his authorisation of the terms and to have a charter drafted. The king sanctioned this, and everything they'd agreed and pledged was set down in the charter. It was a very wise arrangement; and so was sealed a marriage that was praised by many people. It would have been a long-lasting union, but Death, ever the divider of the good, allowed them little time together. Gluttonous, all-devouring Death beset and seized the lady and she died: nothing – her wealth, her station, her intelligence or anything else – made any difference. When Death goes to work She won't consider ransom: crazed, senseless, She doesn't care whether She's loved or loathed; in Her haughty pride, She pays no heed to kings, dukes, counts: She has her way with them all; rich and poor alike are Hers! It's rightly said that there's no escaping Death. But I shan't go on: it's not relevant to my theme, and I don't want to be diverted from my story of the Marshal – and God grant that I treat it in such a way that it may be an example to all who hear it.

The Barons' War

But I must pass over the war which now took place in England between the king and his barons, for it involved many things unworthy of record, and it might get me into trouble. But the upshot was that the barons came to the king and demanded their privileges, but he refused. So most of those present declared outright that unless their demands were met they would serve him no more; they made it clear that he could have no faith in them: thenceforth they would give him grief at every opportunity. And they were true to their word: they abandoned his service, and these allied barons came to London to oppose

---

[534] Baldwin de Béthune, who had become count of Aumale through his marriage to Hawise (above, p. 125, note 301).

THE BARONS SEND FOR LOUIS OF FRANCE

him.[535] But you should know that the Marshal had no part in any of this: he greatly regretted the intemperance of both sides – he didn't approve or wish for any of it. Nor was he involved in the agreement made between the barons and the citizens of London: with the approval of the latter, the allied barons came to London and sent, I understand, for Louis, the king of France's son. They had great confidence in him, and sent for him to be brought to England, promising to make him their lord. What a foolish enterprise!

But before all this the king had laid siege to Rochester, squandering a fortune in the process. What happened was this: he made his way to Dover by sea – why by sea rather than land I shan't go into now; it's not important to my story – and sent for an army of Flemish knights and foreign mercenaries, who wanted just to loot and pillage every day. They weren't interested in advancing his campaign – only in ravaging his land! That was clear from his treasury: in five weeks he'd spent all the riches and the money that he had. But that's what happens when you carry on like that: if you throw money around with little gain, and get involved with the wrong people, it doesn't take long to be cleaned out! But he stuck at it anyway and finally took Rochester by force.[536]

And then the Londoners succeeded in bringing Louis from France.[537] He was in control of the land for quite some time, taking Farnham, Winchester, Portchester and Southampton. Those wretched French braggarts were drinking by the tun and barrelful, and claiming England was theirs and that the English had no right to the land and should clear out! The French were going to have it as their own from now on! But their bragging did them little good: later I saw a hundred of them eaten by dogs, killed by the English between Winchester and Romsey. In that sense they ended up occupying English ground! And the same thing – and worse – happened in many parts: witness the deeds of Willikin of the Weald.[538]

It's worth saying that once the king was out of cash, few of those who'd come for money hung around! Off they went with their booty! But the loyal-hearted, constant Marshal stayed with him through the darkest, hardest times. He wouldn't desert him, and his heart never wavered: he served him in good faith as his lord and king. He never left him till the day he died, and I declare he stayed with him and his followers even then, in death as well as life, good and loyal man that he was. It's a proven fact, very frequently observed, that, no matter how he'd been treated by the king, he could never be persuaded to forsake him.

All the same, the war raged on till the realm had suffered much, and those opposed to him inflicted grievous losses. Finally he was heading for Lindsey[539] when grim misfortune struck him, for it was in those parts that the grievous

---

[535] In the middle of May 1215.
[536] Rochester fell after a three-month siege on 30 November 1215.
[537] In May 1216.
[538] 'Willekin de Vauz'. In 1216 and 1217 William of Cassingham (now Kensham) in Kent, a minor nobleman otherwise known as Willikin of the Weald, gathered great bands of archers (in almost Robin Hood fashion) in the woods and wilds of the Weald in Kent and Sussex and harried the French repeatedly, killing considerable numbers. He was later rewarded for his guerrilla exploits with a royal pension and made Warden of the Weald.
[539] One of the historic divisions of Lincolnshire.

sickness of which he died took hold, gripping him so dreadfully that he was incapable of moving, a sickness so bent on crushing him that at Newark he could go no further and that was that.[540] The bishop of Winchester[541] was in attendance, and, most certainly, Sir John of Monmouth stayed with him till his death, as did Sir Walter Clifford and Sir Roger,[542] very moved, and John the Marshal,[543] upset likewise to see him suffering so, and, in short, many other eminent men and knights; and all those present were in great distress. As his sickness worsened, giving him no respite from dreadful pain, he summoned the very closest to him and said:

'My death is upon me, sirs: there's no escape. I can endure this pain no more. In God's name, ask the Marshal to forgive me for all the harm and wrongs and troubles and woes I've caused him, for which I sorely repent. He has always served me faithfully and never wronged me no matter what I've done or said to him. By God who made the world, sirs, crave his pardon. And because I trust in his loyalty above all others, I pray you, let him be my son's protector, his guide and guardian in all matters: without his help and his help alone, he'll never govern these lands of mine.'

Such were the king's words. And then pitiless Death, intent on inflicting all possible pain, began a final assault, rendering him powerless, robbing him of all strength and sense, reducing him to a sorry state indeed. I've heard a number of people say that he was truly repentant; but harsh, cruel, ruthless Death took him in Her grip and wrung him till he died. So the king was dead; there was no remedy. He was taken from there to Worcester.

When the Marshal heard that his lord the king had died he was deeply saddened. He left Gloucester[544] and set off to meet the party bearing the body to Worcester. The legate Guala[545] was among them, and a great host of clerics and knights were gathered about the bier. It was borne into the cathedral where a splendid service was held, befitting a king and according to due rites and divine decree. And so it was that Merlin's prophecy about him, assuring us that he would rest among the highest, had been fulfilled;[546] for indeed, he lies between the bodies of Wulfstan and another saint, almost side by side.

[540] He reached Newark on 16 October 1216 and died there two days later.
[541] Peter des Roches.
[542] John of Monmouth and Walter Clifford (from Herefordshire) were both Marcher allies of Marshal; the identity of 'Sir Roger' is not clear, though the flow of the sentence suggests he was another Clifford.
[543] William's nephew, as noted above, p. 140.
[544] Marshal had been based at Gloucester Castle since the summer.
[545] 'Wales': Guala Bicchieri, papal legate to England since the beginning of 1216.
[546] This is puzzling: it is hard to see that any of Merlin's gnomic prophecies – in Geoffrey of Monmouth's *History of the Kings of Britain* (c. 1135) – could be interpreted as referring to John.

Protector of King and Realm

After they'd laid the king to rest, the great lords agreed to leave Worcester and headed straight to Gloucester, where they rightly decided to send for the earl of Chester[547] and other barons who they knew were loyal to the king, wherever they might be in England, bidding them come – if they dared despite the war – and join them at Gloucester without fail. When they arrived they met in council, and all agreed as one to send Sir Thomas of Sandford to Devizes to fetch the king's young son;[548] they would then follow God's guidance and do what was right and proper. And they sent word to all the child's entourage that they were to let no one stop them coming with him.

The Marshal went and met them in open country outside Malmesbury; there was a large armed escort for the child, and rightly so. Ralph de Saint-Samson was there; he had been – and still was – the child's guardian, responsible for his upbringing, and was carrying him in his arms. The Marshal went forward to meet him; he greeted the child, who replied most graciously, saying:

'Welcome, sir. I entrust myself, truly, to God and to you, praying you in God's name to care for me; and may the true God who bestows all blessings grant that you manage our affairs successfully and keep us safe.'

'My dear lord,' the Marshal said, 'I faithfully swear upon my soul, as long as I am able I shall be your loyal servant and ever mindful of your safety.'

The king and all around him were moved to tears, as was the Marshal.

They set off then and made their way to Gloucester, where the principal lords discussed whether to wait for the earl of Chester or to undertake the coronation without him. Some said they should wait for him, but others thought they should press on quickly with making the boy king, for no one knows what's around the corner.

'The sooner the better,' said one. 'There's no point in waiting – by my life, if we delay too long we may end up with nothing! And I tell you, the earl's so good and worthy and wise that he won't object to us crowning the prince: he'll be pleased to see us get on with it! He knows how much it matters.'

And so it was resolved. Then, when it came to the child's coronation, the members of the council debated who should knight him; and one said:

'Who else but the one – even if there were a thousand of us – who's more worthy than any, of higher standing, and has done more deeds of valour? That's William the Marshal, who girded the sword of the Young King. God has favoured him so much – none of us can match him! I think I've proved he should gird the new king's sword – it must be so: then he will have knighted two kings.'

This was agreed by all. Then they dressed the prince in royal apparel, made to fit his little frame: a fine little knight he was! And the great lords present bore him to the cathedral, where he received the gift of succession through anointing and

---

[547] Ranulf de Blondeville, 6th earl of Chester, a staunch supporter of John.
[548] Prince Henry was nine years old.

crowning.[549] The legate Guala sang the mass and crowned him, with the ready and willing assistance of the bishops present there.

Once he'd been crowned and anointed and the service was done, the attendant knights didn't stand on ceremony but took the child, of such tender years, in their arms: Sir Philip d'Aubigny[550] and William de Ferrers[551] in particular – though many of those who lent a hand proved later to be little help to the king.[552] They carried him to his chamber where they took off his coronation robes – sensibly so, as they were very heavy – and dressed him in other clothes.

But then, after he'd entered the hall, grim news arrived. They were seated at table and about to dine when a messenger came to the Marshal; he can't have been the brightest, as he blurted out in the hearing of all:

'Sir, your constable sends word from Goodrich Castle that yesterday before none* it came under siege, and he begs you send help this very night, at once!'

The Marshal withdrew and didn't delay: he sent knights and men-at-arms and crossbowmen who marched right through the night. Meanwhile there were some in the hall discussing the news and saying:

'This is a sign, and it's far from good! On the very day that the child is crowned, the Marshal's castle is besieged just a few leagues away!'[553]

Then all the great lords present gathered in council and said to the Marshal:

'Hear us, sir. You have knighted your lord, which is much to your honour, and thanks to you he has now been crowned. We have decided – rightly, in our view – to ask you to take in hand the guardianship of the king: we know you'll do it far better than we, and we've no doubt you'll govern the land, in both peace and war, better than anyone.'

But he replied: 'I cannot. I've no longer the strength and vigour to fulfil such a task. I'm old now – I can't accept the office: it needs to be given to someone else. Come what may, wait till the earl of Chester's here. Then we'll be in a better position to decide.'

That's how it was left that night, and everyone retired to his lodging or wherever he had business.

The Marshal returned to the castle[554] and quickly called to his rooms Sir John the Marshal, Sir Ralph Musard[555] and John of Earley. There were just the four of them present, and he said to them:

'These men are very eager that I be the king's guardian and assume the care and government of the realm. Before committing to any of that I'd like your advice – it's a weighty task!'

Sir John the Marshal answered, saying: 'For many a day, sir, you've enjoyed great esteem and honour in the world – not least the honour here of knighting

[549] Henry's initial coronation took place at Gloucester Cathedral on 28 October 1216.
[550] Soon to be a leading commander in the royal army.
[551] The MS reads '*Ricart de Ferriers*', but this is surely a reference to William de Ferrers, 4th earl of Derby.
[552] i.e. in the crisis that was about to follow.
[553] Goodrich is only twenty miles or so from Gloucester.
[554] i.e. Gloucester Castle.
[555] A Gloucestershire baron, Marshal had made him castellan (and sheriff) of Gloucester.

your lord the king. And it's deemed an even greater honour that he's been crowned by you, thanks be to glorious God. It comes down to this: a man, they say, who doesn't finish what he's started has laboured in vain – his time and efforts are wasted! So do it! God will assist you, and it will bring you great honour indeed.'

'God save me, sir, he's spoken well,' said Ralph Musard. 'Accept this office and enhance your standing. The way I see it, it'll be the best for all! It'll be splendid! You'll be in a position, if you choose, to make all your followers – and others, and us three here! – rich men!'

'And you, Sir John of Earley?' said the Marshal. 'What do you think? I'd like your approval.'

'I'll give you my opinion, sir, indeed I will. God save me, I really don't see how I can advise you to accept. Your body's strength is waning – through exertion and through age. And the king has scant resources, so anyone wanting anything from him will be coming to beg it from *you*! I'm very worried: I fear the pressure and the trouble will be hard for you to bear.'

'Let's wait for the earl to come,' the Marshal said. 'We'll have better guidance then. Let's to our beds now – and may God bring peace and resolution!'

The next morning after mass the good earl of Chester arrived and came before the king and bowed to him. The king stepped forward and greeted him graciously and accepted his homage, as he did from others present who rightly owed it to him. Some of the earl's followers were offended that the decision had been taken to crown the king before the earl's arrival; they thought it disrespectful, a disgrace, but the earl himself said:

'That's enough! I think it was wisely done: I'd have been less pleased to see it delayed.'

Then all who'd come and were present in the city were summoned to assemble in the king's hall without fail. They did so at once, allowing nothing to detain them, and when they were gathered the great lords discussed the choosing and appointment of a worthy guardian for the king and for the kingdom: careful consideration was needed to determine who would be best. The bishop of Winchester said to Sir Alan Basset:

'I lay it on your shoulders, Sir Alan! The decision rests on you!'

'In faith, good sir,' Sir Alan replied, 'the only contender in my view is the Marshal – either he or the earl of Chester it should be.'

Then the Marshal said quite reasonably and in all sincerity: 'Truly, sirs, I can't assume such a great responsibility. I'm too worn and frail now – I'm more than eighty![556] In God's name, my lord earl of Chester, accept it – it should be you! You'll have my support as long as I have strength: I'll be faithfully at your command to the best of my ability. As long as God gives me grace I'll do whatever you bid in person or by letter.'

'No, Marshal! It cannot be!' the earl of Chester said. 'My good, dear sir, I know you to be so fine a knight, so worthy, accomplished, feared and loved

---

[556] Marshal was in fact about seventy, having been born c. 1146. It's probable that the author didn't know Marshal's exact age, only that he was unusually long-lived for the time.

and wise – you're one of the finest in the whole, wide world! You should be the protector, sir – accept the role: that's my sincere advice. I shall serve you, undertaking if it's in my power whatever mission you ask of me, without demur, wherever it may be.'

Then the legate drew the Marshal to one side, and called the bishop of Winchester and some of the great lords present and took them to a chamber to confer; but try as they might, no matter what they said, they could reach no resolution. So the legate took charge and implored the Marshal in God's name to assume the guardianship in return for forgiveness and remission of his sins, for which he granted him total absolution before God on Judgement Day.

'In the Lord's name,' said the Marshal, 'if it saves me from my sins, this office suits me well! Much as it pains me, I'll accept it!'

So the legate duly bestowed the position upon him, and the Marshal accepted guardianship of the king and of the realm. And he performed it well, I'd say, as long as he lived. But we were robbed of him too soon. And that was a great loss for England, for the land declined much in consequence – and will decline still more shamefully unless God soon intervenes! Declined? That's all too plain! Iniquity has overtaken Prowess and swept it to the rear, thrusting its own banner to the fore! I shan't say too much, though it has to be said that in God's good time the root of the evil will be revealed! But I'll leave it at that – it's not part of my theme.

Having accepted the office, the Marshal spoke thus: 'The king is young, sirs, of tender years; I wouldn't wish to take him with me around the land. If it please you, with your help I'd like to appoint a worthy man to keep him somewhere in comfort and safety. I think that's essential: I don't want to take him with me, and I can't stay in one place. He needs a guardian while I go around the marches keeping order. So I'd like your considered choice of one to whom I can entrust him safely and with confidence.'

The legate answered, saying: 'Let it be whomever you wish, sir: we've no doubt you'll appoint the right man.'

'If you're leaving it to me,' he said, 'I think I know who'll be a fine guardian: I'll entrust him to the bishop of Winchester, who's lately been most attentive and cared for him splendidly.'

The worthy lords present thanked him and thoroughly approved, and the bishop duly took the king under his wing and cared for him well.

When those outside heard what had transpired – that the Marshal had been made protector of the king and of the realm – they were overjoyed. 'God is watching over us for sure!' they said. 'There's no man in England more fitted to the task or better able to fulfil it.' They stayed there, greatly cheered, till evening.

And to come straight to the point, the Marshal reconvened his trusty council in the same place as he had the previous night – the same three who'd been with him then – and leaning against a wall he said:

'I need your advice, by the faith I owe you. I've ventured into the wild sea where even the most experienced sailors find no shore or anchorage – it's a wonder that anyone ever comes safe to port! May God come to my rescue! I've been entrusted with a ship that's already close to sinking: you can surely sense it. Our child-king's treasury's empty – it's disastrous – and I'm a man well on in years!'

His heart was so afflicted that tears welled from his eyes and ran down his face, and those with him, their love for him sincerely felt, shed tears of pity. Then he looked up and said:

'Have you nothing more to say?'

'Yes,' said John of Earley, who'd grasped the situation fully. 'You've assumed a task that can't be shirked on any account. But in seeing it through, even with the worst outcome you'll win great honour! Let me propose the worst, and show what honour will befall you: suppose all your side desert you for Louis, and stoop so low as to surrender every castle, to the point where you've no refuge left in England and have to abandon the land, and Louis pursues you and you flee all the way to Ireland; even then you'll have won great honour! So, then: if the worst result is honour, the best is elation and the highest prestige! You'll know joy indeed if God sees to it that the best befalls you! Even the dimmest will have to admit that no man of any lineage ever won such honour in this world – that's a prize worth winning!'

'By the Holy Lance,' the earl replied, 'that's good and true advice! It stirs my heart, so much indeed that if all the world had abandoned the king but I, do you know what I'd do? I'd carry him astride my neck and bear him unfailingly from isle to isle, from land to land, even if I had to beg for bread!'

'By God, good sir, you couldn't have spoken better!' said his fellows, applauding his words and saying he was sure to succeed, for God would be on his side.

'Let's to our beds now,' he said, 'and may God who governs all send help and inspiration, as he surely aids those committed to goodness and loyalty.'

The king and his attendants, including the Marshal and the other worthies, left Gloucester and made their way to Bristol. Sir Savari de Mauléon[557] was there, I understand, and he came before the king and asked leave to return to his own land.[558]

At this point[559] Prince Louis was besieging Hertford, where the defenders were in low spirits with no prospect of relief. The king's men went to Louis to request a truce for twenty days, which he granted in return for the surrender of Hertford and Berkhamsted. So rightly or wrongly, they fell into his hands.[560] It was a short while after this that the justiciar[561] and Sir Faulkes (who was working his way to prominence)[562] joined the king at Bristol with a fair number of other eminent

---

[557] See above, pp. 154 and 158. He was at this time the keeper of Bristol Castle.
[558] In Poitou, from where he then set off to the Holy Land.
[559] November 1216.
[560] Hertford Castle surrendered around 6 December; Berkhamsted Castle was handed to Louis in return for a Christmas truce that ran till the middle of January 1217.
[561] Hubert de Burgh.
[562] Faulkes de Bréauté was a notably loyal royalist but later fell out both with the king and with Marshal – hence the author's use of this phrase insinuating that Faulkes was a smooth and possibly devious operator.

men. When the truce expired, those who'd negotiated it agreed to another, again for twenty days, without consulting the Marshal; this was not well done: they gave up in return two fine, strong, splendid castles, at Norwich and Orford.[563] They did this on their own, without a word to the Marshal, and it was a bad move: Louis had thus won possession of four castles. And he didn't even keep the truce as he'd promised – the French, more overweening than ever (and in too strong a position), wouldn't condone it and refused to let him!

Louis now decided he would return to France,[564] and the Marshal, aware that Louis, far from observing the truce, had broken it, said:

'Tell him *we* won't keep it, either! We'll not treat with him and that's that! Let both sides make the best of what they can!'

The Marshal mustered all the good true men who were loyal to the king and still sincerely loved him, till none capable of bearing arms remained behind, and headed for Chertsey.[565] Meanwhile Louis made straight and fast for Winchelsea,[566] but he couldn't put to sea with his barons: he found himself blockaded. The Marshal had discussed with the great lords what they should do, and how they could crush the pretensions of Louis, whose presence in the land was not their doing; and now you can hear the shrewd, valiant, noble plan the Marshal had proposed to the loyal lords, which led to the deaths of a thousand of the rogues who'd got ahead of themselves! He took Philip d'Aubigny and a body of good knights and tried and tested men-at-arms, and with this fine company he garrisoned the town of Rye;[567] then he sent a well armed and provisioned fleet to blockade Winchelsea. He now advanced on Louis swiftly with a mighty force of knights and men, and when they drew near they penned him in so tightly that he didn't know which way to turn. He was stuck: on one side was the Marshal and on the other the good and brave Sir Philip, who was doing a deal of damage, killing a great number of his men; and the fleet at sea was a problem, not to mention Willikin of the Weald, who was giving him nothing to laugh about, harrying his men at every turn and having many of those he caught beheaded. Louis was hard pressed indeed – he felt well and truly cornered. Around a thousand of his men were killed, their confessions heard only by the swords and spears that came their way the moment they strayed and were isolated. So that band of rogues who'd bragged that England would be theirs were battered and almost destroyed: none remained in the land laying claim to any part of it – and I can't say that's a shame. Two eminent vavasors were captured there, I believe, who'd abandoned Louis and were heading home – Anselm de Pont-de-l'Arche and John FitzHugh[568] – and with

---

[563] In Suffolk, north-east of Ipswich, and an important port in the Middle Ages.
[564] Under threat of excommunication by the Pope, who was intervening on Henry's behalf.
[565] On the Thames in Surrey.
[566] In late February 1217. At this time Winchelsea was a thriving port in Sussex.
[567] Less than five miles from Winchelsea.
[568] '*Alsemen de Poent de l'arche e Johans...filz Hue*'. FitzHugh was a knight from Northumberland who had sided with Prince Louis; Anselm was probably a member of the same family as Robert de Pont-de-l'Arche mentioned above, p. 103. Both later received pardons for their disloyalty.

them quite a few Englishmen who are still despised for their conduct: at least, that's the view of many.

Louis himself would have been caught and captured had it not been for chance and Fortune – who frowns on England's heirs and robs them of their birthright! How harsh Fortune can be! But how She advances those She decides to favour! No one, regardless of wealth or beauty, royalty or the support of friends, can withstand Fortune's blows if She's vowed to strike; against Her we're all defenceless! But enough. What happened was that Sir Hugh Tacon,[569] dead set against us, came with a great fleet to rescue Louis – which he succeeded in doing, arriving in such force that he was able to bear him back to France. He wrecked our ships, I have to tell you, while Prince Louis rode with a great body of knights to Rye, where the king's garrison, seeing they couldn't resist them (they numbered more than three thousand), abandoned the town – there was no point staying: they couldn't have defended it, so they withdrew. And Louis rode on to Dover and took ship.

But that's enough of him for now. I'll say no more; I want to return to the Marshal. When he learned that Louis was headed back to France he made his way to Shoreham[570] with most of his army. They stayed there that night, and as they left next day they met the young Marshal[571] and the good, fair, worthy Earl William of Salisbury, who loved each other like brothers.[572] Then together they marched on Knepp[573] which was barely defended and quickly surrendered. So that was that; and next day the young Marshal left his father, and he and the earl of Salisbury, staying ever close, went swiftly with their men to Winchester and laid siege to the castle immediately, wanting to make a telling show.[574] The army was now divided, as some of the great lords set off with Marshal the father, tireless as ever, to lay siege to Farnham. The young Marshal and the earl of Salisbury took lodging at Hyde[575] as they laid siege to Winchester, doing little on the first day but mounting an assault on the next. But the day after that, according to the record I have, the father sent word that they and their forces were to rejoin him without delay. So off they went; but when they reached Alresford[576] it seems they ran into messengers who told them that Farnham Castle had been taken! Hearing this they turned back once again, riding in good, tight order, telling their men to be alert and proceed with care, in case the defenders of Winchester launched a surprise attack.

And let me tell you, when they'd seen the besieging army leave, the Winchester garrison had been jubilant, and stormed from their castles[577] and into the town, looting and burning, enraged that the townsfolk had defied them and harboured

---

[569] Hugh Tacon d'Aubigny, a baron from Picardy.
[570] A small town on the Sussex coast. Marshal was there on the night of 4 March 1217.
[571] i.e. William, his eldest son.
[572] The author chooses not to mention that they'd been siding with Louis but had now defected.
[573] A castle in Sussex north of Shoreham.
[574] i.e. to show their commitment to their new cause, though the author plays that down.
[575] Hyde Abbey, just outside the city walls.
[576] 'Aurfobest'. Alresford is in Hampshire, not far up the road from Winchester to Farnham.
[577] There were two castles at Winchester, the larger built by William the Conqueror and the smaller belonging to the bishop.

their attackers. But they didn't have time to do the job as thoroughly as they'd have liked, for the besiegers suddenly reappeared, and they had to leave their work undone and flee back to the castles. (Unfortunately for the people of the outer town, the suburbs outside the walls, they'd sided with the garrison and were made to pay the price.) The earl of Salisbury besieged and took the smaller of the castles, while the young Marshal boldly, bravely laid siege to the bigger, committing so many men to the assault, both day and night, with strength and valour for eight whole days, maintaining such relentless pressure, that the defenders couldn't rest and didn't dare show their faces. Once the earl of Salisbury had taken the first castle, he hurried to give his full support to the young Marshal at the other. These two firm friends attacked with such resolve, launching such a barrage of arrows and missiles, that the defenders were aghast, dismayed indeed. And at this point the elder Marshal arrived with a mighty host and company of knights that filled the riverside and the country all around the town. The garrison in the tower now saw that they hadn't a chance of holding out – there was no way they could resist.

As soon as Marshal the father arrived, he met with the others to make plans. It was clear that the garrison couldn't hold out or mount a defence for long – they would have to surrender; it was decided that the elder Marshal would stay and continue the siege, the defenders being utterly trapped, and following his father's proposal the young Marshal and the earl of Salisbury marched swiftly with their forces to Southampton. Without a word of a lie or a shadow of a doubt, the spoils from that town were so great that the poor who took part in the plunder made themselves rich from the wealth of their foes; and the young Marshal and the earl of Salisbury and their men then set to work and took the castle and appointed a constable and governor before returning to Winchester.

The Marshal now sent a body of fine knights – Sir Philip d'Aubigny and a good number of others – to take the castle of Rochester, which they duly and swiftly did before rejoining him at Winchester. And it was shortly after this that the young Marshal came to his father, who was still continuing the siege, and said:

'Truly, sir, I say we should be more concerned with taking Marlborough, for it's ours by right.[578] If it please you, while you stay here I'll go with my men and besiege it and garrison it with friends who've promised me their aid.'

This was done and carried out to the letter – the record I have bears me out: on the very first Friday after Easter[579] the young Marshal advanced on Marlborough and besieged the castle till he took it, though not without great difficulty. Prince Louis, seven weeks and five days after he'd left, I believe, returned to England with a fierce and mighty army, but the Marlborough garrison, in a sorry trap and not knowing he'd come, surrendered in return for their safe release.[580] But the Marshal had heard of Louis's return and wasn't happy; he had all the castles he'd captured destroyed at once with the sole exception of Farnham. Meanwhile

---

[578] Marshal's father had held Marlborough Castle in the previous century (see above, p. 30) – it had been granted to him by King Stephen – though Henry II had in fact taken it back in 1158.
[579] 31 March 1217.
[580] Louis returned on 22 April, so Marlborough Castle evidently surrendered shortly after that date, the siege having lasted nearly a month.

the men who'd surrendered Marlborough, hearing that Louis was back, were downcast and ashamed of what they'd done!

For his part, Louis was less than pleased to learn that the castles he'd thought were his had been taken. With his mighty army – and a great rabble of carters, foot soldiers, crossbowmen and other thugs and hangers-on eager for war – he by-passed Farnham without more ado, not wanting to spend time or bolts and arrows there, heading instead straight for Winchester,[581] for the damage it had suffered upset him greatly. In a matter of a few short days he rebuilt the keep and high walls splendidly with stone and lime, and repaired the breaches and all the damage till the defences were fine and strong and looked as good as new. With the castle restored to strength and splendour he departed, leaving the count of Nevers,[582] a cruel and overbearing man, with a very strong garrison; he went on to commit many wicked acts which earned him great shame, but I don't want to talk of them here.

On leaving Winchester Prince Louis divided his mighty host into two great armies. He marched swiftly to lay siege to Dover and sent his other force to a castle called Mountsorrel,[583] which was being besieged by the earl of Chester and, I believe, Earl Ferrers[584] and many other fine knights. When they heard of the great body advancing on them, bent on their destruction and capture, the earls didn't dare wait to face them, assuming that if they were coming in such numbers Louis must be among them; so they withdrew, and little wonder, and headed for Nottingham, leaving their camp and all their siege engines in flames. They wouldn't have returned for all the wealth of Limoges! Then the French, having relieved Mountsorrel, made with all speed for Lincoln where they prepared in earnest to besiege the city and the castle.

The Battle of Lincoln

When the Marshal learned that the siege of Mountsorrel was lifted he was enraged – and the others were none too pleased; and then, when word came that this large French force was at Lincoln, and that Louis wasn't among them, he was very disturbed and tense and troubled.

The day before the eve of Pentecost[585] he was with the king's men at Northampton; and it was now that God, who ever supports and aids and guides the loyal, steered them wondrously to great success and honour. Hear now what happened. All who have ears, attend and listen! You're about to hear how God lent guidance to that worthy man who was trusted, esteemed and respected above all others.

'Hear me, true and noble knights,' William the Marshal said, 'who remain loyal to our king. Heed my words, in God's name, for what I have to say is vital. Since

---

[581] It was now the end of April 1217.
[582] Hervé IV of Donzy.
[583] North of Leicester. The earl of Chester had begun a siege of the castle at the end of March.
[584] The earl of Derby (see note 533 above, p. 183).
[585] 13 May 1217.

we're about to take up arms in defence of our names, our land, our lives and the lives of those we love, our wives, our children, and to win the greatest honour, and to restore the peace of Holy Church which our enemies have shattered and violated, and to earn redemption and forgiveness for all our sins, be sure that none of you lacks courage this day! Part of our enemy's force has entered Lincoln, intent on besieging our castle, I know. But not all of them are there: Lord Louis, it seems, has gone elsewhere. His followers have made a grave mistake! And we'll be sorely wanting if we fail to take revenge now on those who've come from France to rob our people of their inheritance. They mean to ruin us entirely! So let's go to it with a will, mindful that if victory's ours we'll enhance our honour and preserve for ourselves and our descendants the freedom that our foes would outrageously steal. They'll not succeed – God wants us to defend our rights! And since they've divided their forces we'll more easily defeat one part of their army than the whole! I'd say that's right and obvious – God wills it, and reason proves it! So it's only right that each of us should strive his utmost – how can we do otherwise? It's surely plain to all that we must cut a swathe with iron and steel! This is no time for idle threats – let's go straight to the attack! God in His grace has sent us the chance to avenge ourselves on those who've come to abuse and wrong us. No one should hold back: a man takes full revenge for the shame and wrong he's suffered when he overcomes his enemy!'

These words fired them with hope and heart and strength and courage, and they couldn't wait to go. On the Wednesday of Pentecost[586] they rode to Newark where they spent the night, and rested on the Thursday. Then the Normans in the army came to the young Marshal[587] and addressed him thus:

'In God's name, good sir, you were born in Normandy; you surely understand that Normans should strike the first blows in any battle! We trust you'll observe that right – don't let us down!'

But the earl of Chester heard this and wasn't happy; he insisted that if he didn't lead the first charge he'd take no part in the battle! They'd have no support from him! The Marshal and the others didn't relish this dispute: they granted him all he wanted, while acknowledging the Normans' rights.

With the matter settled, the legate duly granted them absolution and remission from every sin they'd committed since the moment they were born, so that they'd be free and clear of them on Judgement Day. And he excommunicated the French inside the city – he truly did: that's a well-known fact. Then he set off and headed for Nottingham, while the army made their way to Torksey[588] where they spent the night.

Next morning, a Saturday it was,[589] after mass they took up arms, preparing with the utmost care; and when they were fully, finely armed they formed their battalions in proper fashion and duly ordered their squadrons. The earl of Chester, a worthy and experienced knight, led the first, and the Marshal the

---

[586] 17 May.
[587] i.e. William the younger, Marshal's eldest son.
[588] About ten miles north-west of Lincoln.
[589] 20 May.

second with his son right beside him, earnestly hoping to do all in their power to advance the cause – as indeed they did: they made a mighty contribution that day; the good earl of Salisbury (may God and His mother receive him to their side in glory)[590] was at the head of the third battalion, and the good bishop of Winchester, commander of another part of the army, led the fourth – he was more than capable. The whole army, when counted, numbered only four hundred and six knights[591] and three hundred and seventeen crossbowmen; but though they were few they made a fine show, for they were a fine, brave body of men. And when they were drawn up in proper array, the Marshal addressed them nobly – he was the master of such speeches – saying:

'Listen now, sirs! Glory and honour are at hand! Right here and now, you can win the country's freedom, truly: so damn any man who fails this day to challenge those who seize our lands and property! And may God see that right prevails! The enemy are here, right here in your hands. They're at our mercy, I promise you, come what may, unless heart and courage fail us. And if we die in this mission, then God who sees and knows the good will set us in His paradise, in that I place my certain trust; and if we defeat them, without a lie, we'll have won lasting honour for all time, for ourselves and all our line! And I tell you, our enemies labour under another grievous burden: they're excommunicated! How much more that shackles them! What a dismal fate they have in store: they'll be going straight to Hell! They're waging war on God and Holy Church, and I swear God has placed them at our mercy. So come, make haste, let's fall on them – the time and the hour are upon us!'

The Marshal, having made this address like the valiant, loyal, accomplished knight he was, entrusted the crossbowmen to the good Bishop Peter of Winchester: he was a fine and skilled commander of such a force, and always strove to excel. He told him to deploy at once to the right of the French[592] in an extended, drawn-out line, ready to bring down the French horses when they advanced. The Marshal also called for two hundred soldiers and ordered them to slaughter their own horses if the need arose, to create defensive barriers. All who heard the earl responded with joy, as cheerily as if it had been a tournament!

Unless I'm much mistaken the French inside Lincoln numbered six hundred and eleven knights and at least a thousand foot, not counting the English who still sided with them. Sir Simon de Poissy, the count of Perche and the earl of Winchester rode out of the city to reconnoitre the king's army and make an accurate assessment of their strength. They were quickly back to report that they looked impressive indeed: nowhere had they ever seen such a well-armed force more ready for battle. Hearing this the French drew back inside the walls,[593] convinced that the royal army wasn't strong enough to attack them in the city,

---

[590] This suggests that this part of the *History* was written shortly after the earl's death in March 1226.
[591] To be precise the MS at this point says 405, but this contradicts a later figure (below, p. 204) which is probably correct as it is used in a rhyme.
[592] i.e. to confront the French right wing.
[593] Through the north gate and into the area of high ground between the cathedral and the castle.

however fine a show they might make, and would be sure to withdraw. But they wouldn't let them calmly ride away without some kind of engagement first, they swore to that; and they were sure they'd win plenty of booty from them, for the king's men's horses were weary from their to-ing and fro-ing, their long and endless marching, bearing their riders night and day. The French were right about that, but it made no difference: the king's knights and the whole royal army made a bold and open advance upon the city, the Marshal exhorting and urging them on, filling them with courage and heart, saying:

'See, my friends: those who were so keen to attack have cracked already – they're cowering behind the walls! God is fulfilling His promise: He's bestowing great glory upon us this day. Here's one victory already: the French, always first to enter a tourney, are hiding from us! God is at our side! They're handing us honour and demeaning themselves, surrendering the fields out here to us! And the city will be ours, too, I promise you! Fight bravely now: it's God's will! Let all who've proved their worth in the past commit themselves to their very best, and have no cause to repent of this day!'

I should add at this point, sirs, that those who've given me accounts of what followed don't all agree, and I can't comply with them all – I'd lose track of myself and be less worthy of credence. No one should tell untruths when recording proper history: falsehoods have no place in such a celebrated story, heard about and witnessed by so many. But I can tell you this much: before the royal army began their advance, as soon as the Marshal saw how things stood – that the French had withdrawn inside the walls – he told his nephew John the Marshal to go and assess the situation at the castle[594] and then come back. Sir John did just as he said, promptly and with a will. He headed straight for the castle, and as he approached, Sir Geoffrey de Serland[595] came swiftly to meet him and showed him an exact way for the army to enter unopposed.[596] Sir John could see he was quite right, and turned back at once, not wanting to dally. But just as he was setting off, French look-outs came rushing to attack him. Undaunted, he boldly met the first of them, and they couldn't withstand his fierce, brave prowess, his skill and speed; he soon beat them off – none dared stay to face him[597] – and so it was that Sir John escaped the French without harm or mishap, having made it plain that he was coming after them to reclaim his land! After sending them packing he rode back to his uncle and told him what had happened. His uncle was delighted with his work, not to mention the news of the entrance. So that's what Sir John did at this point, and I'll tell the rest in my own good time: what he did in the battle that followed I'll explain in due course as the story requires.

The bishop of Winchester, wanting to reconnoitre further, now headed boldly for the walls with a large body of crossbowmen, but told them to stop

---

[594] i.e. how the castle's defenders and defences were withstanding the French siege.
[595] One of the castle's main defenders.
[596] Presumably through the castle's west gate, which abutted the town wall, standing as the castle did on the very edge of the medieval city: see map of the battle of Lincoln, above, p. xv.
[597] This seems to be the general sense of a passage in which unresolved rhymes indicate at least two missing lines.

and wait a little: he'd be straight back. Then accompanied by a single soldier he entered the castle, and as he did so he met Sir Geoffrey de Serland in a fearful state. They could see the walls being battered, devastated, a distressing sight indeed; the bishop saw the wreckage of the walls and houses and the plight of the townsfolk, bombarded now by catapults and trebuchets. Some of the defenders were warning the bishop, begging him in God's name to take cover, for the mangonels and catapults were smashing everything in sight. Into the keep he went, where he found the good lady of the castle[598] – may God preserve her, body and soul – who was doing her utmost to defend it. The lady was overjoyed by his coming, and he comforted her greatly with the news he brought. But he didn't stay long, I assure you: he stepped out through a postern into the town, wanting to see how things stood. And as he looked about, he spotted an old gate – of great antiquity, it was – which connected the walls of the town with those of the castle.[599] He was thrilled by this, but it had long ago been walled up with rubble and mortar, making it quite impossible for anyone to enter. So to strengthen the castle's position the bishop bade that this gate be broken through, demolished, so that the army could see a safe way in. He first prayed to God that this would work – and God answered his prayer. Then the bishop returned to the army who came and greeted him with joy, raucously singing as if victory were already theirs!

The bishop, in high good humour, joked about why he'd pulled this stunt: it was so he could claim the bishop's palace to sleep in that night – he'd every right to lodging there! 'It can hardly be refused me – not when I've arranged a safe way in for all our valiant men!'

When Faulkes's men[600] heard this they were exultant, and swept forward into the town; but they met with fierce resistance and made little headway – it all went quickly wrong.

'By my life!' the bishop said to the Marshal. 'What have they done? They've clearly not found the way in I intended[601] – they could have entered unopposed: no one's defending it; there's nothing to fear. I promise you, there's a breach in the wall that's open to us and hidden from the enemy. I'll lead you there: come!'

And the good Earl William Marshal replied: 'By the Holy Lance, bring me my helm!'

But the bishop said: 'Hear me, sir: we mustn't attack in such haste. Let's send two men from each of our battalions to scout around the castle and see if there are any more surprises. Then we can act according to what they find.'

---

[598] Nicola de la Haye, who had been castellan of Lincoln for many years following the deaths of her husband and son.
[599] The author is almost certainly describing the ancient west gate of the Roman city of Lindum. This gate was sited in the town wall just to the north of the Norman castle.
[600] The royal battalion led by Faulkes de Bréauté.
[601] According to Roger of Wendover in his chronicle, Faulkes had entered through the castle; he had initially stationed his crossbowmen on the battlements to shoot at the French in the streets below before sallying forth into their midst, whereupon Faulkes himself had been captured in the fighting but later rescued.

The Marshal agreed and set off, while the bishop of Winchester [took ten men],[602] two from each battalion, and headed for the castle. When they ran into the throng of troops who'd basely turned tail[603] they gave them a deal of abuse.

The Marshal now cried to all his men: 'Onward! Victory will soon be ours, you'll see! Shame on anyone who lags behind!'

But the bishop said: 'A moment! Hear me, sir: wait for the rest – it'll be better and safer if we all attack as one rather than separately. Our enemies will be more daunted if they see us all together. And we'll make them pay!'

But the Marshal, truly, took no notice. He thrust in his spurs and started forward faster than a merlin, and all his men who saw him were fired with courage. Then a boy interjected:

'Wait, good sir, in God's name – you haven't got your helm!'

Earl William realised this was true! And he said to the young Marshal: 'Wait here while I get my helm – I nearly came unstuck!'

It didn't take him long, and as soon as he was helmeted he looked the grandest of them all. As swift and light of movement as a bird – a sparrowhawk or alerion* – he spurred his horse forward, eager to make his presence known, and no ravening lion, falling on its prey when he sees it at its mercy, ever attacked with the speed of the Marshal on his foe. That performer of so many feats of prowess plunged fully three lance-lengths into their massed ranks, breaking and scattering the press, densely packed and determined though they were, driving a path clean through them as he sent them reeling in disarray. The bishop followed behind, crying at the top of his voice in all directions:

'Come! This way! God help the Marshal!'

I mustn't forget to mention that in the course of our knights' attack the master of the enemy's catapults, bombarding the castle keep, was killed. At first he was cheered by our men's approach, thinking they were on his side. All the better, he thought, and set another stone in his catapult; but in the middle of giving the command 'Let fly!' the second word never left his lips, as the knights riding up behind him unceremoniously took off his head.

Meanwhile the young Marshal had made it clear that he'd no wish to lag behind: his banner was ever at the forefront – he made his presence felt that day! Our men advanced fiercely, and the enemy defended with a will at first – but didn't choose to stay there long, for no time was being wasted on idle threats! While the Marshal was having his helmet laced, his son had entered the city through the breach with a great body of his men – he had many able followers. The enemy were in a strong position, outnumbering the attackers, but the young Marshal charged straight in. Their resistance was soon broken; both sides performed some splendid feats of arms, but before all was done the defenders came off worse: the young Marshal, I assure you, sent them packing.

And his father charged forward with the good earl of Salisbury (may God and His mother graciously grant him pardon for his sins),[604] and together they turned

---

[602] The probable content of an uncompleted line.
[603] i.e. Faulkes's men, retreating from their battering.
[604] As noted above (p. 197), this may well help to date the composition of this part of the *History*.

right, leaving the cathedral[605] on their left, and found a great body of the enemy in alarm and consternation. Robert of Ropsley[606] seized a lance and prepared to joust, come what may; he struck the earl of Salisbury so hard that his lance smashed to pieces; he charged on past, but as he wheeled and was about to return the Marshal met him with a fearsome blow between the shoulders that almost felled him; realising his luck was out, Robert dropped to the ground and scurried off to hide in an upper room, not daring to stay in the street below. They paid no more heed to him, and headed on to pursue the battle, and found the count of Perche right in front of the cathedral, looking proud and fierce indeed: he was a fine, tall, impressive figure, backed by a great body of men. They defended stoutly, while our men assailed them with all their might, filled with hatred for the French. The fighting was intense, with many wounded, trampled, battered, maimed or seized and captured – our side suffering as much as those found in the city, for no one was asking for favours or respite: they were all intent on battle.

It was a mighty mêlée and combat, and the count of Perche fought splendidly indeed and began to inflict real damage on our men – though he wasn't to last long. Then the Marshal saw his men forcing the French back in no uncertain manner, driving them down the hill,[607] so he reached out and seized the count of Perche's bridle – rightly so, the count being the most eminent of the French. But the count had already taken a mortal wound from a sword, thrust in a fearful lunge through his visor by Sir Reginald Croc;[608] and now, as he saw our forces driving his men back, he let go of his reins and gripped his sword in both hands; then William the Marshal dealt him three successive blows upon the helm, so strong and fierce that they left clear marks upon it, whereupon the count collapsed and went tumbling from his horse.[609] Seeing him fall, the Earl Marshal thought he'd lost consciousness and feared he'd be held to blame. He said to William de Montigny:

'Dismount and take off his helm – it's giving him trouble: I fear he can't stand up.'

When the helmet was removed and the Marshal, at his side, saw that he was stone-cold dead, there was much consternation; but from the moment the blade had been pulled from the wound dealt through his visor, his death had been inevitable. It was a grievous pity that he died so.

---

[605] '*un mostier*' ('a church'): this is without doubt the cathedral, which stands close beside the castle.

[606] '*Rob. de Ropelei*'. Ropsley had been a prominent member of King John's household but had joined the rebel barons.

[607] The streets of Lincoln slope steeply downhill to the south of the cathedral.

[608] Previously a knight of King John's household, Croc is cited in Roger of Wendover's chronicle not as the slayer of the count of Perche but simply as 'a brave knight of Faulkes de Bréauté's retinue' and as being one of only three knights killed in the battle on either side.

[609] The preceding part of the paragraph is badly garbled in the MS. The scribe's jumbled syntax and phrasing and subject-shifting suggest inattention and, I would argue, almost certain misreading. He seems to have understood that it was the mortally wounded count who had struck Marshal's helm three times, but this makes little sense of the passage as a whole, and I have chosen to re-interpret and reconstruct an original meaning.

And when the French – despite their numbers – saw our forces assailing them so vigorously, they were dismayed and realised they could resist no longer. Unable to withstand the onslaught, they fell back down a street to the left, towards Wigford.[610] It proved to be a good move, as they ran into others of their side still there; they were greatly cheered, I'm sure, and rallied their forces and prepared to resume the fight – though they'd have been better advised to beat it, as some were soon to do: according to my sources, they looked to their right and saw the earl of Chester and his fine company and were filled with alarm.

Meanwhile the young Marshal came to his father who gave him a joyful welcome, delighted at what he'd seen and heard of his splendid contribution to the battle.

'Have you any wound?' he asked him.

'No, sir,' he replied.

And the worthy earl said: 'If it please God, today we're going to win back much of what we'd lost. I do believe we're going to crush the foe – or they'll give up the fight. And the rebels will see how misguided they were to side with the French.[611] Let every man fight with firm resolve: we're offering no truce.'[612]

At that moment the French advanced with the English who'd sided with them; they were coming up the hill in tight, serried ranks. But before they reached the top they were none too pleased to see our men appear in fine formation between the cathedral and the castle. Our forces attacked with such ferocity that they sent them pouring down the hill in all directions. Then, to their rear, Sir Alan Basset and his brother Sir Thomas roared their battle-cries and charged with all their brave, fierce men; the French were dismayed to find themselves surrounded, and were hard pressed, without a moment's break, all the way to the bridge at Wigford.[613] There they had soft ground to fight on,[614] so they didn't have to look far for chivalrous contest: anyone seeking deeds of arms had his hands full! And nothing less was at stake than heads and lives! It was no place for the boasts made indoors at night – it was time for real business! Both sides fought long and hard till even the strongest were tiring: there was no respite or hope of help – nothing but the giving and taking of blows.

There are some men who hold forth about deeds of arms who, if they held a shield by the straps in a battle like this, wouldn't know what to do with it; and if fully armed they'd think they were under a spell: they'd stand in a trance, no matter what happened! What's involved in performing deeds of arms? Is it like wielding a winnowing fan,[615] or swinging a mallet or an axe? No indeed –

---

[610] The southern suburb of the town, beyond the River Witham.

[611] This is a conjectural reconstruction of an uncompleted sentence; unresolved rhymes indicate at least two missing lines.

[612] '*Nos nes volons mie atrère*': literally 'we don't want to attract them'. This is possibly an ironic and absurd understatement, to be translated as something like 'I'd rather like to see the back of them'; but that does not sit well in context, and I suggest '*atrère*' is a misreading of '*atrever*' (agree a truce with) and have translated accordingly.

[613] This must surely be High Bridge, which crosses the Witham between the lower town and the suburb of Wigford.

[614] As opposed, presumably, to the Lincoln streets.

[615] Literally 'a sieve or winnowing basket'.

it's a great deal tougher than that. Most men can rest after labouring a while; but the work of a knight? It's a mighty business, demanding courage and so much application that none of little worth dares undertake it. But are all knights the same? No. There are quite a few who perform no deeds of arms but swan about all high and mighty! Any knight who seeks great honour needs to be thoroughly schooled in arms, and at the battle of Lincoln there were some who'd learned enough to achieve the highest renown. Prowess wasn't hidden in that engagement: you'd have seen an array of knights all armed, mounted on their destriers, shields braced; no one equipped with a good and worthy steed and a stout lance in hand would have swapped them for all the gold in Blaye[616] – or lent them on this occasion: they'd have taken some recovering! And you'd have seen mighty blows exchanged, and helms resound and ring, and lances flying into shards, and knights taken captive and saddles emptied. All around you'd have heard great blows of sword and mace on helms and arms, and knives and daggers drawn from sheaths to stab and slay the horses, a caparison as much protection as a cowl. Hands were thrusting on every side, reaching to seize bridles; some knights were racing to aid companions, or to rescue those they saw in trouble – though attempts at rescue came to nothing. So great was the din that you wouldn't have heard God's thunder if a storm had struck – or taken any note of it. At the cries of 'For the King! For the King!'[617] you'd have seen the traitors so stricken, stunned, cowering, awestruck, that they didn't know what to do – and there was no question of retreat. The king's men began to take prisoners, and there was little or no resistance: the rebels could see that all was lost. William Bloet, the young Marshal's banner-bearer, eager to be at the forefront, charged into the heaving throng, with such headlong force that he and his horse went plummeting over the bridge! No laggard, he! And he certainly wasn't looking for a rest: anyone seeing how he sprang straight up would have deemed him a knight of vigour, valour and prowess indeed.

The fighting now continued there, but wasn't sustained for long by the French – who'd previously been boasting that they'd chase all the English out of England! Among those taken prisoner were Saer de Quincy, earl of Winchester, and Sir Robert FitzWalter. Promptly taken too was Sir Robert de Quincy,[618] along with numerous others, I'm not sorry to say. The rest took to flight, all the way down the road that leads towards the Hospital.[619] They had a hard time reaching the outer gate,[620] and there they fell foul of a wretched stroke of luck: a cow had wandered through the gate and triggered the bar, closing the gate so that no one on horseback could get through:[621] they were well and truly stuck. In

---

[616] 'Blaive'. Blaye was an important stronghold in Aquitaine, but no doubt is mentioned here primarily because 'Blaive' rhymes with 'glaive' (lance).
[617] Literally 'Royals! Royals!'
[618] The earl's elder son.
[619] The Hospital of Holy Innocents Without Lincoln: a leper hospital outside the city to the south.
[620] Great Bargate, at the far edge of the southern suburbs, close to the Hospital.
[621] A bar automatically closed the gate after each person entered. A rider would have to dismount to re-open it.

their desperation to escape they killed the cow, but that just made the shambles worse, and many of their knights were captured there, as easily as could be.[622] The gate was then smashed in, and Sir Simon de Poissy fled through with all speed, followed by the castellan of Arras, scurrying like rats back to London, to the ladies who'd yielded and cleaved to their side.[623] The others who managed to escape rode night and day, never stopping in house or town – they imagined a Marshal behind every bush in hill and vale! The thought filled them with dread! They showed that well enough at Holland Bridge;[624] it was broken and unsound, and so desperate were they to get across that they killed their horses to make a bridge!

When Sir Richard of Sandford[625] saw the utter chaos and that all the French who could escape were fleeing, he realised all was lost, and took his wife and sat her on his horse before him to see if he could carry her to safety. A knight cried out:

'Leave her! You're not taking her away!'

Sir Richard was none too pleased by this; he gently put her down and turned and charged the knight who'd challenged him, and met him with a lance-blow high on the chest to send him crashing to the ground. Then he picked up his wife again, truly, and carried her off to safety.

The good bishop of Winchester, Peter des Roches, who commanded our forces so ably that day, was neither idle nor slow and knew how to fight. He set off in pursuit with his fine company, capturing numerous knights in the process, and those of his men who were after spoils won them in abundance: no knight intent on booty and prisoners could fail to win them that day. But no one in the end won more than that knight so full of qualities, being noble-hearted, valiant and loyal: Sir John the Marshal; before he left the battle Sir John, truly, captured seven barons, men of power and the highest status, all of them flying their own banners, along with a good few of their companion knights.

As I mentioned before, the number of knights, precisely counted, who'd stayed loyal to the king was a mere four hundred and six, while facing them were exactly six hundred and eleven; but it was the latter who met with disaster – and rightly so: that's what happens to those who are not on God's side.[626]

---

[622] Literally 'as if they'd been handed over'.

[623] This is a conjectural rendering of a strange couplet which is either severely corrupt or a barbed comment of which the significance and reference are not clear. It plays upon the rhyme of 'rats' with 'Arras' (and the fact that the coat of arms of Arras at that time featured three rats). Simon de Poissy and Hugh, castellan of Arras, were two of the very few French lords who managed to escape the battle.

[624] Near Horbling in southern Lincolnshire, at what is now named Bridgend, was an important causeway called Holland Bridge which provided the only good route between the parts of the county known as Kesteven and Holland.

[625] Either the elder brother of Hugh, the member of Marshal's household (above, p. 125), or his nephew, the son of Thomas (above, p. 167). Both were named Richard, but one stayed loyal to the king and was constable of Devizes and the other – mentioned here – had sided with Prince Louis.

[626] The French having been excommunicated – above, p. 196.

The Battle of Sandwich

When the Marshal and his men had utterly vanquished and routed their foes, and seized and captured many of the highest rank, those loyal to the king returned to the city to decide the best way forward. But everyone involved had a different opinion: some proposed going to lay siege to London, which was still held against them; others said they should advance on Louis and force him to raise his siege of Dover. But opining and knowing aren't the same thing – why? Because that's not how God sees it. And the Marshal, whose knowledge and experience of war were greater than anyone's, advised them all to take their prisoners and keep them securely captive till they'd given their assurances, and then appointed a day when they were all to meet without fail at Chertsey. He sent word to the legate [Guala], too, asking him to be sure to join them there to discuss the future defence and protection of the realm and decide how best to proceed.

Louis was dismayed and furious when he heard his forces had suffered such a rout at Lincoln, with the loss of so many prisoners and the death of the count of Perche; he knew he'd come off worse for sure! He lifted his siege of Dover and headed for London with all speed, deeply worried and afraid that the royal army might take the city by surprise or force, or come and confront him in battle.

Such was his alarm that he sent to France for aid. And when King Philip of France heard of the disaster that had befallen his men, defeated and crushed at Lincoln, he was sorely troubled. And here's what he said:

'Is King John dead?'[627]

'Yes,' replied the messengers, 'and his son is already crowned king. And the Marshal is committed to protect him.'

'Then we can win nothing in England and that's that! With that worthy knight's acuity the land's defence is assured! Louis has lost! I tell you, if that valiant knight's involved we're sunk! It couldn't have turned out worse for Louis: he'll soon be driven from the land and his plans'll be scuppered once the Marshal gets to work!'

That's what he said. Then he set about assembling a huge force to be sent to support his son. And they would surely have been able to rescue him and help him to conquer the kingdom – if, that is, they'd been able to invade with the numbers that set out. But that was not God's plan. Louis's wife,[628] truly, went to every city in France and garnered support, both men and money, with such energy that she mustered a force which, had they all arrived armed in London, would have conquered the whole realm.

When the Marshal heard that such a mighty force was preparing to invade and conquer the kingdom he was most disturbed, and thought long and deeply

---

[627] The question works in the context of what follows, but cannot be authentic: John had by this time been dead for several months.
[628] Blanche of Castile.

about how he could mount a defence of the realm, for the king was young indeed and quite devoid of money, and most of the barons had sided with Lord Louis – and now the most eminent barons of France were on their way with plenty of cash and fully equipped to seize the land! If you wish to hear the names of some of the greatest lords who were preparing to sail from France – though they were to be disappointed! – I've learnt the names of the foremost: Sir Robert de Courtenay, Sir Ralph de la Tournelle (who'd encountered many a chivalrous adventure in his time but was to have the worse of this one), and William des Barres,[629] too, was one of the company, a knight of the highest standing and noblest conduct. And with them was Eustace the Monk,[630] unstinting in his wicked works and as deceitful as could be; but God was to show him the error of his ways: he made himself commander of the fleet, but that day proved to be his feast-day[631] – he ended up beheaded! There were a great many more of high degree whose names I don't know: I've only learnt the names of those taken prisoner.

But regardless of this, nothing was going to stop the Marshal riding swiftly to the coast with such forces as he had. He summoned mariners from the Cinque Ports,[632] and others came, too, with speed and in good numbers, according to God's will (He was to show how much He approved). The Marshal, shrewd as ever, won them over with words and gifts and promises of rich rewards, till they were all fired with a fierce, brave will to go and engage the French. And they met them boldly indeed, as you're about to hear as my tale unfolds. The mariners, who loved the Marshal and trusted his every word, headed straight for Sandwich without demur; there they fitted and rigged their ships with ropes and shrouds and stays, and good anchors and strong cables to hold them fast outside the ports if a battle were needed to crush the presumption of the French.

The Marshal and his men made for the coast with all speed – he couldn't wait to confront the French. But he wouldn't be allowed to embark – all his companions insisted he shouldn't, and explained why it was vital he should stay behind: if by chance he were killed or captured, who then would defend the land?

The Marshal now planned assiduously, devoting all his energies to the task: he assembled a fleet of twenty-two ships, both large and small; they were sound, strong craft, splendidly stocked with arms and good men, and he'd promised the mariners that he'd gladly compensate them for any losses by replacing lost ships with those they won – so now they should go to it with a will. They heartily agreed, and vowed and swore they'd suffer death or capture rather than be found wanting. But they complained bitterly of the wrongs and losses and damage

---

[629] William III des Barres, son of the William who appeared earlier in the *History*.
[630] Eustace was the younger son of Baudouin Busket, a lord of the county of Boulogne. Having been for a time a Benedictine monk, Eustace became a pirate in the English Channel and a mercenary in the service of England first and France later. His notoriety was such that he became the subject of a thirteenth-century romance biography (translated by Glyn Burgess in *Two Medieval Outlaws* [Woodbridge, 1997]).
[631] A saint's feast-day typically marks the day of his death.
[632] Hastings, New Romney, Hythe, Dover and Sandwich.

inflicted on them by King John, who'd reduced them all to wretched poverty:[633] that's what the mariners said.

With the great French fleet now on its way, these men prepared to confront them as they'd vowed. But then, realising they were leaderless, they were stricken with fear, losing their nerve so badly that they abandoned their ships, truly, with the sails still set, and shamelessly, in terror, they took to their rowing-boats and made for the shore. But the Marshal put them back on track! He urged them to recover their resolve, exhorting them to do their duty and take courage, for they'd be accompanied by a fine body of men – good knights and soldiers, valiant, bold and daring. He swore that if his men had let him he'd gladly have ventured forth with them to face whatever God planned, for it was clear to him that if the French fleet could make landfall it would be disastrous: England would be lost.

On the feast of Saint Bartholomew, towards the end of August,[634] the Marshal returned to Sandwich with a strong, impressive army: he had his son's knights with him, fine men indeed, and King John's son Richard,[635] and the earl of Surrey,[636] too, and Philip d'Aubigny, and other very worthy knights not all of whose names I know. They'd spent the previous night, I'm told, near Canterbury, but they hadn't slept for long: as soon as they saw day break they were up and ready, and took to the road very early. They pressed on swiftly till they reached Sandwich. It was a fine, clear day and you could see far out to sea, and the wind was soft and pleasant. Then our men caught sight of[637] their ships as the enemy fleet approached in serried ranks, exactly like an army in the field. Driving forward at its head was the ship of their guide and leader, Eustace the Monk; but he was to die that day unshriven. The French fleet, truly, numbered at least three hundred vessels.

The Marshal didn't dally; he ordered his men to embark at once. He'd have joined them himself most gladly if they'd let him, but that wasn't for the best, indeed it wasn't: he would be the only hope if the French made landfall. But Hubert, justiciar of England,[638] did embark on a splendid, well armed and well provisioned ship, as did Sir Richard, King John's son, and a fine company with him. Some of the Marshal's own soldiers had embarked the previous day. The men aboard the other ships provisioned them as best they could. Then the Marshal rose to his feet and exhorted them all to take courage and fight well, saying:

'We should all be heartened, sirs, mindful that God gave us the first victory over the French on land![639] Now they're returning to England to claim the kingdom against God's will; but He has the power to aid the good on land and

---

[633] Literally 'serfdom'.
[634] 24 August.
[635] His illegitimate son by his cousin Adela, a daughter of Hamelin de Warenne, 4th earl of Surrey.
[636] 'li cuens de Garene': William de Warenne, 5th earl of Surrey (and therefore Richard's uncle).
[637] The MS reads 'charchient' ('boarded'), which may be right, but since we are about to be told that Marshal then 'ordered his men to embark' I have followed Meyer's emendation to the more logical 'perçurent' ('perceived').
[638] Hubert de Burgh.
[639] i.e. at Lincoln.

sea alike, and once more He will aid those dear to Him! No empire can endure against men who have God's guidance: you have the upper hand – you will vanquish the enemies of God!'

With that they set sail and headed straight for the French with a stiff wind and a rising tide. When the French saw them leaving the harbour and coming towards them they held them in contempt. They furled their sails at once and said:

'A bunch of common foot soldiers, that's all they are! There's not a knight among them, that's for sure. We'll take the lot – they're at our mercy! Fortune has dropped them in our hands – they'll be powerless to resist! They'll cover our expenses! We'll cart them off with us to London – or leave them here fishing for flounder!'[640]

Such was their bold bragging; and how they gloated, seeing how few ships we had and recalling the hefty beating our men had suffered at their hands on their last visit.[641]

Nonetheless, Sir Hubert de Burgh's ship sailed ahead of the rest, giving every sign of intending to attack; but she surged on past, as both sides saw, as if avoiding battle. So the French rogues, crowing, yelled:

'In for the kill! In for the kill!'

They were full of it. But they were soon to be outmanoeuvred, cornered, and full instead of water.

As chance would have it the great ship of Bayonne[642] was sailing at speed, well ahead of the rest. On board were the king's treasury and the most eminent of the French I named above, along with others who shouldn't be forgotten: the castellan of Saint-Omer and the count of Blois,[643] who came with an impressive entourage. Sir Richard, King John's son, was first to move to the attack, boldly bearing down on the ship with the men at his command, though he didn't launch a proper attack till he was joined by a cog[644] carrying soldiers and plenty of other good men. The cog sat high in the water, being not too laden, but the Monk's ship, truly, was overfull, sitting so low that the waves were almost washing in. This wasn't surprising: it had far too great a load, carrying the trebuchet and all the horses that were being sent to Louis. It was so heavily laden that the sides were barely out of the water. The men in the cog took advantage of the height: they had huge pots full of quicklime that they hurled on those below, creating havoc – it blinded them: they could see nothing. Renaut Paien from Guernsey, a valiant soldier, quite fearless, now leapt from the cog aboard the ship – and his landing was none too soft: so mighty was his leap that he brought William des Barres and

---

[640] Flounder being bottom-feeding flatfish, the implication is obvious.
[641] The French had earlier landed at Dover and given the English a battering. See above, p. 193, where 'Sir Hugh Tacon ... came with a great fleet to rescue Louis ... [and] wrecked our ships...'.
[642] 'la grant nef de Baone': a 'nef' was a ship with three or more masts, the medieval forerunner of the galleon.
[643] Theobald (Thibaut) VI.
[644] Primarily a trading vessel, the single-masted, single-sailed cog was widely used in medieval Europe.

Sir Robert de Courtenay crashing down before him: a splendid feat it was! And he sent Sir Ralph de la Tournelle tumbling three times – he couldn't get out of his way! And it got better: this soldier Renaut went for him in no uncertain manner; it was quite a fight, but there was to be only one outcome: that fine knight of lofty status was taken prisoner! After Renaut, Theobald[645] leapt aboard, and no hunting dog ever went to work so keenly! They fought together splendidly. And all the others jumped from the cog on to the ship and laid about the foe, and took the whole lot prisoner.

Captured with them was Eustace the Monk, commander of the fleet. He offered ten thousand marks for the sparing of his life, but in vain: he'd met with a fearsome master, Stephen of Winchelsea by name, who told him an unforgiving tale, listing all the cruel, unwarranted, treacherous acts he'd committed against him on land and sea. Now he'd have to pay. And he offered him a dreadful choice, and there was nothing else for it: he could be beheaded, there and then, whichever way he liked – either across the trebuchet or across the side of the ship. It's hard to see a soft option there. With that they cut off his head; and so it was that it proved to be his feast day.[646] Thirty-two knights would have suffered the same fate if the English knights hadn't stepped in and – with a good deal of trouble – forbidden it.

Once this great ship was captured, our side displayed such prowess and daring and bore themselves so boldly that the French were unable to resist; they didn't stay to face them but fled as fast as they could. Away they went; but our fleet stuck with them all the way and created havoc, killing and capturing great numbers: whenever they managed to take a ship they didn't hesitate to slaughter all aboard and feed them to the fishes, sparing only one or two or three at the most on each vessel – all the rest they slew. They pursued them almost to the port of Calais. Some thought they had rich and easy pickings, and went to hook great bolts of scarlet* from the sea; how cheated they must have felt to find they were congealing slicks of blood. According to eye-witnesses, it's reckoned there were at least four thousand slain, not counting those who leapt in the sea to drown, whose numbers no one knows. But I wasn't there myself, and I'm not going to make rash claims when numbers are uncertain: no one likes or respects a man who strays into falsehood and speculation.

When the battle was over, our men blessed by Fortune sailed homeward with abundant booty. Sir Hubert hadn't been the first to engage but returned with two captured ships. It had turned out as God wished. And some of our boats, truly, had won such spoils that the mariners were doling out money in bowlfuls: they had handsome shares indeed. And the Marshal ordered that the gowns and horses, arms and equipment should be divided in such a way that all the mariners could declare themselves well satisfied. Then he gave praise and thanks to God for having granted him and his knights and his household and all the rest

---

[645] *'Thibaut'*. This is clearly not Theobald count of Blois – it is someone fighting on the English side. The lack of an identifying phrase suggests that this 'Thibaut' may have been someone well known to the Marshal household for whom the author was writing.
[646] See note 631, above, p. 206.

such grace – and praised *them*, too, for what they'd achieved, for they'd fought magnificently. Then he decreed that with the rest of the spoils, to commemorate the triumph, a hospital should be established in honour of Saint Bartholomew, who had given them the victory there that day.[647] So the records tell me; and the seamen have properly observed his command: they've built the fine house of high renown for the shelter, support and relief of God's poor.

You should have seen those mariners the following day! Decked in finery, bulging with cash, they strutted up and down the streets clad in silk and samite, scarlet and purple,* thronging around and vying with each other; one said:

'My gown's worth two of yours!'

'Come off it!' said another. 'Mine's superior by far! My whole outfit – tunic, surcoat, mantle, cloak – it's all made of cisimus!* There's none finer from here to Aleppo!'

'Oh, yes there is!' said a third. 'Mine's of ermine, superbly made and embroidered with gold! It's richer and better than any of yours! There's none to compare at all!'

While they were busy arguing, others, I believe, were bringing ashore all manner of provisions – meat and wine and grain, and vessels of iron and steel, and all of the highest quality – for the relief and benefit of the whole surrounding country.

When the Marshal had completed the fair division of the rich spoils taken on the ships he departed, and the prisoners were led away to Dover. Thirty-two French knights, men of the highest rank and power, were escorted there as captives and left with the justiciar.

Rumour, ever fleet and quick to spread, took no time to make its way to London. The news reached Louis there before next day – and it was far from welcome! – that the forces coming to his support had been destroyed and come to utter grief at sea, and all those taken aboard their ships had been killed, except the knights of high degree who'd been miserably led away to imprisonment at Dover. Those who'd managed to escape had vanished in shameful flight. Louis was aghast, crestfallen to hear of the loss of his most valued men.

To France, too, eye-witness reports soon came, distressing indeed for Louis's father King Philip, of how his forces had sailed straight to a crushing defeat. He immediately summoned the council of France, very afraid that his son would be betrayed and among those captured. When they assembled he said to them all:

'Well, sirs, wasn't I right? I said from the start: once the worthy, noble, loyal William the Marshal was involved, he would put paid to Louis and his ambitions! What should I do now, sirs?'

They advised him to send word to Louis bidding him find a way back, however he could: he didn't care what he did as long as he got back safely. He sent this message secretly, and Louis gave no sign that he'd received it.

---

[647] The Battle of Sandwich had been fought on Saint Bartholomew's Day: see above, p. 207. Saint Bartholomew's Hospital in Sandwich exists to this day as almshouses with a thirteenth-century chapel.

AGREEMENT REACHED WITH PRINCE LOUIS

The Marshal now left Dover with the earl of Surrey and the other worthy lords; and shortly after the return of the good Marshal and his fellows who'd stayed loyal to the king, Louis consulted with his close advisors and decided to seek a meeting with the Marshal and those who'd been fighting at his side. He sent word to request this, and the Marshal met to discuss it with his fellow faithful king's men. And let me tell you, there were some who'd stayed well away from the sea in the hour of danger who had plenty to say for themselves now:

'We've no reason to treat with Louis! Let's not waste time talking – let's go and lay siege to London!'

They were full of it now, but they'd kept very quiet when it had come to the crunch: they'd stayed well clear of the sea! The worthy men who'd been there, however, spoke more moderately. Wanting to see an end to strife they urged and prayed the Marshal, good men that they were, to have the French who'd been causing so much trouble cleared from the land, and not to be deterred by want of money, for they assured him they'd devote their hearts and bodies and their wealth as well to aiding him to the utmost.

The Marshal, convinced that their advice was sound, granted Louis the requested meeting, proposing a date that was accepted. But I'm not saying – by God I'm not – that all was settled on that first day; conferences were held over several days as they struggled to reach an agreement that would be acceptable to all. The French were very keen that the English who'd sided with them should be kept out of the negotiations and in the dark about their dealings, as they didn't see eye to eye. So they stopped them coming. Finally, at a grand conference between the French and the king's men[648] it was resolved as follows: Lord Louis would leave the country in return for a substantial sum of money, and on condition that he was first given absolution. This was a good move by Louis, well advised indeed. They met on an isle near Kingston[649] to conclude this, but the legate wasn't happy: he refused to give him absolution unless he came barefoot, shirtless, stripped to his braies; the French pleaded for a concession, that he should come in private, with a coat to cover his linen. And so it was that he and all who'd sided with him, French and English alike, were given absolution, which seems only right and proper.

They now set a day, I understand, for escorting Lord Louis from the land, and conducted him to Dover and then returned.[650] And first it was arranged that the English who'd sided with Louis in the war should have their lands restored to them – except those who'd sold or ceded them to pay ransoms. Once Louis and the French had gone, the Marshal took charge of the king's castles, placing garrisons in each according to its importance; this was essential. He was acting, I assure you, following the counsel of the most eminent and loyal men present.

I've forgotten to mention that after the negotiations had secured the truce, accepted by all parties, Lord Louis sent word to his allies – French, Scots, Welsh

---

[648] Literally 'some of the English'.
[649] There are several islands in the Thames not far from Kingston. The meeting took place on 12 September.
[650] Louis left England on 29 September.

and English alike – commanding them to observe the truce absolutely. The earls and barons duly did so – all except Morgan of Caerleon. He waged war on the Marshal and inflicted no end of harm and trouble, until Llywelyn[651] sent him word through William of Coleville[652] insisting that he stop creating mischief by breaching the truce. But Morgan wouldn't desist on his account; he said he'd never keep the truce: while the Marshal held a single foot of his land he'd continue waging war on him and wreaking all the havoc that he could. That's what Morgan said, truly – and he meant it: as everyone knows, in the period of the truce agreed by Louis, Sir Roland Bloet[653] was killed along with Walter,[654] and Robert de Colombières[655] likewise – and with him we know for certain at least seven other noble men died in a single day. It was a grievous loss and sorrow for their kin. And after Louis had returned to France Morgan kept on waging war, never letting up for a single day: his heart was ever full of malice. But the following year, after Michaelmas, he suffered a heavy blow: the Marshal's bailiff summoned his friends and allies and besieged and took Caerleon. After that the war raged on and on and the land and many people suffered greatly.

At last a conference was held at Worcester;[656] the archbishops were asked to attend, and bishops were present, too, as were the legate Guala and Llywelyn of Wales and a number of earls, viscounts and barons all of whose names I don't know. Anyway, they met, I understand, to address the wrongs and excesses committed, and once they'd all assembled they spoke of many matters. In the course of this Llywelyn and his followers resolved that he should send word to the king – by way of the earl of Chester and the bishop of Winchester – asking that all that had been taken from his kinsman Morgan should be returned; the Marshal was currently withholding it contrary to the peace terms made with Louis, whereby all should have the lands restored that they'd held before the war. The Marshal rose and said he'd consider this. He gathered together all his faithful counsellors and asked them what was best to do. You may be sure that, had they so advised, he wouldn't have hesitated to hand over what Morgan had asked; but that's not what they advised at all: rather, they immediately set forth all the reasons why he should keep it for himself. The Marshal left it to one of his most lucid men to make his case; back he came before the king and modestly and calmly said:

'Hear, good sire, what my lord wishes to say: he maintains that Lord Morgan should not have the land he wrongly claims. He has no right to it, for when Lord Louis ordered his allies to observe the truce and do nothing to infringe it, Morgan refused, choosing instead to pursue his proud, outrageous, wicked ways. The

---

[651] Llywelyn ab Iorwerth (as above, p. 178), prince of Gwynedd and the dominant power in Wales.
[652] Coleville had sided with Louis and been captured at Lincoln but released in June.
[653] Brother of William, who is mentioned above (p. 203) as the banner-bearer for Marshal's son at Lincoln. He and Morgan were cousins. He had sided with Louis for a while but soon returned his support to the king.
[654] The text is garbled here and the identity of this Walter, if he is not another Bloet, is unknown.
[655] Probably related to Philip de Colombières (above, p. 119), but the relationship is not known.
[656] In March 1218.

Marshal is aggrieved at his continuing refusal to comply, and is ready to prove that during the period of the truce agreed by Louis, Morgan killed a number of his knights along with other gentlemen and common folk. Others of us here are ready to prove it, too; and Morgan can't deny it: his wicked deeds and crimes are all too foully plain! He has burned twenty-two churches and ravaged lands – for which he's been punished with excommunication! What more proof is needed? It's as plain as day!'

Every earl and baron accepted this; and in view of Morgan's crimes and excesses his land and all its appurtenances, including the castle of Caerleon, remained with the Marshal. With that the conference was dissolved.

I shan't go into everything that was decided there (to the benefit of many), as it's not relevant to my theme; but with regard to the date, I can tell you it took place in the year after the Michaelmas[657] when Louis left the land.

Marshal's Death

It was only the following Candlemas[658] that the Marshal was taken with the illness which brought him to his death. What a grievous pity it was that he had to die. Suffering as he was he rode to London, to the Tower, where doctors came from far and wide but could do little for him. Their coming is hardly worth mentioning – they were of no use at all. What more can I tell you? His illness grew much worse, I understand, from then till Lent; he was suffering much pain and trouble, and the countess stayed ever at his side. And as it took even fiercer hold he called for his son[659] and his household and addressed them, as lucidly as ever, doing his best to comfort them as far as his sickness would allow. A number of those who loved him dearly implored him in God's name to make his will, which he did, and very wisely, I assure you – as we see to this day, thanks be to God. And it wasn't done hurriedly – a will is not best drawn up in haste. He did all he could to give it due attention, and showed his great clear-sightedness.[660]

At last he chose to send for his son, and Henry FitzGerald with him, and bade them have him taken without delay to his manor at Caversham: he didn't wish to stay a moment longer in that unhealthy city which was making his illness worse. He felt he'd endure his sickness more comfortably at home, and if his death was inevitable he would rather die at home than anywhere else. They did his bidding instantly; boats were prepared, and those who were to accompany him carried him aboard a craft and gave him all due attention, giving him every comfort. The

---

[657] The MS reads 'two years after', in which case the chronology is awry, but the scribe seems to have been confused by these lines and they read awkwardly. Louis left England in September 1217 and the treaty of Worcester took place only the following March. But the author, too, is confused about the conference just referred to: this was probably not part of the transactions at Worcester as his account suggests but occurred later, in London (though still within a year of Louis's departure).
[658] i.e. early February 1219.
[659] His eldest son, William.
[660] The last two sentences are a reconstruction of a passage from which at least one couplet is missing.

countess, quite disconsolate, boarded another, and they sailed gently and calmly upriver to Caversham.[661]

It was around this time that the legate Guala left England and headed for Mont-Joux,[662] and Pandulf[663] came in his place. I've heard – and it's a fact – that a council was convened at Reading on account of the earl's infirmity.[664] The king, they say, was present, along with the legate and the justiciar, and many of the greatest barons gathered there with them. When they were all assembled the earl sent word to the king, the legate and the earls, all the most eminent, asking them to come to him if they would; if they didn't mind he very much wished them to see him and speak with him as soon as ever they could. They duly came as he'd asked, without delay. They went to him at Caversham and greeted him when they arrived, as he did them, very graciously. They sat around him most respectfully, and he said to the king:

'My good, dear sire, in the presence of these lords I wish to say that when Death beset your father till unavoidably he died, the legate Guala, as we know, went to Gloucester with many of the great lords who were loyal to you and defending your honour, and there, by God's grace, you were crowned. It was decided then that you should be entrusted to my care, and so you were. As protector of your land in a time of crisis I have served you, I swear, loyally and to the best of my ability, and I would serve you still if only I could, if it pleased God that my powers endured; but it must be plain to all that it is not His will that I stay longer in this world. So now, if it please you, the barons must consider who should be your guardian and protector of the realm, in a manner pleasing to God and to the world. And God grant you a master who'll bring you honour!'

The bishop of Winchester rose then and said: 'Now listen, Marshal: you were charged, I grant you, with the protection of the kingdom and defence of the land, but the king was entrusted to me!'

'What!' replied the Marshal. 'Not so, lord bishop! How can you say that? You know very well what happened! It's not that long ago: you were in tears and begging me – you and the good earl of Chester – to be guardian and protector of the king and of the realm together! Your memory's shaky, it seems! And the legate begged and implored me earnestly – and he was speaking for you all – to take charge of the king and of the kingdom. It was common knowledge that I'd taken the king into my care. I assure you, I passed him over to you because he was too young to travel: he was in your hands for no other reason!'

Then the Marshal, who was suffering greatly, said to the legate Pandulf: 'Go now, and take the king with you; but come back tomorrow, I pray you. I'll discuss this with my son and with my men, and try to determine who'd be best. God send us good counsel!'

So they took their leave and left him, taking the king with them.

---

[661] Caversham is close to the Thames, just north of Reading. It was now mid-March 1219.
[662] The Great Saint Bernard Pass (as noted above, p. 57) – i.e. he was returning to Italy. He had left in November 1218.
[663] Pandulf Verraccio.
[664] On 8 and 9 April 1219.

When the next day dawned the Marshal called for his son, the noble, faithful countess, Sir John the Marshal and his other most trusted advisors, and shared his thoughts with them.

'Sirs, I've been considering what we spoke of yesterday: who should be made the king's new guardian. There's no land whose people are more contrary than England! Whoever I entrust him to, others will resent it, you may be sure! So I've decided, if you all agree, that he should be entrusted to God and the Pope – and to the legate: let him be his guardian on their behalf; that would be best. No one can reasonably censure my decision; my thinking is this: I tell you in all honesty, and I want you all to understand, that if the Pope doesn't protect our land at this juncture, I don't know who will.'

And everyone present agreed.

Then the king and the legate arrived, and other great lords with them, their hearts heavy with sorrow. The Marshal propped himself on his elbow and called the king, and in the sight of all he took him by the hand and said to the legate:

'Sir, I have pondered and deliberated long about the matter we discussed yesterday. I wish to place my lord here in the hands of God and of the Pope – and in your hands, truly, for you are here in his stead.' Then he said to the king: 'Sire, I pray to almighty God that, if I have ever done anything pleasing in His sight, He may grant that you grow to be truly worthy; but if you should be otherwise inclined, and emulate some wicked forebear, I pray God the son of Mary will see you live not long but die before that happens.'

'Amen,' the king replied; and with that they all rose and took their leave and departed.

Then the earl, in grave pain, said to John the Marshal: 'Tell my son, on my behalf, to go and entrust the king to the legate – in the presence of the barons.'

He didn't want anyone accusing him of having arranged it behind closed doors.

The son gladly followed his father's bidding: he took the king by the hand and offered him to the legate in full view of everyone. But the bishop of Winchester leapt up and threw his arms around the king's head, whereupon the young Marshal, ever courtly and steadfast, said:

'Let go, my lord bishop! You're wasting your time. I'm carrying out my father's bidding and I want it plainly witnessed.'

The legate was furious with the bishop, and rose and received the child king into his care, as he'd already agreed to do. Then the young Marshal returned to his father and mother and reported what he'd done – and the bishop's outrageous behaviour.

They spent the time in this sad state till morning: there was nothing to be done. Then the Marshal wished to summon his household and the countess; and he said to them:

'I can confidently say, sirs, thanks be to God, that, whether I live or die, I am now relieved of a heavy burden. It would be good now to complete my will, and since my body is in jeopardy I must take great care of my soul. With you as my witnesses, I must dispose of my earthly possessions and turn my thoughts to heavenly matters: it's high time.'

He provided first for his children, dividing his lands between them following the promptings of his heart; and he said:

'Sirs, one of my sons, Ansel, is receiving nothing, yet he is very dear to me.[665] If he lives long enough to be a knight and succeeds in achieving high honour, then landless though he may be, he'll find someone who'll love him and bestow surpassing rank upon him, truly! God grant him prowess and wisdom!'

'Oh, sir!' said John of Earley. 'You can't do that! Leave him enough of your wealth at least to shoe his horses! It's only fair!'

So he granted Ansel, without further pressing, land worth one hundred and forty pounds per year to live on and support himself. Then he said:

'Now I am at ease. But I worry about my daughter Joan; it troubles and upsets me that I haven't given her in marriage before I die. If she were married my soul would rest forever more content; it's the only thing that bothers me. I wish her to have land enough to yield thirty pounds, and two hundred marks to live on until God takes care of her.'[666]

Having settled his affairs to his satisfaction, he said: 'John, don't dally now; go quickly and take charge in Striguil.[667] I'm worried about my people in Netherwent,[668] and especially about your son:[669] I'm afraid that if he listens to the wrong voices he may launch some foolish mission in which our people would suffer. So go, good sir,' he said, 'and by the faith you owe me, make no delay! My sickness is growing ever worse. When you return, bring me two lengths of silk I gave to Stephen[670] to keep for me: it's always good to plan well ahead. Whatever happens, be sure to come back quickly.'

And so he did: he carried out his orders well, riding exceptionally long and hard each day. By the time he returned the earl's condition had worsened – and was growing ever worse. The moment he arrived the earl asked:

'How is it with my people?'

'All's well, my lord, thank God: there's no trouble at all. And here are the lengths of silk you wished me to bring.'

Hearing this he took them and said to Henry FitzGerald: 'See these beautiful sheets, Henry.'

'Indeed, sir, but I have to say they look a little faded, unless my eyes deceive me.'

'Unfold them,' said the earl. 'Let's take a closer look.'

And when the sheets were unfolded they were handsome and precious indeed, of the finest, most exquisite work. Then he called his son before him and his knights likewise; and when they were all assembled he said:

---

[665] This is a reconstruction of an oddly uncompleted sentence; there may be a missing couplet.
[666] Joan did marry after her father's death (see above, pp. 183–4), though the date of her marriage is unknown.
[667] '*alez tost a vostre baillie*': literally 'go quickly to your bailiwick' – i.e. go back to Striguil (Chepstow) and act as 'bailiff'.
[668] Netherwent (Lower Gwent) was part of the lordship of Striguil.
[669] Probably John of Earley's elder son, also named John, acting as seneschal or deputy-seneschal of Netherwent.
[670] Presumably Stephen of Évreux.

'Look at these, sirs: I've had these sheets for thirty years. When I returned from Outremer[671] I had them brought back with me to fulfil the purpose they're about to serve: I've kept them to be draped over me when I'm buried. That's their promised role.'

'Sir,' said his son. 'There's one thing that's a mystery to us: we've no idea where you wish to be buried.'

'I'll tell you, my son, and I'll tell you true. While I was in the Holy Land I committed my body, wherever I might be when I came to die, to burial in the Temple.[672] That's my wish and that's where I'll lie; and I'll give the Temple my fine manor of Upleadon[673] in perpetuity. That's my wish and that's where I'll lie;[674] it's what I've planned and vowed.' Then he addressed these good, wise words to John of Earley: 'As you love me, John, and by the faith you owe me, take these sheets and spread them over me when I die; use them to wrap and cover the bier that bears me. And another thing: should it be snowing or inclement weather, go and buy some grey burel* – never mind what kind: I don't care what it looks like – and cover the sheets to save them from being spoiled or damaged by the wet. And once I'm buried, give the sheets to the brothers of the Temple for their use, to do with as they wish.'

On hearing this his son wept piteously, as did all the knights present, filled with grief; the pages, the servants, the whole household, were weeping and grieving bitterly, and with every reason. Then his son rose; he was distressed at the pain and torment he could see his father suffering, and when he'd left the chamber he called the knights to him and said:

'You can see my father's enduring ever more pain; truly, we should be far more attentive than we've been. We must arrange to keep watch over him, three of us each night: in God's name, sirs, don't complain! In the morning three will take their place and stay at his side and keep close watch till dinner; then three other knights will be ready to watch over him till evening. This really must be done.'

They all agreed that this would be good – no one objected at all. And as well as the knights there were servants and other gentlemen who kept watch with them, devoting great care and attention.

Having arranged this as I've described, the young Marshal, so noble, kind and loyal of heart, said: 'If it please you, sirs, I wish to take each of the night watches over my father; as his son it's only right and proper. His suffering pains me greatly. Sir John of Earley will join me – I know I can depend on him – and Sir Thomas Basset. The others will keep watch during the day, in turns, three at a time.'

---

[671] Meaning simply 'overseas', Outremer was the name generally given to the Crusader states established in the Holy Land after the First Crusade. Marshal had returned from 'Outremer' in 1186: see above, p. 104.
[672] i.e. the Temple Church in London, the English headquarters of the Knights Templar.
[673] '*Opledane*'. Upleadon is a village north-west of Gloucester; the manor had been acquired by Marshal's father in the middle of the previous century.
[674] There is no apparent error in this repetition: the same line provides a rhyme in two different couplets, and is presumably repeated by way of deliberate emphasis.

And from that point on, as long as the earl remained alive, his son kept vigil over him every night with devoted commitment. That's how it was arranged.

Next morning the earl summoned his household and his almoner, Brother Geoffrey; he was a Templar, and he came most willingly. Then the earl set his affairs in order, dictating letters; and when that was done he called also for Brother Aimery of Saint-Maur, Master of the Temple and a most worthy and devout man. And he sent out his will, sealed with his own seal and the countess's and that of his son, whom he loved as dearly as a father can love a son. With these three seals attached he sent it to the archbishop [of Canterbury], to the legate – who now was regent – and to the bishops of Winchester and Salisbury. He asked them in the name of God the Father to be chief executors of his will, and out of love for him and in God's name to attach their own seals to it. They gladly did so, and declared excommunicate anyone who disputed the will or tried to alter it. So that was done, and then the document was returned to the earl, for they wished him to see it before he died.

In the meantime Brother Aimery of Saint-Maur had come, and the Marshal called again for the countess and his men and said, in brief:

'Listen now, sirs, in God's name. A long while ago I pledged myself to the Temple, and now I wish to go there – I've no desire to wait longer.' And turning to Geoffrey the almoner he said: 'Dear brother, go to the wardrobe and fetch my mantle and bring it here to me.'

I should explain that he'd had this mantle made a year before and kept it secret: he was the only one who knew of it. Then he said to the countess, to whom he was always loving, kind and good:

'Kiss me now, my dear love: you will never do so again.'

She drew close and kissed him; he wept and so did she, and all the good people present shed tears of love and pity: the whole household grieved piteously at the sight. Then he quickly called for the mantle to be spread before him. His daughters were there, lamenting bitterly over him; no one could find a word to comfort them, and so desperate was their grief that the countess and his daughters had to be led from the room: they were inconsolable. Everyone was downcast and in tears. Then Brother Aimery said:

'Hear me, Marshal: I'm glad that you're surrendering now to God, and laying aside your worldly goods to ensure that you be not distanced from Him and His company. I tell you, in both life and death you've been held in higher honour than any knight at any time, for your prowess, wisdom and loyalty; and when God has so endowed you with His grace in life, you may be sure He wishes to receive you at the last. You leave this world with great honour: you've lived nobly indeed, and nobly you depart. I shall go to London now, to prepare for what you've bidden.'

With that Brother Aimery set off; but no sooner had he arrived in London than he fell ill and died – there was no saving him. But before he died he asked for the love of God to be buried before the cross in the [Temple] Church, 'alongside the good knight, Brother William the Marshal, whose prowess has won him such a great name in this world, and who wishes now to win equal renown in Heaven. I dearly loved his company in this life, in this world, and I wish to remain close to him, lying side by side. And may God grant both of us His company in the life celestial!'

When he died, the news of Brother Aimery's death was taken to Caversham. It was hardly welcome. They didn't dare tell the earl for fear it would cause him yet more pain, but the knights said:

'God truly loves the earl, that's plain to see: Brother Aimery has gone to take his place in Heaven next to the Marshal's; that's what's happened – that's why he wished to be buried at his side. God grant that they may be together in Heaven, close enough to see God face to face.'

I don't know what more to tell you. The earl was now so sick that he lost all appetite: he could neither eat nor drink. His strength was exhausted; his natural functions ceased, having less to work on than would have fed a sparrow: he could manage nothing more. Someone thought of crumbling soft bread very small so he didn't notice, or he wouldn't have been able to eat it. He was in this woeful state for at least a fortnight before he died.

One day he was lying in bed, supported by Sir Henry FitzGerald who was deeply upset to see him suffering; many of his knights were about him, too, all sharing in the pain they saw him endure: it was causing them great anguish – they were all distressed and filled with grief. Sir Henry said:

'By glorious God, sir, you must think now of your soul – we're most concerned. You know that Death respects no man: no matter how great his nobility, his wisdom, his prowess, no one can defend himself from Death. And the clergy insist that no man is safe unless he returns what he has taken.'

The Marshal replied: 'Bear with me a moment, Henry. The clerics are too hard on us! They shave us too close! I've captured five hundred knights and kept their arms, their destriers and all their gear. If that means the kingdom of God is barred to me then that's that – I can't give them back! I can do no more for God, I'd say, than yield myself to Him repentant of all my misdeeds, of all the wrongs I've done. Unless the clergy mean to see me damned they should stop their harrying! Either their claims are false or no man can have salvation!'

'That's absolutely true, sir!' John of Earley said. 'I swear you've hardly a single fellow who could say otherwise at his death!'

So matters stayed till the following day when his daughters came to see him. They were terribly distressed to see how weak he was. They didn't come all together every day, but on that day they did, I understand. And Lady Maud Bigod[675] was nearly crazed with grief, for she loved him very deeply; she kept crying to God, asking why He was robbing her of the one that was dearest to her heart. No lamenting could be greater than the countess of Gloucester's,[676] and Lady Eva's and Lady Sibyl's grief was indescribable. As for Joan, she kept fainting – and she can hardly be blamed, for she was still unprovided for, though the one to whom her father entrusted her has since seen to that, in very worthy manner.[677]

I understand that his son was sitting before him, and a great gathering of knights, when he called John of Earley and said:

---

[675] His daughter Maud had married Hugh Bigod, 3rd earl of Norfolk (above, p. 183).
[676] Isabel, who had married Gilbert, 5th earl of Gloucester (above, p. 183).
[677] Her eldest brother William later married her to Warin, lord of Munchensy (see above, pp. 183–4).

'Shall I tell you something extraordinary?'

'Yes, sir, but you mustn't exert yourself.'

'I don't know what to make of this, but I swear that never for three years or more, I'd say, have I felt such an urge to sing as in the last three days! But I don't know that God would be pleased.'

'Sing, sir, in God's name,' said John, 'if you've the strength and inclination! If it restored your heart and spirits it would be grand! Go ahead – you must! Please God, you might regain your appetite!'

'Enough, John,' said the earl. 'Singing would do me no good: the people here would think me mad! They'd all be saying my mind had gone!'

He didn't want to sing – and couldn't; but then Henry FitzGerald said: 'By glorious God, sir, call your daughters: they'll sing something to cheer and comfort you.'

So they were sent for and they came, only too willing to do his bidding. And the earl said:

'Maud, you sing for me first.'

She was hardly in the mood, being bitterly upset, but she didn't want to go against her father's wishes. So she started to sing, wishing to please her father, and a good singer she was indeed: she sang a verse of a song in a sweet and charming voice.

'Your turn now, Joan, no matter what.'

And Joan sang a verse of a rotrouenge,* but timorously.

'Don't be bashful when you sing,' said the earl. 'It doesn't come out well that way! It didn't sound right – the words didn't flow.'

And he taught her how to deliver it better.

When they'd all sung he said to them: 'My daughters, go to Jesus Christ, who guards and protects His own. I pray He will have you ever in His keeping.'

They took their leave in fitting fashion, and after they'd gone he said: 'Five of them there are, those daughters of mine; if they all live, it may well be that great good will come of them, if it please God.'

They returned very properly to their mother. Then the earl called his son once more and instructed him: 'I want you to be sure, my son, to be ever close at hand. When I enter London you must stay right next to me, and when you see all the poor who'll come in search of alms, distribute so much of my riches that God Himself will hear of it! Be sure likewise to give food and drink to one hundred paupers, and clothes and shoes also.'

After all this had been settled, the head of the abbey of Notley[678] arrived. In welcome and timely fashion he'd just returned from his chapter – black canons they were, of the Arrouaisian order;[679] he followed the order's precepts well, being the good, devout man that he was, and he cared well for his abbey. He came to the earl and greeted him, and the earl bowed his head in return; then he said:

---

[678] Notley Abbey is near Long Crendon, between Oxford and Aylesbury. The manor of Crendon was owned by Marshal at this time.

[679] As the head of an Arrouaisian house, he had attended the general chapter at the abbey of Arrouaise itself (in the forest of Arrouaise in Artois).

'Sir, I've been speaking to our abbot superior[680] and to the brothers of our order. Let me tell you, I informed them in chapter of your illness, and proposed that you be included in the prayers and good works of the order[681] for as long as it endures, and the abbot said: "Without fail. I know the Marshal well: I've known of his reputation for a long while – he is a man of the highest worth and honour." The abbot knew all about you, and kindly and gladly included you in all the good works, past and future, of the entire order.'

This was a fine association indeed! I can't name all the houses of the order, nor do I mean to: I don't want to weigh my story down with details that don't matter; but the head of Notley said:

'I've brought you sealed letters from the abbot, to verify my words.'

'A thousand thanks!' said the earl. 'That is a welcome boon indeed, a mighty favour – and it won't go unacknowledged: if you have kept me in your thoughts, I've kept you in mine. I've left five hundred marks to your house in my will, as I have to every abbey whose name I knew in my lands overseas:[682] I've left five hundred marks to each, bar none. And to every chapter of high repute I've left ten marks, in the hope that I may share in their good works and prayers both night and day eternally.'

The head of Notley, with tears in his eyes, said: 'That's a very rich endowment, sir; and God will repay you more richly still, I'm certain, in the glory of Heaven! You've been wisely counselled, have trusted that counsel admirably, and put it into perfect practice.'

So matters rested till the following day, when his son and his men gathered round him in great numbers. Then John of Earley, who'd been keeping devoted watch, said:

'Sir, what would you like to have done with your fur-lined gowns upstairs? I notice no one has mentioned them.'

The earl wasn't sure what Sir John meant; so Philip the clerk butted in and said: 'God save me, sir, there's a hoard of gowns up there, fine and new, of scarlet* and vair,* and eighty or more of cisimus besides! Being so handsome, fresh and new, those furs could fetch a lot of money – to use as atonement for your sins!'

'Quiet, you wretch!' said the earl. 'You've always had a miserable heart! I've had enough of you – I'll not hear another word! Damn all bad advisors – they're best ignored! Those words of yours have riled me! Look: it'll soon be Pentecost; my knights have a right to receive their gowns – I know it's the last time I'll give them any – and here *you* are, trying to wheedle them out of me!' Then he said, very wisely: 'Step forward, John of Earley. I bid you, by the faith you owe God and me, take charge of the distribution of the gowns, and if there aren't enough for everyone, send straight to London for more so that no one has cause to complain on my account.' Then he turned to his son and said: 'I pray you, dear son, take leave for me of all those who are absent but have served me well. Thank

---

[680] i.e. the abbot of the abbey of Arrouaise.
[681] i.e. they would share with him the blessings they might gain by their good works.
[682] i.e. both in Normandy and in Ireland.

them sincerely; may they have thanks and blessings for all they've said and done, from God as well as from me.'

And so the robes were distributed, in such a way that no knight in his household was without one – and if any knight was absent, it was given to one of his servants. And I'm not joking when I say that all his remaining clothes were promptly divided up and given to the poor. This carried on till morning – his son and his fellow watchers didn't sleep at all that night.

When morning came and everyone rose, those who'd been keeping vigil went away to sleep while others took their places before the earl to see how he fared – not that his son slept much, any more than his fellows: he was too worried and distressed. The day I speak of now was the Monday before Ascension Day.[683] Then the young Marshal came and knelt before his father and said:

'For the love of Christ, sir, eat something: we're sure it would do you good.'

'Come then,' said the earl. 'I'll gladly eat what I can.'

And he sat up, with a knight supporting him. And then, just as the cloth was spread before him, he called John of Earley and said: 'Look here, John: do you see what I see?'

'I don't know what you mean, sir.'

'Two men in white, by my life – look! One is just here to my right and the other to my left. I've never seen such handsome figures anywhere.'

'A company is coming from God to attend you, sir – and more will come yet. God is sending them to escort you on your rightful way.'

Then the earl said: 'Blessed be our lord God who has granted me His grace thus far!'

The fact is, Sir John didn't question who these figures were, feeling sure he'd discover in time – but regretted ever after that he hadn't asked: it grieved him that he never knew.

Day passed into evening, but the earl's sickness never waned but ever waxed, much to the distress and pain of all his friends. Then the young Marshal came to keep watch for the night once more – it was a dear labour to him.

It's foolish and tiresome to go on about the sleeping and the watching – there's little point; but one thing's for sure: at exactly midday on the Tuesday before Ascension[684] young Marshal and a group of the barons returned, and entered to find the earl lying peacefully, turned to face the wall. He looked so at ease, they were sure he was asleep, and his son said:

'No talking now, in God's name! Let my lord rest.'

I don't know if he'd heard them, but he stirred and asked: 'Who's there? Tell me.'

'I am, in faith: John of Earley.'

'Is that you, John?'

'Yes indeed, my dear lord.'

'I just can't sleep,' he said.

---

[683] 13 May 1219.
[684] i.e. the following day, 14 May.

'How could you hope to sleep, or rest or feel at ease? You've eaten nothing to my knowledge for at least a fortnight!'

The earl stretched and made to turn over; and as he did so he was seized by the final, inexorable throes of death.

'Hurry, John!' he said. 'Open the doors and windows! And tell my son to come – the countess and my knights likewise – for I'm dying, truly: I can stay no longer! I want to take my leave.'

John leapt up that instant and threw open the doors and windows, then hurried back and took the earl in his arms. The earl leaned back and rested on his breast, and the best I can say is that he closed his eyes and lost consciousness. When he came to he opened his eyes, confused; and when he spoke he said:

'Did I faint then, John?'

'Yes, sir.'

'It's years since I've seen you at a loss like this! Come! Won't you take that rose water and sprinkle it on my face, that I may share a few words with these good people here? I haven't long.'

Then John, feeling the rebuke, took the phial of rose water and sprinkled the earl's face, now piteously pale and wan with the pangs of death that were striking at his heart. Young Marshal and the countess came, followed by all the knights, crowding in to witness the scene that grieved them so. Then he addressed them all, saying:

'I'm about to die; I commend you to God. I can stay with you no more: against Death I have no defence!'

His son approached and sat in John of Earley's place. He took his father in his arms and – how could it be otherwise? – shed tender, heartfelt, silent tears. A crucifix was brought before the earl and he worshipped it, earnestly praying to God to take pity on him and grant him a good end. And when he'd finished his adoration of the cross, the abbot of Notley gently came to him, followed by a large company of monks.

I don't know what more to say. The earl now curled into the cradling arms of his son, who was in grave distress, for his father was no longer talking: he'd lost the power of speech. There's no question: never was there greater cause to weep for any prince on earth than in that house.

Now truly, sirs, many great and glorious adventures befell the Marshal in this life, and the finest of all befell him at his death, as you're about to hear – and all who've enjoyed hearing of his splendid deeds will relish this. In the middle of their inconsolable grieving, a boy ran up to John of Earley and tugged at his arm and said:

'Listen, sir. The abbot of Reading wishes to come in and speak to you.'

Sir John didn't hear him – his heart and mind were quite elsewhere – and he pushed the boy away. But the earl had heard his words and opened his eyes; he beckoned to John who went to him, and signalled that he should send for the abbot without delay. John jumped up and went to fetch him, and brought him back to the earl. As the abbot arrived he said:

'I bring greetings, sir, from the legate, who spent the night at Cirencester. And he bids me tell you that in the night he had a vision that filled him with awe. It was about you; and it struck him so forcibly that he commanded me to come and share it with you without delay. I swear it's been engraved in my heart throughout my journey – four and twenty leagues at least. The legate sends you word through me that God gave Saint Peter the power to bind or release all sinners, and that same authority has been passed down to each succeeding Pope: so it is written in Rome. And the Pope bestowed that power on the legate when he came here to England. That being God's will, he sends word that he absolves you of all the sins you've committed since the hour that you were born – those you've truly confessed: I unburden you of them all.'

The earl turned to him, clasped his hands together and bowed his head. Regarding confession, I can tell you that since the moment he fell ill and his sickness grew ever worse he'd been shriven every week.

But to return to the matter in hand: the abbot of Reading began to pronounce the earl's absolution, assisted by the abbot of Notley and many other worthy clerics. When he'd been absolved, he bowed to them and raised his hand and crossed himself; and with hands joined he worshipped the crucifix before him. And moments later God did His will with him, as it pleases Him to do with the good whom He takes to His side. Of that we should all be mindful. Let us pray to God that He sets him in holy glory and in Paradise, in the bliss enjoyed by those dear to Him.

Such was the Marshal's passing, and we believe him to be safe with God and His company, for he had a good life and a good death.

His body was now prepared and clad and shrouded with the honour befitting so worthy a man; and when all was done, before he was carried from the manor, a mass was conducted for him in the beautiful, glorious chapel the Marshal had built. While mass was being sung it was clear that the countess was struggling to support herself, her head and heart and limbs overwrought from the strain of grief and lack of sleep. But the mother and the son between them gave Reading Abbey an annuity of one hundred shillings, that his father's soul might share in their good works.[685] This gift was made when the body had been taken to the abbey and was resting there. On leaving Reading they carried the body to Staines, where the good earl of Surrey came to meet them, along with the good Earl William of Essex, whose largesse is unceasing, winter and summer; Earl Robert de Vere[686] came likewise, as did the earl of Gloucester, deeply saddened that things had to be so. Many other great barons were in attendance, too, and all those present were filled with grief at the sight of the Marshal's body. But there could be no recourse: everyone, fools and the wise alike, will die, and all one can do is suffer and endure it, and do all the good one can for the souls of the dead – they've no need of anything more.

And truly, God, who'd granted the Marshal so many blessings in life, did not forget him in death, for they found the archbishop in the city[687] with another

---

[685] See note 681 above, p. 221.
[686] 3rd earl of Oxford.
[687] i.e. the archbishop of Canterbury (Stephen Langton), when they reached London.

bishop and a number of great prelates of the Church. By order of the archbishop a vigil was conducted with all due pomp and honour, with a service gloriously lit by candles and beautifully read and sung, the priests singing to great effect.[688]

And to the burial the following day[689] came a great host of knights, I promise you. And according to God's will, and as the earl himself had requested, his grave lay before the cross and beside his friend, Brother Aimery of Saint-Maur. After the masses had been sung with all due splendour, the archbishop came in full vestments, accompanied by the bishop and numerous abbots and monks, canons and archdeacons, and conducted the service of burial, so elegantly and gloriously that all who were present to witness it rejoiced in their hearts, and praised God for the honour and love He had long shown by His grace, both in life and in his passing, to the worthiest man in their age from there to Rome. Then, as the body was about to be interred, the archbishop said:

'Behold, sirs, how it is with this life: when each of us comes to his end his senses all are gone, and he is nothing more than so much earth. You see before you the finest knight in the world in our time, and what is there to say now, by God? This is what we all must come to: everyone must die when his time comes – it cannot be otherwise. We have before us our mirror – it is mine as much as yours. And now let us all say our paternoster, praying that God may receive this Christian in His heavenly kingdom, in glory with His elect, believing as we do that he was truly good.'

After the burial, those who'd been charged with dispensing alms ensured it was properly carried out. It took place at Westminster because of the crowds; truly, there wouldn't have been room inside the city: the poor were thronging in countless numbers. And wondrously, almighty God saw to it that there was enough of all for everyone, and when the sharing of alms was over not a coin or scrap of bread remained: there had been just the right amount. And when gowns were given to one hundred paupers, faithfully following the Marshal's bidding, it was found that there were three still left.

And bear with me, sirs, while I add just one more thing. News that Death had taken such a worthy man, of such high renown, sped abroad to many lands. It was swiftly borne, you may be sure, to the king of France, who at that time was in the Gâtinais[690] with a great company of men. The king replied to the messenger:

'Wait: it would be best not to speak of this till Richard the Marshal[691] has dined with the others – he'll be most distressed, you'll see.'

When the tables had been cleared, those who'd been serving sat down to eat.[692] Meanwhile King Philip beckoned to Sir William des Barres to come and sit beside him; then he said:

'Did you hear what this man told me?'

---

[688] A vigil and mass were conducted in Westminster Abbey on 18 May.
[689] In the Temple Church, on 19 May.
[690] The region south of Paris and north-east of Orléans.
[691] Marshal's second son, evidently at the French court and not in England with his mother and elder brother.
[692] It was usual for the king and his principal courtiers to dine first, served by younger members of the court who then took their turn to eat.

'What was that, my lord?'

'In faith, he came to tell me that the worthy, loyal Marshal is buried.'

'Which marshal?'[693] asked des Barres.

'Marshal of England – William! So full of prowess and so wise he was.'

'Truly, sire, that is a great pity,' Sir William said then. 'In our time there has been no finer knight anywhere nor one who so excelled in arms, so talented a warrior.'

'What's that you said?' said the king.

'I said, sire, so help me God, that I've never seen a greater knight in all my life. I don't know what more I can say.'

'You've said a lot, in faith, and said it well! The Marshal, I swear, was the most loyal knight I ever met in all my travels.'

And Sir Jean de Rouvray[694] said: 'For my part, sire, I say he was the wisest knight seen anywhere in our time: I'll stand by that.'

God! He was born and raised under a lucky star to have such tributes paid him after his death! And what an inspiration it is to all worthy knights who can hear about his life!

Here ends the life of the Earl Marshal, a story so remarkable that it should be loved and enjoyed wherever it is heard. All those responsible for commissioning this work should be acknowledged, that those who hear a reading of this book may know who it was that provided the material, and had it written and met all the cost – regardless of the expense. First to be named shall be his good son Earl William,[695] renowned by all for his fine deeds – a good tree brings forth good fruit. Once the writing of the book had been proposed, truly, nothing was going to stop him seeing it done – that's plain to see now and will become plainer yet. And it's been plain throughout, both night and day, that the one who arranged the material and has seen the work to fruition, thank God, loved his lord the Marshal dearly: that, truly, is John of Earley, who has devoted heart and thought and money to it for sure – let no one be in any doubt. Sincere love, they say, is proven through good deeds; and it's no idle adage: John has proven his in his making and composing of this book.[696] And may God, who rewards the good for their good deeds and bestows all joy, grant the bliss of Paradise to everyone involved.

When the family line – both brothers and sisters – hear that their brother, the good William Marshal, has commissioned such a work as this about their father, their hearts will be deeply touched. And God grant that it may give them joy. But I know it will give them joy indeed when they hear this book with all the honour and great deeds it records about their forebear.

---

[693] The '*mareschal*' being a position in a noble household (see Glossary), des Barres has perhaps not immediately registered it as being a name.

[694] A Norman knight who had joined the king of France in the 1190s. He was now a major figure at Philip's court.

[695] Marshal's eldest son became 2nd earl of Pembroke.

[696] For discussion of whether the 'John' of this sentence is John of Earley or the otherwise unknown author, see the Introduction, above, pp. 22–3.

Here ends the history of the earl, and God grant that his soul be placed in eternal glory, seated in the company of His angels. Amen.

Glossary

Alerion	In medieval bestiaries the alerion (or avalerion) is described as being larger than an eagle, flame-coloured and having razor-sharp wings. It was deemed lord of all birds, and there were believed to be only two living at any one time.
Braies	Underbreeches, usually of linen, the innermost layer of a man's garments.
Brattice	A *bretèche* or brattice was a battlemented projection from a tower or gatehouse.
Burel	A thick, resilient fabric of woven wool.
Chausses	Chain mail leggings.
Cisimus	A rich cloth lined with the fur of the souslik, the European ground squirrel.
Coif	The hood of mail worn under the helm.
Compline	Night prayer, the final office of the day.
Constable	The constable ('*connestable*') was an important member of a medieval household, effectively a 'security officer', organising protection and maintaining order. In *The History of William Marshal* the word is often used for the keeper of a castle and commander of its garrison.
Destrier	The finest of all warhorses, very costly and by no means common.
Electuary	The medieval equivalent of a 'digestif', taken after a meal.
Galantine	A dish of pressed meat or fish; in modern cuisine the galantine is usually covered in aspic.
Gisarme	A pole weapon similar to a halberd, combining a hook with a point or axe-blade.

Hauberk	A shirt or coat of mail, sleeved and usually reaching at least the middle of the thigh.
Mareschal	The 'marshal' was originally the servant in charge of the care and feeding of horses in a noble household.
Mark	250 grams of silver; in England a mark was worth 160 silver pennies (two-thirds of a pound).
None	The ninth canonical hour, in modern terms about three in the afternoon.
Prime	The first canonical hour of the day, in modern terms about six in the morning.
Purple	Purple ('*porpre*') was a fine dyed fabric, usually but not always of the deep colour that has taken its name.
Rotrouenge	A lyric poem characterised by frequent refrains or repeated phrases.
Rouncey	The rouncey ('*roncin*') was a tough, multi-purpose horse, lacking the *cachet* of the finest warhorse (the '*destrier*'), and costing only a fraction as much, but still a fine mount, used in combat by squires or less wealthy knights.
Scarlet	A fine and costly woollen cloth; scarlet was produced in various colours but most often in red.
Vair	Grey and white squirrel fur.
Vavasor	'Vavasor is sometimes thought to mean the vassal of a vassal ... [but] it does not seem ... that its original meaning had anything to do with a position in a "hierarchy of tenure" ... Vavasor may generally have denoted something more like a social status: a vavasor seems normally to have been part of noble, military society, though near the lower end of it. The status seems to have varied from place to place and time to time ...' Susan Reynolds, *Fiefs and Vassals* (Oxford, 1994), p. 23.
Ventail	The section of mail, attaching to the hood, that protected the mouth and neck.
Vespers	The 'vespers' were usually the hastiludes (a generic term for all martial games involving lances) that took place on the evening before a tournament. They were often considered to be a non-

serious trial for the following day, but there is evidence that they could easily become a tournament proper. This, Juliet Barker observes, is reflected in Wolfram von Eschenbach's *Parzival*, where 'the vespers began in the morning of the day before the tournament and involved all those who were going to participate then. During the skirmishing tempers were lost and the vespers became a full-scale combat ... [and] the tournament for the next day was called off because too many knights had been captured and the rest were too exhausted to fight again.' Juliet Barker, *The Tournament in England, 1100–1400* (Woodbridge, 1986), pp. 140–41.

Index

Abel, *son of the Biblical Adam* 81
Acre 130
Adam, *the Biblical first man* 81
Adam de Melun, *French knight* 74
Adam de Port, *Norman knight, father of William's sister-in-law* 132
Adam d'Yquebeuf, *Norman knight* 77, 81
'Advocate of Béthune', Robert V 89, 91, 93
Aimery Odart, *Poitevin knight* 118
Aimery of Saint-Maur, *Master of the Temple* 218–9, 225
Alan Basset, *English knight* 140, 189, 202
Aleaume de Fontaine, *Flemish knight* 75
Alençon 120, 159
Alençon, Robert III, count of 159
Alexander (the Great) 164
Alexander de Arsic, *Norman knight* 77
Alexander Malconduit, *Norman knight* 177
Alexandre, Le Roman d' 37n, 116n
Alice of Courtenay, countess of Joigny 63
Alresford 193
Amaury de Meulan, *French knight* 74
Andrew de Chauvigny, *Poitevin knight* 117–8, 125
Anet 56, 68, 162, 163
Anglesqueville (-sur-Saane), 154
Angoulême, Adémar III, count of 152
Anjou 40, 43, 44, 48, 50, 56, 60, 77, 80, 90, 94, 104, 112, 113, 138, 152, 157, 158, 180

Ansel Marshal, *brother of William* 31, 76
Ansel Marshal, *William's fifth son* 183, 216
Anselm de Pont-de-l'Arche, *English knight* 192
Aquitaine 43, 44n, 50, 100n
Arques 153, 154, 155
Arras 53, 75, 89n, 204n
Arras, castellan of 204
Arrouaise, abbey of 220n, 221n
Arthur, duke of Brittany 151, 154, 157, 175n
Arthur, King 64, 180
Azay-le-Rideau 120

Baldwin de Béthune, *Flemish knight, later count of Aumale* 75, 89, 92–3, 97–8, 102, 111, 117–8, 125, 133, 165, 184
Baldwin de Caron, *Flemish knight* 75
Baldwin de Strépy, *Flemish knight* 75
Baldwin de Vernon, *member of Henry II's retinue* 120
Baldwin de Wartenbeke, *Flemish knight* 75
Ballan-Miré 121n
Ballon 115, 157
Ballygowran 168
Barfleur 44, 53n, 105n, 136, 161
Bayeux 136, 161, 162
Bayonne 48, 'the great ship of', 208
Beaudemont 149
Beaumont, Matthew, count of 58
Beaumont-le-Roger 137, 161
Beauvais 143, 145

Beauvais, (Philip of Dreux) bishop of 145, 148
Berkhamsted 191
Bernard of Saint-Valéry, *Picard knight* 36
Bertrand de Verdun, *companion of William Marshal* 113
Blanche of Castile, *Philip of France's queen* 153n, 205
Blaye 203
Blois, Theobald V, count of 58, 59, 69, 73, 96, 108
Blois, Theobald VI, count of 208
Bon-Abbé de Rougé, *Breton knight* 42
Bonneville (-sur-Touques) 158, 160, 161
Bonsmoulins 35, 112
Bouère 42
Boulogne, Matthew, count of 36, 38
Boulogne, Renaud de Dammartin, count of 117, 139, 163, 180–1
Bourg-le-Roi 157
Boutavant 139
Bouvines 181–2
Bradenstoke 133
Breteuil 158, 161
Bréval 109
Brian of Wallingford, *English knight* 29
Brie 56
Brionne 161
Bristol 191
Brittany 40, 43, 60, 80, 90, 104, 138, 152
Brittany, Constance, duchess of 50n, 157n
Broglie *see* Chambreis
Brut, Roman de 55, 110
Burgundy 60, 80, 104
Burgundy, Hugh, duke of 57, 59, 78, 89, 90, 91, 93

Caen 44, 87, 136, 158, 161, 163
Caerleon 212–3
Cain, *brother of Abel* 81
Calais 209
Canterbury 207
Cardon de Fressenneville, *Flemish knight* 75
Carrickfergus 176
Castledermot 170
Caversham 213–4, 219
Châlus 150n
Chambreis (Broglie) 137, 161
Champagne 56, 64, 80, 89, 90
Châteaudun 111
Châteauroux 104, 109, 125
Chaumont-en-Vexin 105
Chepstow ('Striguil') 114, 132, 167, 216
Chertsey 192, 205
Chester, Ranulf de Blondeville, 6th earl of 134n, 187, 189, 195, 196, 202, 212, 214
Chinon 48, 110, 114, 120, 121, 123, 150n, 157, 158–9
Cinque Ports 206
Cirencester 132, 223
Clermont, Ralph, count of 58, 59, 65, 67, 106
Cologne 91, 96
Compiègne 163
Conches-en-Ouche 52, 159
Corin of Saint Servin, *French knight* 75
Courcelles (-lès-Gisors) 141
Cyprus 130

Damme 180
Dangu 142
Daniel, *Biblical figure* 84
David de la Roche, *baron of Wexford* 173, 177
Derby, William de Ferrers, 4th earl of 188, 195
Derby, William de Ferrers, 5th earl of 183
Devizes 187
Dieppe 126
Dover 53, 180, 185, 193, 195, 205, 210, 211
Dreux, Robert, count of 74, 96, 106, 108, 182

Dreux de Mello, *French knight*   106, 107
Drincourt   *see* Neufchâtel-en-Bray
Dublin   168, 176
Dunamase, Rock of, *castle in County Laois*   175, 177

Elbeuf   137
Eleanor (of Aquitaine), *wife of Henry II*   44, 46–7, 126, 131
Emenidus, *Alexander the Great's general*   116
Engelger de Bohun, *Norman knight*   150
Engelram d'Abernon, *English knight*   127
Engerran de Fiennes, *Flemish knight*   75
Enguerrand de Préaux, *Norman knight*   76
Épernon   72, 79
Équiqueville   126
Eu   37, 60
Eu, Henry, count of   76
Eu, John, count of   36
Eu, Raoul d'Issoudun, count of   154, 155
Eustace de Bertrimont, *William's squire*   97–8
Eustace de Campagne, *Flemish knight*   75
Eustace de Canteleu, *Flemish knight*   75, 117
Eustace 'the Monk', *pirate in the service of Louis of France*   206–7, 209
Eustace de Neuville, *Flemish knight*   75
Eva Marshal, *William's fourth daughter*   183, 219
Évreux   137

Falaise   160
Farnham   185, 193, 194–5
Faulkes de Bréauté, *Norman knight*   191, 199
Flanders, Baldwin IX, count of   139, 140, 181
Flanders, Philip, count of   36, 53, 55–6, 58–9, 61, 65, 74, 79, 86, 89, 90–1, 93, 102, 106, 108, 120, 150n
Florent de Hangest, *Picard knight*   69
Fontevrault   123
Fresnay-sur-Sarthe   119
Fréteval   138–9
Fulcher of Grendon, *English knight*   134

Gadifer du Laris, *character in the 'Roman d'Alexandre'*   37
Galen, *Greek physician*   46
Gascony   104, 138, 152, 157
Geoffrey, *'count of Nantes', 'duke of Brittany', son of Henry II*   50, 78, 93–5, 157n
Geoffrey de Brûlon, *Angevin knight*   77, 115, 117
Geoffrey FitzHamo, *Angevin knight*   77
Geoffrey FitzPeter, *justiciar*   129, 180
Geoffrey FitzRobert, *knight of Leinster*   168, 177–8
Geoffrey of Lusignan, *Poitevin knight*   44, 46, 94–5, 154, 158
Geoffrey Plantagenet, *illegitimate son of Henry II*   125
Geoffrey de Serland, *English knight*   198–9
Geoffrey de Vienne, *French knight*   75
Gerard de Canville, *commander of King Richard's fleet*   128
Gerard Talbot, *Norman knight*   77, 117
Gerberoy   143
Gilbert FitzReinfried, *English knight*   125
Gilbert Marshal, *half-brother of William*   28
Gilbert Marshal, *William's third son*   183
Gilbert Pipard, *English knight*   124, 125–6
Girard d'Athée, *favourite of King John*   169–70
Gisors   52n, 104n, 105–9, 142–3, 149

Glascarrig 173
Gloucester 178, 186–8, 214
Gloucester, Gilbert de Clare, 5th earl of 183, 219n, 224
Gloucester, Robert, 1st earl of 34
Goodrich Castle 188
Gournay (-en-Bray) 143, 145
Gournay (-sur-Aronde) 53, 85
Grandmont, *chapel of* 160
Guala Bicchieri, *papal legate* 186, 188, 190, 196, 205, 211, 212, 214
Guildford 171
Guizelin de Wartenbeke, *Flemish knight* 76
Guy de la Bruyère, *Flemish knight* 144
Guy de Châtillon, *French knight* 58
Guy of Lusignan, *king of Jerusalem* 104

Haï del Val, *lord of Rathtoe, County Carlow* 174
Hainault 43, 60, 74, 76n
Hamstead Marshall 31n
Harduin de Fougeré, *Angevin knight* 77
Hattin, battle of 104n
Hawise of Aumale, *wife of Baldwin de Béthune* 125n, 184n
Heloise of Lancaster, *William Marshal's ward* 104
Henry II, *king of England* accession 35; at war with Louis of France 35; expedition to Poitou 43–4; crowns his eldest son 47; rift with his son the Young King 48–52; hears the slanders against Marshal 87–8; at war with the Young King 93–6; hears of the Young King's death 101–2; goes to war in Normandy with Philip of France 104; the defence and burning of Le Mans 114–20; falls gravely ill and dies 120–3; burial 125
Henry III, *king of England* accession 187–90; visits the dying Marshal 214, 215

Henry 'the Young King' crowned 47; tutored by Marshal 48; rift with his father 48–52; engages in tournaments 53–7, 65–6, 74–9; epitome of knighthood 55, 64–5, 80; believes slanders against Marshal 84–8; in conflict with his father again 93–6; recalls Marshal to his side 95–6; falls ill and dies 99–100; burial 102
Henry FitzGerald, *member of Marshal's entourage* 165, 213, 216, 219–20
Henry Hose, *English knight* 168
Henry de Longchamp, *Norman knight* 77
Henry Marshal, *half-brother of William* 31
'Henry the Northerner', *English knight* 82, 88–9, 92
Henry Russell, *English knight* 134
Herlin de Wavrin, *Flemish knight* 79
Herman de Brie, *French knight* 75
Herod, *Biblical king* 85
Hertford 191
Hippocrates, *Greek physician* 46
Holland Bridge, *Lincolnshire* 204
Hubert de Burgh, *justiciar of England* 191, 207–8
Hubert Walter, *archbishop of Canterbury* 114, 135, 150, 161–3, 166
Hugh Bardolf, *English knight* 129
Hugh de Corny, *Norman knight* 142
Hugh de Coulonces, *Norman knight* 77
Hugh de Hamelincourt, *Flemish knight, companion of Marshal* 75, 97, 98, 102, 111, 117
Hugh de Malaunay, *Flemish knight* 75, 117–8
Hugh of Sandford, *member of Marshal's household* 125, 167n, 177
Hugh Tacon (d'Aubigny), *Picard baron* 193
Hugh of Wells, *archdeacon* 162
Hugues de Boves, *Picard knight* 182

Huntingdon 133
Huntingdon, David, earl of 76

Innocent III, Pope 173n, 178n, 192n
Isabel de Clare, *'the damsel of Striguil'*,
  William's wife 114, 125, 126, 167–9,
  171–2, 174, 213–4, 215, 218, 223–4
Isabel Marshal, *William's second
  daughter* 183, 219
Ivry (-la-Bataille) 109

Jacques d'Avesnes, *Picard knight* 58,
  91–2, 93
Jaquelin de Maillé, *Angevin knight* 77
Jean de Rouvray, *French knight* 226
Jean le Roux, *King Richard's host at
  Chambreis* 137
Jehan d'Alençon, *vice-chancellor of
  Normandy* 136
Joan Marshal, *William's fifth daughter*
  183, 216, 219, 220
John, *king of England (initially 'Count
  John')* with his father at Le Mans
  117; revealed to have betrayed his
  father 122; his behaviour in King
  Richard's absence 130–1; alarm at
  Richard's return 133–4; forgiven
  by Richard 136; campaigns
  with Richard in Normandy 137;
  crowned duke of Normandy and
  king of England 152; success in
  Gascony 152; marriage to the count
  of Angoulême's daughter 153;
  makes concessions to Philip of
  France 153; victorious at Mirebeau
  153–4; breaks his word to William
  des Roches 157–8; short of money
  and support, slips back to England
  158–61; sends Marshal on a peace
  mission 162–4; accuses Marshal
  of treachery 164–6; demands
  hostages of Marshal 168; falls out
  with William of Briouze 169; plots
  with Meiler against Marshal 170–2;
  banishes Briouze 175; campaigns in
  Ireland 176; charges Marshal with
  treachery and demands hostages
  again 177–8; recalls Marshal from
  Ireland 179; expedition to Poitou
  180–2; lays siege to Rochester 185;
  his death 186
John of Bassingbourn, *English knight*
  165
John of Earley, *squire and close
  companion to William Marshal* 110,
  117–8, 151, 165, 168, 171, 173–4, 177,
  179, 188–9, 191, 216–7, 219, 221–3,
  226
John FitzHugh, *English knight* 192
John Maleherbe, *Norman knight* 77
John Marshal, *father of William* 27–32,
  34
John Marshal (2) *brother of William*
  31, 132–3
John Marshal (3) *William's nephew,
  illegitimate son of his brother John (2)*
  140–1, 186, 198, 200, 204
John of Monmouth, *English knight*
  186
John de Préaux, *Norman knight* 76,
  142
John of Saint-Michel, *English knight*
  76
John de Seeneis, *Norman knight* 107
John of Subligny, *Norman knight* 42
Joigny 63
Jordan of Sauqueville, *member of
  Marshal's household* 168, 170–1,
  173, 177–8
Joubert de Pressigny, *member of Henry
  II's court* 101–2

Kay, *Arthurian knight* 110
Kilkenny 169, 171–2, 174, 176
Kingston 211
Knepp Castle 193

La Ferté-Bernard 114
Lagny-sur-Marne 74, 89
Laigle 137, 158
La Marche, Hugh de Lusignan, count
  of 152–3, 154

Le Bec-Hellouin 162
Le Dorat 114
Le Goulet 146, 152n, 153n
Le Mans 102, 112, 114–20, 158–9
Le Vaudreuil 137, 150
Leicester, Robert, 4th earl of 162, 166
Les Andelys 138, 143
Lillebonne 125
Limoges 94, 195
Lincoln 34, 195–205
Lindsey 185
Lisieux 44, 136, 158, 161
Llywelyn ab Iorwerth, *prince of Gwynedd* 178, 212
London 47, 126, 152, 153, 179, 184–5, 204, 205, 210, 213, 218, 221, 224
Louis VII, *king of France* 35, 49, 51
Louis, Prince of France 153, 185, 191–3, 194–6, 205, 210–11
Louis d'Arcelles, *Picard knight* 69
Louvrecaire, *mercenary* 159
Ludgershall 29, 30
Lyons-la-Forêt 104

Macaire de Châlons, *French knight* 74
Maine 40, 43, 44, 50, 56, 112–3, 126, 138, 157, 158
Maintenon 65
Malmesbury 187
Mamers 159
Mantes 109
Marlborough 30, 131–2, 133n, 134n, 194–5
Martel 100
Matilda, 'the Empress' 27–9, 32
Matthew le Gros, *mayor of Rouen* 156
Matthew de Walincourt, *Flemish knight* 61–2
Maud Marshal, *William's sister* 103
Maud Marshal (2), *Marshal's eldest daughter* 167, 183, 219–20
Maurice de Craon, *Angevin magnate* 124
Meiler FitzHenry, *Lord Chief Justice of Ireland* 167–72, 174–5
Mercadier, *mercenary* 142, 143, 145

Merlin 55, 186
Messina 129
Miles de Châlons, *French knight* 74
Milly (-sur-Thérain) 143–4
Mirebeau 153–4, 157
Montfort-le-Rotrou 115
Montfort-sur-Risle 161
Mont-Joux (the Great Saint Bernard Pass) 57, 74, 214
Montmirail (Sarthe) 110–11
Montmirail-en-Brie 97
Montmorency, lord of 50
Morgan of Caerleon 212–3
Mortagne-au-Perche 88
Mouliherne 125
Moulins-la-Marche 112
Mountsorrel 195
Munchensy, Warin, lord of 184

Nantes 182
Netherwent 216
Neufchâtel-en-Bray ('Drincourt') 35–9
Nevers, Hervé IV of Donzy, count of 195
Newark 186, 196
Newbury 31
Nicola de la Haye, *castellan of Lincoln* 199
Nogent-le-Roi 65
Nogent-le-Rotrou 114
Nontron 150
Norfolk, Roger Bigod, 2nd earl of 166
Norfolk, Hugh Bigod, 3rd earl of 183
Northampton 195
Norwich 192
Norwich, John de Gray, bishop of 175, 177
Notley, abbot of 220–1, 223, 224
Nottingham 131, 134, 178, 195, 196

Odo du Plessis, *French knight* 74
Okencelath 168
Orford 192
Orival 137

INDEX 239

Osbert de Rouvray, *Norman knight* 107
Ossory 168
Otto IV, Holy Roman Emperor 181
Oxford, Robert de Vere, 3rd earl of 224

Pacy-sur-Eure 109
Pandulf (Verraccio), *papal legate* 214–5, 218, 223–4
Paris 114
Pembroke 176
Pembroke, Richard 'Strongbow', earl of 114n, 169
Perche, Thomas, count of 197, 201
Peter of Capua, *cardinal* 146–9
Peter of Courtenay, *brother of Louis VII* 49
Peter FitzGuy, *member of Henry II's court* 115
Peter FitzHerbert, *knight from the Welsh Marches* 177–8
Peter de Leschans, *French knight* 69, 70, 74
Peter de Préaux, *Norman knight* 76, 80, 83, 140, 159, 161, 162
Peter de la Rivière, *Norman knight* 137
Philip d'Aubigny, *English knight* 188, 192, 194, 207
Philip Augustus, *king of France* 96, war with Henry II 104–9, 112–22; on crusade 129–30; no interest in helping Prince John 134; war with Richard 136–46; truce finally agreed 149; receives John's homage 152; relentless pursuit of goals 153; alarmed by defeat at Mirebeau 155; lays siege to Conches 159; demands homage of Marshal 162–3; takes Rouen 162; prepares invasion fleet 178; reaction to defeat at Damme 180–1; dismayed by defeats at Lincoln and Sandwich 205, 210; reaction to news of Marshal's death 225–6

Philip de Colombières, *Norman knight* 29
Philip de Colombières (2), *Norman knight* 119–20
Philip of Prendergast, *Irish lord* 172–3
Philip de Valognes, *Chamberlain of Scotland* 41
Pierre Mauvoisin, *knight in the service of Henry II* 117
Pleurs 57–60
Poitiers 109
Poitou 40, 44, 50, 56, 60, 80, 90, 93, 94, 104, 113, 138, 152, 157, 158, 164, 166, 180, 182
Pont-de-l'Arche 137
Ponthieu 94
Ponthieu, John, count of 36
Portchester 185
Porte-Joie 138
Portsmouth 53n, 136, 161, 162, 164, 166

Ralph d'Arderne, *Norman knight* 150, 163
Ralph Farci, *favourite of Henry the Young King* 83–4
Ralph FitzGodfrey, *chamberlain to the Young King* 95–6
Ralph de Hamars, *Norman knight* 77, 82
Ralph Musard, *castellan of Gloucester* 188–9
Ranulf de Glanville, *justiciar of England* 113–4, 126
Ralph de Plomquet, *Flemish knight* 75, 117
Ralph de Saint-Samson, *guardian of King Henry III* 187
Ralph de la Tournelle, *French knight* 206, 209
Reading 214, 224
Reading, abbot of 223–4
Reginald Croc, *English knight* 201
Reginald de Quetteville, *knight in the service of Marshal* 128
Reims, archbishop of 51, 96, 120, 149

Reinaud de Vassonville, *Norman knight* 76
Renaud de Dammartin *see* Boulogne, count of
Renaud de Nevers, *son of the count of Nevers* 66–7
Renaut Paien, *soldier of Guernsey* 208–9
Ressons-sur-Matz 53, 85, 90
Reynard the Fox (*from the Roman de Renart*) 173
Richard (Lionheart), *count of Poitiers, later king of England* 69n, 75n, 76, conflict with his brothers 93–4; campaigns with his father against the French 107, 109; connives with the king of France 112–3, 115; Marshal kills his horse 119–20; behaviour at his father's death 123–5; crowned king 127–8; on crusade 128–30; taken captive and ransomed 130–2; returns to England 132–5; forgives John 136; war in Normandy 136–46; negotiates favourable peace 146–9; his death 149–50
Richard 'the king's son', *illegitimate son of King John* 207–8
Richard d'Argences, *Norman knight* 106
Richard (Roger?) of Berkeley, *English knight* 76
Richard Clifford, *English knight* 110
Richard FitzHerbert, *English knight* 117
Richard FitzReinier, *Marshal's host in London* 127
Richard Marshal, *William's second son* 167, 179, 181, 183, 225
Richard of Sandford, *English knight* 204
Richard de Villequier, *Norman knight* 106
Robert de Beaurain, *Flemish knight* 75
Robert de Bloc, *Angevin knight* 77
Robert de la Borne, *English knight* 76
Robert de Bouvresse, *French knight* 75

Robert le Breton, *English knight* 76
Robert de Buisson, *Norman knight* 77
Robert Chaperon, *Norman knight* 77
Robert de Colombières, *Norman knight* 212
Robert de Courtenay, *French knight* 206, 209
Robert of Dreux, *son of the count of Dreux* 74
Robert d'Estouteville, *Norman knight* 76
Robert FitzWalter, *English knight* 76, 203
Robert of London, *English knight* 76
Robert de la Mare, *Norman knight* 77
Robert de Pont-de-l'Arche, *Marshal's brother-in-law* 103
Robert de Quincy, *son of the earl of Winchester* 203
Robert of Ropsley, *English knight* 201
Robert de Sablé, *commander of King Richard's fleet* 128
Robert de Souville, *marshal to Henry II* 115
Robert de Thibouville, *Norman knight* 77
Robert de Tresgoz, *Norman knight* 77, 117
Robert de Wanchy, *English knight* 76
Rochester 185, 194
Roger de Boudeville, *Norman knight* 77
Roger de Gaugy, *Flemish knight* 62, 75, 94
Roger de Hardencort, *Flemish knight* 75
Roger de Lacy, *constable of Chester* 177
Roger Malchael, *keeper of Henry II's seal* 121
Roger de Préaux, *Norman knight* 76
Roger Thorel, *lord from the Norman Vexin* 115
Roland Bloet, *English knight* 212
Romsey 185
Rouen 44, 51, 87, 100, 101, 102, 127, 150, 151, 152n, 156, 158, 160–1, 162

Rouen, Walter (de Coutances), archbishop of 130, 132
Rye 192–3

Saint-Brice 42
Saint James 'Intercisus' 108
Sainte-Jamme-sur-Sarthe 40
Saint-Omer, castellan of 208
Saint-Pierre-sur-Dives 102
Saint-Pol, Hugh IV, count of 90–1
Saint Susanna 84
Saint Wulfstan 186
Sainte-Suzanne 120
Saladin 104n
Salisbury 28, 43
Salisbury, Patrick, 1st earl of 28, 30, 44–5, 95
Salisbury, William 'Longsword', 3rd earl of 154–5, 180–2, 193–4, 197, 200, 201
Sancho de Savannac, *mercenary* 100–102
Sandwich 206–10
Saumur 125
Savari de Mauléon, *Poitevin knight* 154, 158, 191
Sées 159
Shoreham 193
Sibyl Marshal, *William's third daughter* 183, 219
Simon de Mares, *English knight* 76
Simon de Neauphle, *French knight* 56–7
Simon de Poissy, *French knight* 197, 204
Simon de Rochefort, *French knight* 74
Soissons, Ralph, count of 75
Soligny-la-Trappe 112
Sorel 56, 68
Southampton 185, 194
Speen 176n
Staines 224
Stephen (of Blois), *king of England* 27–35
Stephen of Évreux, *member of Marshal's household* 168, 170–2, 216

Stephen Langton, *archbishop of Canterbury* 173n, 218, 224
Stephen Longchamp, *English knight, brother of King Richard's justiciar William* 160
Stephen de Marçay, *seneschal of Anjou* 110, 111, 123
Stephen de la Tour, *French knight* 75
Stephen of Winchelsea 209
Stockbridge 34
Striguil *see* Chepstow
Surrey, William de Warenne, 5th earl of 154–5, 207
Syria 103–4, 130, 132, 147

Tancarville 35, 39, 40
Tancarville, 'the Chamberlain', lord of 35–6, 38–43
Theobald de Vallangoujard, *French knight* 74
Thomas Basset, *English knight* 217
Thomas Bloet, *English knight* 170–1
Thomas de Coulonces, *Norman knight* 81
Thomas FitzAnthony, *knight of Leinster* 168
Thomas Malesmains, *Norman knight* 182
Thomas of Sandford, *English knight* 167, 177n, 179, 187
Torksey 196
Touraine 60, 112, 113
Tours 48, 113, 120, 121–2
Trianon 160
Trôo 48
Tuboeuf 137

Ulster, Hugh de Lacy, 1st earl of 171, 176n
Upleadon 217

Valennes 40
Vendôme 48, 138
Verneuil 51, 52, 136–7, 158, 161
Vernon 139, 146
Vézelay 129
Vierzon 139

Walter Clifford, *English knight* 186
Walter of Ely, *English knight* 76
Walter de Lacy, *earl of Ulster's brother* 135, 175–6
Walter Marshal, *half-brother of William* 28
Walter Marshal, *William's fourth son* 183
Walter Purcel, *knight of Leinster* 168, 177–8
Walter Scudamore, *Welsh knight* 144
Warenne *see* Surrey, earl of
Wherwell 29
Wicklow 168n, 175
William I ('the Lion'), king of Scotland 41
William des Barres II, *French knight* 49, 69–71, 74, 108, 155
William des Barres III, *French knight* 74, 206, 208, 225–6
William Bloet, *English knight* 203
William Brewer, *English knight* 129
William of Briouze (1), *English knight* 169, 175–6
William of Briouze (2), *Marshal's son-in-law, grandson of (1)* 183
William de Cayeux, *Flemish knight* 75
William of Coleville, *English knight* 212
William de Dives, *Norman knight* 77
William de l'Étang, *Norman knight* 133
William FitzRalph, *English knight* 106, 107, 129
William FitzRoger, *English knight* 76
William de Garlande, *French knight* 106
William le Gras, *Norman knight* 77
William Longchamp, *justiciar of England* 114, 129–30
William Maillard, *knight of Leinster* 168
William of Mandeville, *earl of Essex and count of Aumale* 36, 39, 107–8, 119
William de la Mare, *Norman knight* 106

William Marshal birth 31; hostage to King Stephen 32–4; his figure 34; sent to Normandy for training 35; knighted 35–6; first combat at Neufchâtel 36–9; first tournaments 39–43; wounded in attempt to avenge his uncle 43–7; tutor-in-arms to Henry the Young King 47–8; knights the Young King 49; career in tournaments 53–80; plot against him at the Young King's court 81–9; great lords seek his service 91–3; meets an eloping monk 97–9; accepts the Young King's cross 99; goes to Holy Land 103–4; alongside King Henry at Gisors 105–10; charge on the bridge at Montmirail 111; defends Le Mans with King Henry 114–9; kills Count Richard's horse 119–20; meets Richard after Henry's death 124–5; marries Isabel de Clare 126–7; asks Richard for return of his land in Ireland 127–8; supports loyalists against Prince John 131–2; grief at his brother's death 132–3; refuses to pay homage to Richard for land in Ireland 135; mounts rearguard for Richard at Fréteval 138–9; aids the count of Flanders 140–1; valour at the capture of Milly 144–5; advises that John should succeed Richard 150–1; sent on peace mission to Philip of France 161–4; loses John's favour 164–6; affairs in Ireland 166–78; summoned back to face French invasion 179–80; arranges marriages for his children 183–4; loyalty to John 185–6; made protector of king and realm 187–91; confronts Prince Louis of France 192–5; victory at Lincoln 195–204; defeats a second French invasion at Sandwich 205–10; agreement with Prince Louis 211; conflict with

Morgan of Caerleon 212–3; final illness and death 213–25
William Marshal II, *William's eldest son*   183, 184, 193–4, 197, 200, 202, 215, 217, 222–4, 226
William Mauvoisin, *French knight*   80
William de Mello, *French knight*   143, 145
William de Monceaux, *French knight*   144
William de Montigny, *English knight*   201
William de Mortemer, *Norman knight*   137
William de Poternes, *Flemish knight*   75
William de Préaux, *Norman knight*   78–9
William le Queu, *knight in King Richard's service*   149
William Revel, *English knight*   76
William des Roches, *seneschal of Anjou*   119, 157–8
William de Sillé, *knight in the service of Henry II*   120
William de Thibouville, *Norman knight*   77

William de Tinténiac, *Angevin knight*   77
William Trihan, *knight in the service of Henry II*   122
Willikin of the Weald, *English 'guerrilla' against Louis of France*   185, 192
Winchelsea   192
Winchester   29, 30, 126, 136, 178, 185, 193–4, 195
Winchester, Henry of Blois, bishop of   34
Winchester, Peter des Roches, bishop of   186, 189–90, 197, 198–200, 204, 212, 214–5, 218
Winchester, Saer de Quincy, 1st earl of   177, 197, 203
Windsor   131
Wissant   53
Woodstock   169n
Worcester   186, 212, 213n

Young King   *see* Henry 'the Young King'